Advising Nixon

Advising Nixon

The White House Memos of Patrick J. Buchanan

Lori Cox Han

University Press of Kansas

For Taylor and Davis

Published by the University Press of Kansas (Lawrence, Kansas 66045), which
was organized by the Kansas Board of Regents and is operated and funded by
Emporia State University, Fort Hays State University, Kansas State University,
Pittsburg State University, the University of Kansas, and Wichita State University.

Library of Congress Cataloging-in-Publication Data

Names: Buchanan, Patrick J. (Patrick Joseph), 1938– | Han, Lori Cox,
  editor, writer of introduction, annotator.
Title: Advising Nixon : the White House memos of Patrick J. Buchanan /
  Lori Cox Han.
Description: Lawrence, Kansas : University Press of Kansas, [2019] | Includes
  bibliographical references and index.
Identifiers: LCCN 2019006708
  ISBN 9780700628292 (cloth : alk. paper)   ISBN 9780700628308 (ebook)
Subjects: LCSH: Buchanan, Patrick J. (Patrick Joseph), 1938– —Correspondence.
  | Nixon, Richard M. (Richard Milhous), 1913–1994—Friends and associates.
  | United States. White House Office—Records and correspondence. |
  Presidents—United States—Staff—Correspondence. | Government
  correspondence—United States—History—20th century. | Memorandums. |
  Presidents—United States—Election—1968. | Presidents—United
  States—Election—1972. | United States—Politics and
  government—1969–1974.
Classification: LCC E855 .B7872 2019 | DDC 973.924092—dc23
LC record available at https://lccn.loc.gov/2019006708.

British Library Cataloguing-in-Publication Data is available.

Printed in the United States of America

10 9 8 7 6 5 4 3 2 1

The paper used in this publication is recycled and contains 30 percent
postconsumer waste. It is acid free and meets the minimum requirements of
the American National Standard for Permanence of Paper for Printed Library
Materials Z39.48-1992.

Contents

Acknowledgments

I first read some of Pat Buchanan's memos in spring 1997 while a graduate student at the University of Southern California. With the help of a Goldsmith Research Grant from the Shorenstein Center on Media, Politics, and Public Policy (part of the Kennedy School at Harvard University), I was able to visit the NARA facility in College Park, Maryland, that housed the papers of the Nixon presidency. My dissertation on White House communication strategies, which I completed and successfully defended a few months later, would include archival data from the Nixon, Kennedy, and Reagan presidencies. Thus my love of research at presidential libraries began, which would translate into numerous visits to all thirteen NARA presidential libraries and animate many of my publications for the next two decades. Throughout that time, I always came back to one thought about all of the files I had accessed and memos I had read, most of which dealt with the public aspects of each of those thirteen presidencies—no memos were as interesting to read as those found in the Buchanan files from the Nixon years and the topic would make a great book someday.

While a faculty member at Austin College in Sherman, Texas, I set aside any ideas of research on the Nixon White House to focus on the George H. W. Bush presidency instead, given that I lived just a few hours from the Bush Library in College Station, Texas. When I accepted my current position in 2005 at Chapman University in Orange, California, a mere eight miles from the Nixon Library, I concluded that pursuing the book about the Buchanan memos might be fate after all, if only the Nixon documents could make their way out to Orange County. They did just that after the Nixon Library officially became part of the NARA presidential library system in 2007. It would still be a few more years before I found time in my schedule to get back to this book idea, but I finally began my research on Buchanan at the Nixon Library in earnest in 2014.

The end result is this book, which represents what I consider to be the most fascinating, substantive, and instructive memos written by Buchanan during one of the most consequential presidencies in U.S. history. While it was not easy to select which memos to include here, I chose those (either excerpted or in full) that provided a unique insight into the political strategies and deliberations behind the scenes of the Nixon presidency. This, however, is far from the final word on Buchanan's political influence during the Nixon years, but merely a small sample of his own words that played a role in shaping the political environment for decades. Whether you agree with Buchanan's views or not, there is much to be learned from studying his time in the Nixon White House, along with the growing significance of the conservative movement during the early 1970s and how the events of that era continue to influence American politics today.

Many people provided support and encouragement as I worked on this project, and all deserve thanks. My editor at University Press of Kansas, David Congdon, was enthusiastic about this book from the moment he heard about it; he and the entire team at UPK have been terrific to work with. Pat Buchanan was gracious in answering my questions about his many memos, both via phone and email, which was an invaluable addition to this book. Thanks also to the Nixon Foundation for facilitating that connection back in 2015. The archivists at the Nixon Library are truly amazing; a special thanks goes to Carla Braswell, Pamla Eisenberg, Craig Ellefson, and Meghan Lee-Parker for sharing their time and expertise every time I spent the day in the research room. I also had a top-notch research assistant in Kyle Koeller, now a Chapman University alumnus, who spent countless hours searching for documents in the Nixon Library for this project (and some future projects as well). I am blessed with supportive colleagues and friends within the Presidents and Executive Politics section of APSA, many of whom have heard me talk about this book idea for years (especially Diane Heith and Victoria Farrar-Myers). At Chapman University, there are numerous people to thank. Bob Slayton, professor of history, provided helpful input on the book proposal and is always happy to share his wealth of knowledge about all things related to academic publishing. Erin Berthon, department assistant in political science, always makes my life at Chapman easier and more organized. Patrick Fuery, dean of Wilkinson College, provided essential funding and support of this and many other research endeavors. I am also most appreciative for the continued support, financial and otherwise, for my research from Provost Glenn Pfeiffer and President Daniele Struppa. My Chapman students, especially those in my presidency course, always remind me that scholarship is most meaningful when shared with those in the classroom who are eager to learn. Finally, my children, Taylor NyBlom and Davis Han, provide unconditional love and support in all that I do. For that, I am eternally grateful.

List of Nixon Advisors

The following individuals are referenced within the memos included in this book, and worked in the Nixon White House and/or as a Nixon presidential campaign advisor:

Spiro Agnew. Governor of Maryland, 1967–1969; Republican vice presidential candidate, nominated August 1968; vice president, January 1969–October 1973

James Allen. U.S. commissioner of education, May 1969–June 1970

Lyndon "Mort" Allin. National director of Youth for Nixon, 1967–1968; special assistant to the president (daily news summary), January 1969–August 1974

Martin Anderson. Director of research, Nixon presidential campaign, 1968; special assistant to the president, 1969–1970; special consultant to the president for systems analysis, 1970–1971

Winton "Red" Blount. Postmaster general, January 1969–January 1972

Arthur Burns. Counselor to the president, 1969–1970

Frank Carlucci. Director of Office of Economic Opportunity, January 1971–December 1972

Henry Cashen. Deputy counsel to the president, 1969–1970; deputy assistant to the president, 1970–1972

Dwight Chapin. Personal aide, Nixon presidential campaign, 1967–1968; assistant to the president, 1969–1971; deputy assistant to the president, 1971–1973; appointments secretary, 1969–1973

Chuck Colson. Counsel, Key Issues Committee, Nixon presidential campaign, 1968; special counsel to the president, November 1969–March 1973

John Dean. White House counsel, July 1970–April 1973

Harry Dent. Deputy counsel to the president, 1969–1972

Robert Dole. U.S. senator (R-Kans.), 1969–1996; chair of the Republican National Committee, 1971–1973

John Ehrlichman. Advisor (advance man), Nixon presidential campaign, 1969; White House counsel, January 1969–November 1969; assistant to the president for domestic affairs, November 1969–April 1973

Robert Ellsworth. U.S. permanent representative to NATO, May 1969–June 1971

Robert H. Finch. Senior advisor, Nixon presidential campaign, 1968; secretary of Health, Education, and Welfare, January 1969–June 1970; counselor to the president, June 1970–December 1972

Max Friedersdorf. Congressional relations staff, January 1971–August 1974

Leonard Garment. Special consultant to the president, January 1969–April 1973; White House counsel, April 1973–August 1974

L. Patrick Gray. Assistant attorney general, civil division, 1970–1972; acting FBI director, May 1972–April 1973

Alan Greenspan. Coordinator of domestic policy, Nixon presidential campaign, 1967–1968; advised President Nixon informally, 1969–1974

Alexander Haig. Deputy national security advisor, June 1970–January 1973; vice chief of staff of the army, January 1973–May 1973; White House chief of staff, May 1973–September 1974

H. R. "Bob" Haldeman. Chief of staff, Nixon presidential campaign, 1968; White House chief of staff, January 1969–April 1973

Bryce Harlow. Advisor, Nixon presidential campaign, 1968; assistant to the president for congressional relations, 1969–1971; political counselor to the president, 1973–1974

Rita Hauser. Cochair, New Yorkers for Nixon, 1968; U.S. ambassador to the United Nations Human Rights Council, February 1969–March 1972

Stephen Hess. Deputy assistant to the president for urban affairs, 1969; national chairman of the White House Conference on Children and Youth, 1969–1971

Walter Hickel. Secretary of the interior, January 1969–November 1970

J. Edgar Hoover. FBI director, May 1924–May 1972

Tom Huston. White House aide, 1969–1971

Kenneth Khachigian. Staff assistant to director of communications, 1970–1971; assistant to Pat Buchanan, 1971–1972; deputy special assistant to the president (speechwriting), 1973–1974

Henry Kissinger. U.S. national security advisor, January 1969–November 1975; secretary of state, September 1973–January 1977

Herb Klein. National communications manager, Nixon presidential campaign, 1968; director of communications, January 1969–July 1973

Noel Koch. White House speechwriter and aide, 1971–1974

Egil "Bud" Krogh Jr. Deputy counsel to the president; deputy assistant to the president for domestic affairs, 1969–1973

Melvin Laird. Secretary of defense, January 1969–February 1973; White House domestic affairs advisor, May 1973–January 1974

Clark MacGregor. Congressional liaison, 1970–1972; chairman of the Committee to Re-elect the President, July 1972–November 1972

Jeb Magruder. Deputy director of White House communications, 1969–1971; deputy campaign director, Committee to Re-elect the President, 1971–1972

John Mitchell. Campaign manager, Nixon presidential campaign, 1968; attorney general, January 1969–March 1972; chairman of the Committee to Re-elect the President, March 1972–July 1972

Toby Moffett. Director of the Office of Students and Youth, Department of Health, Education, and Welfare, 1969–1970

Clark Mollenhoff. Special counsel to the president, 1969–1970

Edward L. Morgan. Deputy counsel to the president, 1969–1970; assistant director of the Domestic Policy Council, 1970–1972

Daniel Patrick Moynihan. Director of the Urban Affairs Council, January 1969–November 1969; counselor to the president, November 1969–December 1970

Lyn Nofziger. Deputy assistant to the president for congressional affairs, 1969–1970; director of the California Committee to Re-elect the President, 1972

Patrick O'Donnell. Staff assistant to Charles Colson, May 1971–February 1973

Leon Panetta. Director of the Office for Civil Rights, 1969–1970

David Parker. Special assistant to the president, 1971–1974

Kevin Phillips. Senior strategist, Nixon presidential campaign, 1968

Herbert "Bart" Porter. White House aide to director of communications, 1970–1971; director of scheduling, Committee to Re-elect the President, 1971–1972

Raymond Price. Assistant to the president (speechwriter), 1969–1974

Elliot Richardson. Secretary of Health, Education, and Welfare, June 1970–February 1973; secretary of defense, February 1973–May 1973; attorney general, May 1973–October 1973

William Rogers. Secretary of state, January 1969–September 1973

George Romney. Secretary of the Department of Housing and Urban Development, January 1969–February 1973

Donald Rumsfeld. Director of the Office of Economic Opportunity, 1969–1970; director of the Economic Stabilization Program, 1970–1972

William Safire. Advisor, Nixon presidential campaign, 1968; assistant to the president (speechwriter), 1969–1973

John Sears. Deputy counsel to the president, 1969–1970

George Shultz. Secretary of labor, January 1969–July 1970; director of the Office of Budget and Management, July 1970–June 1972; secretary of treasury, June 1972–May 1974

DeVan Shumway. Director of public relations, Committee to Re-Elect the President, 1972

Maurice Stans. Secretary of commerce, January 1969–February 1972; finance committee for the Committee to Re-elect the President, 1972

Herb Stein. Chair of the Council of Economic Advisors, January 1972–August 1974

Randolph Thrower. Commissioner of the Internal Revenue Service, 1969–1971

William Timmons. Deputy assistant to the president for congressional relations, 1969–1970; assistant to the president for congressional relations, 1970–1973; assistant to the president for legislative affairs, 1973–1974

John Veneman. Undersecretary of the Department of Health, Education, and Welfare, 1969–1973

John Volpe. Secretary of transportation, January 1969–February 1973

John Whitaker. Deputy assistant to the president for domestic affairs, 1969–1973

Rose Mary Woods. Personal secretary, 1951–1968; personal secretary to the president, January 1969–August 1974

Ron Ziegler. Press secretary, January 1969–August 1974

1 Introduction
Pat Buchanan as Political Wordsmith

While it has been more than four decades since Richard Nixon resigned the presidency, various aspects of his time in office remain salient for scholars. Some have argued that Nixon permanently altered the political environment for each successive presidency, particularly when considering the public aspects of the office (including White House communication strategies, the presidential-press relationship, and public opinion). For better or worse, Nixon and his advisors changed the way that the White House attempted to manage the press (through the creation of the daily news summary) and manage the president's public image (staging made-for-television events to highlight presidential activities). Most of these strategies still exist, in one form or another, as they have evolved through each successive administration.

Among the many advisors in the Nixon White House, Patrick J. Buchanan served as an architect of Nixon's public strategy. First employed by Nixon in 1966 to help lay the groundwork for the 1968 presidential campaign, Buchanan became one of Nixon's closest advisors. He managed the daily news summary, prepared briefing books, wrote speeches, and served as a political strategist from the first day on January 20, 1969, until the last, when Nixon resigned the presidency on August 9, 1974. In the decades since, numerous books have been written about the Nixon years, including biographies, memoirs, and various scholarly analyses on both the policies and politics of this administration.

This book, however, is unique in that it offers a close examination of Buchanan's role in the Nixon White House, previously untouched as a topic of a book-length scholarly study. This behind-the-scenes analysis relies on Buchanan's White House memos, one of the most important tools available to a presidential advisor attempting to influence both strategy and policy.

Housed at the Richard Nixon Presidential Library and Museum in Yorba Linda, California, the Buchanan memos offer a fascinating perspective on the inner workings of the White House through an in-depth analysis of a key advisor during one of the most consequential presidencies in American history. The memos provide a blunt yet detailed analysis of the most salient political issues of Nixon's presidency. As Buchanan himself recalls about the roughly 1,000 memos he would write while working for Nixon, "I could write swiftly, tersely, wittily, and well memos that Nixon loved to read, on matters he cared about most: politics, policy, and personalities. . . . Nixon asked for and welcomed my missives. It became our primary means of conversation."[1]

The Buchanan Memos

For some scholars, it is the documents written by the president himself that offer the most insight into an administration, as presidential words can "provide a window into the world of those men chosen by their fellow Americans to lead the nation."[2] For others, the inter- and intraoffice memos of those who work in the White House offer the best day-to-day analysis of how political and policy battles play out in an attempt to influence the president's decision-making. Access to presidential documents, including the memos, notes (sometimes handwritten), and other documents from those who worked in the White House provide a unique perspective into the decision making and thought processes of some of the most powerful figures in American government.

The Buchanan files at the Nixon Presidential Library are no exception. Buchanan wrote numerous memos each day, many of which were long and detailed. In them, he gave Nixon advice on communication strategies, press relations, policy positions, and how to navigate the political environment; memos sent to other White House figures were integral to the internal debate on how to create administration positions and plans. Buchanan recalls:

> From the first day I went to work at Nixon Mudge at 20 Broad in Manhattan in January of 1966, they had been the way I communicated ideas and recommendations to the ex-Vice President. During these three pre-presidential years, Nixon would have me into his office to talk politics, policy, and personalities for hours on end. Back in my own office, with Rose Woods, I would write memos for him to take with him in his briefcase when he left and went uptown. In the White House almost all of my memos would go through Haldeman as Chief of Staff, who would take them in to the President. Bob often acted like a Marine Drill Sergeant, but honestly conveyed my views—even those with which he disagreed—to Nixon. That was the way Nixon wanted to communicate in many cases. In personal relations, President Nixon often phoned me in my office, or out at dinner, or at home when he wanted to talk directly. Meetings in the Oval Office alone between the two of us—other than working together on speeches—were more rare than meetings there with others present. . . . The overriding purpose of my policy and strategy memos was to argue, persuade, convince the president to adopt a course of action which I viewed as consistent with conservative principles and beliefs and in the interest of creating a great new coalition of Republicans, conservatives, Southern Protestants and Northern Catholics—the latter two being Democratic blocs.[3]

Throughout his political career, including many years as a political commentator and three-time presidential candidate, Buchanan has been known for fiery rhetoric that does not mince words regarding his traditional or populist conservative (sometimes called paleoconservative) views. His memos during the Nixon years were written in the same style and tone, either counterpunching against views from other White House advisors Buchanan viewed as too moderate or providing Nixon with a take-no-prisoners approach to every political battle that presented itself. If you read anything that Buchanan has written or hear him speak, there is never any doubt about exactly where he stands.

Born and raised in Washington, D.C., Buchanan graduated first in his class at Gonzaga High School and then attended Georgetown University on a full academic scholarship. From there, he earned a master's degree in journalism from Columbia University, and at the age of twenty-three he became an editorial writer for the *St. Louis Globe Democrat*.[4] In 1966, he was an early hire by Nixon in preparation of the former vice president's eventual 1968 presidential campaign; he traveled the country with Nixon throughout the 1966 midterm elections to build support for the candidate within the Republican Party. By 1968, Buchanan played a significant role with both media strategy and messaging, as well as opposition research, in helping Nixon win the White House.[5] After Nixon resigned the presidency in August 1974, Buchanan returned to journalism with a syndicated column, a radio show, and eventually regular television appearances on PBS's *The McLaughlin Group* and CNN's *Crossfire* and *The Capital Gang*. He returned to the White House in February 1985 to serve as Ronald Reagan's communications director, a job he held until March 1987.

Buchanan then resumed his syndicated column and role on *Crossfire* until he launched his first presidential campaign in 1992. Challenging President George H. W. Bush for the Republican nomination, Buchanan surprised the incumbent with a strong showing in the New Hampshire primary, winning 38 percent of the vote. He would go on to win more than three million votes throughout the nomination process, signaling dissatisfaction within the Republican Party at Bush's failure to expand on Reagan's conservative legacy. Buchanan would run for president again in 1996, sharpening his populist conservative message, highlighted by his opposition to policies such as the 1994 North American Free Trade Agreement supported by President Bill Clinton. In addition to winning the influential early state of New Hampshire, Buchanan would win three additional contests (Alaska, Missouri, and Louisiana) before the eventual nominee, Senator Robert Dole of Kansas, wrapped up the Republican nomination. Buchanan sought the presidency one last time in 2000, eventually securing the nomination of the Reform Party after leaving the Republican Party in October 1999. He received more than 440,000 votes (0.4 percent of the popular vote), and it is believed that many of the more than 3,400 votes he received in Palm Beach County, Florida, a strong liberal area, were by mistake due to the disputed "butterfly ballot." Supporters of Democratic nominee Al Gore believe this cost him the state of Florida and thus the presidency; Buchanan has stated the same belief.[6] Buchanan then returned to cable television (with MSNBC and later Fox News) and continued his work as a columnist. He has authored fourteen books, including one about his years in the Nixon White House.

Whether as a presidential advisor, political pundit, or presidential candidate, Buchanan has never been at a loss for words. As a candidate, Buchanan's speeches were known for their "ideological fervor" as well as offering "fiery oratory and vigorous public debate," encouraging listeners to join his "crusade" for traditional conservatism.[7] Some dubbed his message "Buchananism," a new populism that put America first with a message that highlighted Buchanan's appeal as both a champion of the common man and an intellectual. After winning the New Hampshire Republican primary in 1996, he was attacked by traditional conservatives for challenging the party's status quo, while his supporters would chant, "Go, Pat, go" and applaud his "conservatism of the heart."[8] Buchanan delivered one of his most memorable lines of that campaign during his New Hampshire victory speech: "They hear the shouts of the peasants from over the hill. You watch the establishment. All the knights and the barons will be riding into the castle, pulling up the drawbridge. They're coming. All the peasants are coming with their pitchforks."[9]

He also made headlines with his speech at the 1992 Republican National Convention, stating: "There is a religious war going on in our country for the soul of America. It is a cultural war, as critical to the kind of nation we will one day be as was the Cold War itself." Buchanan's rallying call to conservative ideals stood in stark contrast to the more moderate message of the incumbent president, George H. W. Bush, who sought to unify the party, instead displaying divided and "politically problematic elements" within the party.[10] Although Bush had easily won the Republican nomination after the initial scare by Buchanan's campaign in New Hampshire, Buchanan's words from the convention would serve as a reminder through the fall campaign that Bush did not have the same support among conservatives as Reagan had enjoyed. According to historian Timothy Stanley, the message was powerful: "Play Pat Buchanan's 1992 convention speech to someone and you can probably tell by their reaction what side of the culture war they are on. Liberals presumed that its ugliness would make Pat Buchanan unelectable and consign his brand of conservatism to the trash heap of history. Moderate Republicans used it as an excuse to try to purge the radical right from their party, with mixed results. But for many conservatives, the speech defined their struggle against liberals in both parties."[11]

In 1996, two Washington journalists writing under the pseudonym of S. Thomas Colfax marveled at Buchanan's effective use of the English language. They labeled

Buchanan's skill with political messaging a "blood sport between Us and Them" due to his choice of words for their "ability to cut and slash" and that his style was "more like a Green Beret wielding a Bowie knife than a heart surgeon a scalpel." They surmised that it was in the Nixon White House that Buchanan perfected his tone and style and that this skill had become a tremendous asset for his presidential campaigns: "He is so good at torching opponents because of his rapier wit; he wins audiences because he amuses and entertains while he shocks. Richard Nixon once observed that Buchanan was the only extremist he knew with a sense of humor, and there are plenty of liberal Washington pundits who would vote for Buchanan as their favorite dinner companion. His stunning ability to paint vivid word pictures gives Buchanan air supremacy over his more pedestrian political foes."[12]

Throughout his career, though, the written word for Buchanan has been just as powerful. In addition to the hundreds of memos that Buchanan wrote during his time in the Nixon White House, he also wrote or contributed to many speeches and other public statements by Nixon and Vice President Spiro Agnew. As Buchanan himself explains, messaging played a significant role for Nixon and his attempt to govern in the divided political environment following the 1968 presidential election, and those messages were often consequential as he "helped to write several of the more controversial speeches of the Nixon era—the President's Great Silent Majority speech in November 1969, Vice President Agnew's follow-up attack on the television networks at Des Moines, and the president's announcement of the U.S. incursion into Cambodia, which was followed by widespread student disorders and the killings at Kent State University."[13]

The lines Buchanan would write for a speech, just like his memos, were always direct and to the point. Buchanan often wrote "long, surprisingly frank memos that said on paper what protocol demanded not be said to [Nixon's] face." Buchanan sought to challenge Nixon on certain policy positions while remaining respectful, though in later years he questioned some of his own language and tactics. According to Stanley,

When the memos were leaked many years later, Buchanan was shocked to read just how rude he had been—often using adjectives to describe his boss like "gutless" and "aimless." It is difficult to think of any other President who would have tolerated Buchanan's polemical abuse. In conversation, Nixon used his "or am I wrong?" technique, but no one could now reply with a flat "yes." Instead Buchanan weighed up advantages and disadvantages of a Nixon-originated idea and concluded, on balance, that the administration might move in a different direction. Nixon once told a staffer to pass on the message to Pat that he was to "stop sending me problems without sending me solutions."[14]

On looking back at some of the memos, Buchanan says some "were even more raw than I recall." He was aware that the president "was reading them closely." Nixon would often write comments on the memos, news summaries, or briefing books to send back to Buchanan. Buchanan's memos to others in the White House were also significant:

> My memos to other staffers were more abbreviated than those to the President. But, again, they were a primary means of communication. I put less labor into these, as the man I was really trying to persuade—with whom I had a personal relationship dating back three years before the presidency—was the man who made the ultimate decisions on political strategy and policy, both foreign and domestic. As for the influence of my memos, they had far more impact than one-on-one meetings.

Many memos written to other staffers were intended for Nixon. For example, memos addressed to Dwight Chapin during the 1968 campaign "were almost always to Nixon," while during the White House years, memos to Haldeman and John Mitchell on political strategy "were intended for Nixon and sent to Nixon." The intent of sending the memos to others was "to give the president cover if they leaked." The memos also played a significant role in major decisions made by the Nixon White House. According to Buchanan:

> Consider. My October 8, 1969, memo triggered, I believe, the President's decision to deliver his decisive "Great Silent Majority" speech. The memo to the President through Haldeman on Nov. 5, 1969, was the origin of the Agnew attacks on the media of Nov. 13 and Nov. 20, the first of which, in Des Moines, was carried live on all three networks and reverberates to this day. My memo in the early fall of 1970 was used as the strategy plan for the off-year elections of 1970. After my memo, Nixon talked constantly about the "real majority" and "social issue" that Ben Wattenberg had identified in his book. Today, critics are crediting me with writing the veto that killed the Family Assistance Plan of 1971, which I was able to do only after a memo persuaded the President and West Wing to give me carte blanche to make the case. Repeated memos, refusing the President's idea, and the West Wing's idea, of having me head up the Ellsberg inquiry kept me from becoming the leader of "The Plumbers."[15]

Presidential Libraries
Thanks to the presidential library system, many memos like those written by Buchanan have been preserved and remain accessible to presidential scholars. One

of the most important sources of information for those who study the American presidency are the thirteen presidential libraries under the auspices of the National Archives and Records Administration (NARA). A presidential library can be "a balanced and engaging history museum as well as an accessible archive where the nation can learn from its history and hold its presidents and even the presidency itself accountable."[16] According to NARA, presidential libraries are repositories for the papers, records, and historical materials of the presidents, working to ensure that items are preserved and made available for the widest possible use by researchers. The goal is to "promote understanding of the presidency and the American experience" as well as to "preserve and provide access to historical materials, support research, and create interactive programs and exhibits that educate and inspire."[17]

The presidential library system first began with Franklin D. Roosevelt in 1939, who wanted to preserve the papers and other materials from his time in office. Prior to this, papers were often dispersed to family members and administration officials, and many were even destroyed. In 1955, Congress passed the Presidential Libraries Act, which established a system of libraries that were to be built through private funds and then donated to the federal government to maintain and oversee. Now when a president leaves office, NARA establishes a Presidential Project until the new presidential library is built and transferred to the federal government. Today, the working papers for each administration since Herbert Hoover are available in presidential libraries. The Library of Congress houses the papers for most administrations prior to Hoover.

Subsequent laws have also been passed that have changed the governing structure of presidential libraries. In 1978, Congress passed the Presidential Records Act (PRA), which established that presidential records documenting the constitutional, statutory, and ceremonial duties of the president are the property of the federal government. While the first presidential libraries built acknowledged the fact that presidential papers were the personal property of the president, NARA had great success in persuading presidents to donate their historical materials to be housed in a NARA-run library.

The Nixon Presidential Library, however, is an exception. Nixon's resignation from office in 1974 brought with it numerous lawsuits over ownership of his presidential papers, which in part encouraged Congress to change the law. In 1974, Congress also passed the Presidential Recordings and Materials Preservation Act, placing Nixon's papers in federal custody to prevent their destruction. Originally dedicated in 1990, the Nixon Library did not become an official NARA presidential library until 2007. After numerous legal battles between the government and the Nixon family, Nixon White House documents held in NARA archives in College Park, Maryland, began to be transferred to the Yorba Linda library in 2004; previously, the Nixon Library was run by the privately funded Nixon Foundation and only housed pre- and postpresidential papers. Unlike contemporary presidential libraries that were opened within a few years of the president leaving office (Lyndon Johnson in 1971, Gerald Ford in 1981, and Jimmy Carter in 1986), the Nixon library has many more documents that await processing for researchers because of the late start in making it a presidential library with on-site NARA archivists.

Plan of the Book

The goal of this book is to view the Nixon White House through the lens of Buchanan's many memos, analyzing his advice to Nixon and how he helped to shape the eventual policies and political strategies employed by Nixon and his administration. Buchanan also served Nixon as the "most reliable representative in his White House of the conservative wing of his party and his coalition"[18] at a time when the more moderate and conservative factions within the Republican Party were battling for control of the party's platform and direction.

Buchanan summarized his role in the Nixon White House in a November 1972 memo to Haldeman, just weeks after Nixon's landslide reelection, in which he talked about his responsibilities during the first term as well as his projected role for the second term.[19] In addition to the news summary, press conference briefing books, and speeches, his "other assignments" had included:

> A) Political liaison with the Conservative Movement and an assortment of conservative writers and thinkers. B) In-house advocate of the "Catholic Strategy," and those policies and position, which in PJB's view, would best advance a politically feasible "new majority." C) Occasional participant in the news planning sessions, and regular and enthusiastic member of the campaign "Attack Group." D) Adviser on political strategy for both 1970 and 1972 campaigns and analyst of the Democratic Party strategies and strengths and weakness of various Democrats in 1972.

Regarding the second term,

> . . . the President has recommended a "free safety" role in coming Administration. This is eminently to my liking—and the areas of immediate concern are: 1) assistance in identifying and removing bureaucrats who have been problems in the past and replacing them with Nixon loyalists, and those who will help us build a permanent majority. 2) An active role in developing Administration posture toward media, inclusive of public television. 3) Prime responsibility for researching and preparing Administration posture toward the Foundations like Ford and

Brookings. 4) A more visible role in the President's attack apparatus—speaking and writing those things which the President needs said—but cannot have Ziegler or Klein say. Other specifics will certainly arise, as did the Child Care veto fight, but the "general assignment" role the President outlined I find comports with my own interests and the President's, I think.

This memo shows the range of responsibilities, especially regarding media and political strategies, for which Buchanan was responsible throughout Nixon's time in office.

Each subsequent chapter will offer a case study of the significant political issues faced by the Nixon administration by providing chronological excerpts of memos that explain Buchanan's perspectives, advice, and suggested tactics regarding specific issues. Chapter 2 considers the 1968 presidential campaign and presidential transition. Chapter 3, on White House communications, looks at topics such as press relations, the use of television, polling, speeches, the daily news summary, and press leaks (including the Pentagon Papers in 1971). Chapter 4, on governing and policy, considers presidential leadership on domestic, economic, and foreign policy issues, as well as interbranch relations and management of the executive branch; this chapter also includes perspectives on Nixon's relationship with conservatives within the Republican Party. Chapters 5 and 6 consider the 1972 presidential campaign, with the former focusing on party nominations and the latter focusing on the general election campaign. Chapter 7 looks at Nixon's second term and the looming presence of Watergate up until his resignation.

Most of the documents in this book are available to researchers at the Nixon Presidential Library, and most come from the Buchanan files. However, the entire collection of Buchanan files at the Nixon Library has not yet been processed and made available. Some of Buchanan's memos, particularly from 1969–70 and 1973–74, were located within the files of other White House advisors as well as Nixon's office files. A small number of documents are also available as part of the proceedings published in 1973 from the Watergate hearings in the U.S. Senate, where Buchanan testified to the Select Committee on Presidential Campaign Activities. Any editing of the memos published here stem merely from minor typos and were corrected simply for the sake of the reader and did not change the meaning or intent of any content. Regarding the style of memos, all underlining, use of capital letters, and other formatting have been retained from the originals.

2 The 1968 Campaign

On December 20, 1967, Richard Nixon appeared on *The Merv Griffin Show*, a talk/variety show similar to *The Tonight Show with Johnny Carson*. Nixon, whom Griffin described as "one of the most astute men in the field of politics in world affairs on the scene today," engaged in lighthearted banter on topics such as his daughter Julie's engagement to David Eisenhower, as well as a variety of policy topics, including his 1959 meeting with Soviet leader Nikita Khrushchev (known as the "kitchen debate") and why he did not support sending U.S. ground troops into North Vietnam. However, the most prominent issue of the evening was the impending 1968 presidential campaign and whether Nixon would soon declare his candidacy. In late 1967, the Republican presidential contenders included New York governor Nelson Rockefeller, California governor Ronald Reagan, and Michigan governor George Romney.

When asked by Griffin about his intentions, Nixon stated that he planned to decide by the latter part of January 1968:

> Now being quite candid I would have to admit that a number of considerations are entering into that decision and that point in that direction. But a man in political life must never make a decision of that importance until the last possible moment. He must not make it finally. That's a candid answer, but I'm sure nobody will believe it, however. They think you've already made it.

Nixon continued in explaining the timing of the decision:

> It isn't just timing for purposes of how it's going to affect voters, but once you decide to become a candidate, and particularly if you should decide to become a candidate for the presidency, then it means that your life changes completely, that must be, that's war, it's a battle, it's a battle for the nomination, and it's a battle for the presidency. I've been through both, so I know something about it. And so that decision must be made only at a time when you're ready to leave everything that you're doing and give your whole life to that great contest for however long you stay alive.

When Griffin asked whether he had been unfairly stigmatized as a "loser" by the press after defeats in the 1960 presidential election and the 1962 California gubernatorial election, Nixon replied, "You combat it by winning something," and then pointing out that while not equating himself with politicians the likes of Winston Churchill, Franklin Roosevelt, and Abraham Lincoln, all three had lost elections before winning "the big ones." A fellow guest, producer David Susskind, asked Nixon about his strategy for 1968 given that Democratic voters outnumbered Republican voters three-to-two: "You can't become President of the United States unless millions of disaffected Democrats vote for you, and to those people you are an anathema." Nixon replied that he had done "rather well" with Democrats in 1960 and 1962, that in 1968 he would need 20 percent of Democrats and half of the independent voters, and that he was confident that his cross-party appeal would continue in 1968 if he chose to run: "People are not thinking in terms of Democrats or Republicans, they are thinking about the serious trouble this country is in."[1]

In some ways, Nixon was accurately predicting the eventual outcome in November 1968. He would win a close election against the Democratic nominee, Vice President Hubert Humphrey, and the independent challenger, Alabama governor George Wallace. Voting behavior experts would note that 1968 marked a "dealignment" in the electorate, characterized by a greater responsiveness among voters to short-term influences, such as the candidates and issues of the moment, rather than long-term influence of party identification.[2] This trend allowed Nixon to win despite registered Democrats outnumbering registered Republicans. In addition, the presence of divisive issues such as the Vietnam War, the civil rights movement, the women's rights movement, protests on university campuses, urban unrest, and the assassinations that year of Martin Luther King Jr. and Robert Kennedy all led to a volatile political environment that eroded party loyalty among voters. Nixon ran on the promise of restoring law and order and ending the Vietnam War, targeting voters that Nixon would eventually call the "silent majority." His campaign also pursued a "southern strategy" designed to appeal to conservative white voters in southern states who had traditionally voted for pro-segregation Democrats. Despite a surge by Humphrey in the polls during the last weeks of the campaign, Nixon won by a wide margin in the Electoral College with 301 votes from thirty-two states. Humphrey carried thirteen states plus the District of Columbia with 90 Electoral College votes, while Wallace won the states of Alabama, Arkansas, Georgia, Louisiana, and Mississippi for a total of 46 Electoral votes. The popular vote was much closer, with Nixon winning a narrow plurality with 43.4 percent, Humphrey with 42.7 percent, and Wallace with 13.5 percent.

As the following memos show, Pat Buchanan advised Nixon on numerous campaign strategies, including press relations, use of television, and overall messaging (in both style and substance). Throughout the summer and fall of 1968, issues of concern varied from significant policy matters like Vietnam to political considerations such as the vacancy on the Supreme Court created by the retirement of Chief Justice Earl Warren, and campaign controversies involving Nixon's selection of Spiro Agnew as his running mate. Agnew made several rhetorical gaffes during the campaign, with some statements labeled racist, and the *New York Times* ran an expose on his financial dealings as governor of Maryland. After Nixon's victory in November, and during the presidential transition, Buchanan turned his attention to organizing the Nixon White House and building the "New Majority" voting coalition for the Republican Party. After having lost a close election to John F. Kennedy in 1960, experiencing a bitter defeat to Edmund "Pat" Brown in the 1962 gubernatorial race in California, and spending 1964 and 1966 campaigning for fellow Republican candidates, Nixon finally experienced triumph in 1968. In considering Nixon's political comeback nearly four decades later, Buchanan wrote, "The rise of Richard Nixon was spectacular."[3]

1. Memo to H. R. Haldeman, "On the Uses of Television," November 15, 1967

. . . I know that in our various institutions, the word has gone forth that television is the medium that makes the largest impact, television is the way to hit some 10,000,000 where rallies don't make a damn bit of difference, etc.

I think we ought to consider the question why we want television exposure and do we want television exposure?

One reason for television exposure is to get identified to the public. But god knows, everybody in the country knows who RN is, and those that don't would know just as much as soon as the convention is over. So we don't want to be identified.

A second reason would be that our personal appearance is an asset. This is a day and age when the TV screen is filled with incredibly handsome young people, and the only politicians I know who are "attractive in their facial expressions and mien on TV are Jack Kennedy and Reagan. Thus, I don't think how RN looks or his personality are reasons for getting onto the tube.

Third, RN might want to get on the tube to get his message across, to talk with the people. Right, this is a legitimate reason. What is RN's message. He knows more about foreign policy than anybody else in the country and is the best qualified man to be President. How can you show this on a one-minute slot? You can't show anything about RN's qualifications; in one-minute RN can say about 150 words on the Mid-East or Vietnam. Can we demonstrate anything in a single two- or three-minute answer on Vietnam, which would lead someone to believe we could handle it better?

Can RN say something which will take one minute on Cronkite's show that will make somebody in his living room say, "He can settle the Middle East better than Rockefeller or Johnson or Reagan" could settle the Middle East.

I don't think so.

No. People have been told repeatedly that RN has had twenty years' experience in foreign policy; they have heard about his travels. (Incidentally, TV shots of RN abroad, pictures, not of RN saying anything, but of RN traveling in Vietnam, in Iran, in Kenya, in Israel, etc. help here at home.)

What RN says about Vietnam on a news clip will not lead anybody to think he can handle Vietnam better—he might, however, remind somebody who already thinks so, but the reminder is really not that important.

(In conclusion on this point, our big assets, experience, qualification, ability, are not things that can be shown on Walter Cronkite or Huntley-Brinkley. So, why do we want to be on those shows at all?)

Let me go further. We don't need TV to prove we are the most experienced, most qualified and most able; we don't need TV to get ourselves known; we don't need it to demonstrate we have the looks and the glibness. Do we need the damn thing at all and do we want it.

Yes. But only to do the job we want it to do. We want it controlled. And we can control it, because while the press can write that RN is doing X, Y or Z, the TV cameras can't show it, unless RN invites them to do so. I say, thus, that TV is a partially controllable medium and we ought to make it work for us.

In these areas. We can use TV to destroy some of the myths about RN. One of those is that RN is mean and ruthless. Another is that RN is a strictly political character who doesn't give a damn about principles or problems, but only about the politics of the situation. (Note: these are the same things that are said, or rather "were" said about Robert Kennedy, and look how he has managed TV to get rid of them. He makes with the shy little boy smile and talk, not about the political situation, but about the starving children in Recife, Brazil. "Can you imagine that; little children growing up without a glass of milk etc. etc. etc."

I thus think that RN's appearances on TV should be of the following kind:

1) He ought not go before the cameras to talk about politics, to talk about the primaries and all that garbage. The people who are astute about the business of politics know RN is a pro, but there is no sense showing you are a sophistical pro to a lot of people who think politics is a dirty business. In short, if we know a TV show is going to quiz you on how the primaries are going to go, or what Reagan and Romney are going to do, or who is moving where—just what good does it do us for RN to go on and explain all the intricacies. Do we make any new converts that way?

Summary of point one. Many people think politics is per se dirty business. Okay, that's the conventional wisdom. Then, rather than show that RN is an excellent and sophisticated politician, why the hell do we want to talk about politics at all on a TV camera to ten million people. We don't need the exposure; and we don't need to remind the prudish that RN is an excellent politician.

Point Two: To destroy the myth that RN is mean and that he places politics ahead of principles, RN ought to get on shows where he can kid himself, where he can talk about family, where he can crack jokes about past foibles. On other shows, he ought to talk about problems, dismiss questions about primaries and say, we have to concern ourselves not with political management, but the goal. In short, use the TV to convey the impression that RN isn't thinking about New Hampshire or Wisconsin, but about Harlem and Appalachia.

Specifically, then, Buchanan would rather see RN on Cronkite telling a joke about himself than being quoted on Vietnam. If a guy doesn't know if RN can handle Vietnam, that minute won't convince him. But a guy who thinks RN is a humorless S.O.B. might be stunned and convinced by a grinning RN telling about his "getting stoned in Caracas." [4]

2. Memo to Richard Nixon, "Research," April 17, 1968

I have given some thought to our research situation and it seems to me that our answer lies somewhere along these lines. First, let us recognize that we have a very small staff, that we cannot expect it to do first tier research in-depth with some great breakthrough. What we can expect is that they will be equipped to brief us on anything we want. We can expect that they will act as harvesters of the available material.

HOW TO USE RESEARCH

Given our situation, with this small staff, we must concentrate upon relevant research, which is quite precisely what RN wants and what RN himself can use. That has got to be our first priority. And the only one who can determine that is RN himself. Thus Buchanan recommends that either Buchanan or Chapin or someone designated get from RN on a regular basis just what RN wants research to do for him.

Right now, research is not getting the necessary guidance, and the necessary guidance can only come from RN. If RN asks for a great deal, then research can expand according to RN's needs, or we can set RN's demands in front of him and have him list priorities.

This sounds elementary, but the problem in research is that they are flying blind; they are too small to turn out everything one associates with a national campaign, position papers from A to Z, etc. etc.

Their first purpose is to service the candidate, and only the candidate can know precisely what he wants done.

Now, for the second purpose.

When no demands are being made, research should yet be moving, continuing to gather and winnow material, and working in anticipation of future needs. For this also, however, Research needs guidance from RN as to just what areas to concentrate in.

(Let me put it this way. The Research Effort we have today is nothing more than an expansion of the one-man operation we ran with in 1966. The research I did was a) specifically what RN requested for his speech material and b) the regular reading and gathering and filtering through. I realize the Big Show requires a hell of a lot more—but the needs of the candidate still come first, and only the candidate can know them exactly, and he is the one who can best project what he will need.)

RECOMMEND: That RN on a regular basis tell Chapin or Buchanan or whomever he designates to be the pipeline just what he wants from the Research people and when. . . .

Secondly, that RN tell research, or rather tell the pipeline to research, what priorities he wants set on long-range projects in what areas he wants them done.

Third, that the Research people be taken out of the Issue Mail Area if at all possible.

Fourth, that the Research People submit to RN on a regular basis a brief progress report of what they are working on and where they are going, so that RN can cut off this or that project and tell them to move in this or that direction.

Let me add here a number of important points. We delude ourselves I think if we are expecting the Research group we have, which is quality in my view and competent, to come up with position papers on a thousand different subjects. Basically what we have here is a small strong arm for the candidate to use as he sees fit.

If we do not keep in communication with it, if we do not provide guidance (which comes directly from RN's demands), then the research effort will be flying blind, and they will miss the mark time after time. I think, however, that with constant instruction from the plane we can get valuable service out of them.

We must remember I think that the only research that amounts to a damn is what gets into the public print and what gets into the public print is going to come nine times out of ten out of RN.

I think it would be a mistake to have a massive operation going here independent of RN and working on great research papers which are never going to get us anything which RN is never going to say. The important thing is that seven paragraphs is all that is going to be run.

This does not preclude the need for more people which exists. It does not preclude the need for more writers which exists. It just argues for effective use of what we have. [5]

3. Memo to Richard Nixon, July 13, 1968

Lying unnoticed before our eyes in the breakdown of the Gallup Poll is the answer to our riddle; RN's landslide victory is sitting right there in front of us. I have already documented the quintessential importance of RN winning the Wallace Protestants—the other wing of RN's victory lies in the Humphrey Catholics.

Everyone is squealing about RN's 7 percent of the black vote and RN's 4 percent of the Jewish vote. The crisis and the opportunity lie in RN's 27 percent of the Catholic vote against HHH. . . .

These statistics are telling us something that we can ignore only at the cost of victory this coming November.

First, let's take the Jewish vote. If we multiplied our present Jewish vote by five, we would be adding fewer than 400,000 new voters. In other words to go from 4 percent of the Jewish vote to 20 percent of the Jewish vote would add to RN's total about 386,000 new supporters.

On the other hand, if RN increased his support among Catholics from 27 percent which he has against HHH to 30 percent (which RN already has against McC), RN would be adding 510,000 new supporters to his cause.

That 3 percentage point increase that RN can easily pick up among Catholics also amounts to more than all the Jews and Negroes combined that RN has right now—which as I pointed out from the current Gallup Poll is under 500,000.

Now let's look at the Catholic vote.

RN is currently running at 27 percent of those 17,000,000 votes, which means RN is reaping about 4,600,000 Catholic votes, or just a shade under that figure. In other words, RN has 46 Catholics for every Negro supporting. RN's Catholic support is nine times RN's Jewish and Negro support combined in terms of total votes.

These statistics are in themselves astounding. But more important is where we get the votes to win this election.

If we look at it cold-bloodedly in terms of votes—we should be putting seven times as much time and money and media and writing in special interest appeals to Catholics and Jews— because they have seven times as many votes.

But even seven times the effort would not be sufficient if we argue from reason and logic—because the Catholic is one hell of a lot easier to win over from Hubert than is the Jew or the Negro. The latter two are the most committed of Democrats. (JFK did better with Jews than he did with Catholics; and since 1964 the Negroes are lost to the Republicans for a generation.)

There is no reason on God's earth why in this day and age HHH, the liberal Protestant Druggist, should be getting twice as many Catholic votes as RN.

Let's put it this way.

Suppose RN has in mind making a speech like Black Capitalism, which is directed to our black friends, or perhaps writing a piece for the Zionist magazine which is directed to our Jewish friends. If RN's purpose is to raise his percentage among these groups he will find that:

An increase of 1 percent among Jewish voters adds 24,000 new supporters to RN's ranks.

An increase of 1 percent among Negro voters adds 55,000 more supporters to RN's ranks.

An increase of 1 percent among Catholic voters adds 170,000 more supporters to RN's ranks.

My contention is further that it is easier for RN to pick up that 1 percent among Catholics, than it is among the traditionally hostile Negro and Jewish communities. The logic seems to me to be undeniable; if we are going to make special group interest, minority interest appeals—let's make them to the Catholics.

It is easier for RN to gain ground here; it is less risky in terms of backlash to make specific appeals to RCs as opposed to Jews and Negroes; and it is a thousand times more promising.

Let's remember too that Cardinal Cushing and Jack Kennedy won't be in this ball game; and Catholics in 1968 are one hell of a lot more conservative and receptive to an RN positions approach, than are the Negroes and the Jews.

In terms of votes, 50 percent of the Catholic vote would mean more to a candidate than to get every Negro and Jewish vote in the United States.

If RN can raise his percentage of the Catholic vote 13 points—from 27 percent against HHH to 40 percent against HHH—the votes he would add would be equivalent to raising himself from 7 percent of the Negro vote to 37 percent and from 4 percent of the Jewish vote to 28 percent.

It is utterly impossible for RN to get 37 percent of the Negro vote; it is next to impossible for RN to get 28 percent of the Jews—but to jump from 27 percent of the Catholics to 40 percent is not impossible; and if we did it, we would have broken up the historic Democratic coalition and won a national landslide.

Hubert's Catholics have half of our victory and the Protestants of George Wallace have the other half. If we get one of these halves back, we win; if we get them both, we can win a landslide—and the two objectives are not mutually exclusive.

It is time to ask ourself—what is the best we can do among Jews and Negroes. I would say 20 percent of the Negroes and 20 percent of the Jewish vote, given our current situation and only four months to go. If we made a Herculean, Jewish-Negro pitch and reached that percentage among both (it would cost us votes to Wallace) we would be adding some 1,100,000 Negro and Jewish votes. We can get the same number of new votes—1,100,000—by raising our Catholic total from 27 to 34—at little or no loss to Wallace. This seems incredible but the statistics are there.

What do we conclude from this memo:

1) Hubert Humphrey will be looking for a Catholic, if he is thinking, to put on that ticket with him—and the case for Teddy Kennedy becomes even more convincing.

2) If RN intends any future special interest appeals—for God's sake, let us give the Catholics some consideration.

3) RN's research staff should find out what is the gut "Catholics" issue which unites them—and I would think it is the question of parochial schools and some [sort] of tax relief for what they feel is an excessive burden of supporting both their own and their neighbors' school. If we go with the tax credit idea—let's make sure we put the Catholics and Lutheran Schools up high in the copy.

4) Let's stop looking around so hard for what the Negroes want to hear, and what the Jews want RN to say on the Middle East—and let's start taking some polls of Catholic voters' interests and concerns.

5) As for the Middle East and Israel—it now becomes clear that there is no mileage whatsoever in a hard-line pro-Israel posture by RN. As noted, if RN's Jewish vote goes from 4 percent to 20 percent, he picks up fewer than 400,000 votes. It's a waste of time and effort.

6) RN should reconsider, if he has already decided, whether we ought not definitely to take the Conservative Party endorsement, and let [Senator Jacob] Javits and his friends squeal their heads off.

7) It would be seven times as valuable for RN to show up at a visibly Catholic event as it would be a Jewish event.

8) It might be in RN's interest to begin to say what intelligent men are already saying—that when it comes to the Middle East or anywhere else—that an American statesman's first duty is to place America first, and not any other country, no matter how strong our times or our commitments.

(I am not arguing for RN to come off anti-Jew and score points that way at all. I just say that quite frankly, slobbering over the Israeli lobby is not going to get us anything, and so we ought to stand tall on the issue. It would appear the same is true of the Negroes.)

9) This offers new thoughts on the Vice Presidential thing—which Buchanan did not mention in his memo on Reagan.

10) Ethnic groups which tend to be Catholic should be given first priority consideration in media and time and RN statements and considerations. Among minority groups religion becomes now a factor in our considerations.

11) Positive efforts should be made to have RN and family and kids in specifically Catholic settings—such settings should take priority over Negro and Jewish settings.

FINAL NOTE: To RN/ From Buchanan

We have come up here in the last two weeks with the Wallace in-depth analysis which no one has to date refuted; and here is a Catholic analysis which would seem to me to be self-evident to any of our people who are supposed to be analyzing the polls. But our poll people, to my knowledge, have never even mentioned either—and our media people have not yet acted on the first—the Wallace threat.

If this kind of analysis—of both Wallace and the Catholic thing—as opposed to the Negro-Jewish approach has not been brought to RN's attention by his poll analysts—then perhaps they are reading our polls through rose-colored liberal glasses—and they ought to be replaced.

My suggestion is that some of us in research be given access to the polls that we are taking—so that we can do some of our own analysis; that Alan Greenspan be instructed to analyze the results of our polls as well as the "media" people; that further, strategy people be asked either to refute the analysis we have come up with—or start guiding the campaign and the advertising by them.

What I am contending in these recent memos and what I have yet to see refuted is that all this endless talk we have been getting about RN losing unless he gets the Negro and Jewish vote is a pile of crap. We have let ourselves be sold a bill of goods. The Eastern liberal Establishment which goes down the line for the Democrats has made the Republican Party dance to its own tune; it has told us that we cannot win without Negroes and Jews—and it continues to feed us this nonsense every day.

The power of the Negro and the Jew to damage RN in this election lies in this: The Negro loud-mouths are given access to the public communications media by a guilt-ridden establishment—and the Jews control that communications media.

We don't want to antagonize or alienate these people—they can damage us.

But they're not our voters; and if we go after them, we'll go down to defeat chasing a receding rainbow. The Irish, Italian, Polish Catholics of the big cities—these are our electoral majority—they, and the white Protestants of the South and Midwest and rural America. That way lies victory.

RN—By dropping to 4 percent of the Jewish vote and 7 percent of the black vote—we have been given a tremendous flexibility; man, we can't get any lower—and so RN is now free of trying to placate these people, of trying to acquiesce their views—and he can tell it like it is to the whole damn country. Let's face it. We are right now at 35 percent of the vote nationally—six points under Barry Goldwater. The way I see it we are just about at bedrock—the guys we have will be hard to lose in any event; they are damn near all Republicans; it is time for RN to start swinging and telling it precisely like it is. [6]

4. Memo to Richard Nixon, July 28, 1968

[. . .] I confess to a good degree of apprehension over this Vietnam thing. Some headlines are invariably going to say "Nixon Softens Viet Position" or "Nixon Shifts Vietnam Position," or something akin to that. For instance, De-Americanization is a code word for a more doveish position than we now have—and it would be legitimate for a writer to say our new position is more doveish. My concern is this. The conservatives . . . might well raise hell on this Vietnam thing, saying RN is making a new "aperture a sinistra," that we are seeing the old Nixon swing to the left, once the right gives him the nomination—and I wonder what the reaction of [Senator Strom] Thurmond et al. in the South will be. In short, I am wondering if our carving out a more doveish position—right now—might not anger some of our hawk delegates in the South and generate enough erosion to jeopardize the nomination. I thought I should pass this along to you before getting together this afternoon.[7]

5. Memo to Richard Nixon, August 1968

When Chief Justice Earl Warren announced his retirement in June 1968, President Lyndon Johnson nominated Associate Justice Abe Fortas to fill the vacancy. Fortas would not be confirmed, due in part to questions about his close relationship with Johnson as well as questionable financial dealings; he would eventually resign from the Supreme Court in 1969. Nixon nominee Warren Burger would instead become the next Chief Justice.

I talked with Austin of <u>Time</u> tonight. He wanted to know if RN's position has shifted on the Fortas thing. I said not a centimeter since Fortas was named. He

said that Herb Klein had led either him or someone to believe that RN's statement about opposing all filibusters was something of a movement toward the
appointment. I don't know what Herb has been told to say, but if I were RN, I
would sit right where we are. We have already gotten the benefit of our position—and paid the price. Why take a new position on this thing?[8]

6. Memo to Richard Nixon, "Strategy, Some Thoughts On," August 15, 1968

1) This period of tranquility has, like the days after the Oregon primary, lost us
some momentum, I think. I think that moratoriums have just about outlived
their usefulness, when we consider it is 85 days to the finish. When we sit idle
like this—without taking the offensive and holding it, to start nit-picking us—
and we have to answer them. Maybe this is inevitable during this period, but I
think that, like the period between May and August, we are letting the others do
the firing, and we are only defending, not an enviable political position.

2) I am inclined to go with RFK's theory of going "flat out to the finish line"
in the fall. Throw Humphrey on the Defensive and keep him right there until
November. Indict this Administration for every sin of which it is guilty, and
they are many. I think we will be making a mortal error if we think that the
Establishment is going to give RN points for running anything approaching a
Goody-Two Shoes campaign. I don't think we need to ever again say that HHH
is a nice and honorable man, in whose hands the country would be well off. We
don't have to be irresponsible—just candid—and as President this weasel would
be a disaster.

3) The ancient complaint. I got a call from some character from Downey,
Cal., who said that the tv spot he heard was an excerpt from RN's acceptance
speech, promising something on law and order—followed by fifteen minutes of
applause. It was general and not specific; he thought it very ineffective; so did
his friends. I know this is old ground—but I think the spots we run ought to
state clearly and tersely what the hell has happened in this country in the last five
years—specifically, what RN is going to do—and then say, damn it, elect him.
Maybe we ought to write the spots ourselves—or get some of Reagan's ad guys
to write them. Honestly, much as I like Len [Garment], he just doesn't have the
instincts to cut the hell out of these people like HHH or to make the gut issues
that anger and concern people. They're all soft sell—telling them to start hitting
gut issues and making gut appeals is like trying to get Mary Poppins to act like
Eartha Kitt. They don't know how to do it.

4) The Republicans are far behind the Democrats in types of appearances. I
am sure we are now scheduling speeches and rallies and the rest of the traditional

crap. What we should realize is what the Democrats do so well—speak not only with their words but with their settings. Where RN appears sometimes says as much to the nation as what he says there. Because Democrats have lower income, lower education supporters, they have to use symbols to appeal to all the senses—as well as to the intellectuals with words. Thus LBJ wanders through Appalachia and RFK inspects an Indian reservation. So, too, [New York mayor John] Lindsay's tours through Harlem are essential symbols. By walking, he is saying he gives a damn.

Thought should be given to issue-oriented appearances by RN. I have sent examples to Whitaker of a number of them. Maybe they are no good—but we should think in these terms. We can speak to poor people—other than by the words from the candidate's mouth.

There will be pockets of unemployment in the Steel Industry in Nov. What about a visit to Union Hall, drop a statement there, talk to these guys about their problem. What about a visit to a prison—to talk about how these places are turning out as many criminals as we put in. What about a visit to some shipyards to talk with some idle workers about the decline in the Merchant Marine. The Computer Job bank thing is in North Carolina—what if RN went down to that thing—and gave the reporters a briefing on how it works—and how it can apply on a national scale.

RN has mentioned at times that a lot of people don't read the papers; they look at the pictures—this, pictures plus captions, is how a number of immigrants learned the language. RN can speak through pictures as well as through words—and there must be one hundred thousand good settings for RN to be in when he drops his statement—so that his surroundings reinforce what he has to say.

For example—RN might stroll into a Catholic School and lecture the fifth grade for a little while—and there drop some statement on the contribution of religious parents who take the burden of education etc. and that this contribution should be reflected and recognized by government.

A visit to a hospital might serve as a background for talking about Vietnam (if war wounded are there) or to talk with the staff about the shortages in doctors and nurses etc.

5) RN has talked about excitement in a campaign. One way to be exciting is to be controversial. I think we ought to give consideration to holding our fire on the likes of these bastards like [Reverend Ralph] Abernathy and others [*sic*] charges RN with racism etc. And just wait on them. And one day, get up on a high horse and kick the hell out of them. Ninety percent of the people in this country think that Abernathy is an unpolished and disreputable clod.[9] The

same is true of those who are saying Thurmond is running the campaign. We ought to give thought to some occasion when we can program a little righteous indignation against these clowns—which will score heavily I think, and stir up the enthusiasm. What we want to avoid is to allow the Establishment to be setting some sort of guidelines of niceness which we are supposed to follow in this thing.

For what they are worth.

I talked briefly with Timmons and the others who are going to be with the Truth Squad group in Chicago [at the Democratic National Convention]. I think I know RN's positions better than anyone—and can write up the attack material rapidly. So, I talked with them and I wondered if I might not be more useful writing for those guys in Chicago during those days, than being in N.Y. watching it on television.[10]

7. Memo to Richard Nixon, September 1968

To reiterate briefly one point on Vietnam. I don't believe most people in this country really know how precisely where either RN or HHH stands. They get impressions of the positions of both—but I am sure they could only give the vaguest outlines of those positions.

But Humphrey has begun to give the impression in recent months and weeks especially as a man who doesn't know where he stands. RN ought—without restating his own position I think—point up its consistency—and indict HHH constantly on waffling on the central issue of our time.

"If you don't like Mr. Humphrey's position on Vietnam, just wait till his next press conference." You might also if you are asked about HHH saying that your position is escalation etc. answer:

"Listen, Mr. Humphrey hasn't even been able to get his own position on Vietnam down right—to his satisfaction—you can hardly expect him to report mine accurately. Essentially, my position now is what it has been for the last etc. etc.

"Mr. Humphrey on the other hand has an advantage in that he has been able to take both sides of every issue involving the war etc. etc. etc."[11]

8. Memo to H. R. Haldeman, September 25, 1968

The Time boys are really hot on this Agnew thing. They seem to think it is something of a disaster the way he is conducting his campaign, the foot-in-mouth disease they think he has contracted.

What I am wondering is if perhaps we may be giving too little attention to this problem. It has not bothered me a great deal, but the variety of different "clarifications" he has issued is bound to be making some impact with the general public.

Agnew ought to be on the offensive, and I would think that all these negative stories are the direct result of uncontrolled situations, press conferences and the like, interviews. What he could use I think is a first-rate writer to hammer the Administration and Humphrey twice a day and not be giving all these reporters other stories to write. He need not be as responsible as we are, thus his attacks can be made news out of the Agnew camp each day rather than having it be some clarification. I wonder if they don't need some more and better staff people over there working for this guy. Seriously, there must be some first-raters on the Hill who could do an effective job for him—with the two a day attacks. The apparent feeling of the <u>Time</u> guys that Agnew is a genuine disaster makes me think that this may have become a middling problem for us. For what it's worth.[12]

9. Memo to H. R. Haldeman, September/October 1968

Not all press are hostile. Last night when we delivered the NATO statement I had a talk with [Jerald] TerHorst, who seems to be an active collaborator in the Nixon cause. Extremely bright. He said that RN might well win the support of the <u>Detroit News</u> for which he works by a properly timed phone call to Peter Clark from the President—as well as to Martin Hayden. Clark is a young guy of thirty-six or so, extremely sharp. They have been for Lyndon but TerHorst says they would be extremely receptive to an RN phone call. Suggest calling both when they are in the area. I have a copy of Clark's speech to a graduating class of which he is quite proud, which I might draft a note of praise for from RN—very briefly saying RN had been given it by an aide, and RN might borrow some lines or ideas from it. You might mention to RN about TerHorst that we seem to have found one just man in Gomorrah.[13]

10. Memo to Richard Nixon, October 5, 1968

The attacks on RN and Agnew have accelerated in recent days—they have become incredibly irresponsible; RN has been accused of being part of an Administration that let people starve in West Virginia. And we continue along our merry way. With no one responding to this thing. I realize that Laird and X surrogate said this and that, and that we have a transcript to prove he said it—but it doesn't make a damn bit of difference if he replied or not—because it sure as hell is not turning up in the news columns.

As for Agnew, he is spending his time these days clearing up the record, or getting chopped up by the Press. He is getting this because he is not making enough hard and tough news to make these bastards sit up and write it as the lead. Now, I don't know about Hess, but from meeting him, I just doubt that he is the kind of nut-cutter RN needs right now.

I don't agree with Finch that the answer for Agnew is to get positive. Our job is not to make the New York Times happy. I think someone needs to kick the living hell out of Humphrey, and if he goes personally after us—then let's go right after him. I think Agnew has got to be that guy. We are letting Hubert off the defensive—he is on the attack every day—this for the most vulnerable candidate and the most vulnerable administration in history. . . .

Maybe the decision has been made for RN to ignore this stuff and perhaps that is right. But my own personal view is that we can't not only for political, but for simply the morale of our troops, let them get away with the type of ir-responsibility they have been getting away with.

My suggestion is that Buchanan go with Agnew for a while, and try to write two attacks a day for him—and have RN call Agnew and tell him this is what he wants done. We don't have any other guns than Agnew—and I think the experi-ence of the campaign shows this. To do the job that needs doing I would need some weight with Agnew, some way to get through his staff if there is resistance there—some press people, just two or so, that would be all we need. The objec-tive is to get Agnew in the headlines every day hammering these people—and let the editorial writers squeal.[14]

11. Memo to H. R. Haldeman and John Mitchell, October 13, 1968

The Agnew staff is wholly inadequate for a national campaign or for an effective Vice President of the United States. It is close to a total loss with George White perhaps the only salvageable member. They lack any grasp of national issues; they lack any knowledge of what a vice presidential candidate should be doing. If they did know, most of them would not be up to the mark—in particular the "press secretary," Herb Thompson.

The de-celeration, in shifting from the Nixon tour to the Agnew tour, is so dramatic as to send one flying through the windshield. There are two typewrit-ers on the plane—and they only get in the way of the stewardesses rushing whiskey to the journalists. No work is done on the plane—I did not observe much being done at the stops. One night when we stayed up until midnight to get the New York Times summary, we came close to provoking a mutiny among the secretaries.

Again, these people are loyal and dedicated to their Governor; but they don't belong in the National league.

The Governor himself is a personable fellow, who comes across quite well at rallies, who handles hecklers excellently, who makes a first-rate appearance on television, and who programs as well as any candidate I have seen. Given 300 to 500 words, he weaves them right into his speech—and he delivers his material in a soft-spoken manner that I find at least quite effective. On local television he is first rate. He is a decided asset to the campaign.

His weaknesses include his candor, his lack of information on national issues, and his lack of sophistication in areas of sensitivity, his unawareness of how an effective national candidate should work his staff to the greatest benefit.

His operation is an effective low-keyed thing on the Governor's part—but it is simply not the professional juggernaut we run on the RN plane—with deadlines met and with copy constantly pouring out. When I arrived there last week, Steve Hess was basically turning out some pedestrian co-ordinating committee-type stuff, on call from the candidate. In confidence, White told me that the Governor is not comfortable with Hess' material and prefers some of the nut-cutting stuff he received later in the week.

Agnew himself is deeply loyal to RN, deeply appreciative that RN did not call and chew him out when he punted a few, willing to do about anything RN asks, on cue.

BUCHANAN'S RECOMMENDATIONS

1) RN should make irregular calls to Agnew to keep his confidence up—and to let him know he has RN's full backing and that RN understands that the press is out to give him a screwing.

2) Since Agnew is going to be made increasingly the target of the HHH operation—with Agnew being portrayed as something of a boob, who is RN's first mistake, and who would be a dangerous man a heartbeat away—Agnew ought to be getting out some substantive in-depth stuff that de facto repudiates that argument. (I don't say Agnew should get off the offensive, but he should be dropping some thoughtful pieces which make the national press sit up and take notice and give the lie of the allegations about him.)

3) The TV people might give some thought to having Agnew put, full face, on national TV spots. He himself and his appearance are the best arguments we have against the kind of attack that is going to be mounted.

4) Keep in the back of our minds the possibility of an Agnew Nationwide TV appearance, for some of the same purposes as the RN Fund speech—apolo-

gizing pro vita sua—if the attacks on Agnew get rough which I think they well might.

5) <u>Do not</u> try to revamp their operation now with three weeks to go. Agnew would see it as a vote of no confidence. It would shake them up, and him up—and we should go down to the wire with the team in the same shape it is in now.

6) My own thinking is that Buchanan can be helpful to Agnew by giving him something of a briefing each morning, by writing materials for him, by acting as liaison with the RN plane who can feed stuff through me to the Governor. I get along well with the staff over there; I represent no threat to any of them; they want help; George White recognizes that they need help. And since this is the front where the attack is going to come, it needs a bit of beefing up—without sending them someone or some group which would lead them to believe we didn't think they could cut it themselves.

7) Agnew is feeling badly about the attacks on him as the weak link in the chain—and RN personally ought to attend to this problem and keep his confidence up.[15]

12. Memo to Dwight Chapin, October 18, 1968

Our early warning system is picking up signs of real trouble in these last 18 days, trouble that can be avoided, as it can be foreseen easily.

We talked with [CBS correspondent] Mike Wallace the other day. He says a consensus is developing in the press corps that RN is inaccessible, that his campaign is super efficient but bland, that we are programmed perfectly, but that we are sort of avoiding controversy and coasting to victory. The press, bored with the rally speech and paying little attention to radio speeches which have been committee-prepared and are sinking without a trace, is now looking for new angles—and finding them. They are going out and they are going to find it and it is going to be damaging to us—seriously damaging unless we counteract it. We have treated these guys with the best of care—but we have fed the stomach and starved the soul—as someone once said.

So, our thinking is this. If our controlled and expected and programmed appearances have lost their news value—as they have—then we must find some controlled and "unexpected" appearances to get our news—and we can do that job.

It is time for a return to the Spirit of New Hampshire, which was one of RN openness and even occasional camaraderie with the press, which was one of the unexpected and the surprising. We can still do it, even with 125 reporters along as opposed to 25.

Possible suggestions:

The unexpected and the unscheduled appearance, at a school anywhere that surprises the press and makes them act as reporters and write it.

The unscheduled RN drop by in the plane to talk to some reporter and too for RN to start ranging off—on his own—into some subject that is of intense interest like the New Majority that RN intends to build or the Successor to the Roosevelt Coalition, how RN hopes to pull together these elements of the old Democratic establishment and put them together with the GOP for a coalition to govern for a decade.

The point in both cases is that the press is rightly tired and bored with re-writing our releases. RN can make them into reporters again at the same time that he gives his own advance thought and care and preparation to his materials and then goes back in the plane, or finds some surprise occasion, to deliver it "extemporaneously."

RN has already demonstrated with [*New York Times* associate editor] Johnny Apple that it can be done. He was reportedly moaning and groaning until his conversation with RN—after which he was genuinely elated, which report came from Wallace—after we had had our conversation.

If RN walks in and controls a situation—then it is not a press conference—and RN can talk about any particular subject that interests him and that is newsworthy.

My point here is that it requires nothing on our parts, but to start using our imagination a bit—and to cease running this show like a Prussian Fire Drill. Unless we get a little of the unexpected and new, and hence newsworthy, in this thing toward the last two weeks—then we are going to find these guys out researching for new and different leads, like "Is Nixon Aloof?" "Where is this Campaign's Achilles Heel?"

The old adage about an idle mind being the devil's workshop is especially true of the press corps, where the devil is always close at hand. So, what I suggest and Ron [Ziegler] suggests, is a simple return to the philosophy of the primaries—controlling the news by providing new and different and exciting and newsworthy events which force these guys to cover them—in order to cover themselves and their competition.

The point we make is that radio speeches and rallies are old hat. They are not going to be reported any more unless they are dramatic and unless we use our collective imagination to find some new and different and newsworthy thing to force them to cover—they are going to write their own stories and, as JFK used to say, "we don't want that."[16]

13. Memo to Richard Nixon, October 22, 1968

In these last ten days I would argue strongly for RN presenting the image of both a winner and a President. I would recommend an easing off in the number of cheer lines, an easing back of the shouted lines at rallies. I would recommend an increase in the depth and substance of the speech—something like Cincinnati, which I did not see but which I heard was extremely effective.

Also, we ought not again I think to have the next President talking about how many rapes occurred in the last five minutes. I think that continued use of broad figures, said not in a shrill but in a serious fashion are fully adequate.

In hitting Humphrey, . . . RN ought I think to do this more as a winner and a President, as we did in New Hampshire with Governor Romney. We needled him, made several jokes about him, but were never bitter, because we knew we would need his support. RN might treat Humphrey in the same manner. We can still stick it in him about Obedience School, etc., but do it in such a way as to leave no impression he has stung us, no impression we are angry or bitter, but rather jab him a few times as though he were a bumbling and ineffective boxer who had been unable to lay a glove on us.

Further recommendation is that RN show a relaxed and confident mood, which could not be better exemplified than a trip through the plane or something like that to needle some of the press people. The little things do more than anything else to show that RN feels confident and thinks things are going well.

As for the stump speeches yesterday, I think they are when RN talks at the audience, or discusses some things with rather than sort of shouting the cheer lines to them. Price points out, the cool as opposed to the "hot" comes over. Also, our campaign is judged not by what is seen of it in person but by how cool the press judges it to be.

Thus, the presidential impression. The aloof but friendly for Hubert the well-meaning clown, the more serious moments, the [*sic*] for support, a cutting back on anything that smacks of braggadocio, and the call for people to join in a common cause, rule out things like a vote for me is a vote for peace, and for Humphrey is a vote for failure. The over-simplistic things we can do without.

Again, a final note. The thing to maintain these last few days I think is "our cool" and our "flexibility." We can get on the offensive without being offensive.

I don't know if RN feels comfortable with it, but if he uses any of these occasions just to get up before the crowd and start [talking] about the kind of country he wanted to build, the kind of nation he wants to see, and we are going to need Democrats, we know there are difficult times ahead. Sort of Wilsonian. If it doesn't come off, we haven't lost anything but a single rally.

One last thought—I think we ought to be now campaigning like the President of the United States and campaigning for election. Above the madding crowd, above Hubert and George.

On the cheer lines and on the criticism, suggest that RN talk them or speak them into microphone, and let the microphone do the amplification, rather than shouting them into the mike. Oftentimes, RN can say the same thing, but if shouted, it sounds like a more bitter attack than if simply said, with the kind of disdain for HHH that he merits and that we should practice.[17]

14. Memo to Richard Nixon (via H. R. Haldeman), November 13, 1968

Some of these thoughts I have already relayed to Bryce [Harlow], but I wanted to get them directly to RN before getting out of town. These reflect some of my views on the White House staff, and RN can discount them given Buchanan's prejudices and predispositions.

1) If RN is going to build a New Majority, we have to get cracking on building and expanding the party in the border states and the South, as well as the Midwest and West. The party has to be united and working together in all these states for us to win—1968 demonstrated the tremendous resiliency and strength of the Democrats. My own suggestion would be to put Sears in as a White House assistant with responsibility to the President for reporting on the condition of the party in every state; he should, as well have some measure of authority for settling disputes and scrounging for new Congressional candidates and for liaison with the Hill and the RNC. Sears is loyal to RN, enormously competent, well liked by press and politicians and without peer in terms of knowledge of the various States' situations.

2) Press Secretary. Directly and indirectly, several members of the press corps friendly to RN have indicated that it would be a grave error for Ziegler to be named press spokesman. First, he is an "advertising man," which turns them off at once; secondly, he is without knowledge on issues and politics, and third, he has no seasoning.

3) RN needs close by him some advisor with "soul" for lack of a better term. By that I mean someone who understands and will counsel RN to utilize the vast powers inherent in the majority of the office and the respect in which it is held. FDR and the Kennedys recognized that you do not speak to the poor in statements and speeches alone, that you speak in symbols and gestures as well. A dramatic and gracious RN visit to the Negro community, done with dignity and decorum, can help more to win the blacks back to the national fold than any of Humphrey's "programs." The same is true of the young. RN, I believe, should

have close to him someone who recognizes and knows how RN can use the tremendous powers, the third and fourth dimensions of communication offered to him by the office he now holds. I don't know who is the man, but RN needs some people of both passion and compassion close by.

4) RN needs to widen his circle of advisors, in my view. The point is not that any particular individual should be there, but that more points of view should be represented. The Congressional Establishment, the Liberal Establishment nationally, the Jewish intellectuals, the conservatives, labor, the Wall Street Crowd and the business community, the stock market: RN should know how all of these various elements are going to react to various moves. And to do that RN has got to have a base of advisors who know something about each of these, who march to the different drums of differing groups of Americans.

There were in my own view a few mistakes made in the general election that might have been avoided if the ideas had been run by a few more people.

Nowhere is this need for reliable backboards more urgent than in the final selection of Cabinet members. I know the requirements of secrecy and time, but I think that these selections should be checked out as exhaustively as possible for both competence and political impact of their appointment. We are going to have to live with these people; they can make or break us, and if we err on any side, for God's sake, let it be on the side of too much checking and too many opinions sought.

5) In selecting the new men around him in the White House, RN must concentrate not only on people who know how to administer things, but on some men who have a clear idea of what they want the Nixon Administration to accomplish. We need some men near RN with fire in their bellies who want to change things, to accomplish set goals, not just to hold power.

6) RN in moving as President should not be a "conservative" in his actions; he should not be induced into any sense of caution or hesitance by the fact of our tiny plurality. That is a myth we can disregard, if we will fill the Cabinet with Big Men. If RN will act with decisiveness and daring, then we will build the majority as President that we did not win as candidate.

7) The greatest asset we have as President is that trust, that bond between President and people which LBJ squandered away by lack of candor and lack of openness. This bond of trust can survive and even prosper in failure, if we maintain it. Remember JFK was never held higher in public esteem than when he took public responsibility for the disaster at the Bay of Pigs.

8) In setting up his White House staff RN ought not let himself be strait-jacketed by any past models, and I for one would like to see on the staff there

perhaps some maverick intellectual like a Milton Friedman responsible for spinning off ideas about how RN is going to accomplish this goal of decentralization.[18]

15. Memo to H. R. Haldeman, December 20, 1968

I have given considerable thought over the last day to the organizational structure of the staff, as you outlined, and unless you left a portion of it out, I don't think it will work to the benefit of the President.

First. You, as I understand, are to sit astride all incoming paper, to read it and to pass final judgment on it. This will tend to be a rather inhibiting factor if we wanted to criticize to the President some element of your own operation, which is really an all-embracive as of now. Suppose the press operation is breaking down, and the press is grumbling about it; suppose special assistants are being flooded with calls about the ineptitude of the appointments operation; suppose there are complaints about "nobody getting to see the President" and the complaints are reaching a point where it is damaging the Administration; suppose someone wants to demand a restructure of the staff. Some of these things the President should judge for himself on the basis of "privileged" input. I am not denigrating your objectivity. In my experience you have always passed things on, where I have felt they "ought" to go in. But the presence itself of a single screen or censor of sorts induces a self-imposed censorship on the writer. Everybody writing memos is going to tailor them to take into consideration the fact that "your Administrative Boss is watching you."

I don't think this a wise arrangement and a bit further on I will mention a few organizational reforms which I think will eliminate what could be a continuing problem in the quality of the paper the President receives.

Secondly, you have in effect told staff that any "end runs," especially to the President, would mean "it's been nice knowing you in the White House."

It seems to be unrealistic frankly to attempt to block all end runs. They are a part of human nature; they represent the oldest play in American politics; on many, many occasions they have resulted in short-circuiting a foolish decision or recommending a brilliant idea.

Even JFK recognized that Bundy and Schlesinger and O'Brien and Sorenson could not be expected to go, hat-in-hand, to Kenny O'Donnell, outside the door, every time they wanted to see the President. So Kennedy deliberately collaborated in their use of Mrs. Lincoln's entrance into the Oval Room, and some grievous staff problems were prevented.

What Kennedy did was to "institutionalize" the end run. As RN is not the type who likes to "chat" with staffers, etc., and our staff is more effective with the written than the spoken word, I would suggest the creation of a <u>Dissenters Pipe-line to the President, a secure pouch in which the staff could get to the President "for his eyes only"</u> real concerns on their mind, whether within or without the White House. The fact that it existed would be an ongoing boost to staff mo-rale; it would not even have to be used regularly. And should it become clogged or heavy with traffic, the President should himself instruct X staffer to tend to his knitting, etc. If you talk with Bryce [Harlow] you will find that Eisenhower had a different arrangement yet with the same motive. To provide automatically 15 minutes with the President to any staffer who requested it, but the staff had damnsite have something significant to say.

<u>Third</u>. The injunction that anything regarding urban affairs or anything re-garding national security be cleared first with Moynihan or Kissinger in effect makes them czars of information in these areas, and it provides simply too much power in their hands without a check, but maybe I didn't get this correctly.

I agree with the need to coordinate the material before the President, to get all proposals, and their pros and cons before him at the same time. But if you leave all coordination in the hands of either of them in these enormously broad areas, <u>then in effect they can make the decision for the President by the manner of presentation</u>. It is a simple thing to accomplish.

I don't argue that they will. I only argue that the President should have his own built-in checks on his own top people, that the President should have dis-sent and vigorous disagreement built into the White House Staff Structure, and it does not appear to be there under the current arrangement.

<u>Of vital importance, it seems to me, the President himself has got to have an independent flow of information so that he can ask informed questions, cogent questions of his top advisers; he has got to have background so that he can throw out another alternative in addition to the two that Kissinger may have presented. In addition, the President should have a brief-case full of his own "ideas" to bounce off the top advisers.</u>

The way the thing is established, RN's only foreign policy ideas will already [have] been screened by Kissinger, upon whom there remains no check.

<u>Fourth</u>. The Press Office. The Ziegler approach to clear every talk with him, or let him know we had it, differs from [LBJ advisor] Marvin Watson's approach of monitoring calls only in that it contains a "public disclosure" clause, with the onus on the staff member.

<u>Now, on all matters on which one talks for public record, I concur whole-heartedly</u>. But with the press since I have been with RN, almost 99 percent of

what I tell them is not for attribution. I think I have always been able to make a good case for the President-elect and for what he tried to accomplish in my own words, matching wits with these people—and we have only been burnt a few times in three years. In those three years, I have been able to soften and improve a hell of a lot of stories, to get good columns written, to get good reports turned out in the public media about our whole operation.

Now, if I am going to have to file everyone I talk with to Ziegler, it is quite apparent that when a bad story or column comes out, and it is found Buchanan talked with the individual, Buchanan will henceforth be watched. It may have been that I screwed up, but it may have been that I improved the column, or prevented a worse one.

The point is that the President, to his own advantage, has to repose a measure of trust in the people around him and loyal to him, not just in their personal loyalty, but in their capacity to deal with these people. I know that Price and Buchanan and Garment and many others have press people with whom they talk to and work with, contacts that are private and which we use in behalf of the cause. If we have to name these people every time they come in, again, that will not be censorship, but everyone is going to say, what the hell, why risk it. If TIME writes a bad article and I've talked with Fentress or Austin, then I'll catch hell and it's not worth it, so I won't talk with them or when I do, I'll give them a lot of crap. You will be inducing that kind of attitude.

I think this was one of the mistakes of Eisenhower. It is the daily press, the Historians of the Present, who are responsible for the fact that he is not rated as a great President. Only the historians can save Ike now—and whether we like these people or not, they are like Communists, we have to talk with them and deal with them and trade with them, or we are not going to be able to really put RN across.

I would hold up as the example the whole primary season where a number of us were open with these people, took risks and chances, but, damn it, it paid off. We won't win unless we get in the game and risk some ships.

Fifth: The emphasis of the meeting seemed to be almost totally how to keep things and people away from the President. Perhaps that is just an impression, but if RN is going to change things, if he is going to turn the government in a new direction, if he is going to innovate policies, as well as simply to react correctly to events, then he has got to have a steady flow of fresh, unadulterated and even occasionally bizarre ideas. He has got to take some risks and chances, and we seem to be structuring this collateral paper-shuffling to minimize the risk and chance. We have to remember I think that we lack what Ike and JFK and FDR had which is that personal following and charisma and trappings of royalty which led the public to ignore or sympathize with failures. We are going to provide our own excitement and drama and our Cabinet and top it off is a Cabinet of highly competent technicians, with Moynihan the only innovator and Kissinger's forte is in penetrating analysis from what I have seen; not in drama or imagination.

Sixth: This seems to be a corporate or para-military, pyramidic structure, which does not lend itself to the office of the Presidency. From my own experience the President is more like a publication or newspaper. "Going over his head to the Publisher" is a way of life there, and it is in that kind of "creative chaos" that you get the kind of dash and color and imagination and boldness and daring that I am afraid we are going to need—and which doesn't seem to be programmed.

Seventh: Let me suggest that RN adopt, on top of the existing pyramid for his own benefit, a circular structure where he, like FDR, draws directly and regularly on the people on his staff for ideas and criticism of what is going on, and for what should go on.

This is something no one can impose on him, but it is needed. RN has about him some twenty or more people in whom he has some confidence I think and whom he should constantly cross check things. The potential [Eugene] McCarthy appointment would have been a disaster in a matter of weeks I believe, with that arrogant messiah up at the UN spouting his own policy and philosophy and anyone of half a dozen of RN's advisers, it would seem to me, would have shot that thing down before it got above the treeline. I don't know how that got so far—perhaps the press is wrong—but it indicates to me decisions are not being put through enough tests.

If RN is not going to have something like this within his staff, how is he going to get the bad news which he has to have, on a regular basis to know where something needs changing. Also, again, RN should know regularly I think what the press is thinking and writing and saying. The Fourth Estate may be the American Institution most in need of reform, but we have to deal with it, because in the short run, and very possibly in the long run, they are going to be grading our papers. TV is now final solution—both Romney and the Vice President-elect can testify.

Eighth: Staff members I think have to have a channel of communication with the President for another reason. To them it is the lifeblood, frankly, which enables them to represent the President's interest, to look out for those interests, to draw information from the press and the Departments. If it is known that some of RN's aides cannot get his ear at any time, their usefulness to the President is destroyed and though the President may have a staff of forty for operational purposes it will amount to only those few who are known to have his confidence and communicate with him.

Similar arguments obtain with regard to salary and titles of the President's aides, a matter which is properly the subject of another memo.

In the last analysis Robert, <u>Structure is Policy</u>; that is why the N. Vietnamese are battling in Paris over the structure of that conference; that is why the structure of this White House staffing can't come off some block chart, because the lines of communication on that chart are going to determine the direction of the Nixon Years.[19]

3   White House Communication Strategies

The start of the 1960s marked the beginning of the television age of politics, and the shift to a more image-based presidency demanded greater attention to White House communication strategies.[1] While Richard Nixon had a reputation as one of the most knowledgeable men in politics, he also brought to the White House a long and difficult relationship with the national press corps that dated back to the earliest days of his political career. Nixon would later recall that while his "battles with the media have been so well publicized, it may surprise people to learn of the good relations I have had with many members of the press in years past."[2] But Nixon's hatred and paranoia of the press was legendary. Washington correspondent Lou Cannon recalled that the animosity was much stronger on Nixon's part than on that of the press: "Nixon hated us. It was reciprocated in some ways, but not as much as he thought."[3]

Pat Buchanan played a prominent role in shaping Nixon's public image, messaging, and relationship with the press. His responsibilities included creating briefing books for Nixon, writing speeches, working on the daily news summary, and providing advice on overall political strategy. Buchanan was also part of the strategic team within the White House that developed a reputation for subversive tactics like intimidating and denying access to reporters and monitoring their activities; many within the White House essentially declared war on the press and spent much of their time strategizing against the "enemy." Speechwriter William Safire recalled hearing Nixon say, "The press is the enemy" on several occasions, which served as encouragement to White House staff to "do battle with what he was certain was an ideological bias against nonliberals combined with a personal bias against him."[4] Vice President Spiro Agnew was instrumental in efforts to call out the press for their reporting on the Nixon administration, most notably by making several speeches (written by Buchanan) to publicly criticize the press for its biased and negative stories.[5] The *New York Times*, *Washington Post*, *Time*, and *Newsweek* were among the top targets for what the White House considered their "Eastern establishment," traditionally Democratic bias. Television networks also were threatened with nonrenewal of broadcasting licenses for important affiliates through the Federal Communication Commission to gain more favorable coverage for Nixon's policies.[6]

By mid-1970, White House staffers had compiled an extensive list of more than two hundred journalists from television, radio, and print and placed each into one of six categories: Friendly to Administration, Balanced to Favorable, Balanced, Unpredictable, Usually Negative, and Always Hostile. Those considered more favorable to the administration came from conservative publications, such as *U.S. News and World Report*, *Business Week*, and the *Chicago Tribune*. Those considered negative or hostile were from more liberal publications, such as the *New York Times*, *Washington Post*, and *Boston Globe*. Specific journalists viewed favorably by the administration included syndicated columnists William F. Buckley and Joe Alsop, while those viewed unfavorably included Tom Wicker and James Reston of the *New York Times*, David Broder of the *Washington Post*, Morton Kondracke of the *Chicago Sun-Times*, Hugh Sidey of *Life*, Marvin Kalb of CBS, and syndicated columnists Jack Anderson and the writing team of Rowland Evans and Robert Novak.[7]

Beyond the attention given to reporters, Nixon's use of television remained a top priority, though the White House kept tight control over his access to the press. Nixon gave one of the lowest numbers of press conferences per year of any president during the twentieth century. He averaged eleven press conferences a year his first two years in office, but that number dropped in subsequent years, and when he left office in 1974, he had held thirty-eight press conferences, an average of seven per year. Nixon did, however, learn how to use prime-time television to deliver important messages to the public. Adopting a strategy utilized by Lyndon Johnson to discuss the Vietnam War, Nixon would request time on network television during the evening hours to make a brief statement about his policies or other events (which occurred thirty-seven times, a higher average than any other president).[8] However, Nixon's advisors would also be criticized for creating a "public relations" governing strategy, particularly when staging made-for-television events to highlight presidential activities, as this contributed to the belief among Nixon's critics that his was an "isolated" presidency. The "PR Campaign," as it was called within the White House, became a tactical concern in May 1971 when news stories started appearing on the subject, including a network news profile on "image makers" in the White House.[9]

The overall communication strategy sought to limit journalists' access to Nixon, whether through the infrequent use of press conferences, making televised appearances where no questioning by reporters was allowed, or having Nixon fade from public view for a time, only to reappear with a dramatic policy announcement. Interviews were also infrequent and usually were only given to trusted and "friendly" reporters.[10] Some communication strategies during the Nixon years were innovative, such as the creation of the Office of Communications (separate from the Press Office and designed to handle long-term public relations for the administration) and the development of the daily news summary (to keep the president informed of how he and his administration were portrayed in print and broadcast media). Both changed institutional aspects of the White House regarding staffing, organization, and the daily responsibilities of communications advisors. For better or worse, Nixon's advisors changed the way that the White House attempted to manage the image of the president as well as manage the press. Most of the Nixonian media strategies still exist, in one form or another, as they have evolved through each successive administration.[11]

1. Memo to Richard Nixon and H. R. Haldeman, "President's News Summary," January 5, 1969

My understanding is that the President-elect wants from Buchanan on a regular basis a "news analysis" or "general appraisal" of how the press is treating the Administration. In particular, following press conferences or television appearances, the President would want from Buchanan broad reaction from around the country.

To accomplish this, I will set up in Washington, in my own office, shelves containing the ten top periodicals in terms of political influence, and eight or so of the nation's best newspapers, representative of the national spectrum.

From a scanning of the press and reading of periodicals, we ought to be able to file an independent regular report on the impression the Administration is leaving.

In addition, on an irregular, perhaps weekly basis, the President would get a briefing on what the columnists are thinking and writing about—especially with regard to the Nixon Administration.

TELEVISION REPORT—On a regular basis, three persons should monitor the evening news shows on the networks and the 11 o'clock D.C. news shows—the latter because they are viewed by national press, national network correspondents, and national Administration.

The three monitors should work for Herb Klein.

They should file daily reports with Klein, Ziegler, and Buchanan. Klein, because he is authorized independently to take up gross outrages with the network chiefs; Ziegler, because he is on hand to take them up with the White House correspondents, if they be the offending party—and Buchanan to report to the President, should any television commentary be consistently prejudiced—either for or agin.

I don't think RN is really interested in a daily report here. Normally, they are worthless, and Buchanan can decide when and if to summarize them and send them along.

Another reason they should be under Klein is simply that to have them work for Buchanan is to provide him with three people in a staff that will have but two half-hour segments of work each day.

NEWS SUMMARY—Any news summary coming from staff to President must—

first—be discounted for what RN is reading in the press, for what RN is getting from Intelligence, and for what RN is going to be getting from the agencies in daily briefings. The news summary may be redundant.

Anyhow, since it consists of one individual marking the papers, and about four typists working full blast for a couple of hours, it is again a function that rightly belongs in communications; this is a routing job involving a number of secretaries; it seems to be rightly the province of the communications division of the government.

They can co-ordinate it with the materials the departments are putting out as well.

However, if this arrangement is otherwise than what the President has in mind—please let me know. If it is acceptable as an arrangement, let me know and I will start working with Herb on setting it up in D.C.—and we can make do up here until then. [12]

2. Memo to Richard Nixon, March 4, 1969
THE PRESS CONFERENCE

The press conference was a masterpiece. With perhaps fifty million television viewers as a captive audience, the President "used" the national press corps as a foil to his strongest suits: knowledge, coolness, competence, and depth.

The major accomplishment was not in news. It was in etching the President more deeply into the American mind as The President, and as a man of stature and wisdom. We could not have asked for more.

The centerpiece was the answer on Vietnam. Resolute without being belligerent. Presidential in tone combined at the same time with that vitally important note of anxiety and concern for the American Troops. No reasonable person on the Vietnam issue can ask for more.

Two added thoughts: First, a question of substance. Having been in the legislative meetings, I realize that the President and Rogers both feel that the Soviets are cooperating to a surprising degree. But given the Soviet position—being raked daily by China for collaborating with the West against the world revolutionary forces—is it not likely to embarrass them to emphasize the hopes we place in their cooperation or the covert assistance they are providing, for instance, in the Paris talks. Secondly, "predicting" Soviet cooperation does not seem to gain us anything even when it comes. Yet it does entail some risk, since a reversal of Soviet policy would leave the President open to charges of unjustified optimism about Russian intentions.

On the Vietnam troop question, the President took considerable pains to predict nothing. That way no hopes are raised, and if troops do come home, we will still get the credit. In Europe, however, we have raised some hopes of Soviet cooperation. Those hopes are obviously justified, but what we are doing is collecting part of our salary in advance of having done the job.

Final point: [ABC News anchor] Frank Reynolds' complaint about the "restrictions on the press conference" should be dismissed out of hand. It is outrageous to insist that the President open himself to questions of "black lung" and oil slicks, following an eight-day and somewhat historic mission to Europe. Stern's griping on ABC reflects the perspective of the press corps that these conferences are for their benefit; we would be foolish to accept their ground rules.

We should look at these conferences, I think, not as some regular "tribute" we owe to members of the press corps, but as opportunities to use our press friends to destroy false impressions in the public mind, and to establish beneficial impressions of the President and his Administration. The vehicle has been used perfectly so far, and we ought not let Reynolds' criticism jog us a centimeter from our course. (Frankly, the right of the press corps to quiz the President on any subject they want—after eight days in Europe—is not one which the mass of the American people are going to go to the barricades to uphold.) [13]

3. Memo to Richard Nixon, June 6, 1969

On June 4, 1969, Nixon gave the commencement address at the Air Force Academy in Colorado Springs, Colorado, in which he defended American military involvement in Vietnam and the need for American leadership on the world stage: "What is America's role in the world? What are the responsibilities of a great nation toward protecting freedom beyond its shores? Can we ever be left in peace if we do not actively assume the burden of keeping the peace? . . . The aggressors of this world are not going to give the United States a period of grace in which to put our domestic house in order—just as the crises within our society cannot be put on a back burner until we resolve the problem of Vietnam." [14]

The accurate term to describe the reception to the President's speech is controversial—not hostile. While [NBC News anchor Chet] Huntley was beside himself, [ABC News anchor] Howard K. Smith thought the President had done a national service. While [PBS news host] Martin Agronsky could hardly contain his chagrin on his TV show, he introduced [columnist] James J. Kilpatrick, who hailed it on the same show as a patriotic tour de force. On the N.E.T. television show, [*Chicago Daily News* Washington Bureau chief Peter] Lisagor said that while it "polarized the Congress," the President "had ably read the sentiment of the nation" and had "cemented his support." Also, it was noted on the same show that a tough speech like this can set the backdrop for a more conciliatory stand on Vietnam. [NBC News correspondent Herb] Kaplow told Buchanan and Garment he thought the speech was a "zowie" in terms of television, that the President had excellent mastery of his material, and this was "good television."

Last night when [Senator William] Proxmire hit the speech hard on television [network news], a young New York Republican Cong. threw Proxmire on the defensive, by an on-site rebuttal which was carried on camera. (The fellow's name is Conable.) It will be in the news summary today which should be in this afternoon.

Talked with Washington this morning. Actually, the speech has produced only a few really outraged reactions, from [Senator J. William] Fulbright and Proxmire—highly laudatory responses from [Senator] Harry Byrd and [Senator] Russell Long. [15]

4. Memo to Jim Allison, July 2, 1969

This memo is a response to a memo from Haldeman to Buchanan on June 24, 1969, that stated: "The President feels very strongly that we need to develop a 'Letters to the Editor' and 'Calls to the Broadcasters' program somewhere within the Administration. He is not sure how this should be set up, but he wants a thorough and efficient Nixon network whose task will be to really raise hell with the people who unfairly take us on, and pour praise on those who take a more productive viewpoint. The President feels this might be something that could be done within the framework of the National Committee, and it certainly should be discussed with Jim Allison and others over there before going off in any other direction."[16]

Basically, here are some outlines of how the thing might be run. First, we get one full-time girl in the RNC to operate the thing. Using your name and mailing lists provided by the National Committee, we send out letters asking likely folks if they would like to be REPUBLICAN CORRESPONDENTS, using the letters to the editor column to get across the President's policy, to defend the Administration, and to put out the philosophy of the Party. (PJB would be happy to draft such a letter.)

When the correspondence comes back in, we would turn them over to this girl, who would then send them a kit explaining how best to go about writing letters, how short they should be made, what issues should be hit now—and regular mailings, perhaps once a month, would go to the Correspondents. The correspondents, in turn, would send in the printed letters from their local newspapers or magazine to be used as examples and encouragements to other correspondents in future mailings.

The girl at the National Committee would keep on file the names of some dozen to fifty whom she would get to write letters on a moment's notice to either national publications or to the networks as soon as word came from the White House. I would hope and expect word to come from the White House quite infrequently, but I can't guarantee this.

If word comes to me, for example, I could get in touch with this girl, who could work immediately writing half a dozen letters herself and who could phone up a number of her correspondents around the country to do the same; or she could phone five correspondents who would take responsibility for phoning five more, etc.

By virtue of regular correspondence with a special letterhead, we might be able to make this a somewhat unique organization—and some of the local people, most of whom would probably be Republican women, might wind up running similar operations in their home states, in local elections and the like.

Also, the Correspondents might be encouraged to write letters from out of state to New Jersey papers, for example, commending our gubernatorial candidate. A number of different individual projects could be undertaken by the girl at the Committee on her own initiative while she was awaiting the "go" sign from the White House for any particular project. [17]

5. Memo to Richard Nixon, July 14, 1969

. . . Under Bill Safire's direction—there has been general approval and a good degree of enthusiasm for an on-going program of <u>White House Dinners</u>, the purposes of which would be manifold.

The dinners would place the President and his family in settings and against backdrops that would reflect favorably upon them throughout the country. They would establish the White House in the Nixon Administration as incontestably the national center of culture, and stylistic pace-setter. They would enable the President to set the standard for the nation, as to what is "in" and what is "out" culturally, to reward and patronize those artists who the President believes are creating what American art should be. They would generate an extra aura of excitement about the White House itself; they would destroy the myth that Republicans are business types whose cultural bent runs to golf and poker. They would provide the President with a host of opportunities to reward his friends with invitations to these great occasions, and to identify and punish his enemies by relegating them to the perpetual darkness outside the manor.

The following are dinners which we have recommended; some of them I understand have already received approval, but they are included nevertheless.

MEDAL OF FREEDOM DINNER: A large dinner hosting a score or so of new winners of the Presidential Medal of Freedom. Among those now being considered are Charles Lindbergh, Arthur Krock, Robert Murphy, Robert Penn Warren, Ray Moley, etc. It would be a golden opportunity to recognize and reward some great Americans who have been loyal to the President, also some great Americans in their own chosen fields of endeavor. In addition, by providing the medal to one or more conspicuous opponents of the President, we could garner national plaudits.

RICHARD RODGERS DINNER: A dinner honoring the great composer would be almost as universally noted and unanimously praised as the one honoring Duke Ellington.

TRIBUTE TO ANDREW WYETH: A dinner honoring this great and more traditional American painter, whose masterpieces could be hung throughout the White House for the occasion; other American artists could be invited to join in the tribute. He is one of the great artists who is of the first rank and who has been a friend of the President's.

ALL-AMERICAN DINNER: A dinner honoring the All-American college football teams of this coming fall and the all-time college football greats of previous days. The dinner could be held after the bowl games on January 1, and after The Coaches and API and UPI All-American teams have been chosen. It could be held in the first week or so of the new year—just before the Super Bowl Game when the nation's attention would be focused upon football.

After these four, Bill Safire recommended a number of other possible dinners—and we discussed them with varying degrees of approval.

Here are a few which might interest the President:

SERENADE TO RUBENSTEIN: A dinner honoring the great pianist—with other great pianists playing that evening.

AN EVENING OF AMERICAN COMEDY: A dinner honoring the best—and most tasteful—of American comedians with Bob Hope and Jackie Gleason as the masters of ceremonies. (One caveat is that although this would be tremendous television, the President would come in for a good deal of ribbing.)

PHOTOGRAPHIC ARTS: A dinner to honor some of America's great photogra-

phers, Dave Duncan, Edward Steichen, etc. Their finest could be hung throughout the White House that day.

CULINARY ARTS: An evening of the finest in American cooking, with great
chefs from around the country called in to each prepare a single course of a
seven-course dinner.

COLUMNISTS NIGHT: A tribute to the greats among American syndicated columnists which might honor Krock and Lawrence and Lippmann or others. (In
this case, as in others, there is always the danger of honoring someone and
slighting someone who may feel himself a better.)

AMERICAN WOMEN'S DINNER: A dinner honoring some selected women who
have achieved tremendous success in their chosen fields.

Most of these ideas were originally Bill Safire's, if not all of them. The vitally
important thing, of course, is that in planning any such dinners they be ones the
President enjoys himself. Are there any here that the President would like us to
pursue and provide for him an appropriate scenario? [18]

6. Memo to Richard Nixon, September 2, 1969

*In 1969, Nixon purchased a beachfront mansion overlooking the Pacific Ocean
in San Clemente, California. Known as "La Casa Pacifica" as well as the "Western White House," Nixon vacationed there while president and lived there after
resigning the presidency until the late 1980s.*

Reception to the President's Western White House, especially at the outset, was
exceptionally good. Reasons are many. The President moved westward just as
the nation was rising in near unanimous applause to the "new federalism," just as
it appeared the President had pulled off one of the master strokes of his career.
Secondly, the "relaxed atmosphere" is not put on but genuine—and it is coming
through. Third, the President scored heavily with his "open" Western White
House featuring the tours arranged for the press. These were the initial reports;
they created the initial impression; as mentioned they were uniformly favorable.
This initial impression was created about a month ago, when the volume of articles came in on the Western White House—and that impression has, by and
large, not been changed.

There have been negatives creeping in, however. Foremost among them is
the growing number of questions being raised about the cost of the move out
there—the price of the month spent there, with staff and Cabinet officers and
the like flying back and forth. Secondly, the predictable left-right sympathies

of various newspapers and writers are emerging in discussion of the WWH. Example, the <u>Chicago Tribune</u>'s columnists are ecstatic the President is in effect sticking it to the East with his Western White House, while there is grumbling at the <u>Post</u>. (Some of this is traceable as well to the style controversy. The President's "middle America," night baseball approach that so many of the forgotten Americans applaud is at best tolerated in the salons of Georgetown or the upper East Side.) While the national publications report the President is identifying well with the common man, the <u>Washington Post</u> broad who covered the Park dinner bitched that "it was the greatest gathering of squares since the last jamboree of the World Boy Scout Federation."

However, though these negatives are reported here—they should not be given the weight that the good reception is given—because they are the exceptions and not the rule.

Finally, there is another problem upcoming from Ted Lewis' [*New York Daily News*] column today, from front-page stories last week, from the lead editorial in the <u>Washington Post</u>. And the direction in which it is headed is likely to influence editorial opinion on the entire Western White House operation. Basically, the disputes between State and Defense over what the troop levels mean, between Burns and Moynihan and the economists and the President over how much the peace dividend will provide, between CIA and the Army over the Green Beret case, between CIA and State over the reports of a Soviet first-strike against China, between Justice and Finch over the guidelines, between Commerce and the CBA over whether inflation is "cooling off," etc., between Finch and Hoover and unnamed White House sources over whether students will be raising more or less hell on the campus—these battles are being waged in the public press; there is a growing call among editorialists that the President put his foot down—and the thrust of the <u>Washington Post</u> editorial indicates that the presence of the public quarrels is at least partially traceable to the absence of the President from Washington, in Bucharest, Saigon, and San Clemente. Other editorial comment traces the public disputes to the tendency of the mice to play when the cat's away. This theme is one that can be picked up—and it is this observer's guess that it will be—regardless of whether or not the President's month in San Clemente had anything to do with it. Anyhow, that is what seems to be coming. For what is in the past, the following:

As for the President's golf game, there have been a good many pictures, and some mention in the hard news (usually noting that the President once called golf a waste of time) and a considerable number of light pieces. Nothing really hostile here, however. . . . The picture of the President on his golf cart riding to work has been played all over—again, I don't detect anybody begrudging the President his time on the links or his means of transportation.

As for the President on the beach, the impression I have is that there is even less comment or reporting on how often the President has been in the surf. A few mentions of the President being banged around by the waves once or twice, but that's it.

THE LBJ VISIT

This received tremendous coverage, press and television, most all of it in this observer's opinion was very good. It was the most widely covered event of the President's western tour, I would say; a number of articles were written noting that the President has used several opportunities to stretch hands across the political divide. All positive here, and very extensive coverage.

THE APOLLO DINNER

This function received as much coverage perhaps as the LBJ visit—though its timing was not so good, and thus the TV coverage was not as broad on the evening news the next day as was the LBJ visit. Coverage in magazines was also favorable—but the dinner did get some negatives. First, the diplomats moaned about inconvenience of having to go all the way to L.A., and their arrangements were apparently rather badly handled. Washington Post took note of this. Secondly, the exclusion of [Senator Alan] Cranston from the dinner was widely noted and not very favorably received. By and large, however, the reception was very good to the dinner.

THE PRESIDENT'S STYLE

If the party line is that the President is relaxed, cool, in command of the situation on the coast, refreshed, feeling and looking better than ever—then, in this case, it is getting across. Every report we have from someone who has seen or spoken with the President reinforces this—as do all of the pictures taken so far, either of the President teeing off, or driving his golf cart, etc. (Also, we get our usual high grades for "efficiency.")

THE CALIFORNIA PAPERS

Our California press is limited here, and since we don't keep the news sections on file, for lack of room, the impressions are more from memory of Buchanan and staff. The impression we have is of a very favorable reception to the President's San Clemente White House and the two dinners—of a little Chamber-of-Commerce pride in the "western tilt," of an attempt to bend over backwards and give a little more than normal in the way of praise and sympathy for what the President is doing. Again, this is a general impression. However, one negative here that most of us recall—a Mr. Stuart Loory [of the *Los Angeles Times*] seems to take every opportunity that presents itself to give the President a cheap shot. One recalls that when the President's office announced that LBJ was coming to California, Loory took pains to note that some people were contrasting the warm reception RN was giving LBJ with the tendency to ignore JFK, the man who defeated him. Noted was the failure to give JFK a proper measure of credit for the Apollo feat. Also, Loory was especially negative in a piece he did on the sports page of the LA Times about the President's former comments about golf and how much he is playing these days.

THE PARK DINNER

My impression is that the state dinner didn't receive a great deal of attention back here—the focus of news and comment was on the arrival, the statements of the two leaders, what the Korean situation is, and what does the Nixon doctrine mean for South Korea. The dinner itself got perhaps more note than it might have if held back here—but not much. Again, the cramming of a dinner with an arrival and departure generally results in the hard news of "what was said" taking precedence in terms of coverage over the soft news fact that a state dinner was held in San Francisco. (Zsa Zsa [Gabor]'s appearance and chat with Kissinger was widely reported.)

(In scheduling these one-day or 36-hour visits, either the President while abroad, or by a visiting President here, we run into the inevitable problem that for most papers there is only one major story that can be headlined from a day's events. If we cram in statements and backgrounders and a state dinner into 24 hours, we are going to get one story—with much of the softer news buried deep in the hard news story. This seems to have been true of the Park visit.)

To keep this a full balanced report, I should note that there has been some "who's minding the store" comment, but it has been sparse. Again, on the whole, the Western White House has been warmly received on press and TV as a presidential innovation. [19]

7. Memo to Richard Nixon, September 28, 1969
Summer TV

As per the President's request Mort Allin went over the summer network reports, and comparing notes, we come up with these general observations.

You could divide presidential stories on the networks into three categories based on amount of coverage. In the first would be the Air Force Academy Speech, Midway Meeting, Clifford remark at the press conference, L'Affaire Knowles, Asian Trip, Apollo II, Welfare Reform.

In second category would be the Park visit, LBJ Birthday Party, Western White House itself, and the nomination anniversary. In the third would be mass transit, birth control, foreign student meeting, and the Haynsworth announcement.

In our view it would not be accurate to condemn all three networks as anti-Administration on these major stories; in some of these stories, generating the greatest coverage like the Bucharest visit and the Welfare Reform speech, the coverage was uniformly favorable; in others like the Knowles incident, we came off quite badly.

If you will note again most of the secondary and tertiary categories, we came off well in almost all of them—simply by nature of the story itself; they are interesting, non-controversial.

In addition, Mrs. Nixon's treatment on all three networks—we recall specifically the Asian tour, the Western swing to volunteer operations, and her trip to El Cerritos—has been consistently, indeed almost without exception, very favorable.

Now to the networks and a few consistent themes.

The one network where we can, on a controversial story, the chances are greatest we will come off badly, is without question NBC. There is a strong and visible bias against the ABM-military-industrial-complex, which comes through in all stories touching on it; there is always a market here for the Saigon-Washington rift type story and the "weakness of ARVN" theme; they do as much or more than any network on the Administration "confusion" over a desegregation policy.

[NBC News's] John Chancellor, we would estimate, is negative toward the Administration and the President's position 90 percent of the time. Because of his frequency on the tube, and because of the time he commands on Huntley-Brinkley, we consider him perhaps the most offensive commentator on the air. A close second is [CBS News's] Daniel Schorr, who specializes in the Finch splits with the Administration.

Huntley and Brinkley take a chunk out of us with some regularity, but this seems more or less their style; they do it to us but they do it to others also, more perhaps because the President and the Administration command more of the news than anyone else. From our point of view, Chancellor and Schorr do more damage to us in the public mind than do Huntley and Brinkley.

As for ABC, Bill Lawrence is rough at times as is Frank Reynolds—but for the [most] part ABC (Reynolds-Smith) has given us the best deal over the summer. CBS is a close second as both [Robert] Pierpont and [Dan] Rather give us as objective a coverage of the White House as we get. (One reason for ABC's lead over the other networks in coverage is Howard K. Smith's hawkishness and no-nonsense attitude on law and order and student disorder.) Smith does hit two themes repeatedly, however, which affect us directly—he is critical of both Congress and the Administration for lack of action on legislation; he will refer time and again to the need for the President to speak out in a State of the Union address or for the President to go to the people with a Presidential explanation of Vietnam. One gets the impression he would want to see the President as more of an advocate and more of an outspoken leader.

Looked at chronologically we were on the receiving end of a lot of criticism at the beginning of the summer from the doveish criticism of Air Force Academy speech, controversy of the Thieu government, Knowles, guidelines, ABM, surtax, and inflation. Once ABM and surtax were out of the way, we seemed to be on the upswing. Even Frank Reynolds began to see a measure of hope in Thieu's government. Presidential participation in the space venture came over very well; the meeting with foreign students, population control message, and the Asian trip all were treated favorably. The Guam-Bangkok confusion—as mentioned in an earlier memo—was the souring note in the entire trip—but the coverage on film of the President was outstanding. Some minor negatives in that trip were occasional comparisons with Ike's crowds—but again this did not figure prominently in the story. Romania, coming as it did at the end of the trip, was the last and most lasting impression.

Welfare, LBJ's birthday, and most Western White House coverage—all favorable. The cacophony of voices in the Administration in Washington which was connected in some commentary with the President being out of touch on the West Coast—is the major problem attached to WWH coverage.

Recently, tax reform and desegregation are the leading negative stories involving the Administration that run on the networks.

One final note. The President's critics [Senator J. William] Fulbright and [Averell] Harriman get a disproportionate amount of coverage in our view; considering their ranks vis a vis a President, they get a good deal more than their peers of "equal time," especially when you consider Mr. Harriman has no official rank at all. For a while there, Harriman was trotted out regularly by the networks to comment on this or that Vietnam or Paris decision or what he would have done. Invariably, Harriman feels what we have done is not enough, or we have missed some opportunity or other which he has seen.

Our general impression—reinforced by Mort [Allin]'s review of the TV over the last four months is that we are doing a somewhat better job than we were of getting Administration spokesmen more time on the tube as compared with the Fulbrights and Harrimans.

As this is based on our impressions—after a summer, and reviewing some 400 pages of TV summary over the last four months, it is necessarily a surface impression. [20]

8. Memo to Richard Nixon, September 28, 1969

The Press Conference was easily the dominant news-generating story of the week. It occupied roughly half of the evening news Friday night; and that evening and the next morning major papers ran three and four stories on the front page alone. The variety of subjects discussed, and the newsworthiness of the subjects, contributed to the lengthy play.

Early in the week, before the conference was announced, there was a spate of stories criticizing the President for not having one—but they disappeared when the announcement came. In our view, the press was institutionally worked up over the lack of press conferences, and the fact that there were few follow-up stories on how well the President handled the thing is one measure of their recognition that he handled it well. (One can be sure if the President had fumbled the ball, there would have been eleven men in the press on top of him this time; they were "up" for this one.) . . .

We are unanimous in this shop that we could be advised to do these news conferences at the same time as the evening news. This does not pre-empt everybody's favorite show. <u>It gives the President a much larger public audience.</u> . . . [21]

9. Memo to Ken Cole, October 10, 1969

In response to your memo to get out the line about the President's press conference—I have gotten it out to all coming in here who asked—and volunteered it to many recently who did not ask. I haven't seen it pop up in print—specifically as a result of what I have said. But as reported in the President's news summary, he is getting excellent copy on the handling of the press conference right now— that is, his personal handling. . . .

The point is: Everybody believes right now that the President handles these things right off the cuff; they are impressed except [Scripps Howard White House correspondent] Ted Knap, whom I braced in a letter which RN saw. We are pushing against an open door on this thing. Everybody I know believes the President does an extemporaneous job—a good job; the fact that he sits and studies background material I find is old hat—that is why it has not cropped up in the media I suppose. It is not news anymore. [22]

10. Memo to Richard Nixon, November 5, 1969

On November 3, 1969, Nixon delivered his famous "Silent Majority" address to the nation, in which he asked middle- and working-class Americans, those not part of the antiwar protesters or counterculture movements, to support his policies in Vietnam: "And so tonight—to you, the great silent majority of my fellow Americans—I ask for your support."[23] Buchanan wrote this memo two days later, in light of what he saw as the media's dismissal of Nixon's address, recalling that it was "among the most consequential I ever wrote" given his recommendation for Agnew to give a speech attacking the networks. Agnew would give the speech on November 13, 1969, in Des Moines, Iowa, in which he argued that Americans had the right to make up their own minds "without having the President's words and thoughts characterized through the prejudices of hostile critics before they can even be digested."[24]

The contrast between the network reception of the President's address and the public's reception offer us a golden opportunity to move in earnest now against the commentators. . . .

An effective battle plan it seems to me would be this:

First, a major address by the Vice President (which I will be happy to draft) that calls for a national debate on the influence of a tiny handful of men elected by no one in the democratic. We could use the Democratic Convention distortions, the horrible question by Frank Reynolds during the last days of the campaign against RN, and the Bill Lawrence commentary after the President's speech—to point up the impact.

Also, the best authority on this is Walter Lippmann—we have plenty of quotes to back up our position. Before the speech was delivered it should be put in the hands of every favorable columnist and every editorial writer in the country.

Step Two: After the counter-attack begins, about a week or two, someone on the floor of the Senate makes the charge that a nationally known diplomatic correspondent for a major network has been in the hire of a foreign power (if we have this.)

Step Three: [Federal Communications Commission chairman] Dean Burch announces in a major address that he is establishing a national network of monitors of the major networks to determine their objectivity.

Step Four: [Senator Hugh] Scott calls on Congress to conduct a similar investigation.

At the same time we have Senators and Congressman saying the same things the Vice President has said in his speech—follow-up addresses, hitting different cases of distortion.

Maybe this effort will run out of steam—but it seems to me that if we can put together a three-week offensive on this one subject—the result will be to terrify the networks; and to discredit their reporting in the minds of millions of people. But it ought to be concerted, coordinated, and it ought to be done in the public arena. While the commentators talk to millions of people, we normally make one-to-one phone calls of complaint. [25]

11. Memo to H. R. Haldeman, November 11, 1969

The Television News Archives at Vanderbilt University maintains a library of televised network news programs dating back to 1968.

This weekend Paul Simpson of Nashville and Vanderbilt University was in my office. Since the Republican Convention of last year, he has kept tv tapes of all network evening news programs. He has these tapes now; and he hopes that they can be kept on a permanent basis—and more important, that, from these tapes, other subject matter tapes on specific issues like campus disorders, ABM, etc., can be made and kept.

The purpose would be to have a file—just like a newspaper's morgue—by specific topic on what has appeared on the network news of ABC, NBC and CBS. If these subject matter tapes were made they could be copied and distributed to scholars and journalists all over the country who could—after a single viewing of a few hours—write articles about NBC's coverage of the ABM debate, for example. By maintaining this kind of network news library, we and others would have instant access to how the great national issues had been treated over a period of months by the network news—we would have a basis on which to build complaints of lack of fairness and objectivity.

In addition, the very announcement that this was being done would be an inhibiting factor on the left-wingers in the network news department. . . .

My suggestion is that we get either Congress or some Federal Agency or even private donors to provide Vanderbilt's current operation with the funds necessary to catalogue and index the tapes they now have and to make "subject matter tapes" from these.

In talking with Simpson, he said this could be done for 125 grand per year. It seems to me it is something which should be done also at the Library of Congress, which might be delegated to keep such film tapes. They now keep microfilm of the <u>New York Times</u>—and the network news is as influential certainly when talking of the great mass of Americans.

It seems to me that an announcement—which hit the front pages—that the Administration was moving to support the idea of keeping complete tapes, and making them available to interested scholars and journalists—would have a dramatic impact on the network news shows, and would in addition be the proper follow-up to the Vice President's speech.

We will be missing a golden opportunity if we don't use the occasion of RN's national address—and the network reaction to begin a sustained counteroffensive. . . .[26]

12. Memo to Richard Nixon, May 21, 1970

Reflections from bedside after a fortnight of reading the <u>Post</u> and <u>Times</u> news summaries and watching the networks. How we have conducted ourselves and what we can expect.

1. The media, the left, the liberal academic community, the Senate doves—whom we overran and routed in November in one of the most effective political offensives of recent memory—have regained the initiative.

Apparently, there are still members of our own White House Staff here who do not realize that what these people want is not some modus vivendi with President Nixon, some consensual agreement on progress. Rather, they want to dominate, discredit, and drive this Administration out of power two years hence—and then write us off as a gang of ineffectual interim caretakers who failed dismally.

Our response to their renewed assault has not been in the November character; it has generally been in the disastrous Johnsonian tradition, too pleading, too conciliatory, gestures of virtual appeasement to our ideological enemies. Word goes forth from the environs of the White House that we will tone down the rhetoric of the Vice President if that will help that we will promise to have American troops out of Cambodia by July 1, that we will move no further than 50 kilometers within the country; we will never go back. We place stringent unilateral limits on our own freedom of action—and to what avail?

What have all these gestures accomplished—but to re-double the enthusiasm of those who despise us and who hope that the President's Cambodian venture will fail ignominiously?

The only thing wrong with the President's move into Cambodia was that

Johnson should have done it four years ago—we have nothing to apologize for or be defensive about; it is something to be vocally aggressive about. Yet, many of our spokesmen one sees and hears seem defensive.

Again, was it not because they were massed and raucous here in D.C. that scores of students were invited in to see and talk with the White House Staff members? They were not all lovable children at the Monument grounds from what I heard from those with whom I spoke; many were close-minded, arrogant and intransigent and engaged in gutter obscenities against the President of the United States.

When we literally ignored the marchers in October and November and let them have their parades and speeches—we won the support of the American people. Now, when we suddenly threw open all our doors to anyone who wants to come in and vent his views here, we gain an appearance of openness but also of a lack of certainty, of being a bit panicked and we merited the increased contempt of those who can spot weakness and uncertainty a mile off. We also confused the millions of Americans who believed deeply the President's strong stand is right.

There is merit in the President and staff making themselves available to students and other groups with different points of view—but the merit lies solely in the public impression conveyed that we are listening. But, why must it be the most vocal and disorderly dissenters who are the ones given the publicity and the audience—as though a loud mouth and a lot of violence is one measure of the justice of a cause.

Having said this, we must begin to take inventory of the country which the President now governs.

THE UNIVERSITIES. Under attack from their own student leaders and student bodies, many of these institutions have capitulated and allowed themselves to become politicized. . . . Rather than risk the wrath of their students, rather than take unpopular positions, which would make daily life miserable for them, university leaders around the country—with [Yale University president] Kingman Brewster the quintessential example of the craven crowd—have decided to throw in with the students, to blame his inability to maintain a spirit of academic freedom on his campus on the war in Vietnam, on white racism, on the Black Panther trial, on anything but Kingman Brewster's lack of courage. Seeking desperately to curry favor with the radical majority, these men have taken political positions as institutions and endorsed strikes on campus, refused to punish violent disorders—in effect abandoned the academic freedom and the traditional neutrality of these bodies for students and teachers alike to hold and express publicly unpopular and heretical views. Some of these universities are now publicly taking what amounts to a party line—and in that sense are ceasing to be universities as we knew them.

This is something the President inherited; something about which we can do little other than to search constantly and find those university presidents and teachers with the courage to stand up and provide them with all the moral and other backing and exposure we can muster. Let's bring the professors and administrators with guts in to see the President. To allow the politicalization of the universities means State Legislatures will react, dissenting views will be shouted, and a new "McCarthyism" will prevail under the auspices of bankrupt liberalism.

THE MEDIA. Some of the television I have witnessed in the last two weeks—conscious efforts to seek out soldiers who didn't want to go into Cambodia, the failure to give the maximum coverage to the tremendous success of our military operation—have raised genuine questions in my mind whether we can seriously continue to let this sort of thing go on without concerted counterattacks. I recall, however, one splendid piece on ABC, showing American tanks and trucks carting off supplies; there have been some excellent stories on back pages of papers like the Star. But they have not been given the enormous treatment they deserve. Had this type of thing gone on during World War II—with American cameramen night after night looking for soldiers naturally frightened and concerned with the war, one wonders how well we could have sustained it.

The left now so dominates the media that they can very nearly neutralize a Presidential presentation or even a military operation as conspicuously successful as the Cambodian venture has been to date. (The national magazines are becoming an increasingly serious hostile and constant source of concern here. They almost acted in concert on the Carswell thing—neutralizing the President's statement. The networks did the same.)

[Conservative columnist Victor] Lasky made a suggestion that appeals to me. When this operation is over the President ought to take live time, five minutes to explain just what we captured and destroyed in there—it ought to be tough and straight—and maybe we ought to fly home the kind of things we captured—rockets, mortars, etc. to show them to the American people.

My feeling is that the media from our post-November efforts has been partially discredited in the eyes of the country; that we should not hesitate to attack and attack hard when it steps out of bounds and we ought to give consideration to ways and means if necessary to acquire either a government or other network through which we can tell our story to the country.

The lens through which our message gets through is a distorted lens—in the national press and the network media, with the exceptions mentioned previously. (A night ago, 1,000 N.Y. lawyers here in D.C. got equal time with 150,000 hard hats in N.Y backing RN and the Veep.)

THE PRESIDENT. With the media, articulate voices of the Senate, the bulk of the academic community, the great foundations, the men of prominence in law and those who have left government service all adamantly against us—we must begin, I believe, again to elevate the people to use more fully and more often the great but few weapons we have, the President and the Vice President and the Cabinet in an aggressive manner. We have the majority of the people in this country with us yet, I still believe. But they are men and women who do not understand sophisticated ideas and the workability of programs and plans—they trust in men and they trust in leaders and our presence is not visible or if we present to the nation any lack of certitude or a lack of conviction in what we are doing—then with all the other pressures boring in, more assuredly they, too, will doubt they are right. In this regard, it is a major and unnecessary concession to our enemies to attempt to muzzle the Vice President who, even when his rhetoric veers off the mark, brings to these people that feeling of strength and conviction and certitude in values they have not heard defended in thirty years.

Neither the President nor the Vice President's statement which are tough are causes of any national problem here—they are explicit response to outrages—and by suggesting or hinting, as some of our aides do, that yes, we'll quiet down; maybe we are talking too loud—we give in effect tacit admission that somehow we are responsible.

THE HARD HATS. Last week a group of construction workers came up Wall Street and beat the living hell out of some demonstrators who were desecrating the American flag in their little demonstration for "peace." Whether one condones this kind of violence or not, probably half the living rooms in America were standing in applause at the spectacle. Yesterday the hard hats marched down Broadway in support of Nixon and Agnew—something no union man would have done for Vice President Richard Nixon for a weekend off ten years ago. There is a great ferment in American politics; these, quite candidly, are our people now—just as the Republican suburbs are. The most insane suggestion I have heard about here in recent days was to the effect that we should somehow go prosecute the hard hats to win favor with the kiddies who are screaming about everything we are doing.

My suggestion was send the Vice President right up to New York, have him say in 200 words that our kids are wiping out sanctuaries that were killing their buddies, that we are marching peacefully, that we are protesting on their behalf, and this is going to be a peaceful demonstration. The message would have hit every blue collar worker in the country and these are our people now—if we want them—and frankly, they are better patriots and more pro-Nixon than the little knot of Riponers we have sought to cultivate since we came into office.

One point I would make here—what have all our efforts and labors to win over the Fulbrights and the lefts, to show them we are reasonable, accomplished? With one decision in Cambodia, it went out the window in a flash—the virulence of the attacks on the President, the genuine brutality of the political assault, must by now tell us we have no converts there now worth the great investment we have made on that side of the fence.

It should be our focus to constantly speak to, to assure, to win, to aid, to promote the President's natural constituency—which is now the working men and women of the country, the common man, the Roosevelt New Dealer. When in trouble, that is where we should turn, not try to find a common ground with our adversaries.

Let me add here—I do not rule out; I strongly endorse symbolic gestures toward groups, especially the blacks, where symbols count for so much—because the President is President of all the people and while they will never vote for us, we must never let them come to believe we don't give a damn about them—or that they are outside our province of concern.

I argue only for a sense of realism, a recognition of who our friends are, where they are and that they being our base—remain our constant course of attention.

THE GOVERNMENT. In point of fact we failed to take control in depth of the Federal Government which is ours by right of victory—and we are paying a heavy price for it now, with State Department letters of protest, with Hickel publicly airing internal squabbles on the national networks, the civil rights revolt at Justice, with Finch and Veneman being called to account for their actions by their own employees, with Thrower refusing to use the political power of his office. We have neither been ruthless enough in eliminating those lower echelon employees who disagree with the President, in rooting out endemic disloyalty, in ridding ourselves of those who—once the President has decided to act—refuse to go out and fight for his position, whether they agreed with it to begin with or not.

The tragedy that has plagued us through this Administration is our well-motivated attempt to bring into positions of responsibility gentlemen like Dr. Allen—who have never agreed with the President on anything. This was based on RN's idea of a "coalition" of point of view. But when there is a lack of discipline among our troops—primarily in the Departments, but also even within the

White House where we find types more than willing to cry on the shoulder of a [*Los Angeles Times* correspondent] Stu Loory just the way [LBJ press secretary] Bill Moyers used to tell the press the terrible time he was having convincing the President to do the right thing. So, they loved Moyers and loathed Johnson.

RECOMMENDATIONS. Thus far, the Presidential posture has been that the Chief Executive, the master arbiter of contesting forces within Society—a task performed with skill and brilliance. On occasions, like the November encounter, the President raised the silhouette, assumed the role of "leader of the people," and rallied the nation to his banner. This power of the Office in my opinion may have to be used with greater regularity and intensity than it has in the past—if the attacks against us stay at the same level. We cannot rely on the Kleins and Zieglers and even the Cabinet types to carry the battle; essentially, their function is less the attack than it is the defense, the rebuttal.

Secondly, we are paying a terrible price now for the appointment or retention in high, but more important, middle public office of men who have never supported the President, and for failing to remove, demote, transfer or fire those individuals who are not first and foremost Presidential loyalists. Dr. Allen has been nothing but a disaster, and the Administration is almost on a suicidal course when it hires a $10,000 a year twerp like Moffett for our Youth Office over at HEW—so that when he resigns, a slobbering and indulgent press puts him on Face the Nation to tell the country that the President does not give a damn about youth.

Third, we have kept the door open to everyone, etc., but keep constantly in mind that nothing will ever come of this other than a little refurbishing of image about "open administration," etc. The Youth Conference we are holding should gather and hail every "square" youth organization and solid kid we can find and keep out every hard anti-Nixon leftist—and if we can't accomplish that, we ought to can the whole damn thing.

Fourth, hard evidence I think indicates clearly that by providing Cabinet officers with a full franchise, turning over the power of appointments to any number of our Cabinet heads—we have gotten some bad returns and now have a government not only hostile in segments to the President—but openly defiant and rebellious. If it takes far-reaching removal of sub-Cabinet types to regain more WH control, I would recommend this kind of dramatic stroke, for if we cannot get greater control of this government, we can accomplish nothing. We can only expect further blow-ups of internal dissent by the media in future months.

Under normal times, the coalition concept of a Cabinet—with everybody popping off—is a fine thing, with different views. But we are an army under fire now—and the actions of Secretary Hickel in publicly airing grievances about WH staffers of the innermost nature on a nation-wide television show—in effect scoring points for himself with the liberal press at the expense of his President—is simply inexcusable.

The President and his Cabinet and his staff must present a greater posture of solid unanimity and strength and confidence than we have to date. There is too much weeping on the shoulders of the press, appearing all over. For Bob Finch to have allowed that slob from the Welfare Rights Organization to occupy his office for two hours was a disgrace—and can only earn us the contempt of those who despise us and the utter bewilderment of those who still believe and respect the American government.

This is no argument for having National Guardsmen shooting 19-year-old girls in the head with an M-1—but we desperately have to present to the nation the impression of a strong government, led by tough people, who know exactly where they are going, and who are not going to be deterred an inch by any crowd of idealistic mixed-up kids running around the streets. It seems that in most speeches one hears from a Cabinet officer, or report of a conversation by a White House staffer, we are pleading with somebody or apologizing for something.

In that evening with Irving Kristol, Henry Kissinger made a point that needs re-making. What we don't need is dialogue and consultation—what the United States needs is a victory. I have read—and it is my earnest hope that it is not true—that the President had an operation ready against the North Vietnamese, which we have called off because of the domestic turmoil. From experience, it seems we gain nothing by denying ourselves military opportunities to tone down a Senator Fulbright or one of the others—who would be destroyed as politicians if Richard Nixon won this war.

So, with regard to our enemies, we need spokesmen—more of them, younger, more aggressive—who will get up when Whitney Young says RN and Agnew were responsible for killing those students and call him a goddam liar.

Young's Urban League, as I understand, feeds high on the Federal trough—has any consideration been given to telling him to fire his fanny or look elsewhere for their fat contracts?

Finally, though this is a discursive and rambling memo, I see us as under very real attack from our enemies with the society, who have many powerful and influential weapons, who are attempting to impose ground rules upon our political warfare they do not impose upon themselves—that our future, if it is going to be successful, may lie in the FDR pattern of engaging them openly in heated political warfare, of not cooling off our supporters but of stirring the fires and passions often. It seems to me here that we are in a contest over the soul of the country now and the decision will not be some middle compromise—it will be their kind of society or ours; we will prevail or they shall prevail. I know these incomplete thoughts and suggestions do not square at all with the calm, cool, dispassionate, orderly executive administration the President has conducted thus far, ably and well. But I think that clearly while the issue is not black and white, the decision is whether we shall be a fighting President in the mold of FDR or the presiding President in the manner of Ike.[27]

13. Memo to H. R. Haldeman, June 27, 1970

Sorry for the delay in getting back to you on this press memo—but the following are thoughts worked out with Mort Allin for consideration in any revised media strategy on the part of the President and Administration.

1. The President already has my thoughts concerning the over-exposure on national television; we should pick our nationwide appearances selectively; we should have something with impact to say before going to the country. This is among our most effective weapons; we ought not to wear it out. The same holds true for the nationwide prime time evening TV press conference.

2. Along these lines, neither Mort nor I would see any objection to the non-televised "impromptu" press conference of which the President has held three, which help us greatly with the writing press and which give them a chance to see RN thinking and ruminating on his feet which we can't do in front of a TV screen where immediacy, brevity and spontaneity are of such importance. (My sole reservation about these is the fact that the preparation of briefing books is a time-consuming endeavor—but then Presidential advances should not wait upon the conveniences of aides. Seriously, RN does these well and it helps us with the press.)

3. You asked "what we are doing right." No need to focus here—but it is true we are doing a hell of a lot of things right and well; we are putting on as good a performance as any group for a President in my view—and the fact that this memo doesn't dwell on that doesn't mean I don't think it to be so. Ziegler does a first-rate job as point man; he takes considerable heat from the Press for feeding them only what the President wants—but that is his job. One suggestion here: Give Ziegler more and more in the way of substance to feed out to the writing press so they will not in turn have to start working for their meals. The more of the good hard news that comes out of our shop, the less pressure on the part of the press to start digging the news out for themselves.

4. The [political journalist and author] Teddy White thing on the environ-

ment was first-rate; I understand Whitaker spilled the whole thing to him. We need more of this. Since Ehrlichman is now the Domestic honcho, suggest that his "six coordinators" be given a broader rein to give this kind of deep back-grounder—coordinated with Ziegler—on what we are doing domestically; what kind of programs we are pushing. Just solid programmatic substance stuff—to those reporters concerned with particular areas—already operating on the Buchanan thesis that as long as you keep feeding them hard news, they will not wander off the reservation in search of other stuff themselves.

What is vitally important in any operation like this, however, if that it be a) coordinated with Ziegler so he knows what is going out and b) that the individuals chosen to do the depth backgrounding know their onions well. But Ehrlichman is the man to decide which of his people should do more of this.

5. Our office, which means in effect Allin & Co., can put together a list of papers—with Washington Bureaus and naming reporters and writers who are in the President's corner constantly. We are not doing enough in the way of leaking major stories to these people, of giving the breaks to our friends. We focus on shafting our foes which is but one side of the coin. We can provide HRH with a list of these papers with their bureaus, and HRH can call a meeting of White House top staff and indicate to them—to help these people where possible, to make a conscious effort to see that they get things first. The _Times_ and the _Post_ are still getting the lion's share of the major news stories—this is partly of course due to the competence and contacts of their reporters—but we are not doing enough to lend a hand to our friends. (Especially TV friends.)

6. I am not one of those who believe that the President's staff should be anonymous. We have some interesting and diverse characters—especially Moynihan and Kissinger—who make for excellent copy; Harlow is doing well in this regard now; we ought to provide more exposure for them. Again, it gives people things to write about; it is generally very good copy; it assists the President's image by showing him to be a man with intelligent, broad-gauged divergent views around him. Kennedy got enormous mileage out of the press about the spectacular staff he got—whereas we have not benefitted adequately from ours, although it seems to me to compare favorably with the people JFK had around him. I would argue this as beneficial to the image of the Administration and also as another means of countering the "isolated President" theme which continues in the media.

7. Tricia, Julie and the First Lady it seems to us get 98% favorable coverage on whatever they do; the more exposure for them, thus the better.

8. We are still grossly deficient in the kind of event where the setting tells the story; we are as weak in this form of symbolic speaking to the country as we

are strong in directly speaking to the country. By this I mean the RFK visit to the Indian village, where he just walked through a country school house; that says more than a thousand million-dollar programs of aid to Indians—about interest in Indians. We did well with that visit to Mississippi; we just have not given enough thought to the kind of "non-hokey, non P.R." type of presidential appearance which shows RN to be the President who is also one of the people, the democrat with a small d.

That visit to Shaw Park in D.C. in the black area was one example. Republicans, especially more conservative Republicans, have never been much good at this or done it at all, whereas liberal Democrats sometimes overdo it. But this is an area where we have much unused capital in the bank. The meeting with Harry Truman was one example of the kind of thing that only helps the President. Just as staff members have been directed to give thought to meetings and dinners of RN with various groups, so a handful should be directed to set aside a few hours and think of settings in which the President's very presence would say something about his concerns.

In this day and age, there is an excess of this kind of thing on the part of some politicians—the New York blintz-eater being the prime example. But serious thought and the occasional use of this can reap great dividends—because like the President's remarks on racial healing before a Jaycee Convention, it catches the media by surprise; it does not fit the stereotype; therefore it is something to be reported in a manner other than the customary cynical monologue in which much of the press tells our story.

9. Personally, I would keep an eye on this fellow [CBS president Frank] Stanton; I am thoroughly convinced that this is a Trojan horse operation; that Stanton's decision of four half-hours for the Democrats represents the first in a series of salami tactics against our strongest political asset. And I am not convinced that a moderate approach to this is the answer—although I concurred in the judgment of Klein, Ziegler in the initial counter-thrust coming from Congress. But we ought not to let them get away with it, [even] if we have to introduce legislation that will send CBS stock right through the floor to prevent it. One of these days there is going to have to be some institutional assault on these networks since our chances of controlling their news operations simply do not exist. But that is in the future.

10. Have talked with the President and Magruder about getting more and better direct mail coverage of controversial Vice Presidential speeches—especially those the orders for which come from on high. On this—we have to get the Veep's full text maximum distribution to our friends; we can win every time

the country hears everything he says, but if they get a truncated AP version and then see it chopped in an editorial, and the networks play a few lines, then chop him in the commentary, we lose. Magruder and I have already worked up a plan on this, which we are taking up with the Veep's people.

11. As you know, on a number of these speeches, the Vice President is directly carrying out presidential orders—yet, within the staff there is a good deal of weeping and gnashing of teeth about his performance, which is understandable, but which seems to me inexcusable when it is leaked to the press as it constantly is. You can hardly pick up a paper without reading of how some staffer is moaning about what the Vice President said or did. This is a form of "Moyerism" where an aide ingratiates himself with a liberal reporter at the expense of his superiors. There is all too much of it within our shop and the Vice President is the target; and I might add from personal contact; he is not altogether pleased with it. He is performing the same service RN performed in the 1950s—willing to take the heat; but he should not be required to be shot in the back by his own people. This might be the subject of discussion at one of the top level staff meetings—simply tell those who disagree with the Vice President to keep their mouth shut when asked about that and invariably they are by the left-wing press.

12. We have failed to bring in the Vice President's staff on planning for our "offensives." It is not enough to designate Buchanan to write a speech for the Vice President without having the Veep or his staff aware that the Veep is to give it. Suggest that in future strategy sessions—like the Kissinger briefing on the Cambodian thing—one of the Vice President's people be there so he can carry back to the Vice President the role we hope he will play. Also, the request for the Vice President to join in the general offensive should come from a top aide (Harlow?)—this is a matter simply of routine communication and coordination in which we have fallen down for no really explicable reason it seems to me.

13. That tour of the campuses by the eight from the Administration resulted in some of our most miserable press. First, they came back home and told the press, without attribution, that RN was more unpopular than ever on the campuses; then there were second day stories saying that they were going to go in and tell the President how unpopular he was and what a disaster the Vice President was; and then there were third day stories with the kids reporting that they had just told the President what a failure his Administration was on the college campus. So, we had a running story for a week—being leaked by our own people—tearing down our own administration. Can someone explain to me any good this kind of exercise does for us? If individuals find it outside their capacity to accentuate the positive in the administration and to down-play the

negative, they should be told to cut off communication with the media. There is nothing a press man likes better than to get an inside story from a White House or other aide, knocking his own Administration. Look at what they managed to do with a GS-11 little nothing like Toby Moffett—one expects this of ideological adversaries, not of White House staff assistants.

14. Kissinger is really the high card we can play as far as rewarding conservative columnists and the like with backgrounders. There are a number of these people who are consistently with us on foreign policy issues—I know Henry is busier than most—but we ought to bring them in by the half dozen for backgrounders.

Again, Buchanan and Allin can get together the list of guys who are carrying the ball for the President in the Daily Media.

15. There should be some kind of meeting between the Klein and Ziegler and Allin shops to set down on paper a list of those reporters and writers who should be on the press list for invitation to presidential dinners; we have not enough coordination on this. Maybe a directive from HRH for a meeting of this kind to gather together a list of those who should and should <u>never</u> be seen around the White House would be helpful. Undoubtedly, many friends are being ignored, while some adversaries, like Mr. Stanton, have been seen sipping whiskey in the East Room. [28]

14. Memo to Richard Nixon, "Chancellor, Smith and Sevareid," June 29, 1970
Because Chancellor does not "comment" officially on the news as do Smith and Sevareid, we are weaker in that Department. However, an analysis of the last month indicates the following interest for the following individuals.

HOWARD K. SMITH
As the President knows, Smith is a hawk who is liberal domestically. He has recently, however, rapped those who talk about re-ordering our priorities to the point where they want to downplay defense spending altogether. Claims Howard, the downplaying of military needs led to two World Wars.

He shows great sympathy for the President—when the President is under severe attack from critics, Smith says harshness of attacks on President are more likely to lead to destruction of the Presidency than to any constructive change.

Smith said not too long ago, it looks like RN may be coming out of Cambodia "smelling like a rose." US had helped build a constitutional structure there in SVN, furthered ARVN's development. "Those who have fought there have helped to build a nation, and if the protestors don't snatch defeat from the jaws of victory, the young Americans who've been in Vietnam might have been successful."

RECOMMENDATION: This is a theme RN could hit if he mentions the patience on the part of the people—something like "Let me tell you; those boys did not die in vain; they may have purchased a chance for 18,000,000 Vietnamese and their children and children's children to live in freedom. Those American boys who fought out there may have bought that; let's not throw it away; let's not snatch now defeat from the jaws of success."

Smith also rapped the Times and the Post when they were outraged at the joint Asian effort to block aggression in Cambodia; isn't this the type of cooperation against aggression we have always wanted, he noted.

On the Middle East, Smith said that if Israel wants peace she should be prepared to give back occupied territory.

Smith long urged Senate to play guts ball and vote Tonkin Gulf Resolution up or down—he now seems disenchanted with the body after the mush mess made of Cooper-Church.

JOHN CHANCELLOR

Don't have much on him, although in talking with Herb, a good point is made: Chancellor is the lightweight on the panel; he is going to want to make himself look good, since he is to be the new anchorman; thus he would be less likely it seems to do something which would embarrass him or jeopardize his new position.

Note: Ziegler says in the last three or four months he seems to have "mellowed," speaks well of the President—this may reflect desire for a "détente" lest we protest his elevation to Huntley's job.

However, at the time of the Air Force Academy speech, he was really hung up on the Arms Race thing—seeing such as MIRV as the next thing to the holocaust. Decidedly leftist in foreign policy—no question about it.

Note: After RN's Cambodia speech on April 30th, Chancellor said that it is not the Indochina War—and as I recall he has hammered home, or tried to, the theme that it is "Nixon's War."

ERIC SEVAREID

Among his positions taken in recent commentaries are the following:

1. Very adverse to U.S. payment of funds to Thais and Filipinos and South Koreans—to the point of being indignant. (Smith generally taking a totally opposite tack on this one.)

2. Pessimistic on the Middle East, regards latest U.S. effort as major effort to get talks underway; it if fails, then Sevareid is gloomy that new efforts can be made soon.

3. Believes Cambodia has involved us deeper than ever in the Indochina War; made situation more difficult to control.

4. Sevareid said at one point that while RN says that Cambodia may have shortened the war—it also shortened the lives of some reporters covering the war. He was most upset as the casualties among the press mounted.

5. Sevareid is a believer in the thesis that we have allowed our power to use us, rather than to control it; idea of reduction of military influence, vis-à-vis civilian and peace sector, strong here.

6. Sevareid does seem cognizant from his comments of the threat RN confronts from the right if there is not some sort of military success—and recognizes the potential from the right in this country from a military disaster.

7. Sevareid concerned a bit about the possibility of "Chinese volunteers" in the Indochina war, has expressed this concern; also has shown interest in the thesis that Cambodian operation upset Russians and provided Peking chance to enhance position in the region.

8. Sevareid seems sympathetic to Senate effort to control the executive in foreign policy—i.e., Cooper-Church—while expressing support for RN getting more control over the Federal government through OBM. [29]

15. Memo to H. R. Haldeman, September 8, 1970

As I understand it, the President does not want the "complete" briefing book—but an abridged version, containing, say, the thirty most likely questions to occur in domestic and foreign policy.

Observations: First, this condensed book, since it is so topical, has a half-life of about three days. As Ron [Ziegler] will confirm, questions that are certain to be asked of the President can change from day to day—one that was key three days ago may have been answered to everyone's satisfaction yesterday. Secondly, right now, and for the foreseeable future, between 60 and 80 percent of any questions asked of the President at a press conference would deal with the Middle East, the hijackings, American-Soviet relations, Vietnam and Cambodia—all foreign policy subjects. . . .

RECOMMENDATIONS FOR FALL BRIEFING BOOKS

1. Ascertain from the President as early as possible when he wants to have a scheduled conference or an impromptu conference. If we can get 72 hours' notice on this, then there should be no problem at all with the kind of book the

President wants. (From Ziegler I understand there is a press conference anticipated in the next few weeks, but nothing is firm.)

2. When I get word, there is nowhere in the country from which I can't get back at this desk, I imagine, in twelve hours or much less, to handle all the domestic questions in the kind of book you want.

3. Since foreign policy is the truly crucial issue right now and has been in most press conferences, suggest that a directive be sent to the NSC to prepare a <u>full</u> briefing book now, that the book be updated every week or ten days, that it either be sent to me on the road or left on my desk. Then the day-to-day questions—which are the most critical here also—can be prepared by the NSC on specific notice of an impending conference. They can be put together easily within 24 hours, and I can have them all gone over in another 24 hours.

4. Strongly recommend that we coordinate the Vice President's campaign speeches with the timing of an RN conference. If we have a good speech ready to go—we ought to hold it off if the President is about to dominate the media.

5. Also, on the road I imagine I will have some hand in preparing the Vice President's briefing book—which will be helpful in terms of keeping abreast of what is likely to be asked of the President.

6. Again, the crucial thing is simply <u>advance notice</u> of an impending conference; the more the better the book, the less time wasted on preparing questions not likely to be answered, and the more time available for other enterprises more fruitful. Also, even if the notice is given a week ahead of time out on the road, I can be working on some question while out there to bring back.[30]

16. Memo to Richard Nixon, "Special Report, Media Coverage, Predominantly TV, During Last 10 Days of Campaign," November 4, 1970
<u>THE ECONOMY</u>

The award for the most effective Democratic Campaigner this fall should not go to [Senator Edmund] Muskie or [Senator Edward M.] Kennedy or [Senator Albert] Gore—but to NBC. A rapid review of our news summaries for the final two weeks of the campaign (October 21–November 3) indicates that no phalanx of Democrats could have done a more effective job of hammering home the economic issue to voters. They not only enthusiastically reported the statistics; they translated them into specific price rises; they had several major film reports underscoring the human problems faced by the unemployed and by consumers. This treatment was in line with NBC's handling of the economy throughout the year. First they reached their apogee just before the election. On one lengthy political report (Zion's District in Indiana) they focused almost exclusively on unemployment and economic problems. On the twenty-ninth, there was a six-minute report on the economic woes of the country—that was in marked and striking contrast to what was presented on ABC and CBS and the following day in the papers.

The other networks made their contribution to the development of this issue—but they were not even in the same ball park with NBC in terms of effectiveness.

LAW AND ORDER

We have no complaints here in the last two weeks. Night after night the networks had reports of violence; there was the second Manson-type killing in California, the La Porte death spill over, Rockefeller against permissiveness, a Panther shootout, police attacks, arson and drug reports, and the San Jose incident widely reported. The networks clearly underscored this issue for us.

THE PRESIDENT

Here again, the coverage was of enormous and unrivaled volume on the network news—we surely have no justification for complaint on the amount of time we received in those final two weeks, although the Democrats might have a legitimate complaint. Out of a possible 29 lead stories in the last 10 days, RN was lead 15 times including a good number of film reports from campaign. (ABC had 19 minutes of RN, NBC 16, and CBS 22. Dems got 7 each on ABC and NBC and 15 on CBS.)

THE VICE PRESIDENT

He got very negative treatment overall for the final two weeks. [Democratic National Committee chair Larry] O'Brien's vitriolic attacks were well reported; Sevareid's "apologia" for the media against the Veep got wide coverage. The V.P. was identified by Democrats with the "politics of fear"; there was a report on NBC—grossly unfair—done by Vanocur which inferred that the Vice President was conducting an anti–young people campaign; Chief Ahern at Kent State, attacking the Veep, was on the air; then ABC had that two-day flap about the Vice President being dropped which was hardly helpful. (Some good reports, however.)

In almost every commentary on the election itself, the networks either inferred or said the campaign was hostile, divisive, and bitter—and the Vice President was charged with being a prime offender in this regard.

CAMPAIGN SPENDING
Both political ads (the volume of them) and spots took a severe beating. Hucksterism was rapped. The final campaign ads in the newspapers identifying liberal Democrats with all manner of violence and anarchy were counter-productive as far as the television media was concerned—since they were denounced as ludicrous and unfair.

"POLITICS OF FEAR"
The Democrats, abetted by the networks, pushed this message across to the public. Democrats pushed the line—that instead of healing the divisions in society, Republicans, especially the VP and President, are trying to profit politically from them. O'Brien has made this a constant theme. NBC ran Lindsay footage making this charge clearly. The Vice President was identified with "McCarthyism" in some reports. The Reston-Sevareid thesis that whatever happens on election night, RN has lost in terms of his ability to unite and lead the country was moved by Sevareid. Generally, the impression was fortified by the networks that this was a dirty, divisive campaign in which both the President and Vice President were deeply involved.

MUSKIE
On the last day of the campaign, must be said he came off very well—was juxtaposed against the President's Phoenix speech, which was technically a disaster. Also, network news shows had him on the air that night. Used low-keyed, "politics of trust" reconciliation line and played it to useful effect for Big Ed. NBC gave him 5 minutes on election night. (In contrast to other reports on individual contests which were quite balanced, NBC had the Muskie job as well as ones on Dellums, Young and Goodell which were done without covering the other candidates in any more than a perfunctory fashion.)

INTERVENTION
Clearly, the nation was kept constantly informed during the final days and on election night that the President's personal prestige and commitment were deeply involved in this election—the unprecedented nature of RN campaigning came through all along. And thus the close identification with results naturally has followed.

MAGAZINES
In the closing days of the campaign, the national magazines—in particular, Look and Time and Newsweek—came out with issues which could only be

considered damaging. The two newsweeklies dumped all over our campaigns, as divisive, vitriolic, fear-oriented campaigns. The theme hit by Muskie, [Kennedy], and O'Brien that we all hate violence, why then do they accuse us of being for it, has come through various media on an increasing basis. Also, the theme that we are taking political advantage of the divisions in the country—and thus making deeper and more permanent those divisions reinforced the O'Brien line. We appealed to men's fears, not hopes, is a theme of the opposition also coming through.

Look in its current issue had one piece by Harriman attacking Vietnamization as immoral—another by [CBS News anchor Walter] Cronkite which identified good old Walter as something of a radiclib—if not a New Leftist sympathizer in some of his views. Very anti-Administration and particularly anti-VP was the thrust of the Cronkite piece.

RECOMMENDATIONS

1) We put together tapes of a) All of NBC's coverage of the economy in the last two weeks. b) Tapes of all of [ABC News correspondent Sander] Vanocur in the last two weeks, c) Tapes of [NBC News correspondent] Jack Perkins gutting Reagan on one of the last nights of the campaign, an especially vicious piece of TV distortion, d) We put together a comparison of how ABC and CBS handled the economic report of October 29—with the 6-minute NBC lynching with the same statistics.

If we get these—look them over—separately, they might serve as visuals for a speech on NBC's very biased coverage. (We could add to it some of the very negative reports done by NBC while RN was in Europe.) Anyhow, the time one would think has come to either fish or cut bait with this network; our courtship of [NBC president] Julian Goldman seems to have produced less than nothing; perhaps the use of TV clips, the naming of reporters with bias back-up, the public call for the Library of Congress to tape these and make them available to scholars and journalists, and taking the case of NBC bias to the FCC might help.

But watching the networks and national magazines, one can readily predict what is in store for us in the final two weeks of the 1972 campaign long before. [31]

17. Memo for the Staff Secretary, "Press Conference Responses," January 13, 1971

Mort Allin and the staff dug up the clippings attached, and from them no one can logically piece together what happened. No "aide" was quoted as saying that we had "anticipated" all the questions asked of RN at his successful meeting with the correspondents. The feeling that one did obviously emerged from the John Roche column three days after that conference—January 8, 1971. But on re-reading Roche's column it is clear he is referring to the President's press conference in December—when all the reporters were gearing up to hit RN. The source of Roche's statement is thus: it seems a <u>Newsweek</u> piece . . . of December 21, in which a White House aide is quoted as saying, "Every one of the 28 questions was anticipated" was it.

From the way that quote comes off, it appears that some "aide" was trying to zing the reporters a bit—by indicating that despite all their planning, they couldn't come up with a single question which we couldn't anticipate. Like the Lisagor quote of a year ago, "We didn't lay a glove on him," this one is liable to recur after every press conference.

Finally, you ought to tell RN that (a) no aide made such a statement following his successful conversation, (b) that Sevareid commented on his tremendous preparation for these meetings and said you can't catch him off guard, and (c) the Roche column which reprints the earlier <u>Newsweek</u> quote was so favorable to the President that Klein's shop used it as "column of the day."

As for <u>Newsweek</u> and Mr. Hubbard who wrote the piece, I have a call into him—although a complaint about the accuracy of a month-old story is liable to make him wonder what the hell is going on.[32]

18. Memo to H. R. Haldeman, "Neither Fish Nor Fowl," January 14, 1971

We suffer from the widely held belief that the President has no Grand Vision that inspires him, no deeply held political philosophy that girds, guides and explains his words, decisions, and deeds. The President is viewed as the quintessential political pragmatist, standing before an ideological buffet, picking some from this tray and some from that. On both sides he is seen as the text book political transient, here today, gone tomorrow, shuttling back and forth, as weather permits, between liberal programs and conservative rhetoric. As someone put it, "the bubble in the carpenter's level."

Nixon, the Plastic President, is a severe, even brutal, judgment, but one held to our disadvantage by increasing numbers of liberals and conservatives.

This impression is reinforced daily by the national media, which invariably discussed in depth the "political motives" behind each of the President's actions—whether it be a visit to a college campus, the appointment of a Democratic Cabinet official, or a meeting with a black leader. Few Presidents have had their "motives" inspected to the degree that Richard Nixon has. (Further, we do not help the President by this very visible campaign to present the media yet another "New Nixon," a campaign whose existence is apparent from reading all the columns and reports of the "changes" in emphasis and goal and purpose of 1971, from 1970.)

Left and right, both now argue aloud that the President and his Administration do not take decisions on the basis of political principle—but on the basis of expediency; that ours is "ad hoc government," which responds only as pressures mount from left or right. Neither liberal nor conservative, neither fish nor fowl, the Nixon Administration, they argue, is a hybrid, whose zigging and zagging has succeeded in winning the enthusiasm and loyalty of neither left nor right, but the suspicion and distrust of both.

This reality, as others see it, lies beneath many of the "p.r. failures of 1970."

More important, this "reality" explains many of the Administration's existing political and "p.r." difficulties, and probably has greater bearing on the President's future—and his place in history—than any successful or unsuccessful "game plan" from Calendar 1970 I can recall.

Thus, I am using the occasion of this memorandum, written "in strict confidence," to focus upon this matter of ideological direction.

SINCE NOVEMBER
The impression among sophisticated conservatives—now being conveyed to the rank-and-file—is that the President, subsequent to the harsh (and unjust) criticism of his 1970 campaign, has moved leftward in force to cover his exposed flank.

The "full employment budget," the open embrace of an "expansionary deficit," the public confession that "Kent State and Jackson State" and the defeat of [Family Assistance Plan] were his greatest "disappointments," the admission "I am a Keynesian now," the enthusiasm for both FAP and for the forthcoming [Family Health Insurance Plan]—these are part of a pattern left and right have both recognized.

The "clincher" for both sides came in the President's conversation with the anchormen. While the booboisie in the hinterlands saw only the President's mastery and skill (74 percent), the sophisticates, on both sides, picked up unmistakable signals. It was not the Nixon deftness in handling questions that made [*Washington Post* publisher] Kay Graham, [ABC News correspondent] Sander Vanocur, and [syndicated columnist] Joe Kraft, watching together, credit the President with his most brilliant performance—or that had astonished conservatives on the phone to each other after midnight.

BALANCE SHEET

A close examination of the early returns, and the projected returns, from the President's recent moves seems imperative before the President sets his compass on the course indicated in that conversation. The State of the Union and the Budget mark the point of no return.

THE DOWN SIDE

In the short run, through 1972, the decision may very well be the necessary and correct one. An electoral cost accountant could argue cogently that Nixon must move leftward to win moderates and liberals from Muskie, and anyway, the conservatives have nowhere else to go. Just as the Gene McCarthy Left eventually came home to Humphrey in November of 1968, so also the Goldwater-Reagan Right must come home to Nixon in November of 1972.

There are problems with this scenario, however. First, it does not allow for the presence of Wallace as an alternative for some on the Right. Second, it does not take into consideration that the Republican Right is not simply a powerful struggling minority in the GOP—as the McCarthy Left is in the Democratic Party—it is the dominant majority, with the power to nominate and veto presidential candidates.

Even more serious in my view than the long-shot possibility of a Reagan-or-Conservative run for the Republican nomination is the certain erosion of the President's historic base—when the accumulated news of the last few weeks filters down to precinct level.

Over the course of two years, but especially in the last month, the President has conspicuously abandoned many of the sustaining traditions of the Republican Party, traditions Richard Nixon rode to triumphant success in 1968 over the defeated "programmatic liberalism" of the New Deal.

Two brief examples. In both "reducing the size of the Federal Government" and "balancing the Federal Budget," the President has swept these traditions aside with an ease and facility that must have astonished millions of Republicans who have held them as articles of faith for forty years.

On his statements and positions of recent weeks, the President is no longer a credible custodian of the conservative political tradition of the GOP. Can one seriously imagine in 1972 those little old ladies in tennis shoes ringing doorbells in Muncie for "FAP," "FHIP," and the "full employment budget."

In the profit-and-loss statement drawn up from the President's move left, we must not overlook the inevitable and considerable loss in morale to the tens of thousands of party workers, the backbone of the GOP, one of the hinges on which the 1972 election will surely swing. The President once rightly identified the Left as the home of the True Believer in the Democratic Party and the Right as the home of the True Believer in the GOP. With Richard Nixon on the ticket, the troops of the Democratic Party will be out in force; where will the troops of the GOP be?

The President's recent moves—if publicized widely nationally—leave the Republican True Believers without a vocal champion. One has to guess that this political vacuum will not go unfilled, that the old political faith will not go unchampioned for long.

Though a minority nationally, many millions of Americans hold fiscal and political conservatism as gospel—and the President's rapid moves have taken him further to the left in a month than the average Republican travels in a lifetime.

Further, in shedding some of the sustaining traditions of the GOP, we have donned the garments of the same "programmatic liberalism" the President scorned as outdated in 1968. Regardless of our rhetoric about "cleaning out the Federal Government" and "returning power to the States, cities and the people," the Federal Government under the Nixon Administration has grown to a size to dwarf the Great Society. What Great Society programs—with the insignificant exception of the Job Corps camps—have been abandoned?

Rather than draw up our own yardstick of success and failure, we have willingly invited judgment by the old measures of the old order. Thus, we proudly point up that we are spending more for "human resources" than for "defense resources." (Most Republicans would argue that Federal spending for "human resources" has proven a failure, and there should be less, not more.) We publicize statistics on how much "integration" has taken place under President Nixon; we argue that our welfare program provides a guaranteed income for families and is bigger and better than anything they have offered; we underscore how much more rapidly we are bringing Americans home from Vietnam and the rest of the world; we congratulate ourselves on each new cut in the defense budget. In short, we ask our adversaries in the media and the academy to judge us on how well we are doing in reaching objectives which liberals—not conservatives— have designated as the national goals.

When the suggestion even surfaces that the President may be disenchanted with [Office of Economic Opportunity], and perhaps ready to scuttle it, Rumsfeld and Carlucci rush to Capitol Hill to swear our eternal fealty to the organization.

Truly, the liberals went swimming and President Nixon stole their clothes—

but in the process we left our old conservative suit lying by the swimming hole for someone else to pick up.

There is another theme abandoned with the new maneuver, the "it's time for a change" theme, on which we had the patent in 1968, and could have maintained through protracted conflict with an "Establishment" during the Nixon Presidency. Roosevelt maintained it through his first two terms in power—running against the "conservative establishment." But, in openly appealing to moderates and liberals, in adopting programs and politics warmly endorsed by American liberalism, we are becoming the Administration of more of the same. On the Democratic side, there is always the alternative available of more and faster—and now, on our right, there is available a clear alternative of a "different road for America." Either Mr. Wallace or Mr. Reagan can apply for the vacancy.

As my own concern with whether the President wins in 1972 is of a piece with my concern for the President's place in history, I have to view the sharp leftward move in disappointing terms.

The President is now abandoning an historic opportunity, the opportunity to become the political pivot on which America turned away from liberalism, away from the welfare state—the founder of a new "Establishment." While the course of a "conservative President" would be more difficult by far, and politically more risky, it would seem a preferable course historically if only because the President would be assured an unoccupied niche in America's history books and a following of millions of men and women to honor his memory.

After observing what liberal journalists, liberal academicians, and liberal historians are doing to the most liberal New Dealer of them all, Lyndon Johnson, I cannot think that they will be paying much grudging tribute to the accomplishments of liberal-come-lately Richard Nixon. One wonders who will be writing our epitaph.

THE UP SIDE

Clearly, among the primary considerations in the President's "opening to the left" was the pressure of advisers that this was the only way to end the daily savaging of the President at the hands of the liberal media.

The national media—television and the national press—dominate the impressions of the Administration conveyed to the nation. From watching the media in the month following the campaign, it was clear they were bent on the destruction of this Administration.

In recent weeks, the assault has abated. The strategy is clearly working; we seem to be succeeding. Having failed to halt the liberal media's attacks by ignoring them until November of 1969, we took to the offensive that month and through the elections of 1970. Originally successful, that policy seems subsequently to have failed and now we have clearly sought an armistice—with major political concessions forth-coming.

A strong case can be made that this new posture is the only way the President can get tolerable coverage and thus perhaps the only way he can survive the 1972 elections.

Over against this, one has to ask, not what the media will say in 1971—about "new initiatives"—but where will it be when push comes to shove in 1972. Where will the liberals, columnists and commentators and reporters go in a Nixon-Kennedy, Nixon-Muskie, or Nixon-Humphrey race? Those who think that Richard M. Nixon, the man who nailed Hiss, can ever win over the loyalty and support of a single liberal reporter belongs, in my view, in that asylum built for those ever-trusting Americans who yet believe that one more gesture to the Soviets will woo them away from the ends and means they have followed unswervingly for a lifetime.

Truly, from watching the three network shows on 1970, they have "had it up to here" with the President.

First, the Nixon Presidency does not even remotely resemble their ideal—a Kennedy-style Presidency, grounded in intellectual and young-poor-black support, a presidency that wages uninterrupted war on Congressional and Southern reactionaries, not consorts with them, an Administration with a heart that bleeds a little publicly, an Administration that will abandon interventionist nonsense from the days of the Cold War, an Administration that will truly re-order priorities. We are not that Administration now. The closer we approximate ourselves to it—the better treatment we shall receive.

Secondly, and as important, the dominant media views the world differently than we do. They look, and everywhere they see crisis—regardless of the merits of the case. Neither statements nor statistics can convince them that poverty is being diminished annually, that the lot of our black citizens is improving monthly, that hunger is being defeated, that war against pollution has begun with a good chance of success.

There are none so blind as those who will not see—and the left intellectual does not want to see the far-reaching successes of the United States at home and abroad anymore. He wants to believe that stupidity and reaction and insensitivity are bringing us to ruin—and so that is what he sees. What confirms this apocalyptic vision is emphasized—what contradicts it is ignored.

So to have ourselves portrayed in a favorable light by the media, and hence to the nation, to win the votes of that "critical margin" of moderates and liber-als, we have determined to compromise with established liberalism, no longer to confront it—to go along in order to get along. Perhaps that is politically the best course of action—historically, I cannot think so—for us or the country.[33]

19. Memo to Chuck Colson, "The 'Isolated President,'" February 4, 1971

When confronted with this myth, in conversation or on the air, an effective rebuttal is the President's own mastery of all the matters of government and the nation, when confronted on live television by the national press. The latter can hardly be considered either sympathetic or magnanimous; yet, despite their tough, accusatory questions, the President has responded not only in good hu-mor, but in as concise and informative a manner as any President in history. One recalls that John F. Kennedy did an hour's show with three correspondents—one of them Mr. Vanocur—a roaring sycophant, and then Mr. Kennedy hauled the 88-minute tape in for clipping and editing. President Nixon went live twice, and on the second occasion, Eric Sevareid, scarcely the ex-chairman of Journalists for Nixon, went away marveling at the President's knowledge and mastery of all the business before him and the nation.

Every one of these live appearances has won plaudits from neutral observers, and has enhanced the President's standing with the American people. And the President does not need "soft balls" pitched up to him by reporters with planted questions. The one time such occurred, the President put his staff on instruc-tions it was never to happen again. He gets tougher questions than any other President—the very fact that the press is so frustrated at being unable to trap him is another good indication that the President is fully in touch with all that is going on in the Departments, the White House, in foreign and domestic policy.

In so doing, we should also hammer home the point that though the pundits write the President off every other week, his personal appearances before the country on television have turned the polls around. Despite the worst a hostile liberal Eastern media can do, the President survives their opposition in good style. If a liberal Democratic President ever had the Eastern media withdraw its "Mandate of Heaven," as it did to Lyndon Johnson, he could not survive. But President Nixon has gone for years without their endorsement, indeed, with their opposition, because his strength, like FDR's, lies with the common man.[34]

20. Memo to H. R. Haldeman, March 2, 1971

Bill Anderson of the <u>Chicago Tribune</u> was in; he is a former City Editor, an older reporter, who says he has twice done and twice torn up a piece on the

White House Staff—mainly because he said it comes off so negatively. He said that the main negatives he was getting from outside (old friends of RN)—which he said was expected, but also from the Hill are complaints about you and John Ehrlichman. He said he was looking for some ideas to balance the piece, if he does it again. (He also mentioned the Ziegler operation.) I asked him the nature of the complaints, and he gave the usual "blocking access," and personal gripes, and a good deal of frustration on the Hill at "how cavalierly" they have been treated, etc. I told him of RN's preference to work through "memoranda," preference for written arguments, etc., that John's job was often resolving disputes where there was a likelihood of one or the other party going away mad; that yours was being responsible for the 99 turndowns out of the 100 requests, etc. I further suggested that he talk with you—and told him I would intercede as I think it a good idea, as I do. It might be well also to get John Ehrlichman to talk with him.

Anyway, his main concern was a piece on the Veep, but he brought this all up before leaving and intends to make, through Ron Ziegler, an approach to see both you and John.[35]

21. Memo to Richard Nixon, "Press Conference," April 23, 1971

Initial research finds that should RN hold a press conference this coming Thursday, televised, the following are the most likely questions:

1. Is your trip tomorrow to California connected in any way with the week of demonstrations planned for Washington?

2. Will you follow through on the Supreme Court decisions with regard to bussing and pairing; how do you feel about the decisions which seem to directly conflict with the course of action you recommend?

3. Did you put the Vice President up to making his statements about China; and are you and he in full agreement on his approaches to Communist China?

4. RN's view of demonstrations.

5. RN's view of Mansfield idea of possibly cutting off funds for the conflict in Vietnam.

6. Questions on Middle East—as per normal.

7. Questions on Vietnam—as per normal.

8. Questions on Soviet Strategic Weapons, coming out of the Laird Conference—and SALT.

RN's decision to hold a televised press conference should be premised upon whether he wants to deal with these issues in prime time TV.

Buchanan's Views:

Plusses: <u>RN standing firm in the midst of a week of turmoil talking about what is going on in the street.</u>

Minuses. Again, Vietnam; again, the economy and Mideast; again, the issues which the nation has seen discussed night in and night out, day in and day out. Also moves into the problem of over-exposure—on the Vietnam issue.

If the President has some things to say—on the demonstrations, and on the Soviets, and on other issues; PJB would recommend go ahead live. But if this is to be just another press conference, for exposure—would recommend that RN not do it live, but make his points with headlines rather than intruding upon the prime time of folks. If we do the latter, it should only be because there is a national interest in seeing RN, or RN sees the national interest—in his going to the country.[36]

22. Memo to Richard Nixon, "Political Memorandum: The PR Campaign," May 3, 1971

We face an increasingly serious political problem in the rising crescendo of news stories about the "image makers" in the White House. It reached a new level this weekend, when [CBS News correspondent] Bob Pierpont went on network television news for the first time with this theme of "twenty-two image makers" now on the White House staff, following the three additions, who are allegedly the ones counseling the President to make the recent spate of public appearances. . . .

Further, both Humphrey and Muskie have touched on the matter (HHH accusing us of "public relations gimmickry"), and if pressed, it could present a serious problem for if there is anything that turns off Middle America, it is Madison Avenue.

Secondly, for every minor color item we have moved into the media, there has probably been one major story on the "new effort to humanize the President." This latter theme coursing through the national media is decidedly not to our advantage. . . .

While I do not have any complete answers to this problem, I think it is a serious one which could become quite serious in the 1972 campaign, and herewith some thoughts:

First, we should de-escalate the time and energy and thought spent on pushing little "color anecdotes" about the President—and shift our emphasis on associating the President with "accomplishments" of his Administration. The President did not get here by being warm and human and witty and charming—he got here by being capable and tough and qualified and politically courageous. And if we stay here, it will be because of those latter <u>virtues and accomplishments</u>—not the former. I <u>do not</u> recommend that we eschew altogether telling the press and media anecdotes and stories which flesh out the President's personality. But if we are <u>relying</u> on that, we are in trouble. And further the efforts to push these to the press becomes at once counter-productive, as Ziegler tells me, for the press room quickly buzzes with the story that we are "pushing" these materials. And they insert in future stories that the "PR campaign" is geared up again.

Again, in speeches and interviews and backgrounders, the colorful anecdote is useful, and should be utilized—but this effort should not call forth the present institutionalized effort. More than one friendly reporter has told me we "are turning people off" with these efforts.

Frankly, the one in the best position to drop the "anecdotes" about a meeting is Ron Ziegler, or some official who has "reason" to be in the meeting—where it occurs—a reason other than there to write up the color. Example: PJB attends the Congressional leadership meetings; it is an easy and natural thing to do when asked about that meeting to relay the anecdotes. But unless it's an extraordinary incident, a phone call from me to <u>Time</u> to "tell" them the anecdote will produce an entry in the "Time File" to the effect that we are out pushing anecdotes. . . .[37]

23. Memo to Richard Nixon, "Pentagon Papers," July 1, 1971

In June 1971, the Nixon administration sought to impose prior restraint on the New York Times *and* Washington Post *when both papers began reporting on the "Pentagon Papers," a 47-volume study on the "History of the U.S. Decision Making Process on Vietnam Policy" that had been leaked by Daniel Ellsberg, a former defense department analyst. The Supreme Court ruled against Nixon in* New York Times v. United States *(1971), but only after the stories had been kept out of the newspapers for approximately two weeks following a restraining order from a federal court judge.*

We are being damaged on three grounds because of these documents:

1. We are being portrayed as "repressive" for attempting to hold up the documents, "political" because we appear to be covering up something, and "ridiculous," in that we have appeared ineffectual and comical with our lack of success.

2. More important, the American support for the war effort is being seriously damaged as the impression is being left to stand that somehow the United States is the guilty party in the entire war. This feeling nationally could affect continued national support for the President's withdrawal program and for US support in Saigon.

3. The whole question of lack of trust in government which is raised by this matter is being used against us as well as Johnson—and we have to build a firewall between the Administrations.

On the necessity side, we have to get clear of the fallout from this entire episode. On the advantage side, the Times and Post are vulnerable, and there is considerable presidential mileage to be gained from speaking out now.

A. The President has yet to address himself to the issue; the timing is just right after the Supreme Court decision; on the other hand, if we fail to speak, people are going to conclude that our case was made and we simply got whipped.

B. We need to somehow divorce this Administration from the onus that is being visited upon LBJ and Government in general. Politically, the "trust" issue is a major issue in 1972, particularly if Muskie is in the field. And we have not succeeded in getting ourselves out of this Tar Baby.

C. Given the verbiage of the Supreme Court decision, its own past statements, and its conduct in this matter, the New York Times is vulnerable. They are at their crest right now—and the President, without an all-out assault, can throw them on the defensive. What they are exulting in right now is a victory—in the minds of the American people—over the Nixon Administration.

D. The President, by being magnanimous to LBJ and JFK, by urging the American people to "suspend judgment" on the basis of simply a biased report—can win plaudits from all those people and their constituency—without losing anything anywhere.

E. There are legitimate, effective answers to all the charges made against the President and the Administration—these answers have not been made, because the media is dominated by the other side in this controversy. Right now, we are the big losers in this enterprise—excepting only the Democrats who preceded us—and question is whether we are even going to show for the second half, or just forfeit on the basis of the first two periods. My view is that we can't lose anything by going on national record with the President's case—and there is a possibility that we can gain enormously, separate ourselves from the onus of the report, and put the Times and Post on the defensive.

Right now we are high among the big losers on this thing. The other side—controlling the networks and the press—have had it all their way. My view is that a speech can be drafted which will sweep the headlines, and if on television, could turn it around. But if we don't go to a confused nation with our side of the entire story, we can't expect them to understand or support our position.

Finally, nationally there is an on-going orgy of self-flagellation; the country is beginning to think itself guilty of the war, and the matter needs to be put into perspective.[38]

24. Memo to John Ehrlichman, July 8, 1971

Having considered the matter until the early hours, my view is that there are some dividends to be derived from Project Ellsberg—but none to justify the magnitude of the investment recommended.

At the very best, let us assume we can demonstrate, after three months' investigation, that Ellsberg stole the documents, worked hand-in-glove with ex-NSC types, collaborated with leftist writers Neil Sheehan and Fox Butterfield [of the *New York Times*], got together a conspiracy to drop the documents at set times to left-wing papers, all timed to undercut McGovern-Hatfield opposition—what have we accomplished?

What benefit would be derived to the President and his political fortunes in 1972—and what damage visited upon his major political adversaries on the other side of the aisle.

To me it would assuredly be psychologically satisfying to cut the innards from Ellsberg and his clique in a major book expose of what they attempted to do, and what they did. But I have yet to be shown what benefit this would do for the President—or for the rest of us, other than a psychological salve.

Most of the returns have already come in on this question—and the media has emerged a two-to-one winner (Gallup). This is not surprising.

First, the media controlled absolutely how the controversy would be portrayed to the American people. Secondly, we decided not to contest the issue where we might have had a chance—in the headlines. The speech drafted for the Vice President—who was prepared to deliver it—was killed. The remarks drafted for the President on several occasions, which would have been an implied and unmistakable rebuke to the New York Times and created a President-Times collision, was rejected, time and again.

An issue that has been decided on the front pages of the nation's papers and on the lead on the nation's network is not going to be turned around in the public mind by a few well-placed leaks to back-page obscurantists. . . .

If we had wanted to contest this issue—and the media would still have held the advantage—we should have done it right out in the open, as the Times dared to do. They made their "Go" decision, pulled out all stops publicly—and we simply did not make an effective response out on the field. No covert back-page guerrilla war is going to take away the Times' victory, which they can claim has been sealed by the Supreme Court.

This is not to argue that the effort is now worthwhile—but that simply we ought not now to start investing major personnel resources in the kind of covert operation not likely to yield any major political dividends to the President.

The lessons of 1969 seem to me to be here apposite. Confronted with a challenge to his Presidency, the Old Man "pushed his skiff from the shore alone" and went directly to the nation via networks, headlines—the works. We overran the opposition, routed them. The Vice President a week later did the identical thing on the networks. Not by PJB letters to the editor, not by Herb Klein chatting with Frank Stanton, not by Ron [Ziegler] talking with Dan Rather—but head-on. That is our forte.

Because the other side dominates the media; because we are limited to a time frame of four years, now diminished—because we have the best podiums in the world—the massive frontal assault is for us the siege gun, the major weapon. We are good at this—and yet most of our resources, as is here being suggested, are utilized for dropping little nuggets to back-page supporters and columnists and the like—the sum total of which is roughly zero. The dividends are to be found in the headlines—and our media resources are geared to the back pages.

That diversion finished—let me provide a future example of what we should do. Rather than . . . leaking attacks about the crowd at Brookings—let's undertake a major public attack on the Brookings Institution.

No one in the country knows what the thing is. We could have it attacked, discredited in the eyes of millions of people, and suspect in the eyes of millions of others—thus, tainting every single anti-Nixon paper that came out of there, subsequent. This is what we have in the works right now; we have West Wing approval and VP enthusiasm. The institutional, rather than the individual attack, the front-page headline, network attack—not the back-page nitpicking—this is to me our strength and our approach. If the President and Vice President eschew an assault on the Times in the major controversy of the decade thus far—Van Shumway cannot reverse the subsequent tide.

Finally, some thoughts.

If Lloyd Shearer is involved in this, a reading should be taken of all the anti-Vietnam positions taken in the Personality Parade section of Parade. ([Columnist] Jack Anderson told me, if I recall correctly, that Shearer did this and perhaps Parade can be discredited—that section is a powerful one in terms of public opinion.)

Neil Sheehan, at the time of [*St. Louis Post-Dispatch* correspondent] Dick Dudman's capture by the VC, sent a telegram to Hanoi all but saying let him go. "Dudman is on our side." Our intelligence intercepted this—and this could be utilized.

Fox Butterfield has visited Hanoi—I just read a particularly slobbering piece by him out of the enemy capital which is being run in Edith Efron's new book on the media.

If Ellsberg is from MIT, his connections with Noam Chomsky might be explored.

In the last analysis, however, the permanent discrediting of all these people, while good for the country, would not, it seems to me, be particularly helpful to the President politically.[39]

25. Memo to Richard Nixon, July 23, 1971

The media on the Vice President's foreign trip has gone from bad to worse. From the start, its purpose has been questioned, the reportage has concluded that it was a junket to get him out of Washington. In the wake of the China initiatives, it is being portrayed and believed that the Number 2 man in the nation was deliberately kept ignorant and away—when the historic steps were taken. From the nature of the reports, also, one gathers that the Vice President is himself reacting personally to his situation.

Now, some of the cheaper shots by <u>Newsweek</u> have been picked up by the Democrats who are making great hay. And his comments on U.S. black leaders—regardless of their truth or advisability—are being parroted in the States and used against the Vice President and by extension the President.

The DNC has already recognized the President's 1972 Vice Presidential decision as an important one—and their attacks on Agnew, and their flat assertions that he has been dumped, are designed now to make the President's decision difficult and costly—no matter which why it goes.

About all these matters, I have some extended thoughts—which I won't belabor here. However, the following seems to me worthwhile.

If the Vice President should suddenly have to take over the nation's duties, there would be a national crisis right now. And the continued media ridicule to which he is being subjected would make it certain that a national crisis would take place. On this ground alone, we should not, without acting, allow the present situation to deteriorate any further.

RECOMMENDATION:

That the President on his own take a helicopter out to the airport to greet the Vice President when he returns. Reasons:

1. No matter what RN's decision in 1972, it is not in the President's interest to have his Vice Presidential choice of 1968 humiliated.

2. It demonstrates that the President is an individual of compassion and concern for the feelings of people, a man who stands by his own, without implying endorsement of everything the Vice President has said.

3. Few, if any, people would condemn such a gesture—one recalls that old Harry Truman only won the support of the common man when he went to Boss Pendergast's funeral, saying, "He was good to me."

4. The gesture would be considered especially well by the Vice President's supporters within the party and on the Hill—with some of whom our relations are somewhat strained over recent developments. While there is great increasing alienation on the "organized" Right, there is still almost 100 percent Presidential support among the Elected Right—on the Hill especially. The Conservative Revolt will go nowhere unless they break that united front for RN on the Hill— and the one thing that would break it would be conspicuously cavalier treatment of the Vice President.

Even those Conservative Congressmen who might think it the President's prerogative alone to choose his Vice President in 1972 would be embittered if they felt the Vice President was being denigrated—and no effort made on the part of the President to stop this.

Thus: If the President showed up at the airport when the Vice President returned, a surprise visit, spoke a few words of gratitude, thanked him for his efforts on behalf of the nation, carrying the President's message to 10 countries, and took him home aboard his own chopper for the flight back to the White House, there would—it seems to me—be only benefits for the President.

My view is that one of the mistakes made in 1968 and on occasion, subsequently, is the assumption on the part of some of our people that somehow by appearing to stand far away from the Vice President, somehow the attacks upon him won't rub off on us. When the Vice President does well, the Administration is greatly assisted—when he is under attack, then we take the casualties as well.[40]

26. Memo to Richard Nixon, September 17, 1971

Understand thought is being given to televising nationally the RN appearance before the Detroit Economic Club. Don't think we should do that—for the following reasons:

1. An hour's show with Richard Nixon answering the concerns of some Detroit Fat Cats does not seem to me particularly good television; it will lack the adversary setting of a press conference, and the sharpness of questions, RN can expect from editors and writers.

2. An hour is simply too long—to sustain the interest of Middle America.

3. We have nothing really new to say, from my knowledge; the President has already covered the "news" in Thursday's conference.

4. The President's greatest political asset is the Presidency—part of the power of that asset adheres in the distance between the Presidency and the people.

Harry Truman as Harry Truman is a clown—as President, he fills the shoes of Lincoln, Wilson, etc. The more we show of RN the individual in front of a camera, the more in my judgment we diminish some of the mystery, the aloofness that surrounds the office. We make the President too "familiar" a figure—and not in the best sense of the word.

5. What makes China such an interesting, important country and De Gaulle such an interesting man—is the aloofness, the distance, from the hoi polloi. Every time we put the President on the camera in a conventional setting—answering Q and A—we tend, I think, to bring him down closer to the average man—and I don't believe that is to our political advantage—partly for the next reason.

6. I have never been convinced that Richard Nixon, Good Guy, is our long suit; to me we are simply not going to charm the American people; we are not going to win it on "style" and we ought to forget playing ball in the Kennedys' court.

This new emphasis on running the President on the tube at more and more opportunities is a corollary to the theorem that the more people who see the President, the more who will become enthusiastic about him. We are selling personality, but we know from our experience with television shows how even the most attractive and energetic and charming personalities don't last very long.

7. As I wrote the President long ago, in 1967, we watched Rocky [Nelson Rockefeller] rise twenty points in the national polls in a year in which he was probably not once on national television. When Rocky took to the airwaves in 1968, running around the country—he dropped in the polls as he did in 1964. In short, what is said and written around Nelson Rockefeller's accomplishments—compared with the accomplishments of others—is invariably better received than the presence of Rocky himself in a competitive situation.

8. The President is going to be on with Phase II in October, and with the Vietnam announcements in November. My judgment is that we ought not to put him on the air, without serious thought, and usually only in context with some significant pronouncement.

9. Finally, I am not at all against some of the more imaginative ideas for presenting the President—but they should come out of a Media Strategy, which I don't know we have right now—or I don't see how this fits into it.[41]

27. Memo to H. R. Haldeman, November 30, 1971

Within the Campaign Strategy session, we have begun the discussion of theme and form, media and approach. One has a sense of déjà vu, as the old dichotomy is there again between those of us who would emphasize the achievement of President Nixon and those who would focus upon the personality traits.

In the 1972 campaign, and for 1972, it seems to me imperative that the Achievement School win out over the Personality School—in terms of advertising and campaign emphasis.

These are the reasons, simply:

a) Our likely opposition—McCloskey and Muskie—will make the personality of the President, the need for a new <u>kind</u> of leader, their battleground. And why not? If one is asked which is the more attractive personality, Pete McCloskey or Richard Nixon, McCloskey will come off infinitely better than if one posed the question—which of these two men is best qualified to be President of the United States in 1972. The area of statesmanship, competence, ability, these are the long suits for the President as they have been throughout his career.

b) Secondly, in times of domestic calm and international peace, the argument for the election of Richard Nixon is simply not to me a convincing one to the majority of the American people. In such times, millions will want to "dare" a little bit, to take a flyer with a "New Frontier," to turn to a fresh, exciting new face. Though some of the finest political minds in the nation have labored thousands of hours in the process, they have not succeeded, in candor, in making Richard Nixon a stylistic exciting "figure" in the Kennedy sense of the word.

However, what are the President's truly strong suits? As source material I give you the confidential report on the Democratic National Committee—based on in-depth research and polls provided by Louis Harris via Charles Colson.

Eighty-five percent of the American people, and eighty percent of the Democratic Party believe that:

"There is no doubt that sympathy works to the President's advantage. Seventeen out of twenty people (85%) believe he (the President) is doing his best in a difficult situation. As shown in this table, there is not too great a difference of opinion along partisan lines. Four out of five Democrats (80%) agreed with the statement.

As long as the President can maintain this posture he rests upon a springboard that could quickly enhance his popularity."

The specific question asked which got this incredible response was:

"HE INHERITED A LOT OF TOUGH PROBLEMS AND IS TRYING TO SOLVE THEM THE BEST HE CAN." Agree or Disagree?

Thus, any political argument which begins with this as its premise already has eighty-five percent of the American people in government and four of every five Democrats agreeing—for openers.

How much better to begin our Political Argument for RN's re-election with this wholly credible, nationally believed argument, than with an argument that deals with the President's personality which starts—according to the same analysis, with only one-half the American people in agreement.

Simply stated then, what I propose is thus—that the campaign be seen as re-electing the President to continue to take America out of the storms, the nightmares, which we were in when he assumed the helm. This means the point of reference for 1972 is not just peace and prosperity now but the living hell of 1968.

There in the spring, five hundred Americans were dying a week, we lived in a time of assassinations, when cities were burning and campuses being destroyed by mobs of radical students. If we can create in the public mind "That Wonderful Year, 1968" and then point to today—the contrast is vivid, the contrast is something that tens of millions of Americans will agree with. The idea is to portray the President as having assumed the helm of the Ship of State, when it appeared that the America we knew was collapsing around us; then to move him through the times of turmoil, de-escalation, demonstration to today, where the seas are choppy, but beyond the storm. And then to point to the port that lies ahead over the horizon.

Film of the horrors of 1968, with the President campaigning in the midst of those terrible days, with something like, "He was the Man for Those Times; He is the Man for These Times. He pulled America back from the brink of disaster; he is the man to lead it now upward into brighter days."

This has roughly stated the idea. As an attack issue against Muskie, for use by others, and in footage—we can tie him and HHH and Harriman and Clifford, and the whole gang as those responsible. The Democratic candidate is brought to you by the same people who gave you the Vietnam War, etc. etc.

As an emotionally compelling argument, this seems to me infinitely more appealing than, say, running on Revenue Sharing and Reorganization and the Welfare Reform.

We can use peace in Vietnam and prosperity—but let us be sure to juxtapose them with 1968. Otherwise, it will be us saying we need a little more time in Vietnam and Muskie saying, Bring the Boys Home Now.

One imagines that the kind of footage you can draw on would be outstanding. Again, from the Democratic analysis, the country believes RN inherited difficult problems and is doing his best. Let's show them graphically just how incredible those problems were—and the present by juxtaposition will seem like Happy Times are Here Again.

Which brings me to the STATE OF THE UNION:

From indirect information, one gathers that the Domestic Council is pregnant and in January plans to give birth to a bouncing New American Revolution—in terms of programs to be the basis for the State of the Union. I do not argue against "targeted" political appeals—which hits groups like the aged, but let us not waste the State of the Union on "Six New Goals," when the six old ones are languishing in the nether regions of the Committee.

Rather, let the State of the Union Address be an address by the President on the State of the Union. In delivering that address, he can deftly turn the clock back three years, and talk a bit about the cooling of America, no more burning cities or destroyed campuses, the boys who have come home, the tasks of peace to which we are turning our minds, the era of confrontation which we are bringing to an end, the possible, hopeful days that lie ahead. "Though three years is short, we have come a long way, you and I." We have come from a time when Americans were calling one another traitors or warmongers, to a time when our differences are over the proper ways to save our environment. I see the State of the Union in the terms the President saw the Acceptance Speech, his first best chance to make his case to the whole American people.

The domestic proposals can go by message; they are things that come off better in the reading than the saying anyhow.

A comment in Ken Khachigian's memo to me on the SOTU is appropriate:

"If there are policy decisions or programs of political importance, I suggest a simple message to the Hill a day or two after the SOTU address.

As for the SOTU itself, I recommend a speech that discusses the "state" of the union in almost a literal sense—a thoughtful analysis of where we stand as a Nation at this point in history. To an extent, this includes an examination of the American culture, morale, and future.

RN could lay the stage for the campaign—against the chronic carpers who look for the worst in America. On the contrary, RN ought to stake out a position not only for a belief in the richness of the national patrimony but also a belief that the future is challenging, not fearsome.

This is a time to lay bare RN as no bashful protector of the Nation and no skeptic of the potential in the last third of the century. Articulation of some key benchmarks of the last three years might be included: a potential for world peace; domestic calm; social problems on the way to recovery (e.g., praise for white and black in South for handling their social transition peacefully)."

In that strategy session, it was interesting. When it got to specific achievement (someone raised the point that the President had increased spending for civil rights enforcement by a factor of five), there is disagreement as to whether that is something to boast about. When you talk about welfare reform, people divide. When you talk about domestic legislation, my friends start up the South Wall. When you talk about turning the Court around, my friends applaud, and the other fellows are climbing the North Wall.

But when you talk about the terrible times in 1968, and how we as a people have pulled through them, how the residue of bitterness has been diminished, how much better the new times are than those old times of rancor and bitterness and hatred—then you have almost the whole nation saying, "Yeah, things are a hell of a lot better today than those days, and maybe Nixon does deserve a hell of a lot of credit; maybe he is the right guy in these times after all."[42]

28. Memo to Richard Nixon, January 13, 1972

Observe . . . the month-by-month Gallup Poll figures for the 14-month time frame from October 1970 to December 1971. Some interesting conclusions emerge; some grave political questions arise; and some thoughts on What's To Be Done follow.

1. First Conclusion: It was not the President's campaigning itself in 1970 that cost him public support—as the media has reported. Rather, it was the media depiction of that campaign—well after it was over—that, subsequently, convinced the American people we had run an "un-presidential" campaign in 1970. The polls bring us proof positive. One week after the 1970 election was already over, the President still stood at 57 percent in the national poll. It was not until December—after the national press corps had been working us over relentlessly for a month as "dirty campaigners" and "big losers"—that the President's approval rating dipped.

Fair to conclude in my opinion that if the media had written that the returns were a "wash," and that the President conducted a vigorous, tough but fair effort on behalf of his party—we would have taken no dip at all in the national polls following the election. It was the media construction of the President's campaign then, not the campaign itself, which cost us support.

2. Despite the tremendous pounding we took in the final months of 1970, for the campaign of that year, the President bounced back in January to a fairly high level of 56 percent support—before the State of the Union and the hoopla of the New American Revolution. Apparently the NAR and the SOTU accomplished "zero" for us—because in the period following, we actually dropped five points, or ten percent of our support. So much for the greatest document since the Constitution.

(Possible explanation of the "dramatic drop" in February is the Laotian invasion by ARVN which received the worst media of any Administration supported exercise since taking office. This February 10–21 poll was taken, as I recall, just about the time the AVRN was "coming out on the skids.")

Nixon's Popularity since October 1970

	Approve (%)	Disapprove (%)	No Opinion (%)
1971			
December 10–13	49	37	14
October 29–November 1	49	37	14
October 8–11	54	35	11
August 27–30	49	38	13
August 20–23	51	37	12
June 25–28	48	39	13
June 4–7	48	37	15
May 14–16	50	35	15
April 23–25	50	38	12
April 3–5	49	38	13
March 12–14	50	37	13
February 19–21	51	36	13
January 9–10	56	33	11
1970			
December 5–7	52	34	14
November 14–16	57	30	13
October 9–13	58	27	15

3. Through the spring, there seems to be no change in our position that could not be written off as simply statistical margin of error. We hovered right around 50 percent for six months.

Further the now famous "Nixon Shocks" of July (the China trip) and August (the economic bombshell) hardly even registered on the Gallup Seismograph. There are two polls on here, taken in August after the second of the "shocks" and neither of them notes any tremor of public opinion rolling in the President's direction. Between the end of August and the first two weeks of October, the President—I know not what the reason—suddenly shot up five points. However, this disappeared in two weeks, and even after the President's Phase II announcement we did not rise in the polls.

4. A crucial point. <u>At the close of a calendar year (1971) in which the Presi-</u>

dent dominated all the news, put on a virtuoso performance by most everyone's standards, and closed out the twelve months by being Time's and everybody else's Man of the Year, the President could find himself between 6 and 9 points lower in public esteem than he was at the end of a year that is considered his worst.

While in the media and among press and TV types, RN may have had a banner year, in fact, during 1971 he suddenly dropped between seven and nine points (10–18%) of his support among the American people—and had not regained it by December of 1971.

5. All the Euphoria about the President's re-election chances within the building, and all the press clippings about the President being almost unbeatable in 1972 thus, in inspection, seems to me to have been made out of thin air. Supposedly, we were frustrated at every turn in 1970, and humiliated in that election—but in three of the four polls at the end of that year, we were seven to nine points above where we were at the end of this year.

The opening of the New Year is thus not a time for self-congratulation on our part, but a time for mild alarm and some serious soul-searching.

While these conclusions seem justified, they are surely frustrating as hell. One wonders just what it is the President has to do to nudge himself back up to, say, 60 percent approval with the American people.

It would appear "bold decisions" have no impact or at least no enduring impact on how the American people view their President. However, one cannot but wonder where we would have been in the national polls without them. Did they make any difference? From these polls, one cannot really say that they did.

A NOT UNPROBABLE SCENARIO

For some months now, PJB has been inundating the West Wing and elsewhere with a blizzard of memoranda, warning about the possibility of a Muskie sweep of the primaries and promenade to the nomination. What was possible before seems probable to me now—and only the Florida Primary stands in the way of the unpleasant scenario outlined below:

Today, according to Harris, Muskie runs head-to-head with the President. Should Muskie roll up the primaries, defeat left, center, and right opposition, remove all doubt that he is the party choice, roll into a Democratic convention, win on the first ballot, stick John Lindsay on the ticket to excite young, poor, and black—he could march out of that convention into a hailstorm of TV and press publicity that could give him a five-point lead over the President by mid-July 1972. That to me is not out of the question.

BUCHANAN'S THEORY OF POLLS

The Great Question is why—after a year of dramatic activity on the President's part, of unrivaled success as judged by friend and foe alike, of bold new initiatives—why the hell is RN at least half a dozen points below where he was at the end of a year, where most observers said he was frustrated and defeated at every turn.

One possibility is that the American people, like all people, get bored with their Presidents, in this day of intense media, and every President is going to suffer an inexorable decline in popularity and support year by year, no matter what the hell he does. If this is valid and I don't know that it is not, then a posture of fatalism about 1972 is justified.

But my own theory is this:

While announcements or pageantry, dramatic bold decisions, and traveling Presidents may win the approval of the people, as registered in the polls, they do not win the standing ovation; they do not win the new converts that we quite evidently need.

Perhaps what the President needs to regain lost strength in the polls is not drama (the China trip), not new initiatives (the New American Revolution), not bold decisions (the economic program), and not even "steady solid performance." Perhaps what is needed is an end to the era of calm presidential leadership and success, and the beginning of a "new era of conflict and crisis" for the President of the United States.

One recalls that the President rated highest with the American people when he was fighting for the survival of the Presidency in November of 1969, against media and demonstrators alike. The HEW veto, with the stroke of a pen, did not lose the President's support; the people hailed it. The Vice President was in deep trouble—until he turned on his critics, and started stomping on them, instead of trying to show them he was not a bad fellow.

THE EMBATTLED PRESIDENT

What I am suggesting is that the President, with value added taxes and revenue sharing and welfare reform and pay boards and price commissions, may be possibly boring the American people.

While I understand that the "Professional President" is being sold to RN as the posture for the campaign, perhaps we ought to consider instead the "Embattled President."

The times when the American people truly sit up and take notice of a President is when he is in a fight, when he is under fire. On such occasions, with a President in full cry, taking after his adversaries, in a great battle, there is the kind of drama and excitement which can stir up the interest and imagination of an American people whose scenes are somewhat dulled. I am not talking about a "war against inflation" or a "war against crime" or a "war against red tape or bureaucracy"—but rather a Presidential duel in the Kennedy versus Big Steel tradition—a political struggle against a despised enemy who is flesh and blood opposition.

They say of the poor miserable people of the subcontinent that the only times they have been truly happy in the last decade was when they were at war with one another, butchering each other by the tens of thousands. This has provided them with the only exciting diversion from an otherwise impoverished, indeed intolerable existence.

Maybe the American people, who have made pro football the greatest spectator sport in history, are bored with revenue sharing and pay boards and price commissions and welfare reform and environmental "programs"; maybe they would like to see a good fight.

Looking back over the Presidents of the Twentieth Century, seems to me they are remembered by the common man for the great battles they engaged in: Teddy Roosevelt, "The Trust Buster," Woodrow Wilson, fighting for the League, FDR, the scourge of "Wall Street" and the "Moneychangers in the Temple," Harry "Give 'em Hell" Truman, and the "no good, do-nothing Eightieth Congress."

This is not to suggest that the President move off the Presidential pedestal, that he engage in partisan combat, or look around for a war to start, political or otherwise.

What I am suggesting is that the avoidance of controversy and conflict with our primary adversaries may be politically wrong—not politically advantageous. Had the High Court disallowed the Amchitka blast, and had the President told them twelve hours later to go to hell and fired off the bomb anyhow, that would have been the kind of dramatic institutional challenge that would have awakened the country and gotten them on their feet cheering.

In short, while the President as President is the best posture for the coming year, we may very well need to consider Great Issues, contested questions, where the President can, as President, throw down the gauntlet to Foreign Relations, to Congress, to the Court, to some massive powerful institution, so that RN will go into 1972 as a Fighting President, not the Professional Managerial President.

We might need to cast the President in a role that not only merits respect and quiet applause, but one that excites people to stand up and cheer, and excites the partisans to go out and fight, bleed, and die.

This is not so much an ideological thing, as it is something within the spirit of the American people, who love a good fight. Perhaps we ought to consider the issues, where we can give them that fight, where the President can draw the line, and draw the sword, and charge into battle on behalf of the best interests of the Republic. Better a howling press and high polls, than a quiescent somnolent press and low polls.[43]

29. Memo to H. R. Haldeman, February 15, 1972

A number of us over here have some concern at the multiplicity of the President's appearances on television, between his formal departure statement to the nation from the White House lawn and his arrival in Peking. Currently, he is scheduled for crowd appearances both arriving and departing Hawaii and arriving and departing Guam. There is no question but that this will interrupt a drama which would otherwise have been the President departing his nation—and next viewed standing down from Air Force One in Peking. Much of the attraction of this trip, much of the drama and history, is not what is seen—but what is unseen. A certain suspense that might otherwise have built up in the days the President departed will be lost if we see him in front of crowds and waving all the way into Peking. Further, if the President is to appear in television shots three or four times—morning and evening—saying essentially the same thing, something is lost in the redundancy. While there is no doubt about the need to have him rested and prepared, and to make these interim stops, our personal view is that the less seen of the President in Honolulu and Guam, the more dramatic and the greater the suspense when he steps off the aircraft in Peking. To see the President just getting off his plane in Hawaii, waving solemnly, and moving into his limousine in Hawaii and Guam would have been best, it seems to us.

Further, we recognize that large crowds are now expected at both stops, coming and going—we would recommend the President's speaking on camera be kept to the minimum—consistent with all other present locked commitments.[44]

30. Memo to Richard Nixon, June 19, 1972

The Administration and the press [are] certain to be a focus of questions. One such question will deal with the "death" of the Press Conference, to which an extended answer is appended. Others could come from any of the directions listed. Suggestion:

Take the press conference question, and then perhaps one of the others—and if they continue in this vein: Suggest the following: "Gentlemen, I am sure that Administration relations with the press corps are very much on your minds, but I am not sure that is what is on the minds of the American people. Are there any questions here relating to matters other than our press relations?"

That should knock it off after the first or second question. [45]

31. Memo to H. R. Haldeman, August 3, 1972

Had lunch with [Tom] Jarriel and [Herb] Kaplow [of ABC News] and in the course of it, I asked Jarriel what was the general feeling of the press toward the President and his Administration, even those who had been in disagreement with the media. He said he felt the relations were now "good," that increased access to the President and staff members was the main bitch and that had been alleviated. Relayed the view that it was our hope to avoid any imbroglios with the press this fall as the contest is with McGovern and if the contest stayed McGovern-Nixon, we would win—and any extracurricular spats with the media only tended to remove the focus from where we would like to see it. They have detected an easing of the media attacks. Following up on this, let me suggest that we move ahead with the "détente" by:

a) RN hosting a press gathering out at San Clemente after his press conference, at which perhaps the Veep might mingle, and even the Haldeman-Ehrlichman-Buchanan anti-press types can shoot the bull, and the President can talk briefly about his dreams for a second term, if he wins one.

b) Word going forth to those of us who talk with the media to open up even to a greater degree than has been the case in the past.

The only fly in the ointment I can think of is that interview PJB did with the New York Times Magazine guy some weeks ago—laying out the line at the time. The story has yet to burst into print and haven't seen the proofs, but will let you have them when they come. [46]

32. Memo to H. R. Haldeman, August 14, 1972

Talked with John Ehrlichman about this, but would appreciate it if you would clear it up for me with the President.

Buchanan was not the source of that Times story about RN directing a halt to press attacks. [Dan] Rather, who said so on CBS, apologized personally to me for having assumed this—and said that the one who told him that I was the source was not [New York Times reporter Robert] Semple, "but someone else." Secondly, talked with Semple in Maine, told him that I was being tagged with this; he not only indicated full willingness to straighten the same out and to testify at my court-martial, but said the story was given to him by others "mentioned in the piece," and the "story was pretty well all put together" by the time he had called me—and I gave him those quotes, which in and of themselves are not disadvantageous.

In any event, my position remains that we ought consciously to hold back on sweeping attacks on the media as a) our concern right now is McGovern and b) any sweeping attacks diminish our credibility when we will have to criticize, that is, this fall—if the nets start favoring George openly. We should await targets of opportunity and not engage in other extraneous enterprises. However, the same thinking would mean that we also ought not to be putting out the line that RN has so ordered because a) it makes it appear that the President is master of the house who calls dogs on and off, and b) this too means a story which is extraneous to what we should be doing right now.

When Semple called me with this "story" already "in the bag," as he put it, I merely reacted much as Ziegler did, saying that we wanted to focus on other matters this fall, and that any such decision did not mean we had given up our "cherished assumptions" or had gone back on what we have said. As for the Jarriel story, know nothing of it at all—except that someone sandbagged Mr. Colson far worse than anyone did to me. Still from the reports coming to me that I have been "fingered" as responsible, I think Buchanan is more sinned against than sinning on this score.[47]

4   Governing, Policy, and Politics

When Richard Nixon took office in 1969, he faced many policy challenges both at home and abroad. He also found himself without a mandate to govern, becoming the first president since 1848 not to carry at least one house from his own party into power, as Democrats maintained their control of Congress. On the domestic front, the American economy was in decline, with lower productivity of American industries, inflation, and slower economic growth. Nixon also inherited Lyndon Johnson's War on Poverty domestic programs, enacted without a tax increase, as well as the continued financial drain of Vietnam. His domestic priorities included welfare reform and changes to the Family Assistance Program (FAP), revenue sharing, crime control, health insurance reform through the Family Health Insurance Plan (FHIP), environmental initiatives, government reorganization, and full employment. In what he called "New Federalism," Nixon sought to shift power back to the states by consolidating categorical grants to block grants and giving the states authority over programs such as welfare. By 1971, in his State of the Union address, Nixon outlined his domestic policy goals as his "New American Revolution," though most issues required legislative approval for implementation and congressional Democrats were not overly sympathetic to Nixon's policy agenda.[1]

Nixon's relationship with Congress also got off to an inauspicious start when the Senate defeated his first two nominations to the U.S. Supreme Court (Clement Haynsworth in 1969 and H. Harrold Carswell in 1970). In many areas, Nixon turned to the prerogative powers of the presidency to affect public policy.[2] By 1971, with many legislative proposals stalled in Congress, Nixon relied on administrative, as opposed to legislative, action to enact policy reforms. In addition, many "recalcitrant bureaucrats" in federal agencies were more loyal to New Deal/Great Society programs and objectives and blocked many Nixon initiatives. In response, Nixon expanded and reorganized the Executive Office of the President, creating numerous White House–based staff positions to usurp the power of departments and agencies in creating domestic and foreign policy. He also impounded funds earmarked for the Office of Economic Opportunity (OEO), responsible for implementing Great Society programs, in an attempt "to challenge Congress for the right to govern."[3] Nixon focused even more of his attention on foreign policy, including the ongoing war in Vietnam, his diplomatic efforts involving détente with the Soviet Union, his trip to China, and ongoing tensions in the Middle East. According to historian Melvin Small, his foreign policy achievements were most prominent in his mind, even after he left the White House: "In his own evaluations, Nixon always began with foreign policy." Yet it is perhaps in the domestic arena where even more policy success occurred despite a Democratic Congress "with which he was often in mortal combat," including creation of the Environmental Protection Agency and the Occupational Health and Safety Administration, ending the draft, increased spending for arts, humanities, and cancer research, and the dismantling of segregated schools in the South.[4]

Those legislative accomplishments, however, would also alienate prominent conservatives who thought that Nixon was governing too far to the left. One of Pat Buchanan's most important jobs regarding policy formulation was in his role as Nixon's liaison with conservative political leaders, both on Capitol Hill and in the news media, as well as leaders within the Catholic community. According to Buchanan, "Nixon knew I was the most reliable representative in his White House of the conservative wing of his party and his coalition, allies whom he often viewed with skepticism and suspicion."[5] As the following memos reveal, Nixon's standing among conservatives would continually decline throughout the first term, with Buchanan lobbying the President and some of his other top advisors (notably Chief of Staff H. R. Haldeman) to take actions to minimize the defections from the right. Areas of policy concern for conservatives included programs within the OEO, reforms/expansions in other welfare programs such as FAP and FHIP, school busing, various issues related to states' rights, and placing strict constructionists who believed in judicial restraint on the U.S. Supreme Court. On the foreign policy front, many conservatives were unhappy with Nixon's historic trip to China in 1972 and policies of détente toward the Soviet Union.

In the following memos, Buchanan mentions numerous prominent conservatives of the time with whom he had regular contact, including William F. Buckley, public intellectual, author, and founder of the magazine *National Review*, as well as his older brother, James L. Buckley, U.S. senator (R-NY, 1971–1977); F. Clifton White, a political consultant best known for the "Draft Goldwater" movement at the 1964 Republican National Convention; William A. Rusher, syndicated columnist and publisher of *National Review*; Russell Kirk, author and social critic who helped to found the *National Review* and *Modern Age*; syndicated newspaper columnists James J. Kilpatrick and Victor Lasky; and John Ashbrook, who served in the U.S. House of Representatives (R-OH, 1961–1982). Prominent conservative publications at the time included *Human Events* (edited by Thomas S. Winter and Allan Ryskind) and *Battle Line* (published by the American Conservative Union and edited by Jeff Bell).

1. Memo to Richard Nixon, March 7, 1969

In response to the President's memo, the term "proselyting" is the wrong one, since these columnists and writers (Buckley, Kirk, Kilpatrick, White, Winter, Lasky, et al.) are already within the fold. They are "our conservatives." They haven't gone over the hill; they only are asking for some ammunition to hold their flank.

From my contacts, and Tom Huston's, with <u>all</u> the focal points of the "Right intelligentsia" in the last week, I think this is our situation now.

On the surface, things look gloomy; the dissatisfaction "runs deep" for lack of any "symbolic" victories. <u>This was the situation as of two days ago.</u> I think, however, from the President's Congressional gathering last night, we may have turned the corner.

First, the Otepka thing is precisely the type of "qualitative" action, as opposed to quantitative, that [Senator] John Tower was referring to.[6] Otepka is to the right of what Oppenheimer was to the left. . . . Also, last night the President noted the Job Corps action to be forthcoming, the eventually revised guidelines, the possibility of Finch visiting Tennessee. Earlier this week came the press conference and the strong statements on Vietnam. Immediately before that came the Berlin visit and the Hesburgh letter.[7] So, the President has put in some labors on this side, for which we have yet to receive payment—but will, I am sure.

(As for long range, the make-up of the Department of Justice and of Defense have been the rallying point for the President's conservative supporters.)

As I say, on the surface we are still in tough circumstances, but as we follow through on what RN said he was going to do last night, a lot of our problems— with conservatives per se—should be resolved.

Another line that has worked well is that the Nixon Administration has thus far completed about three and a half percent of its first term—and there sure as hell is no justification for anybody to jump ship at this point.

These arguments are working to a degree—and if the Administration moves in the areas mentioned last night or if the President decides on an address on campus disorders, our most serious concerns with this political wing should ease substantially. . . .

RECOMMENDATIONS:

(1) That Buchanan get some advance notice on things like the Otepka thing, which I found out the same day it happened. We can see that sort of thing—and use it if we get a little notice.

(2) That the President find some opportunity to include Buckley in a group coming to the White House or something. Bill is not immune to flattery, and the invitation might tend to hold off for a few needed weeks some criticism that might otherwise be forthcoming. I can't overemphasize the value of having his continued backing and solid support, as far as holding conservatives in line.

(3) That we take a second look at Buchanan's proposed ad hoc committee of Sears, Timmons, Ellsworth, Buchanan, and Dent. The purpose of this group would not be to dictate policy. It would be to gather together the major gripes of the conservatives, the party machinery outside of the East, and the Congressional establishment—and get the President a once a week undiluted memo on precisely how serious his problems are with these groups and what we recommend to help solve them. When the problems go away, the committee can go away.

My own view is that Saturday's group is awfully unwieldly; there must be fifteen in attendance and some of those in attendance are not really in touch with this specific problem. Again, I know the small group recommended is oriented heavily to the GOP right—but that is where our problem is. When RN wanted to build bridges to the Jewish community in New York, he didn't call me in and rightly so; he gave the project to Garment and Rita Hauser. This proposal seems in that tradition.

One final note. None of the conservatives Tom and I talked with were critical of anything that the President himself has said on the issues. They all admitted that his statements at the three press conferences have been reassuring to conservatives. Their complaints seem to be about actions taken and statements made in the name of the President by members of his Administration and staff. The sins of the sons are, in this case, visited upon the father.

Essentially, it strikes me that the problem is—as [Nixon political strategist] Murray Chotiner used to say—"a lack of communication" and sensitivity. Somewhere in the decision-making process, the conservative voice is not being heard—statements are issued and appointments announced which political sensitive antennae would immediately detect as likely to upset conservatives. Often, in such cases, the tone is as important as the substance. The President should not have been placed in this position where he is on the defensive with some of his staunchest supporters. . . . It would help, I think, if the President had an early warning system which identified in advance the policies, statements and appointments likely to arouse ill-will or misunderstanding among key elements of the President's political coalition.[8]

2. Memo to Richard Nixon, March 13, 1969
THE PORNOGRAPHY EXPLOSION

Filthy movies are pouring out of Hollywood and entering the United States from abroad like a plague of locusts. All legal barriers to what can be shown on a movie screen seem to have collapsed. Many of the things now showing at the

neighborhood theatre would have merited a jail sentence for the producer just a
few years ago. Unless one has been to the movies lately, it is impossible to gauge
how far we have come in so short a time.

Even the <u>New York Times</u>, which can find "redeeming social value" in most
"stag films," seems to have choked a bit on the latest—I AM CURIOUS (YELLOW).
This piece by [film critic] Rex Reed . . . follows a <u>favorable</u> review of the movie
by one of the <u>Times'</u> own critics. The marked passage will give the President
some idea of what is being put out today.

In any event, from the reception of the President's acceptance speech in Miami, it is clear that pornography and filth are gut issues with millions of decent
people; it also seems clear that even those who would eliminate any form of
decency code or standard whatsoever are somewhat on the defensive because
of the kind of filth that is moving onto the screen now that the barriers are
discredited and down.

Perhaps the President would want to drop by some meeting of movie producers or something similar, and comment quietly and briefly, but strongly, on
their responsibility to the people and children of this country—and just what
the President thinks personally about what is going on. <u>No need to threaten
laws or jail sentences or outrage—just presidential disgust, the exercise of the
moral leadership of the office.</u> Would be happy to research and draft remarks,
which should be made briefly and off the cuff—as something "on the President's
mind." [9]

3. Memo to Richard Nixon, April 11, 1969

Talked with Cardinal-Elect [Terence] Cooke at length in New York. <u>He wants
to be of assistance to the President.</u> He volunteered to serve as the President's
eyes and ears with the American church or to convey the President's thoughts
to and from Rome.

On Vietnam, I said he might convey to the Pope the President's appreciation
over the moratorium of Pope, Church press, and American bishops on criticism
of Vietnam, while the President tries to work this difficult problem out. He
agreed that withholding criticism or pressure gave the President a freer hand to
work out a more just settlement guaranteeing a better future for Vietnam. Cooke
indicated his belief that we have stakes there, and his view that a precipitate
withdrawal would bring about the loss of all Southeast Asia.

<u>His main concern is the acute crisis in Catholic Education. I told him I would
find out the status of the President's "Commission" and get back to him on that.</u>

<u>He is a good and useful prelate who wants to lend this Administration a</u>

hand—and if the President wishes to communicate with him, he would be delighted to use Buchanan as the go-between.[10]

4. Memo to Richard Nixon, "Committee of Six," April 29, 1969

Catholics and the RNC

The establishment within the RNC of a CATHOLIC DIVISION, not specifically designated as such, would be a wise investment. The purpose of such a group would be to promote constantly the President and the party through the Catholic press, and to serve as a Republican and Administration point of contact for Catholic lobby groups and Church pressure groups. We have in mind one or two individuals whom we think would make the promotion of this Administration with Catholics a full-time effort. If the President indicates he wants this, we can carry the specifics to Morton.

Inflated Census Counts

FYI. Reportedly, a number of "new methods" are being discussed, at lower echelons in the Census Bureau, for counting the inner city folks. One idea has surfaced to have OEO-type community action people do the counting, which would result in an inflated headcount of Negroes, which would mean stronger Congressional Representation for 10 years for heavily Democratic areas. According to Kevin Phillips, a fair count should aid the suburbs at the expense of the cities. We have sent Secretary Stans a copy of Phillips' cogent memo.

Crisis in Chrome

Two major American corporations own chrome ore mines in Rhodesia. Since the sanctions, they have been unable to bring their ore into the country and have been forced to purchase Russian ore at prices which have increased 50% in two years. Our companies have a year's supply of ore stored in Rhodesia which they bought and paid for prior to sanctions, but which State refuses to let them bring into the country. There is strong pressure on the Administration to act, conservative columnists are picking the thing as an example of a particularly outrageous U.S. policy abroad, and the evidence indicates that the hardship on the U.S. chrome industry is excessive.

Huston has staffed the problem, consulted with the appropriate officials at Commerce, OEP, and Treasury, and found them in agreement that the President should over-rule State's objections and allow the chrome to come into the country. State will raise hell that we are eroding the sanctions, but the fact is that by removing the chrome from Rhodesia, we are denying Ian Smith a valuable asset, an asset for which American companies have already paid hard dollars.

Huston has prepared a four-page briefing paper on this problem for the President to review if he wishes. We strongly urge that the President instruct Treasury to issue a special license to import this ore. The national interest would be well served; in our view we would win some valuable friends in the business community, and avoid some serious domestic problems which OEP fears will develop if nothing is done to ease the pressures on our domestic chrome industry. We would, perhaps, get some flack from the left, but we feel it would be short-lived, since such a strong case can be made that we are hurting, not helping, Ian Smith by hauling off a valuable asset which he might be able to sell on the black market for badly needed foreign exchange.

The Single Issue
Bill Timmons suggests that we begin now to quietly talk with marginal Republicans to determine what single thing it is they consider most important to their re-election. Without promising them anything, we can then see if the Administration can lend them a hand in getting it. The side benefit of the whole exercise is to get these Republicans to thinking of them—not just asking all the time. [11]

5. Memo to Richard Nixon, September 12, 1969
TAX REFORM
We're being whipped from pillar to post on this issue. It is not just that [Rep. Wilbur] Mills and the Democrats have expropriated it. In the last ten days, during Senate hearings, [Senator Albert] Gore chewed our people up with his demagogic allegations about favoring the right and the corporations as against the workingmen and women of the country; the Democrats picked up the chant; the networks ran with it; the headlines played it that way and left-wing interpretive writers gave us a fearful beating—on front and inside pages.

However, surprisingly we are getting good marks for being responsible from many editorial writers in major publications not always friendly. . . . But that does not balance out the negatives appearing on front pages.

One yardstick of our difficulties is that the cartoonists, who have been somewhat charitable to us, considering past history, have rallied around this issue and ganged up against us. The cartoon, here, is not untypical of the type of beating we get. [12]

6. Memo to Richard Nixon, "My Lai Incident," December 5, 1969

The My Lai Massacre occurred in March 1968 when U.S. Army soldiers killed approximately 500 unarmed South Vietnamese civilians, including women and chil-

dren. Twenty-six soldiers were charged, but only Lt. William Calley Jr., a platoon leader, was convicted.

In addition to the answer on My Lai suggested in here, I am not recommending—since I lack knowledge of the facts—but am laying out here some suggested possible approaches to the questions which Ron Ziegler says in his memo may come up about My Lai.

1. If pressed on when you became aware of the My Lai incident, Ziegler has said August and that the Defense Secretary's office undertook their investigation in April. A possible way to fudge any real trouble here is this:

The President was informed of the magnitude and the full nature of what was alleged to have happened in August, immediately following the investigation of the Defense Department. Prior to that there was awareness that an investigation was taking place, but it was not known the charges would be of any such seriousness or magnitude. This was brought immediately to White House attention—when we learned the full facts in the case which eventually produced the indictment.

2. Why the delay before the President was informed?

The President is not informed of every such investigation as it is taking place. There are probably some going on now he is unaware of. The President was immediately informed when the full facts were in—and the extent of the charges and gravity of the case was clear. (To my knowledge, there is still nothing that prevents us from saying—if necessary—that the President was aware that some investigations were being conducted, but that Defense brought it directly to the President's attention when it was learned what a grave situation it was.

3. Why didn't we make it public?

Once the investigation was completed, and the facts known and the legal process begun, it was certain to come to public attention, no question about that. There are the rights of the accused in such a case which have to be respected. For us to lay the story out in the public press would have prejudiced the case against the defendants.

4. Will the President form a public commission to investigate the incident?

No, we intend to bring out the facts; the trial will bring them to the attention of the American public. A commission would only duplicate their efforts. It is this Administration's policy—and it will continue to be—to investigate in the future of any allegations, true or false, which seem to have merit.

5. What about a standing commission to investigate all reports of atrocities by Americans?

To set up something like that makes the assumption that atrocities are the common occurrence by American soldiers in combat, whereas the history of the American army in this war and every war in my memory is the precise opposite. They are the isolated exceptions to the rule that the United States Army is the most humane great army in history. If you look at the history of World War II, or any war in which we have been engaged, you will find that it is always to the Americans that the enemy prefers to surrender, when they do surrender. And the reason lies in the character of the American soldier.

6. Is the President aware of other incidents similar to My Lai or has the President ordered an investigation to determine if there have been similar incidents?

I am aware of no such incidents and consequently have ordered no such investigations.

7. Is the President aware of the methods used by U.S. forces in South Vietnam to interrogate enemy prisoners?

Revolutionary wars are always the most bitter of wars; none of them in my memory has taken place without some atrocity of some kind; the Israeli war for independence, the Algerian war, the Soviet Revolution—all have been marked by great horrors. Nothing of anything near approaching that magnitude is true of Americans in Vietnam. As I told you earlier, those men we have sent to Vietnam are the finest soldiers we have ever produced; they are the finest fighting men in the world. [13]

7. Memo to Richard Nixon, December 18, 1969

In 1962, fourteen countries, including Laos, signed the International Agreement on the Neutrality of Laos. The other countries included Burma, Cambodia, Canada, China, France, India, North Vietnam, Poland, South Vietnam, the Soviet Union, Thailand, the United Kingdom, and the United States. The so-called Ho Chi Mihn Trail, which ran mostly through Laos, became an important logistical weapon to the North Vietnamese in providing manpower and supplies. Nixon approved secret bombings in Cambodia and Laos beginning in 1969. On November 3, 1969, Nixon delivered his "Silent Majority" address in which he outlined the "Nixon Doctrine," which sought global peace through a partnership with American allies and the "Vietnamization" of the war to gradually bring home U.S. troops while shifting responsibility to South Vietnamese soldiers: "First, the United States will keep all of its treaty commitments. Second, we shall provide a shield if a nuclear power threatens the freedom of a nation allied with us or of a nation whose survival we consider vital to our security. Third, in cases involving other types of aggression, we shall furnish military and economic assistance

*when requested in accordance with our treaty commitments. But we shall look to
the nation directly threatened to assume the primary responsibility of providing
the manpower for its defense."*[14]

There is a prima facie case to be made that the North Vietnamese have violated
both the 1962 Laotian agreement and the terms of the full bombing halt over
North Vietnam. The United States made major concessions in both instances,
concessions that have not been withdrawn, in the wake of abrogation of the
agreement by the other side.

It seems to me that the Vice President's return from Southeast Asia affords
the Administration a golden opportunity to lay this record of U.S. adherence
and enemy duplicity right on the line—to make it clear to the Communist world
that when they do not live up to their terms of a bargain, the bargain is no longer
binding on us.

A motive behind such a speech is this: The war can never be "won" so long as
the enemy is accorded sanctuary for his soldiers in Laos and Cambodia and the
lower segment of North Vietnam. Currently, because we control the war—wisely
or not—we have imposed restrictions upon ourselves and the South Vietnamese.
As we withdraw our control and manpower support of the South Vietnamese, it
seems likely and not unwise that they would no longer follow ground rules for
prosecuting a war for their survival set down by John F. Kennedy.

They can win the war in the South, but to terminate the menace they are
likely to have to one day root out the base camps along their frontier in Cambodia, along the Ho Chi Minh trail, and perhaps in the southern half of North
Vietnam, essentially the bases of aggression, many of which have become once
again—thanks to LBJ—sanctuaries for aggression.

It seems apparent, given the conditions in this country, the American people
would not sustain for long any large movement of United States troops into
Laos, or Cambodia, or across the DMZ. But who—besides our political enemies anyhow—is going to get outraged if the South Vietnamese should make
a foray into the jungles of Laos in strength and engage the Communists on their
supposedly safe grounds.

RECOMMENDATION: When the Vice President returns, he can lay out the record once again of American involvement in Vietnam; he can lay out the various
agreements—1954, 1962 and the bombing halt; he can show our record of good
faith and the Communist record of duplicity; he can state that in his view the
agreements are no longer binding upon us; that it is now not any agreement,
but only American restraint [and] Presidential desire for peace that prevents a

resumption of bombing; he could argue that no American combat troops are going into Laos or Cambodia, but that as far as our allies fighting for their own survival, we no longer intend to impose upon them arbitrary and artificial conditions in a fight for their life.

Both the potentiality and/or the actuality of a threat on the part of the South to slice off and take home a chunk of the North might be a better inducement to North Vietnam to negotiate than anything being done now.

Would be delighted to write up a draft while the Vice President is on his tour of the Far East; when he returns, we shall have in the bank considerable capital in terms of foreign policy speeches—which has to be spent rapidly to do us some good.

Added note: If there is anything the President wishes to have stressed in terms of the Nixon Doctrine in Asia, or other points, this is the time and the place to hammer them out into the public record. [15]

8. Memo to Richard Nixon, January 30, 1970

School desegregation and busing were prominent and divisive civil rights issues during the Nixon years. The U.S. Supreme Court ruled in Swann v. Charlotte-Mecklenburg Board of Education *(1971) that busing was an appropriate remedy to achieve racial balance to ensure that schools were properly integrated and that students would receive equal educational opportunities regardless of race. While Nixon opposed busing, he stated during an April 29, 1971, press conference immediately following the Swann ruling that he would nonetheless implement the laws according to the Court's ruling: "Now that the Supreme Court has spoken on that issue, whatever I have said that is inconsistent with the Supreme Court's decision is now moot and irrelevant, because everybody in this country, including the President of the United States, is under the law."[16]*

On Sunday, the National Observer had an in-depth piece on the decline of integration in the Northern Schools—and the pattern of re-segregation appearing there.

It is based on a Federal School Survey which shows

1) Racial isolation exists in every section of the country and its growth is most rapid in the big northern cities. It is raising doubts among longtime integrationists about the wisdom of trying to enforce de-segregation in the public schools.

2) In city after city when a school reaches somewhere between 30 percent and 50 percent black—there occurs a tipping and within a few years, it is 95 percent or 100 percent black.

3) Only 25 percent of the Negroes outside the South attend majority white schools, as contrasted with 18 percent of Negroes in Southern Schools.

4) Seventy-two percent of the Negro students in the State of Illinois attend schools that are 95–100 percent black, and there are no court orders compelling de-segregation in Illinois.

5) Southerners are objecting to what they call "the dual system of justice."

6) Alexander Bickel, a constitutional law professor of impeccable credentials, has a book coming out this coming month—based on his Harvard Law School lectures—which says the Supreme Court should have contented itself with out-lawing legally enforced segregation as unconstitutional.

7) [Civil rights activist] James Farmer said recently he has stopped trying to sell Negro audiences on integration because "They don't agree on it anymore."

The above are items the President may be interested in or may use if he talks of the need for understanding and compassion in this enterprise; and when it says it is an easy but unfair thing to throw stones at one section of the country when what we are dealing with is a national problem.

Asked about de-segregation in the North, the phrase "dual system of justice" might be dropped into the context. [17]

9. Memo to Richard Nixon, March 9, 1970

Re: Your request that a report be submitted on Leon Panetta's letter to the Editor of the New Republic regarding Alexander Bickel's article on desegregation.

Mr. Panetta's letter reads like some game and doggedly optimistic battle report from a junior officer in a single sector—when at headquarters we can see the whole front collapsing before us. If we can credit Leon with one quality, it is his unflagging belief not only in the rightness but in the progress of a cause that seems everywhere to be collapsing.

Let me begin by conceding—on paper—every strong defense he makes of integration. The Coleman Report [a 1966 U.S. government study on education equality] does say that a black kid from the slums who goes to school in a middle-class environment is aided, while the white child does not suffer. Let's concede his figure of some 750,000 black kids in white—and better—educational environment. Let's grant that school integration has produced more integration than public accommodation laws, housing laws, and job opportunity laws. Let's concede that some Southerners are saying, as Leon contends they are, that integration "is much better than we thought."

If the country were today in the spirit of August of 1963, with an era of good feeling among all Americans on race questions—Leon's points could well be the most significant and most prominent. But we are in 1970—and court decisions are not riding along behind an era of good feeling—they are having a backlash among blacks and whites.

Mr. Panetta points to "the" authority—the Coleman Report. In an abstract situation, black student X going to school with white student Y might indeed benefit while Y did not suffer. But the Coleman Report does not add into the equation the hard fact that exists in thousands of schools around the country—the presence of racial tension and racial bitterness that are breaking out in violence with growing frequency. . . .

Secondly, Mr. Panetta quotes white folks as saying, in the South, that integration is "much better than we thought." Now is this really genuine feeling in the South, or, in the North—or rather, is the national feeling one of rising hostility and anger among both black and whites toward each other and among white toward any kind of racial mixing of their children. Panetta talks about an "emerging positive attitude among children, parents, and teachers in 13 Southern School Districts surveyed by HEW." Is this the same South whose Governors are railing against the Courts and Washington; is this the same South where Red Blount says the Administration has lost the entire power structure in the integration fight; is this the same South where hundreds of teachers are quitting rather than take jobs in black schools, where private academies are springing up, where whites are dropping out of school altogether; is this the South where Senators are unanimously fighting for a national freedom of choice amendment. . . .

Panetta's nice little quote simply does not reflect reality. Of course, there are Southerners trying to make integration work, no matter how excessive the court orders are; there were millions of Americans still trying to make Prohibition work when it was repealed.

What about the three-quarters of a million black children in desegregated schools? Certainly, this is progress. However, my argument is that the current effort to raise this figure further is running into tremendous resistance; it will require "racial balance" in most cases; and as Bickel contends—in today's environment—advocates must prove that both the advantages to education and the advantages to race relations are worth the investment this would demand. No one wants to go back to officially segregated schools (although re-segregation is occurring in the North), what we are contending is that to plunge ahead seems a course certain to end in social disaster, without any visible social or education benefits in the current environment. . . .

The brutal reality of 1970 runs against the grain of Mr. Panetta's liberal ideology. When racial violence is the rule in the nation's integrated high schools, how does integration remain "essential to a sound education policy." When black-white relations are deteriorating, when blacks are desirous of more and more separatism, and whites are losing all enthusiasm for integration—how, in those circumstances, does integration now form a "sound basis for American Society." Only, I suggest, if you believe that "integration is good; separation is bad" unqualifiedly.

Compulsory mixing of the races in the United States right now would be about as wise as compulsory mixing of Greeks and Turks on the island of Cyprus—we would have bloodshed—and for what.

"The alternative Professor Bickel suggests, that black schools be retained without further attempts to desegregate them, and that we 'try to proceed with education' constitutes in fact a conscious policy of isolation of black children, and mandates further isolation of the black community as adults."

Crap. It is not a "conscious policy of isolation of black children" to simply recognize that residential separation of the races exists all over America and, rather than spending tens of millions of dollars in a fruitless effort to integrate the schools, we ought to improve them where they are. Rather, it is simply common sense in the current environment.

Panetta, as the article closes, says that "on the basis of the record to date and the willingness of thousands of American citizens to make it [desegregation] work," we should plunge ahead.

In the current national environment, those Americans, like Mr. Panetta—who want racial integration and are willing to accept any imposition to get it—should have it. But those who don't want it should not have it forced upon them or their children. Compulsion in this area is counterproductive. As Santayana said, it is only the fanatic who redoubles his efforts when he has lost sight of the goal.[18]

10. Memo to H. R. Haldeman, March 10, 1970

Your note assumes that the editors of Battle Line are pragmatists.

Far from it. They are the hard right ideologues; they were for Reagan at the convention; reluctantly, Nixon in the election; and they bolted as long ago as May 1969—because of the drift of the Administration they felt they detected.

Being candid, the President is simply not ever going to satisfy these people—he is an activist in domestic policy, and they are going to object unless he reverses the course of domestic policy. We shouldn't lose too much sleep over that.

The real problem would arise if Human Events, the conservatives on the

Hill, National Review, and the key conservative columnists would suddenly begin taking this line. They are not doing that now—so, our problems here are certainly not grave. But there is a noticeable and rising disenchantment among portions of our conservative support, which we are watching.

As for Battle Line itself, they made a great tactical blunder last May when they bolted ranks with a wild free-wheeling attack on the President which every conservative recognized as a drastic over-reaction and which identified ACU as militantly anti-Nixon, which is not the most effective position from which to criticize the Administration.

The thinking of Battle Line is that the best way to bring Nixon to the conservative position is not to work with him—but to bring pressure on him from the outside. The same reasoning is applied by the left ideologues (Galbraith, Steinem & Co.) on Humphrey and the others.

Incidentally, if RN would follow that recommendation I sent over—to gather up the worst programs in OEO that are outraging people in various states, and announce publicly that they are being abolished, saving even $100 million—it would provide some red meat for the fellows to chew on for a little while. [19]

11. Memo to H. R. Haldeman, June 16, 1970

On May 4, 1970, four students were killed and another nine injured at Kent State University when members of the Ohio National Guard shot protestors demonstrating on the campus four days after Nixon announced the extension of the Vietnam War into Cambodia.

URGENT & IMMEDIATE

When in Florida I first read of the constituency of our "commission" to study Kent State and campus disorders, I was appalled. The last two days have convinced me that a serious mistake has been made that will be damaging to the President when the report comes out, and may be used against us both on the campuses and in the fall elections.

1. Attached is a New York Times article on the young black we named—we have some idea of what we can expect from him. [Edward] Banfield of Harvard, with whom I spoke yesterday, author of The Unheavenly City, told me he was himself appalled by this appointment, felt the commission itself a dreadful mistake, and that we had invited serious trouble as a result of the report.

2. The obvious and flagrant over-representation of blacks is ludicrous—not only that, but every vocal black these days is a captive of his black constituency. . . . It is simply not realistic to expect any one of them—with the constituencies

they have to serve—to come up with other than the stock conclusions, which I predict will be:

The campuses are alienated; Nixon has his priorities mixed up; we have to get out of Vietnam now; too much is being spent on defense; the youth do not feel they can participate in the democracy; they are losing confidence in their leaders; ad nauseam.

3. We have invited upon the President's head the same thunder that fell in on LBJ when he let that Kerner Commission [the U.S. government report that studied race riots in 1967] blame America's problems on "white racism," a commission which never even credited Johnson with the enormous steps he had taken.

4. Our group is undistinguished in terms of the prestige of its people.

5. Why was not the Sidney Hook Academic Group—which has gathered hundreds of professors, liberals of prestige among them, from around the country who are speaking up for an open campus and academic freedom brought in—indeed, why do they not dominate it?

6. There must be some inherent suicidal tendency or death wish which would allow the creation of the kind of animal we have put together to report on the problems of the campus. <u>The reason this is sent to you rather than the President is simply that right now I don't know just what the hell we can do about this commission</u>—now that we have announced it; RN has enough things to worry about right now—but it sure as hell is something we ought to be worrying about.

7. What about this—one proposal—let me see if I can get lined up some four or five top flight academicians—there is a group meeting regularly with the Veep, which has real credentials—and then paste them on. Other alternatives: circumscribe the operations of this little group to perhaps Kent State, and get another group to report later on the larger problem. [20]

12. Memo to Richard Nixon, August 21, 1970

On August 14, 1970, National Security advisor Henry Kissinger briefed reporters on U.S. foreign policy, expressing optimism for world peace: "We are at a point where except for the war in Vietnam, there are possibilities of bringing about a more reliable peace in the world than we have known in the whole post-war period. We are at a point where . . . it may be that even the Soviet Union has come to a realization of the limitations of both its physical strength and of the limits of its ideological fervor. But none of these possibilities can be realized except by an American Government that is confident that it knows what it is doing . . . and by an American public that has enough confidence in its leaders so that they are

permitted the modicum of ambiguity that is sometimes inseparable from a situa-
tion in which you cannot, at the beginning of a process, know completely what all
the consequences are."[21]

In the wake of the New Orleans briefing, several papers (<u>Washington Post</u>, <u>NY Daily News</u>) wrote of the near "euphoria" that seemed to dominate the Administration's view of the world. This could lead to the kind of serious problem that Democrats had at the time of Czechoslovakia. I suggest that—regardless of how hopeful the situation may be in Europe, the Mideast, and Vietnam—we knock down the euphoria and re-adopt the posture of sober realism which has always served us well. If things go well, we will get credit anyhow; if they go badly, the excessive optimism can be used against us—by both the left and right. What brought this to my attention is that William White, the columnist, is genuinely stunned at the reports he has read of the Administration's view of the world.

Possible solution—in the campaign of the Vice President, I have been desig-nated to write the speech in San Diego on the Administration's Defense Policy. We could easily key it to the Vice President's "conversations" with the President in which the latter has reminded him of the tremendous strides in sea-power and strategic weapons by the Soviets and that while we are moving with caution hopefully toward settlement of outstanding conflicts—let us never fall victim to euphoria.

What concerns me is that the Russians could easily pull the rug out from under us this fall anywhere in the world, and if we are on record, solid, as urging Americans to maintain their skepticism and realism, then we would be in a more readily defensible political position.[22]

13. Memo to Richard Nixon, August 24, 1970

Published in 1970, The Real Majority: An Extraordinary Examination of the American Electorate *was a best-selling book by Ben Wattenberg and Richard M. Scammon that analyzed voting data after the 1968 election. The authors argued that the American electorate was centrist and that electoral victories for a candi-date and/or political party would come from appeals to the "real majority" in the center of the political spectrum.*

THE VEEP AND THE CAMPAIGN OF 1970

Given this Scammon-Wattenburg thesis—which I believe is right on the mark for Democrats—we are in serious danger of being driven back to our minority party posture. Our needs seem crystal clear.

1. <u>We cannot allow the Democrats to get back on the right side of the Social Issue</u>. This they are attempting to do right now with tough talk, etc. They have to be branded—and the brand must stick—as permissivists, as indulgent of students and black rioters, as soft on crime. This can be accomplished with their record in the last Congress, I believe. But for us to contest with them primarily on the Economic Issue—Big Spenders, etc.—as the major assault seems to be not a prescription for success. Republicans for forty years have been tarring Democratic Congresses with "Big Spender" labels, and Democrats have been winning those Congresses, lo, these same Forty Years.

The focus should be on tarring them with "ultra-liberalism" and "radicalism"—especially on the Social Issue where we are strong and they are weak.

2. Where are the swing voters in 1970? We must assume left-wing Democrats are going for their Democratic Candidates and Republicans are going for Republicans, come hell or high water. <u>The swing voters are thus Democrats—law and order Democrats, conservatives on the "Social Issue," but "progressive" on domestic issues.</u> This is the Wattenburg thesis—and I think it is basically correct. How to conduct ourselves then.

<u>Tar the Democratic Leadership specifically with the "radical" label on social policy; tar them as well with the "obstructionist" label on the President's programs for reforming society, for getting America moving.</u>

Frankly, we should go after the "<u>Daley Democrats</u>." No one can do this better than the Vice President—but we cannot get these voters by using rehashed Republican arguments or stale Republican rhetoric.

"Big Spenders" is a theme that might work, will work, with our Republicans—we are using it in all our GOP literature—but <u>will it have any real bite with the union guy to whom big spending may mean the medicare for his mom or old man?</u> (Foot-dragging Congress does not seem charged with much electricity, either.)

3. Scammon contends that a hard-line on riots, etc. by Democrats may anger "liberals," but liberals have no place to go anyhow except the Democratic Party. Just so, regular Republicans have no place to go in 1970 (no Wallace) but the GOP. So, let's go straight after the Daley Democrats.

4. The Vice President should win these Democrats to the Presidential banner by contending that RN is a progressive on domestic policy blocked by "obstructionists" in the left-wing leadership of the Democratic Party; that RN is a hard-liner on crime, drugs and pornography, whose legislation is blocked by "ultraliberals" in the Senate who care so much about the rights of the criminal that they forget about the rights of society; that the President is a man trying

with veto after veto to hold down the cost of living but is being thwarted by radicals and wild spenders who would, given the chance, create the kind of inflation that would put Indonesia in its heyday in the shade; that the President is a man in foreign policy who is moving toward peace with honor but whose efforts are being attacked and undercut by unilateral disarmers and isolationists who think peace lies in an abject retreat from the world and the dismantling of the army, navy and air force. This is said strong—but these I would think would be the ways the Vice President could best appeal to the patriotic, hard-line pro-medicare Democrats who are the missing element in the Grand New Party.

5. There is move afoot to "low-key" the Vice President's campaign in 1970—to have him focus specially on the local issue and not seek the national publicity. There is no conflict between garnering national publicity and helping local Senate candidates—the two are thoroughly complementary.

The Democrats—see Scammon's book—are only now coming around to recognize what we knew in 1966 and 1968—that a strong statement in Oregon is more effective in getting to voters in New Jersey than a banal statement in Trenton, Tenafly, Newark and Elizabeth. The way for the Vice President to help the Senatorial Candidate is to praise him to the skies, fine—but to hammer the national Democratic leadership in a manner that will keep our big press corps excited and with us, that will get network time every night if possible with our message; and so help every Republican Senatorial Candidate while we are helping the local one.

Right now the Agnew tour is getting tremendous publicity as the potential best show in town. All we have to do to forfeit that national publicity is run around talking about "cattle and oil" in Casper, as has been suggested already. We ought to remember also that when we give up the television time—on the networks—someone else, namely our Democratic friends, gets it.

Mike Mansfield says the Democrats have no one to compete with the Veep on the hustings. We have a tremendous advantage here—which we should use, not throw away by talking about local issues that carry no national wallop.

We should have something topical and tough for the national media every day. If the Vice President can raise the Republican Administration a few points in the polls and the President by his decisions and actions raise it several more, the effect will be like raising the water level and all the boats in the lake will rise at once.

A hard-hitting tough campaign can help bring home Senators and Congressmen who live or die on a few national percentage points.

6. Clearly, from the Scammon book, we should tar the Democrats as being

not only the party of "bugout" but the party of bussing, the advocates of "compulsory integration," the party whose last Attorney General banged down the door in Chicago in order to testify on <u>behalf</u> of the Chicago Eight, the leadership that let this country turn into the porno capital of the world, and is blocking RN's effort to change that. Also, the Democratic leadership has altered its historic foreign policy position to kow-tow to student radicals who bully-ragged those same leaders in the streets of Chicago, etc. The Democratic Leadership should be portrayed as selling out to the crazies in their own ranks—and selling out the interests and views of the good patriotic Democrats who number in the millions. We might even say LBJ was destroyed by the "ultra-liberals" in his own party.

7. We should stay on the offensive, take the "out" (and offensive) position even though we are the "ins" (and defensive) by hammering at the "liberal Eastern Establishment" that is responsible for what has happened to America, the "Establishment" that is frustrating our efforts to right the wrongs in Society, the Establishment whose wards are tearing up the colleges, the Establishment that indulges rioters, etc. (Of course, said in better phraseology, but the need to be on the offensive, to act as "outs," seems to me vital.)

8. The Economic Issue. To get into a debate on whether or not we are in a "recession" seems to me a utterly foolish idea—since the very discussion of "recession" is surely not going to help us and since anyone who is hurt in the current economic situation is not likely to be convinced he is not being hurt by anybody's rhetoric. Rather than debate whether or not the investors and brokers and unemployed are being hurt, let's go after the Democratic radicals whose wild schemes are frustrating our efforts to stop the rise in prices. This is the Big Spender theme—but in different rhetoric, tougher rhetoric, equating the Democrats with the same kind of ultraliberalism in spending that they follow on the Social issue.

9. Finally, to change the Vice President now into the traditional Republican campaigner is to change a winning strategy for a losing one. [23]

14. Memo to Richard Nixon, January 6, 1971
TROUBLE ON THE RIGHT

We have a serious political problem developing on the Right. For some months, the American Conservative Union (Ashbrook, Jeff Bell, the old [Young Americans for Freedom] crowd, Bill Rusher, et alia—the Reaganites at the Miami Convention) has been harboring a growing cynicism toward the Administration. The disaffection has now spread to include a majority of the younger conservatives. Lately, it is being given national publicity through [syndicated columnists] Evans & Novak; now [Nicholas] Thimmesch, and coming up, David Broder. Originally localized, the infection is spreading and now being broadcast, through the press, to the party structure nationally.

We should anticipate some severe criticism of the Administration at the Annual Conservative Awards Dinner—which will bring together the entire leadership of the Conservative Movement in Washington in late January.

Briefly, a list of the on-going and new grievances against the President and the Administration would include:

1. The President is adopting a liberal Democratic domestic program, indistinguishable from what an Ed Muskie or Ed Kennedy would propose—and the President's ability to drag the GOP along behind his proposals makes him a more effective "President Liberal" than any Democrat could possibly be. . . .

2. The Right, which had felt that RN was luke-warm about FAP, and "understood," now finds the President 100% committed to the program; they see a verbal abandonment of the "workfare" aspect of FAP; the President pushing a national health insurance program of the kind conservatives have fought for years, and actively pushing a "full employment budget" which will deliberately produce deficits that violate the First Article of GOP Dogma ("balanced budget") for forty years. (In this light, while some of the more knowledgeable and sophisticated Republicans can appreciate the need for economic stimulation, in the form of deficits and "full employment budgets," one has to think the little old ladies who work in the precincts are going to be demoralized by an approach that seems to say while the old Democratic deficits were evil, this new Republican deficit is good. Similarly, with other Administration initiatives in the social arena, these would have been considered a few years back as hemlock to a good many Republicans—and we have to be aware of the perplexing impact they are certain to have on our folks in the hinterland.

3. There is no identifiable conservative left in the policy-making position in the Nixon White House. Every conservative remaining is in some form of liaison or P.R. position; thus the hope of a "conservative alternative" in domestic policy is groundless. This complaint has been made with increasing vigor since the departure of Arthur Burns. The original "balance" in the White House staff is now felt to be gone with the departure of Burns and Harlow and the arrivals of Finch, Rumsfeld, Shultz, and MacGregor. Further, a general sense of despair over this situation is traceable to the fact that the domestic structures are now frozen for the duration. Ehrlichman's shop is seen as a small group of pragmatic technicians who can teach it either way; Schultz's operation as Budget Bureau career types who have always leaned to Big Government and statist solutions; and the Cabinet Departments as dominated, in the lower policy-making areas,

by liberal hold-over in the bureaucracy. Thus, the options that come up are solely "liberal" in orientation—and the President no longer has another "point of view."

4. One of the constant complaints heard is that RN "takes the conservatives for granted; he doesn't think we have anywhere else to go." They feel that they are the dominant force in the Republican Party; yet, the President seems sensitive to them only at election times; they feel themselves to be the "niggers of the Nixon Administration." While they get the "rhetoric," the liberals within the party get the policies and programs. Further, they view the President as ever solicitous of the point of view and sensibilities of the left and the media—but not so much so of the Right. Their conclusion is more and more that the squeaky wheel in the Nixon Administration gets the grease—and there are a variety of plans floating about for them to start squeaking publicly.

5. One of the problems emerging is that the party people, the workers, the backbone of the Nixon support for twenty years must be increasingly disheartened by (a) the liberal activist domestic policy of the Administration being pushed so strongly and (b) the reports coming increasingly from columnists of conservatives, party people, even Republican Congressmen and Governors disenchanted with the Nixon White House. Without the party, without the basically conservative workers enthusiastically and energetically behind us, 1972 will find us in "deep kimshee."

Other points that should be noted:

A. The Evans-Novak column indicating that Reagan was black-listed from a White House established international meeting was damaging, in that it refuels the sub-surface talk of a Nixon-Reagan coolness, in the face of Nixon-Rockefeller warmth.

B. While [William F.] Buckley's influence nationally is enormous, his influence among the hard-core right politicos is being diminished, and we cannot count on his bringing them over. Some of them are caustic—and Buckley gets a bit of the same constant criticism that conservatives in the White House do—that they've "sold out."

C. The only criticisms I have received of RN's performance the other night are from the Right. Reportedly, Buckley was disappointed, [James J.] Kilpatrick expressed the same feeling, and half a dozen or more conservatives have called saying that while the President helped himself nationally, conservatives were appalled at the new emphasis on FAP (away from incentives, and towards "helping minorities"), the comment about Kent State and Jackson State as though the Administration were somehow connected and the enthusiasm with which RN seemed to speak of his "full employment budget," and "expansionary budget . . . a budget in deficits."

D. There is serious talk heard now among conservatives to urge Governor Reagan to begin to become a focal point of public opposition to the President's domestic initiatives. Some conservatives close to Reagan don't believe he will move in this direction—as he is basically not that type. But at the Awards Dinner, the one annual gathering of the most important conservatives, these kind of things are certain to be talked up—and promoted.

E. These are sentiments being picked up from the conservative right with which I have some communication. One would imagine that they are also prevalent on the Hill—and the President should take some soundings from his own people to ascertain if this is not so.

F. Having investigated the Evans-Novak column thing as requested, I am unable to learn who made the quotes—but have been told repeatedly they are not unrepresentative of a general mood out there.

Buchanan's View and Thoughts

The situation on the Right is as bad as I have known it since joining RN. Some of the departing Right are not coming back—given the nature of the new domestic program. But we have to act to retain the allegiance of those drifting off; to retain the support, at least occasion[ally], of the writers—who are now increasingly dubious. Also, we have to take the steps to stop this constant bickering in the press within the Party and on the Hill—about the President not caring, or not consulting, or not listening to the Congressional and Party Regulars.

How this last is done is a problem for our Congressional and political people.

Some suggestions on all these matters:

(a) The need to bring the Congressional wing of the Party in on the take-off of these domestic programs we are contemplating; let the President hear their views on FHIP before it goes and we demand their backing.

(b) There may be a need for RN to get together with the party types on their visits to Washington and to take a more active role in putting down the complaints that lead to all this negative leakage in the press.

(c) The Conservatives need to be put on notice that their policy alternatives, their program suggestions, from without can get a hearing within. Right now, it is felt there is no conservative programmatic recommendation that can get a hearing in the policymaking procedures of the White House.

(d) There may be a need for the President to bring an identifiable "conservative" in at the Rumsfeld-Finch-Ehrlichman level—who can be visible as a voice of the Right to which the President will listen and to whom the Right can take their complaints.

(e) While the President's decisions and directions domestically may be locked in—perhaps there can be more media emphasis, in terms of speeches and statements and appearances—on the "Conservative" side of the RN policies.

A foreign policy speech, which explains the need for greater defense expenditures based on Soviet activity and Soviet spending—would be most welcome. A presidential or White House emphasis on what is being done for the Veterans of Vietnam—which is considerable—might be helpful. In short, while recently RN has been given public emphasis to the "liberal" side of the Administration, a corresponding emphasis on the "conservative" side of the Administration could help with the party folks and the country.

(f) The President might himself meet with a representative group of ideological conservatives—in the writing community, in the Congress—to hear out their grievances. Many I am sure, having been out of power and favor in Washington for so long, want to be an integral part of the Administration. Given the opportunity, they become the best defenders of the White House in the conservative community we have.

(g) Some reports from within indicate that RN plans to do no party meetings whatsoever this year—not the GOP women, not the Young Republicans in the East Room as last year, etc. I feel this would be a great mistake, since no one condemns RN for being a party leader; that is a natural and expected role for a President. What the media objection is is to the "partisanship" of the campaign.

(h) Many of the conservative objections to Administration policy have been and are being refuted on the grounds that conservatives rarely come up with "programs" of their own to present to the President. They recognize this to a great degree—the idea of a conservative Brookings is always mentioned, and enthusiasm for this kind of idea from the President in a meeting with conservatives like Buckley would be most useful. It is something which needs to be done; it is a conservative short-coming which the Right recognizes.

Finally, I think the problem contains enough potential harm to the Administration, and its future, that I feel that RN should draw the views of other conservatives within on all these subjects—people like Bill Timmons, Harry Dent, Tom Huston, Lyn Nofziger, Martin Anderson—and all the political types who have lines out in the conservative community.[24]

15. Memo to John Ehrlichman, February 3, 1971

Having read Martin Anderson's memo on welfare reform, to which the President referred in conversation, I have to endorse it. I am very concerned about two basic things:

1. RN is liable to go down in history in the 1976 elections—or even by 1972—as the President who doubled the welfare rolls; the man who did more than anyone else to destroy the work ethic in America, by bringing the "working poor" into welfare, men and women who were themselves moving into the lower middle class before being dragged back.

2. Without the working poor, we have something that can go through and satisfy most of the liberal demands. I have never heard anyone proclaim the "working poor" aspect as the be all and end all.

Has any thought been given to the Banfield idea of providing the incompetent poor with services, i.e., Food Stamps, medical stamps, transportation stamps, etc., instead of with cold cash, which they are unqualified to spend wisely?

I know this thing is mighty far down the road—but I have still great reservations about its efficacy and political wisdom.

Also, even if we do move, we should be on the lookout for a Democrat—i.e., Wilbur Mills—flanking attack on the Right. In short, Mills gets up some morning and accuses the President of giving away billions without work incentives, which he and the House then stuff into the Bill. Considering what they did on food stamps, this is not an altogether impossible eventuality.[25]

16. Memo to H. R. Haldeman, February 5, 1971

The following are proposals suggested by Jeff Bell and passed along as an input from the conservatives, as requested.

1. Nomination of an Italian American to the Supreme Court, for the first vacancy after the President's pledge to the South has been kept.

Merits: Italian Americans, though a disproportionate number go into law, have rarely been rewarded with high Federal judgeships. Though they are more than three times as numerous as Jews, no Italian has ever sat on the Supreme Court, as compared with five Jews.

Politics: Such a move would accelerate and perhaps (with the voucher system) complete the Republican trend among Italians already in progress. Italians are by far the largest single Catholic subdivision and are rankled by the high office attained by Irish Americans.

2. A massive simplification of the Federal income tax structure. One proposal: no exemptions other than for the first few thousand of income (more depending

on size of family); <u>no one's tax rate on taxable income more than twice as high as anybody else's.</u>

Merits: The present tax structure is now recognized as a morass. Nominally steeply progressive, it actually favors those who can afford tax lawyers—in other words, the well-off. It needlessly consumes billions of man-hours a year and has created a bloated national bureaucracy.

Politics: Almost the entire nation would breathe a sigh of relief if such a bold but simple plan were adopted. Opposition even among liberals would be scattered, since so many of them recognize how easily the very rich can get off. Aside from the fat cats, the only negative groups in this equation would be the nation's army of tax lawyers and bureaucrats.

3. Mandatory minimum sentencing for serious Federal crimes like murder, rape, and armed robbery.

Merits: Because of the extreme flexibility of sentencing law, in Federal law and in the States, punishment varies widely from judge to judge. White criminals have gotten better breaks than blacks, but permissiveness is spreading to the inner cities as well. Instances of comparative injustice are scandalous. Criminals are becoming increasingly confident of good representation that can win "suspended" sentences, a device that is particularly blameworthy.

Politics: Taking the ability to suspend or radically reduce sentences away from judges, and <u>putting minimum sentences in the Federal law, would do more than anything I have heard of to reduce crime in the District, and state legislature would not be far behind in adopting the reform. The political benefits of a declining crime rate are incalculable.</u>

4. Because of the skyrocketing relief rolls, the nation will sooner or later have to change the approach to welfare benefits embodied in both the present law and in FAP. Inevitably, that change must come in the direction of strictness.

The only way to move toward strictness is to repudiate the so-called incomes approach to welfare benefits. It is far too late in the day for other types of solutions—e.g., work requirements and increased house checks by welfare agencies—to work or even be enforced.

I don't like the "working poor" aspect of FAP, but in this area the "incomes policy" is at least tenable; families whose head is working have shown the minimum stability required to spend money acceptably.

But as suggested by Dr. Banfield in <u>The Unheavenly City</u>, the non-working poor who make up the <u>bulk of our welfare problem are for the most part incapable of spending cash to the benefit of themselves and their children. Families whose heads do not work should receive most of their welfare benefits in goods and services</u>, rather than in cash. This would involve, in addition to Food Stamps, such innovations as Housing Stamps, Clothing Stamps, Transportation Stamps, and perhaps Medical Stamps.

Merits: Again quoting Banfield, the heart of the welfare crisis is people who are "present-oriented," who do not plan more than a few hours in advance and are truly interested only in the present moment. Because they are bound up in a "<u>lower-class culture" (which can be either black or white) their decisions do a disservice to themselves and their children every day of their lives. If there are only certain (essential) items these people can purchase with their welfare payments, this damage can be minimized</u>. A family whose head went to work would begin receiving its benefits in cash immediately.

Politics: Liberals would not like it. Neither would some libertarian rightists (such as Dr. Milton Friedman) who believe that the ability to spend cash on the market is the answer to all social problems. But the realism (indeed the necessity) of this step would recommend itself to the vast majority of working Americans—particularly those who realize that they could, in certain circumstances, realize more income by going on welfare (which is true of both the present system and FAP). The attractiveness of that option (and the resentment felt by those who resist it) would be considerably lessened if most welfare benefits came in goods and services to those not working. In view of the present problem, this step is not only just and necessary, but could become a winning political issue for the President who propounds it.

5. Reprivatization of all government insurance programs, including Social Security. These programs would remain mandatory.

Merits: Governments are bad at running businesses. Private concerns—whether existing insurance companies or a special quasi-private corporation (like RAIL PAX) set up specially for the purpose—could administer mandatory insurance programs far more efficiently, and for less money.

Politics: Nobody really likes government bureaucracy any more—not even the liberals. Retaining the principle of mandatory participation from the outset would tend to diffuse any reminiscences of Goldwaterism. If objection is made to the possible profits ("from the people") of reprivatization, <u>lower</u> taxes with increased benefits could be guaranteed by statute. Different private plans could compete with government regulation of standards in the context of mandatory coverage—as is presently the case with automobile insurance.

6. <u>American support for a European Defense Community which would possess an integrated, independent nuclear deterrent.</u>

Merits: This is an old idea, which came close to reality before the French veto in the 1950s. It has merit now because it dovetails so perfectly with the Nixon Doctrine of indigenous defense. The conservative-nationalist governments of Britain and France would find this an attractive option, and since these two nations would be responsible for the specifically nuclear deterrent, there would be no conflict with the Non-Proliferation Treaty in American nuclear aid to EDC. This independent structure would by no means supersede the American alliance via NATO—it would simply give European defense more anti-Soviet credibility than it now has in this era of parity.

Politics: Any move which appears to reduce America's world burden would have great appeal domestically, regardless of whether U.S. troop reductions in Europe are immediately possible. Furthermore, bold moves in foreign policy are generally popular in themselves. <u>Attacks on American-fostered "spread" of nuclear weapons will fall flat, since Britain and France are already independent nuclear powers. If our major allies are going to deploy their own nuclear weapons in any case, why not give those weapons credibility?</u>[26]

17. Memo to Richard Nixon, "J. Edgar Hoover," February 12, 1971

J. Edgar Hoover served as director of the Bureau of Investigation beginning in 1924 and became the first director of the Federal Bureau of Investigation when it was founded in 1935. He would serve in that position until his death in 1972. In his later years, Hoover became a controversial figure over his harassment of political dissenters and activists and the secret files he kept on politicians, including presidents.

While this may appear unorthodox coming from me, I think the President should give serious consideration to replacing Hoover as soon as possible—for his good, for our good, for the country's good. First, Mr. Hoover has already passed the peak of his national esteem. At one point I would guess that ninety-five percent of the nation felt he was doing a phenomenal job; he has had nowhere to go but down, and he is going down steadily. He cannot possibly reverse the trend in my view; the attacks on him are mounting and mounting and the deterioration in his standing in the country are necessarily going to diminish in face of these attacks. His own place in history is secure; but, with each of these new picayune battles in which he involves himself, his place is being sullied. It would be a crime if these battles at the end of his career brought his end of office at a time when it was widely desired that he go.

Mr. Hoover stands today with the American people as an almost unvarnished symbol of what is right with American law enforcement. He must retire in a matter of a few years anyhow—and now in my view will be better for that symbol, for his place in history, than anything hanging on a handful of years could help accomplish.

Secondly, Hoover is under terrific heat; and instead of his former practice of ignoring his critics, he is responding, which is what they want. On more and more of these quarrels, Mr. Hoover is not totally right—and comes off as something of a reactionary. Among young people, especially, who do not have anything near the esteem for him as do their parents, he is increasingly becoming a villain; and he is tied totally to us. McGovern is making him a focal point of attack—this is certain to continue; and on one of these issues one of these days soon, one can guess that the public is going to think Mr. Hoover wrong and McGovern right.

Finally, if Hoover goes now, he can be retired in full glory, at a time of his own choosing. If we wait, it will be something like the departure of General Hershey which had all the appearances of a forced departure.

Again, I would think we would want Hoover's replacement—the President's man—in that job, before the choice of such a man becomes an issue in 1972—as Fortas became an issue because of the timing of his replacement.

There is the possibility—although looking down that roster on the other side I don't see any of them even in our league—that we may not win in 1972. God forbid that we should then have a Ramsey Clark or some politically oriented Democrat placed in that job for the next fourteen years.

My strong recommendation would be to retire Hoover now in all the glory and esteem he has merited and deserved, and not let him—for his own sake and ours—wind up his career a dead lion being chewed over by the jackals of the Left.[27]

18. Memo to Henry Kissinger and H. R. Haldeman, "Full generation of peace," March 12, 1971

Repeatedly in recent weeks, the President has been hitting the theme of a "full generation of peace," which now seems to be moving from a vague hope to a near commitment, with RN's "our last war" statement to [*New York Times* publisher Arthur] Sulzburger. While this has some appeal, surely, to a war-weary people, there are serious dangers in this.

The first is for the President's place in history. The United States has only partial control over whether we are going to war again—the other half of the debate belongs to those who may desire to test our commitments. By making these statements—especially the "our last" war statement—the President is leaving it to some dictator or Communist government to make a fool of him by limited aggression against one of our treaty allies. What is the impact of this kind of statement on those who are our allies, and those who may be our potential adversaries?

Secondly, while a remote fear, I am concerned that the President's "last war" statement may turn out to be as foolish as Chamberlain's "peace for our time." We are promising something which we alone cannot deliver.

Finally, this repeated talk of "a full generation of peace" and again "our last war" tends to induce a sense of serenity and calm and even complacency among the American people which (a) hardly seems justified by the situation and (b) is certain to undercut our own arguments for more dollars for strategic defense. We ourselves seem to be contributing to the on-going psychological disarmament of the American people, which itself is the major obstacle to our getting the dollars needed for maintaining parity and preventing Soviet superiority.[28]

19. Memo to Richard Nixon, "Political Memorandum," May 7, 1971

Evident from the attached, there is a new strain of bitterness, frustration and alienation among younger conservatives, toward the Administration. Increasingly, it has focused on the White House Staff—especially in attacks directed at John Ehrlichman and his staff. . . .

First, younger conservatives, more <u>True Believer</u> than the older <u>National Review</u> columnists crowd, are distressed at the departure from the White House staff of conservatives Burns, Harlow, Freeman, Anderson, Allen, Nofziger, Huston, Mollenhoff, etc. They do not see anyone replacing the departing conservative voices.

Second, they are convinced that the White House staff has been structured to systematically exclude "conservative" input in domestic policy—thus the recent attacks on John Ehrlichman from the Right in recent months.

Third, they believe that the President makes his decisions, not on the basis of who he sees, but what he reads, and they contend there is no conservative view presented in the day-to-day paper going in and out of the President's office.

They feel that the President's instincts are basically conservative, but he just does not get enough conservative proposals and conservative views, and they feel this is the reason for what they see as the mistakes (i.e., FAP) of the Administration. As for conservative ideas (i.e., special revenue sharing), these seem to them to be dying without any major Administration concern.

Fourth, they believe that the golden opportunity to build a "new Republican majority" of conservative Democrats and regular Republicans is being lost because of the Administration's domestic policies, which they see as by and large extensions and refinements of the Great Society, only more so.

Fifth, they are all Nixonites, but they contend that if the President is re-elected <u>with</u> his existing staff structure without conservative representation—then they will have totally lost their leverage with the President and Administration—the dream of the New Republican Majority will be gone forever, "we will be out of the ball game completely."

In short, they are convinced . . . that "structure is policy" and with those Congressman who believe that the "White House Staff" is responsible for the leftward direction of an Administration whose President has basically conservative instincts.

What they have in mind, if they don't see some changes, is to try to co-ordinate a conservative attack on the White House staff, to persuade some of the older columnists to join it; in the hope that the attacks will bring about some changes in the present staff structure, perhaps force the addition of political conservatives to the President's top staff.

While the number of individuals involved in the effort is not great, they do have at least one columnist among them—and they are determined to win as many Congressmen and columnists and publications to their effort as possible. Some of the far right anti-Nixon conservatives would probably join the effort.

The whole effort has been building for months. We have managed to stave it off—arguing that the exercise would be counter-productive, that you cannot attack the President's staff without striking the President, and that any damage done to the President only enhances the possibility that a Muskie or Kennedy will be sitting in the White House in two years, and if that happens, the Western World can close up shop.

All of those involved, incidentally, were to my knowledge Nixon Conservatives in 1968, not Reagan conservatives.

I have passed this along, as these fellows consider me their "conduit" to the President and as I think their present spirit, mood, and plans could present us with some serious problems in the months ahead. [29]

20. Memo to Richard Nixon, July 16, 1971

On July 15, 1971, Nixon announced in a brief address to the nation that he would visit China in 1972. A staunch anti-communist since first elected to Congress in 1946, Nixon's decision was influenced by Henry Kissinger's advice that opening relations with China would help bring peace in Vietnam, provide opportunities for U.S. trade and investment, and improve relations with the Soviet Union. Nixon stated: "Our action in seeking a new relationship with the People's Republic of China will not be at the expense of our old friends. It is not directed against any other nation. We seek friendly relations with all nations. Any nation can be our friend without being any other nation's enemy. I have taken this action because of my profound conviction that all nations will gain from a reduction of tensions and a better relationship between the United States and the People's Republic of China. It is in this spirit that I will undertake what I deeply hope will become a journey for peace, peace not just for our generation but for future generations on this earth we share together."[30]

After the euphoria passes, the following seems a sketchy diplomatic profit-loss statement.

FOR THE UNITED STATES

(1) Confusion, astonishment in Hanoi, fear of a Chinese double-cross; suspicion of Sino-American collusion—perhaps producing the impetus to do a NVN deal with the United States, on the best terms possible, so as not to have Hanoi's interests subordinated to Big Power decisions.

(2) Paranoia in Moscow that their foremost ideological and military adversaries are dealing behind their back. But will this not produce upon Brezhnev enormous pressure with his ultra generals and marshals to provide them with the wherewithal necessary to "protect the Soviet Union from any combination of powers anywhere on the Globe." Will this meeting not prove a spur to rapid Soviet expansion of strategic missile strength—that search for absolute security, which only strategic superiority can provide.

(3) Loss of China's ideological virginity; blow to morale of Communists everywhere (i.e., Cuba)—not dissimilar to the effect of Nazi-Soviet pact upon Warsaw Communists. If anti-Communism suffers a blow to morale—so, too, does Communism—when the leading "imperialist" power sits down to talk with the capital of militant Asian Communism.

(4) A startling, imaginative stroke in American diplomacy—re-asserting the United States' diplomatic leadership of the West; and strengthening the President's global credentials a bold and unpredictable statesman.

FOR THE COMMUNIST WORLD

(1) Acceptance "with pleasure" of Chinese invitation by US President <u>gives China enormously enhanced respectability and standing in the world</u>, and the West. Formerly, the outlaw Nation and outcast of the non-Communist world, she is now seemingly being chaperoned into the United Nations by her ancient foremost adversary, the United States. If this is a victory for American diplomacy, it is a triumph for Peking to have the Western leader come to Peking to pay his respects, and negotiate as equals.

(2) Clearly, as American Eastern Establishment is salivating in anticipation over the visit, as the President has considerable personal stakes invested, <u>hostages have been given to Peking</u>. President Nixon would be under enormous pressure to grant minor concessions, to concede middling points, to be "flexible" on major demands—if the alternative were "cancellation" by Peking and despair and disappointment in a hopeful world, and hopeful West.

(3) A significant degree of psychological and moral disarmament of the world and American anti-Communist movement, to whom Hitler's Germany was but a scale-model of Mao's China, must ensue. Impact of RN negotiating with a Communist fanatic who imposes fascist-like discipline on 800 million, who is responsible for the death of 25 million Chinese cannot be fully estimated.

(4) Will surely be used to reinforce arguments left that China is not a hostile aggressive power, that China represents no danger to the United States—<u>thus, why the need to continue the build-up in strategic weapons</u>? Will added weapons not destroy the chances of SALT, antagonize new relations with China, prevent the hopeful moves toward détente taking place. Fear of Chinese attack—one of the arguments for ABM—will be difficult to make, as well all defense requests in lieu of "generation of peace" rhetoric, coupled with RN's "breakthroughs."

(5) In Vietnam, "how do we ask more American troops to die fighting the evil of aggressive Asian Communism—when the President is hailing as a triumph his prospective visit to the capital of Asian Communism?" The pressure for total pullout of American troops, now, will be increased; perhaps begin even from the Right.

(6) Of particular concern is that up-coming trips may effectively restrict our options in Indochina. If NVA moves across the DMZ in force, and the President must bomb the North, say, up to the 20th parallel, to halt the advance—China might well publicly demand a halt to the bombing of their neighbor—or other military concessions—as price of consummation of the visit. (i.e., K demand for U-2 apology from Ike.)

(7) Peking has already received a "security deposit"—RN's world-wide acceptance "with pleasure" of an invitation which RN sought—while Unites States'

dividends come in on completion of the deal. If broken off now, China retains the deposit, while United States and President suffer a net loss.

(8) Unless something has been locked in in advance to come out of the Pacific Summit—then Chinese intransigence at the talks could rally Communists the world over—and produce a dramatic letdown in the West and the United States, not unlike the collapsed summit in Paris in 1960. In an enterprise of such hopes, the diplomatic risks of failure are as dramatic as those of success.

(9) Just as Hanoi must be stunned—so, also, must the smaller non-Communist powers of Asia, our friends and allies, who have followed the American lead, and who do not want to be the last to reach an accommodation with Peking if that is where the future lies.

(10) Chinese embassies will likely begin sprouting in those Latin American, African, Asian nations which had heretofore followed America's lead, and withheld recognition. Similarly, the impact may well be traumatic among the millions of overseas Chinese, who had heretofore seen the mainland as contained—but who now see China on the diplomatic move all over the world.

POLITICALLY

No one need belabor the political benefits of the President's having diminished to near-zero or ended American involvement in Vietnam—while having set America out on a historic new era with China. And a sitting President making peace in Peking is a more attractive figure to all the American people than some squabbling politicians in the snows of New Hampshire. Then—to the political negatives and how to deal with them.

EUPHORIA

This will subside in a week or so—as the second-thought columns are written; it should subside; there is only folly in seeking to "collect in advance" political dividends for what has not occurred. Thus, the President and Kissinger should specifically warn against national euphoria. If the President's visit is a success to the world, we will not heed anymore to tell the American people. If the plans bring disappointment—then we want not to have created the euphoria.

THE RIGHT

This broke the camel's back—for some. For others, like [Senator] James Buckley and [Senator John] Tower, it forced them into open opposition. The previously confined right-wing opposition to RN—it has been held to the "organizations"—has now found some major political voices. But the President should not write off the conservatives—though some are gone for good. The columnists, if Kissinger can address them Monday or Tuesday may still be salvageable. The strongest argument we have—if we cannot state explicitly that we are engaged in a move with anti-Soviet overtones—is that they look at RN's background, look at his record as President—there is no justification in the world to think that he is a "Harriman." The President is not going to China on a spree—he does not think that the veterans of Yenan have suddenly "mellowed"—the interests of the United States will be what he is bargaining for—and finally, the nation has a tough-minded, hard-line bargainer in whom it should have confidence. There is no reason to believe that we cannot sit down at a table with Mao and come off much or more a winner than the Communists.

POLITICS

The worst charge, and most serious—it will come from Left, as well as right—when the euphoria passes is that RN is playing with the national interest—to advance his political interest. The argument used on the wires today—that specifically a post-May meeting was ruled out for political reasons—should be repeated and repeated and repeated.

RN can argue, rightly, that a visit during the campaign season in that environment would have had little chance of success. And had we waited until after the campaign—it might have been 1973—and peace and the reduction of tensions cannot wait that long. As many have written, for the world it is "five minutes before midnight"—and in such a world, President and Prime Ministers must move more swiftly—if that is what the hopes of peace require.

ATMOSPHERICS

The sense of elation, and delight, that seemed to emerge partially from the aftermath of the President's address is to me politically alarming. It leaves the impression that we think we have scored a "coup." The atmospherics surrounding any discussion of these matters, seems to me, should be sobriety and gravity—more consistent with a hope for peace—than that elation which surrounds a political victory.

Finally, the best argument we have for anti-Communists is "Trust Nixon"—he has hung tough in Vietnam; he took the risks in Cambodia; he did not cave in the Middle East; he has fought for ABM—his record entitles him to trust, to the confidence of the nation—that he will sell no friend, no ally down the river for political gain. To suggest that outrage is to suggest something for which there is no precedent in the political career or presidential history of Richard Nixon.

What enables the President to make such far-reaching moves is the confidence in him of the national anti-Communist community, which would never trust a Democratic President who so acted. That confidence is there—but it has been shaken—and the President in a press conference, in a statement to the nation, should speak directly to it. His aides should likewise build on it, in assuring the concerned—who today are legion. [31]

21. Memo to H. R. Haldeman, July 28, 1971

The right met secretly in New York Monday, with security tighter than normal, and are distributing today a "suspension of support" for the President. While passing over domestic policy critically—hitting inflation, unemployment, welfarism, etc.—the statement focuses on foreign policy. Basically, the lack of American response to German policy toward the Soviets, the lack of response to the Soviet build-up in the Mediterranean, the initiatives toward China—without visible concessions on Peking's part—but most important, indeed "above all" in their terminology—the lack of American response to the Soviet conventional and strategic arms build-up. While praising the President for standing up to those who want him to abandon South Vietnam, while extending all manner of personal courtesies, etc., they indicate that they are "suspending support." And they leave the door open to political opposition in the primaries—while not asking for political support right now. Signatories include members of six conservative organizations or publications—but the crucial one is William F. Buckley, Jr. The press can be expected to give them the kind of ride on this one they would never receive with an endorsement.

The signers are Buckley, Burnham, Myer and Rusher for National Review; Winter and Ryskind for Human Events, Mahoney for the NY Conservative Party; Teague for YAF, Anthony Harrigan for the Southern Industrial Conference. John Jones for the American Conservative Union, Neil McCaffrey for the Conservative Book Club; there were others present, however, as my source told me. Some pushed for a primary candidate. But they are looking at this as a "two-step" arrangement—not asking for politicians to step forward until they have "cleared the field."

Important to note—[Senator] James Buckley's people did not participate—and some others I know of did not—because their security was so bad on the recent meetings.

The impact of this will be I would think to "energize" the conservatives outside of Congress.

Some consideration ought to be given as to how to handle this. Do we use

Reagan and Jim Buckley—are they the most effective political spokesman? But some thought should be given to this right away; whether to low-key, tend to ignore it; and work quietly—or what? The problem is that the press will be all over the Hill—asking for "off the record" comments if they cannot get on the Record ones. . . . [32]

22. Memo to Richard Nixon, August 4, 1971

The White House, in my judgment, should take these conservative defections more seriously than we have to date.

First, all of the individuals who broke with the President were RN supporters in 1968—many, if not most of them, supported the President for the nomination.

Secondly, the meeting at Buckley's apartment brought their opposition together, brought it into the open, and added the support of William F. Buckley, whose influence on the Right—nationally—can hardly be overestimated.

Third, Ronald Reagan was informed of the meeting and what transpired prior to the public announcement—and from my source, was not unhappy with the action and decision taken.

Fourth, the younger right-wingers, both in the political organizations and among the activists, have now reached a point where their attitude toward us is little short of bitterness and contempt. . . . They feel they have been had—and some of them have made the decision to go after the President in the primaries.

Fifth, political realism indicates to me that we are vulnerable to a conservative assault in the primaries on half a dozen issues, regionally and nationally. Example: A Republican who ran a Conservative campaign denouncing the President for (a) "surrendering US strategic supremacy," (b) producing inflationary budgets and monstrous deficits, (c) going along with Court-imposed "forced integration" and busing in the South, (d) giving welfare clients a "guaranteed income", (e) expanding the Great Society, (f) slashing defense and space. Such a fellow could not take the nomination away from RN. No one could. But he could carve us up so badly that the election would be over before it started.

To me, currently, this is a potential—not an actual danger. But if someone had told me, during the campaign of 1970 that in mid-1971, we would be facing this bitterness on the Right, I would not have believed him.

What makes it a potential, not an actual danger.

(1) The group consists of writers and publicists, not politicians, with the exception of the NYCP (Cliff White was not there). (2) They have not yet crossed the Rubicon—for many reasons—in terms of a "Dump Nixon" political movement. (3) They have no horse to ride. [Governor] Ronald Reagan and [Senator]

James Buckley are the "viable" candidates of the Right who could score heavily against the President in a primary—and neither is so disposed.

My great concern is that if the deterioration in relations continues, if they come to assume that all is hopeless with the Nixon Administration, some <u>voice</u> just might emerge to articulate their bitterness—and then the thing will snowball, and we will have ourselves a serious problem.

Further, my view is that, just as we needed a 100 percent united party in 1968, so we will need it in 1972—if we are to take advantage of the centrifugal forces (McCarthy, etc.) now at work in the Democratic Party.

What is developing now—and especially among the younger conservatives looking to the post-Nixon era—is a bitterness, a Kamikaze spirit of, "Let's help defeat Nixon and then pick up the pieces." The same attitude on the Left plagued Humphrey all the way through the 1968 election, and his party was a good deal larger than our own.

RECOMMENDATION—As the conservative writers and thinkers and political organizations are now divided into hawks and doves when it comes to opposing RN, as we hope not only to stop the attacks, but to bring them back in—as we did in 1968—<u>nothing is gained by attacking them. Nothing is gained by attempting to discredit people we hope will return to the fold</u>—except to <u>further alienate them.</u> We should use the olive branch, rather than the stick—especially where conservatives like the Buckleys are concerned—who are uncomfortable opposing the President, and who prefer to remain within the only Administration they felt they could support in their adult lives.

Secondly, their major concerns are not cosmetic; they are not personal—<u>they are substantive</u>, i.e., deep concerns over the strategic and conventional arms balance with the Soviets, what is happening at SALT]—and the RN mission to China.

Now, by the spring—<u>these matters will of themselves be resolved one way or the other</u>. By then, conservative fears that we will be frozen into inferiority at SALT will be alleviated; as should conservative fears that we are making overtures to Peking at the expense of our Asian allies. The outcome of these will be evident by the spring.

So, at this point, it seems to be that our interests would be served by privately alleviating their concerns to the degree possible.

This would be especially important today with James Buckley whose major address at the Press Club was on defense. Further, Kissinger might well go ahead with a briefing for conservatives on SALT, and the arms balance.

Nothing, however, would do more to calm the Right than (a) increases in the strategic arms sector of the defense budget for 1972 and (b) a Presidential address on the Defense requirements of the United States in light of the Soviet advances.

The President's speech. Let me argue the "political" case for this—as I believe strongly in the national case for it.

The "Peace President" is a strong political posture in an election year; there are few better. And the Presidential credentials in this area have been established to the satisfaction of all—except those who would not believe.

However, let us assume the China trip aborts, SALT miscarries and that, instead of an era of negotiations, we are in the midst of a Mediterranean confrontation with the Russians in mid-1972. Does this destroy RN in the election?

Hardly, the opposite would be the case. In times of crisis the American people (a) rally to the President in office, and (b) look for a strong leader. In a crisis atmosphere, ala November 1956, the American people were not interested in a soft-headed liberal Democrat, but a hard-headed anti-Communist who knew what he was doing in foreign policy.

My view is that the Peace President theme co-opts a traditional Democratic position—but the "President in Crisis" is a posture that will appeal not only to our own party, but across the board.

Again, my opinion is that if the Russians or Chinese try to "hold us up" at an exorbitant price for cooperation—the option is open to turn around and tell them that while we want peace it is not at the price of selling America's friends down the river, or disarming in the face of an adversary's buildup.

When security of the country is at hand—the President has the whip hand.

Now, as for the defense speech—first, the groundwork has been laid, not just by right-wing columnists. Life, Reader's Digest, Newsweek, moderate columnists, networks all have pointed ominously at the Soviet build-up in the Med. The American Jewish community, which controls the liberal media is not unaware. There is a basis on which RN could make an address on a "generation of peace" depends upon American power. Also, we could gin up the unions on this—after all, it means jobs as well as defense—they have normally been favorable to both. It would divide the Democrats once again. It would draw the line with the other party—and are we not going to have to draw it in the dust, anyhow, before 1972.

Clearly, however, a strong speech calling for increased preparation for defense would rally the entire right back into the presidential camp.

To move on, we should maintain our lines of communication. And while cosmetics and goodies will not end the opposition—it will ease the transition back. Appointment of their respected intellectuals to boards; providing them with a quota of political victories inside in terms of minor and major appointments; continued friendly discussions with the leaders like Buckley especially; briefings for their columnists with the others. All of these things can help.

Some of these fellows are so bitter that they want us beaten badly. But this is not the majority. Others are not enthusiastic, now, about a position against the Administration. They are like the editors at the Richmond News to whom Herb [Klein] and I talked who said, "Give me some reasons so we can be for Richard Nixon."

We ought, then, not to write off people we had and need in 1972, people who would like to be aboard and enthusiastic, but who are confused and de-spondent—whether white collar National Review conservatives, or blue collar Wallace right-wingers.

Further, on this question, there is no one with more credibility in both those camps than the Vice President.

Rather go into brief details—they have been contained in a number of memos over some months—my suggestion is that I get together with the Conservatives in here, and on the Vice President's staff and provide a list of specific positive actions for the President and HRH that can be taken, and can be promoted, to help with this thing, before it deteriorates. [33]

23. Memo to H.R. Haldeman and Charles Colson, September 13, 1971

The correspondence between the two offices sent to me for review underscores part of our problem with the Right—a lack of understanding of what they are about, and what motivates them.

Within the Colson memos there are repeated references to "see what Sops are available to conservatives," discussion of "cosmetics," the use of appointments for "therapeutic value," and the "need to make some significant gesture. . . . That is what they are playing for." . . . .

That is not at all what they are "playing for," like their left-wing counterparts, they are ideologues concerned with substance and policy, more likely to be alien-ated than appeased by gestures and cosmetics in the absence of action.

After canvassing the Right, and especially, those who have "suspended" their support for the President, this seems to me the situation.

They themselves do not yet realize their own potential to damage the Presi-dent in the primaries; the Right is divided between "hawks" and "doves," the former of whom are currently bent on attempting, not to unseat the President in the primaries, but to defeat him in the general election . . . believing more and more that the defeat of Richard Nixon is the necessary condition of restoring some unity and strength to the conservative movement, within the GOP.

The doves on this issue—who have yet to write off the President—like Bill Buckley, are being pushed by their own constituency further and further from us. Individuals like Reagan, Goldwater and Jim Buckley are being disparaged by the hard Right for "selling out." They are themselves under continuing and increasing pressure. Along with the conservative columnists, they remain our most effective bulwark against any further attrition on the Right.

If those three should openly break with the President, we would be in grave jeopardy in 1972. What the President has going for him right now is that no rec-ognized major conservative political leader has publicly broken with him—thus the erosion is contained within the small circulation right-wing papers—ex-tending into the major media only through Buckley. If any of those three broke with us, however, the whole conservative revolt would be in the national media on a regular basis and we would, as I say, be in deep kimshee. The obvious point is that these three should be constantly apprised of any Presidential decisions or moves likely to further antagonize the Right.

To simplify, three things are preventing an effective open challenge to the President in the primaries. First, the logical candidates of such a movement—Reagan or Buckley—are with us. Second, there is a reluctance among many con-servatives to break publicly with a man and administration they have supported enthusiastically and often in the past—they don't want to cross the Rubicon, and unless pushed into the river, they probably won't. Third, there is a present mood of despondency among the anti-Nixon conservatives, somewhat surprising lack of determination and drive. There is enough support on the right, in money, tal-ent, manpower and youth to present some grave problems for the Administra-tion—and the failure to "get it all together" I have to trace to lack of either drive or appreciation of their own strength.

What should be done?

We are past the point where gestures and rhetoric will be sufficient. To bank upon that is to delude ourselves and insult these conservatives. We are not going to buy them off with beads and trinkets. Most helpful would be a major politi-cal confrontation against the Left, where the President was clearly and visibly upholding the Right position.

Examples:

1.) The Administration co-sponsorship of the seat on the Security Council resolution will be costly—but in the wake of that the Administration is seen as fighting and winning the battle to keep Nationalist China within the UN, that battle itself will be helpful.

2.) The nature of the President's fight for his defense budget, if spirited, is certain to bring the Right in as allies on his behalf. Sometimes in the heat of a common cause, old differences are submerged and forgotten.

3.) Should a Supreme Court seat open, this would be a golden opportunity for the President to go to the wall for his belief in a strict constructionist.

4.) Conservative fears today focus on SALT, the Soviet buildup, and the President's visit to China. In all three instances, what is feared is a "deal" to the disadvantage of the United States and to the political advantage of the President.

My view is that time itself will show that these fears unjustified, the lack of trust in the President without justification, and that thus the steam will go out of some of the conservative anti-Nixon drive.

5.) The inevitable chasm between the views of the President on defense and foreign policy—and those of his Democratic opponent—will it seems to me obviate, for most of the thinking Right, the old chestnut that "there's not a dime's worth of difference between them." Once the conservatives see RN and Muskie side by side, they will see the difference, and most of them, if grudgingly, will support the President in my judgment—considering the situation as of now.

6.) Though the anti-war mood, in the face of the disintegrating American army is broader than ever—what happens to Vietnam is still a concern to the silent right-wing in this country, and the prevalent war-weariness in this country should not be misconstrued as a carte blanche for total American freedom of action in bringing the troops home.

Looking dead ahead, the fight to keep Taiwan in the United Nations seems a golden opportunity for the President to rally the Right. Red China is being brought in, with U.S. assistance, on two grounds; one universalism (all peoples should be represented) and two, realism (Peking controls one-fourth of the globe's human beings). The same two arguments can apply to Taiwan—despite recognition of Peking, Taiwan is de facto in control of Formosa, and controls some 11,000,000 people—more than two-thirds of the nations in the United Nations.

Thus, if Peking is brought in on the grounds of universalism and realism, Taiwan should be kept in—on the same grounds.

And with all the millions America puts up for that organization, with all the contributions we make over and all dues, no conservative is going to believe we can't get our way—when we are both right and the vital interest of an old friend are at stake. In short, if we lose, and Taiwan is thrown out of the United Nations—no one is going to believe that "George Bush did his best." If that happens there will be a "Dump Nixon" movement on the Right.

If we are behind Taiwan, then it seems to me there is political mileage to be gained in the President's fighting for their seat in the UN. Surely, even the Times would concur with the rules of "universalism" and "realism". Further, we could surely use the kind of arm-twisting, and neck-wringing, if need be, of our little African, Latin and Asian friends to swing it, and some good nationalistic pro-America, anti-UN rhetoric on the part of the President would be as well received as his America Firsters address to the Congress.

Some thoughts on our current situation. Finally, as to "speakers", the idea of a . . . "Conservatives for Nixon" committee is ridiculous. It would be called the "Uncle Tom Conservative Committee" within days; it would have no stroke and less credibility on the Right, would simply be taken as proof that the President has written off conservatives and was engaged now in cosmetics into convincing people he had not.

Paul Harvey has been helpful on this—but none more so than Reagan, Goldwater and Buckley (Jim). The more we can get them and Dole and the Vice President and Uncle Strom speaking out for the President's controversial foreign policies especially—the more we guarantee that the rebellion is confined and contained to the farther Right.

Further, re: the Colson contention: "I've talked several times to Buchanan about it who does not offer any positive suggestions; I have the feeling that Pat feels hurt we have not heeded his advice before."

Considering the half dozen memos sent in the first half of 1971—to prevent just what occurred—the first half of that statement hardly seems justified; as for the second, Pat does not feel "hurt" that his advice was not followed; he is, however apprehensive right now that widespread anti-RN sentiment on the Republican Right in 1972, that might have been avoided, coupled with an inevitable pro-Muskie media campaign by our friends at the networks may well get us defeated in 1972. [34]

24. Memo to Richard Nixon, September 20, 1971

Between 1969 and 1972, Nixon would fill four vacancies on the U.S. Supreme Court: Chief Justice Warren Burger (1969–1986), and associate justices Harry Blackmun (1970–1994), Lewis Powell (1972–1987), and William Rehnquist (1972–1986); elevated to Chief Justice by Ronald Reagan, 1986–2005).

The political imperatives argue loudly for a rapid appointment of a Southern conservative to the Supreme Court. All the arguments are on the President's side:

1. If a Southerner does not go on the Court, it will be the first time in a century the South has not had its own justice on the Bench.

2. RN can argue that the October session needs a full nine-man Court—thus hopefully preventing the delaying actions that would enable Democrats to hold the appointment off to next year—and then to the election.

3. If [Rep.] Richard Poff is the President's man, which is widely reported, the sooner, the better. For Poff has reportedly already gone through the laborious clearance; it would be exceedingly difficult for Democrats in the Senate to reject one of their own from the Hill. Indeed, if they did, it would clearly put the Democrats in the position of anti-Southern bias—fix them in that posture for the coming election. The President might even be able to get a massive bi-partisan House Resolution, endorsing Dick Poff's nomination—to pressure the Senate.

4. We have to move fast—14 months before election—lest we allow the Democrats to use the "griffin Argument", that a "new" President should name the Court.

5. Vital, for the long-run future of the country that the President name younger Justices than [Warren] Burger or [Henry] Blackmun, if we want to have a "Nixon Court", all the way into the 1980s and 90s.

6. My recommendation is that this week the President call in the Press, announce Poff, have him present for photographs, call for speedy action, and in his remarks:

a) Point out that RN's pledge to name a Southern strict constructionist to the Court, to a new Senate, is with this nomination being fulfilled. President believes that Poff will clearly and quickly be ratified by his colleagues in Congress.

b) Congressman Poff as a legislator is a strict constructionist who believes that nation's social problems should be worked out by elected legislators, which he is now, not by unelected Justices, which he will be tomorrow. . . .

c) President can use the occasion to further outline and define in some three pages what he means by a "strict constructionist." If President has Poff in mind, seems to me we can put Senate into a box. President can say that his prediction that a New Senate, with a different balance and point of view, would accept a Southerner he is confident is going to come true. If Senate approves Poff, no one will believe it was not an expression of anti-Southern bias. (One assumes that Poff has passed muster with [American Bar Association] and FBI—and is "clean as a hound's tooth".)

7. We have a golden opportunity here to join in an effort in which conservatives can again rally to the President.

8. Further, if any other Supreme Court appointment comes up, suggest strongly that the President appoint a conspicuous "ethnic Catholic" like an Italian-American jurist of conservative views. Not blacks, not Jews, but ethnic Catholics—Poles, Irish, Italians, Slovaks, etc. are where the ducks are. We ought now to be canvassing the best legal and judicial conservative minds in the Italian-American, the Irish-American and the Polish-American community—and the fellow ought to be a Holy Name Society Daily Communicant.

Would be happy to draft for the President the statement accompanying the appointment, a statement which might elucidate and deepen the Presidential position on "strict constructionists". This is the kind of Court the whole country wants with the exceptions of the Eastern Establishment, and the President's political opponents. . . .[35]

25. Memo to Richard Nixon, "Supreme Court," September 29, 1971

The Southern Manifesto, formally known as the Declaration of Constitutional Principles, was a document signed in 1956 by 101 members of Congress opposed to racial integration in the wake of the Supreme Court's 1954 decision in Brown v. Board of Education. *The signatories, who believed that the Court had abused its judicial power, included the entire congressional delegations from Alabama, Arkansas, Georgia, Louisiana, Mississippi, South Carolina, and Virginia. All were Southern Democrats except two Republican House members, Richard Poff and Joel Broyhill. The only three Southern Democrats who refused to sign were Senators Albert Gore and Estes Kefauver of Tennessee and Lyndon Johnson of Texas.*

1) RN should move as quickly as possible on both nominees—to head off mounting lobbies of women, blacks and labor. To delay is to allow them more time to build public support to work the Senate.

2) Southern Judicial Conservative presents a grave political problem for Muskie, especially—if he hopes to carry any state in the South. He may be able to explain away votes against Haynsworth and Carswell—but how can he explain three straight anti-Southern votes for the Supreme Court—especially if the third candidate is right out of Congress.

3) HHH made a serious error in ruling out all signers of Southern manifestoes for the Court— [Senators] Sam Ervin, Bill Fulbright, [Richard] Russell, etc.—as well as some fifty others, mostly Democratic, still on the Hill this ruled out.

4) If RN goes with Judiciary Committee type for one seat—other should be the most distinguished strict constructionist we can find, a real heavyweight in everyone's eyes. ([Irving] Kristol strongly urged this.) Reason is that even those papers that agree with RN feel that two giants have departed—and men of like caliber should be placed.

5) Poff has gotten a good review from the New Republic, and is getting some fairly good ink from responsible liberals.

6) <u>If RN plans to send up the nominations, not together, but in series—send up the Big Rock first, the Southern Strict Constructionist first</u>. Otherwise, the Senate Committee might immediately pass what they will call the "moderate"—seat him on the Court, to RN's embarrassment. <u>If they go one at a time, the tough one should go first</u>—so that if they are chomping on him, we can line up another.

7) Would not be averse to a Senates mini-rebellion on this issue—if the Southerner is impeccable, it is a bitterly divisive issue for Democratic candidates—either they kick their black friends in the teeth, or they kick the South in the teeth. In any event, so long as they cannot get an "out" by accusing us of naming an unqualified man, they are on the hook. Thus, again, urge strong strict constructionists for both appointments—coupled with a Southern Conservative for one of them.

Kristol recommends Edward Levi, the President of Chicago University, Jewish, for the second seat. My view is that as stated before, we ought to get the most brilliant and qualified Italian-American strict constructionist jurist or attorney in the nation—and then name, play up his Italian background—and let the Democrats chop him up, if they want. [36]

26. Memo to H. R. Haldeman, October 1, 1971

We are taking a public relations beating on this woman on the Court thing. First was the near unavoidable controversy; then came the raising of hopes by the President and Mrs. Nixon and other top officials saying they were considered. Some of this came by accident and necessity, i.e., in response to a question; thus unavoidable.

But last night, some cluck obviously told Dan Rather on background to knock down the report, that we were backing away from a woman. That exercise was only damaging to the President, as Rather went on the air to "tell" the Nation's women we were backing down, and then to "tell" them that this would adversely affect the President at the polls. Clearly, Rather used the opportunity to impress upon women that they were being ignored by the President and the thing to do is retaliate at the polls. What should have been done, it seems to me, once the women thing was raised, was say nothing—until the appointments—when the new names, if not women, would be the "lead" on the story—while the fact that a woman was not chosen was buried. If hopes had to be dashed, they should have been submerged in the news of the appointment itself—not as was done. [37]

27. Memo to Richard Nixon, October 26, 1971

Politically, both Sears and I would be <u>against</u> the President enacting <u>any</u> new taxes in 1972—let alone one of the magnitude proposed, and despite the fact that one objective is to provide some tax relief.

1. Taxes are far more a gut issue than education—as is evident from the fact that voters time and again knock down bond issues for schools. The American people would simply not understand how it is the President is going to raise their cost of living four percent—in order to provide them with tax relief.

2. We would be raising "taxes for all of the people in order to provide relief for some of the people." The prospective tax increase would loom, in my personal judgment far larger in the voters' consideration—than the prospective cut in property taxes. If he voted this "issue," my guess is that he would vote <u>against</u> the man proposing the increase; and that is certain for the millions of individuals who do not own their own homes.

3. We could not avoid the headline, as John Ehrlichman put it, that
NIXON PROPOSED $__BILLION TAX HIKE FOR EDUCATION
Relief Promised for Home Owners

4. Education is simply not a sexy political issue. First, it is a nebulous thing; when RN vetoed spending for education on television, the country backed him by a margin of five-to-one.

5. The education lobby that would benefit, and that would push for such a proposal—these are not our people.

6. As a practical matter, there is no correlation . . . between an increase in spending for education and an increase in the quality of education. Education has been eating high on the hog for a decade; the number of children going into the school systems each year has leveled off; the baby boom is over. Surely, if we are going to raise $20 billion to spend—we can do it for some distinctly <u>Nixon Programs</u>.

7. Congress is likely to grab our tax relief idea, our aid to education idea—and leave us sitting there fighting it out <u>unsuccessfully</u> for the new tax, in 1972.

8. Why these "huge" sums recommended—unless there is really something we want to, or think we can, accomplish with that kind of money.

Should these funds be taken to build more schools, to raise teachers' salaries (God forbid)—what is the hard, tangible benefit that one can see in the education of children. Education needs discipline and reform—throwing twenty billion dollars at the present public school system seems to me to be approaching the old "rathole" metaphor.

Would an increase in pay for teachers, principals and the like really increase productivity any? I can't imagine how.

Both Sears and I feel that if we get some new money (we both oppose any RN tax increases at all in 1972) we should spend it on new "Nixon Programs." . . .

Why not set aside a billion dollars in College Tuition and Room and Board Scholarships—for individuals in mid-career who only finished high school, or who have a high school equivalent.

Example. You could provide a billion in those scholarships to tens of thousands of auto mechanics, union and non-union machinists, aerospace and defense workers. The grants would come in the wake of competitive exams. They might be for four years—to bachelors or masters and make engineers out of mechanics.

Re-opening colleges and universities to some of these individuals who would appreciate and use the golden opportunity, it seems to me, is the type of thing that would energize the unions whose membership participates and win the President some friends.

Just an example, but it is something that would be the "President's" program—not just more money for the same old causes. . . .

What we should be looking for is things that are targeted right on groups we hope to win, union men, Catholics, ethnics, etc. Specific, hard and immediate. [38]

28. Memo to H. R. Haldeman and Charles Colson, October 26, 1971

The Twelve Apostles, also known as the Manhattan Twelve, were a dozen conservative leaders who would meet in William F. Buckley's New York apartment; in July 1971, they issued a statement to suspend support for Nixon. [39]

Last week, the Twelve Apostles met again in New York and elected a subcommittee to draft "recommendations" to the WH in exchange for which they would terminate their "suspension of support" of the President. In the absence of a favorable response, their present intention is to make an open break to attempt to create a political alternative to the President, whether in the primaries, at the convention, or in the general election I cannot learn. . . .

As for the twelve (prior to the UN vote, which I am afraid is going to be a crippling blow to our efforts) their view as of last week was to seek out and find some common ground for re-joining the President's camp.

Prior to the Taiwan vote, the climate was perfect. The conservatives have won a few within the White House; the President appointed two first-line conservatives to the Court; the OEO-Child Development-Legal Services bill is headed for a veto, Ronald Berman, a conservative and National Review Book Reviewer, looks to be our new Humanities man, instead of Steve Hess. . . .

My recommendation is that the President give the United Nations—at the least—the worst blistering—ever accorded that whorehouse by an American President. This, it seems to me, should be done on grounds of the cynical betrayal of a loyal honorable member who has met all its obligations for a quarter of a century. Methinks the nation would not be averse to this kind of standing up on behalf of a friend and ally of long standing. As for Peking, they probably think less of the UN than most conservatives do; and they can hardly be offended at our excoriation of the world body.

In any event, in my absence, the conservative group said they would prefer to meet with Chuck Colson—and present to him their "recommendations."

Basically, they will focus on defense, where they would like to see the budget of 1973 reflect Laird's expressed concerns in 1971; they would like to see FAP strung up on the Hill, without any prevailing intervention on the part of the Administration. They want to see some indication that the Administration truly wants to curb federal intervention in American society and federal growth on the body politic; (OEO-Child Development veto will help) and they may have something to say about the Vice President.

In any event—prior to the Taiwan vote—they were prepared as of last weekend to find a common ground for conciliation with the Administration. In my judgment their support is essential in all their publications and their associated columnists means that many thousands of hard-line conservatives in many Republican bastions like Orange County are going to be sitting on their hands in 1972—or worse.

Second Recommendation:

Since the veto of OEO-Legal Services—Child Development will anger the sociologist lobby, we should derive the President his rewards. This can be done by a strong statement focusing first on Child Development and secondly, on Legal Services. . . .

Rhetoric about the primary responsibility for raising children lies not with the state but with the parent—and the camel's nose of government must not be allowed inside this tent unless all America is aware of what we are doing. Also, we can point to sixties legislation enacted in haste, where we repented in leisure.

In any event, this thing should be knocked down hard—as should the expanded legal services concept, which amounts to little more than subsidization without strings of thousands of anti-Nixon, radical, and liberal lawyers—half of whom are out to overthrow the President, the other half to overthrow the country.

Suggest that in working on Legal Services, and on the OEO bill—contact be made with Dave Keene in the Vice President's office who has done considerable research on these issues—and who also has contact with the conservatives. Further, Chuck might want to counsel with Dave before meeting with the conservatives.

Again, on the OEO matter, the argument can be used as well that "when we ask working men to cutback, then government should likewise hold back."

The arguments will be raised that RN has made statements which imply support for Child Development, i.e., "the first five years of life," and the President's favoring of a "creation of a comprehensive family-oriented child development program." These statements should no more inhibit a reversal and strong veto than past statements with regard to the admission of Communist China to the United Nations. Further, the opportunity is present to get us off the hook on this legal services program which we have been supporting.

The sting of the message, however, is all important. If strong and tough enough we can knock this thing out of the park—and the President can win high marks for protecting the family from a "regiment of bureaucratic intruders" and for holding the line of inordinate federal spending.

Back to the conservatives. Again, I think the time is (was) ripe for healing the breach; unless their meeting aborts over Taiwan, they will be approaching him. And we should see what can be done to bring them back into camp. Sorry about the rambling nature of the memorandum; was written in considerable haste. [40]

29. Memo to H. R. Haldeman, December 1, 1971

Would be happy to put together The Conservative Case for Richard Nixon— but the time to do that is not now. Definitely not.

First, The Conservative Case for Richard Nixon, if it is to be effective, would have to be comprehensive. What Nixon has done for Conservatives in three years. Thus, we would throw the book at them (Four Justices on the Supreme

Court, the unleashing of the Vice President, ABM, Vietnam, Cambodia, Middle East crisis, Law and Order, etc., etc., etc.)

Methinks a very convincing case could be made—but once made, the job can't be done again, with the same dramatic impact. And we don't need it done so much now—as we are going to need it done later. The reasons are these:

a) Coming up are the trade with the Soviets decision, which is going to outrage them further, but Budget which they will look at extremely closely in the defense area, the trips to China and the Soviet Union, about which they are deeply apprehensive, the decision on FAP, and the outcome of SALT. These are the Big Rocks.

The time to make the case for the President is after these are <u>behind</u> us.

If we shoot our wad now, many conservatives will say, "Well, that's a powerful argument; I think we have to be for Nixon." But then comes some supertrade deal with Moscow, and FAP—and any gains we made go right out the window—and the Conservative Case for Richard Nixon cannot be made again; and <u>then</u> is when it will be most needed.

We ought to compile all the materials for The Conservative Case for Richard Nixon, but go with a piece for massive mailing—only when the crunch comes and we need it. Not a year before the election.

Right now, the Manhattan Twelve have decided upon a course of action, I know not what. And if they go the primary route, which I suspect they desire, then, when the primary date approaches, we will have to go with it.

But there are yet more arguments to be heard, with months to go before the convention, before the time for a summation of the Conservative Case for Richard Nixon. We will lose some of those battles in the interim, with conservatives; we will win some. Let's wait until the conservative case for the prosecution of Richard Nixon has completed its closing arguments, before we make our pitch in his defense. [41]

30. Memo to John Mitchell and H. R. Haldeman, December 3, 1971

The Manhattan Twelve gathered again Wednesday. From the White House point of view, the convocation was the least constructive to date. They were not dissatisfied with the Administration (Colson, Buchanan) response to their list of "demands;" they were outraged. For some the meeting served as a catharsis, a point of final departure from the Nixon Administration. My friend, Bill Rusher, the most hawkist, leader of the group and designated spokesman, would tell me nothing other than they were heading off, and "you are welcome to join us." Rusher as he told me some time ago, made a personal commitment to sever any remaining ties with the Administration, if Taiwan were expelled. By written memorandum, Rusher has argued upon the twelve the case for the defeat of Richard Nixon—"at all costs" as they put it—even if it carries with it the certainty of electing Teddy Kennedy. His memorandum, which argues the case that this is the last best hope for conservatives, is reportedly witty and well-written—but badly argued. Have been unable as stated, to lay hands on a copy, so that I could write a rebuttal for the next meeting.

The Twelve have maintained an utterly close-mouthed attitude about both proceedings and decisions. From outside sources, however, have learned the following.

1) A number of options are being explored; they run from an open challenge to the President in the New Hampshire, Florida and California primaries to a Third Party effort in the General election. My source indicates that they have already made contact with Bill Loeb of the [New Hampshire] Union-Leader; their political man, Jerry Harkins, has explored the possibility of running a primary candidate against the President.

2) Some of them are now so anti-Nixon that they cannot, under conceivable circumstances, be brought back into the fold. Among the twelve and their other colleagues assembled, the following are the anti-Nixon hawks:

William Rusher (Publisher, NR)
M. Stanton Evans (Indianapolis Trib Ed Page Editor; ACU Chief)
James Burnham (Columnist, NR)
Frank Myer (Vice Chairman, N.Y. Conservative Party)
Ron Docksai (YAF Chairman)
Neil McCaffrey (Conservative Book Club)
Jerry Harkins (Political Operative—Crane's Campaign Manager)
John Jones (ACU Exec—was not present Wednesday)

3) In the middle, those perhaps amenable to an accommodation, but still disenchanted, are Dan Mahoney of the N.Y. Conservative Party, and Jeff Bell, Editor of ACU publication. Anthony Harrigan was not present; don't know where he stands.

4) Doves include the Human Events people, Allan Ryskind and Tom Winter, and William F. Buckley, Jr. (Apparently, Bill regaled the gathering with his wit; his political recommendations, however, were themselves the subject of some humor. My guess is that since Bill is such an independent spirit, he must be a bit uncomfortable being yoked in harness in a twenty-mule team whose direction he alone cannot possibly control.)

5) The YAF leaders are reportedly anxious to make a go against the President, both to show their youth turn-out to the media and for organizational and other purposes.

6) The elements upon which any challenge to the President would be raised would include the editors and writers here involved, their publications, the New York Conservative Party, the Michigan Conservative Party, the United Republicans of California, Phyllis Schlafly and her women supporters, and the ACU organizations that seem to be popping up, in New Jersey and elsewhere.

7) My source indicates that they have covert support within the Republican Party in the Congress; and that there is no problem from a money standpoint. A number of traditional GOP moneymen, whose names I could not acquire, are said to be willing to fund the effort, when it goes.

8) F. Clifton White was _not_ present at this meeting.

9) Am unable to determine just _who_ they would focus upon as a candidate, should they decide to go either in the primaries or the General. Got a soft—not a hard—impression that Reagan is privately concerned about trends within the Administration. There was no negative word with regard to Jim Buckley (whose defense man, Bill Schneider) was present—but there is a feeling among them that Senator Goldwater did his job in 1964 and could not be expected or counted upon to support them now.

10) The major issues which concern them, despite the laundry list are a) Defense and b) FAP. One source indicated that if there were some way we could indicate something positive from the Defense Budget, that might help create some dissent from the prevailing view within the ranks. They are cognizant, however, that the Budget is not presented until after the filing deadline for New Hampshire is passed.

11) From comments from those who refuse to talk, one gets the impression that they are readying some media-making event in the near future. Don't know what it is or what form it will take—but something nice I am sure.

BUCHANAN ASSESSMENT: This seems a fairly serious problem. Right now, we could win without these conservatives and their train; but right now, is not October of 1972. So long as they continued meeting and talking, there was no great problem. But, should they "get it all together" and announce something rather exciting, then their efforts would take on a new momentum of their own. A National Conservative Party in the General Election, if the threat is to be taken seriously, could be a problem (there was talk further of canalizing efforts and running a conservative candidate only in those states where it would be sure to cost the President the state.)

While the possibility exists, it would be an error to write these fellows off as blunders or talkers without follow-through. Currently, they resemble a milling herd of cattle, making considerable noise and doing little harm; but if they start moving off together in one direction—picking up every stray anti-Nixon conservative in the country—they would be difficult to stop.

My hope had been that something like Child Development-OEO could be brought down here for a Presidential veto, with a tough message, which might then cause at least some of them to say, wait a minute, the returns aren't all in. But that does not now seem in the cards, as the House is to do the honors. . . . [42]

31. Memo to John Mitchell and H. R. Haldeman, "The Manhattan Twelve," December 13, 1971

Sunday, for five hours at the Watergate Apartment, Chuck Colson, Dave Keene, Max Friedersdorf and I met with five members of the Manhattan Dozen; they included Jeff Bell and John Jones of ACU, Wayne Thorburn, one of the two leaders of YAP, and both Tom Winter and Allan Ryskind of Human Events. In our judgment the meeting was a success. Of the conservative "planks" which had been set down, Chuck Colson answered the majority of domestic questions to their satisfaction; and indicated that the "thrust" of the Defense Budget coming up would be clearly in the directions that many of us inside, as well as the Conservatives outside, would like to see.

The President's veto of Child Development, the nature of that vote, clearly established our credibility with the Conservatives, and set a positive framework for discussions.

As a consequence of those five hours, the following:

1. The conservatives agreed to talk to Ashbrook and try to convince the rest of the Twelve that this week Ashbrook—when he makes his promised statement—should state that he needs far more time to think over the requirements and complexities of a primary run, and will make a final decision at a press conference "before the First of January."

2. The conservatives agreed, after considerable debate, that Ashbrook—in light of the day care veto—would not "move his candidacy forward" this week—if the five conservatives could prevail on the others. They agreed that the best approach would be not to give a "go signal" at this point. They agreed further that Ashbrook's New Hampshire effort should take no public forward steps—and that the conservatives themselves should make no subrosa efforts, except those currently essential to Ashbrook's running—should that decision come before the First of January.

3. What the conservatives are looking for is a) Signals of intention to move in the domestic direction, which we indicated the President was moving and most specifically b) Solid evidence that the new Defense Budget will be what we indicated it would be—i.e., "thrusting" in the direction of stronger defense posture for U.S., especially in the strategic sector which is their most immediate and direct concern.

4. They will get back to me to indicate whether or not the objective conditions in New Hampshire (i.e., time needed for petitions and lining up delegates) permits them to hold back any public action until the last minute; which as of now we agreed should be as close as possible to the first of the year.

My reading of them is this:

There is a disposition among most of them there (especially the Human Events people) not to run anyone against the President if they can possibly do that. What they are interested in is some policy direction changes—not in a primary challenge. If we can come through on the Defense side, and can send some public signals, then my view is that Colson, Buchanan and Keene have convinced this group that <u>not to run</u> is the best possible course for the future effectiveness of the conservative movement.

We indicated that the leverage of conservatives within the White House and the Administration would not be enhanced by an Ashbrook candidacy; it could well nigh be terminated; further that any open public moves right now toward candidacy would not lead toward the objectives they want within the Administration. Rather such a course would induce a "To hell with the Kooks" attitude in the White House, which would militate against the very objectives they pursue. In my judgment, again, we persuaded the majority of those present of the wisdom of this course—and they will attempt to so persuade the balance of their delegation.

However, if we cannot deliver anything of substance on the Defense Budget—despite the doubts of some of them about this course of action—they will gear up a campaign against the President in New Hampshire and elsewhere. Whether or not they want to go against the President, and many of them like Bartleby's Scrivener "would prefer not to," they will have to; indeed they have to go to vindicate their threat, if nothing is forthcoming. . . .

In my judgment we should immediately send out a signal to them. . . .

1. Appointment of a strong security man like John Foster to the empty Packard post as Assistant Secretary of Defense.

2. Public announcement by a high Administration official, that, given some of the abuses to which the Legal Services Corporation—in legislation—was

being opened we intend now to "ask for a Governors's veto" of all legal services programs. We could argue this on the grounds: a) majority of Governors are Democratic; and for Congress to be against this provision implies a lack of trust in their own state leaders b) the possibility of abuses which could injure the program's effectiveness and diminish its support are so rife, that a veto now seems essential.

Finally that, considering the principle of accountability we believe that any such controversial program as Legal Services should win the support of a Governor of a State, as, after all he is the highest elected official of that state, and the one who must necessarily be responsive to the people. This is democratic principle; this is the essence of majority rule.

Last point: Methinks the groundwork, at this point in time, has been ploughed to abort the Ashbrook candidacy. There are "hawks" among the conservatives . . . who would like to "go" under any conditions. But if we can produce something tangible in the Defense Budget (reportedly Goldwater has already been given such assurances) then we can abort this candidacy before it is born. In my view that is surely in the President's long-term interest. If the Far Right of our party goes charging off in New Hampshire, and is humiliated and routed, a good many people will be embittered; wounds will have been opened within the party which may not have healed in time for November when we need everyone.

On the other hand, if we can provide these assurances on defense, I think perhaps we can program Ashbrook in the end of December to give a ringing endorsement to the President, and to call on all conservatives everywhere to maintain his principles, build for the future, and work out their problems within the framework of a Nixon Presidency, which is the most effective vehicle for the kind of changes we want. If Ashbrook used the occasion for a "let's get aboard speech" instead of an announced candidacy, it would truly help us in resolving our difficulties with the Right—and unite the party for an election where we are going to have to be united. [43]

32. Memo to Richard Nixon, December 15, 1971

Recommend against a veto of the Welfare Reform Bill which the President has been sent by the voice votes on Capitol Hill.

a) If the President should veto this measure he will be portrayed, with some justification, as "soft on work requirements" and we will be vulnerable on perhaps the most sensitive of domestic national issues.

b) Why veto this measure when it precisely accords with the President's "workfare" requirements. They have tailored their bill, quite apparently, to RN specifications, to test if the President really means what he says when he says,

"My objective is to get people off of welfare rolls and onto pay rolls in these United States." That specifically is what this bill is designed to do, and if the President does not sign it, we will be vulnerable to criticism from the Democratic Right, while one can be sure the Democratic Left will not stand up and praise the President.

c) We can argue that this is only "half a loaf" but "half a loaf" is better than nothing at this point.

d) This message presents a golden opportunity for the President to issue a major signing message, which would assume credit for all the tough, work-requirement elements of this legislation. We could claim credit for them and take what is clearly the popular side of the welfare reform question.

The President's problems in his own party have been since even the 1970 election, the appearance that he has been behind some welfare giveaway program. Here is the opportunity—in a signing message—to make it crystal clear that the President, while still favoring "helping those who cannot help themselves" yet believes that "any job is better than welfare."

e) A Presidential veto of this thing would please no one but the Welfare Lobby; it would be a veto of something the President himself has loudly proposed and talked about as "workfare". It would do us no good, only harm politically; would make the President vulnerable to attack as being against putting "able-bodied welfare types to work." On the other hand, Presidential seizure of this measure could be used to great advantage for the President politically with the majority of Americans who are in favor of tough work rules; it could help dismiss the impression that RN is "soft" on work requirements; it could help resolve many of our political problems within our own constituency; it would be politically inexpensive, as Congress has done it—we could take the credit. A veto of this would destroy much of the good done by the "honey of a veto" of Child Development.[44]

33. Memo to H. R. Haldeman and Charles Colson, January 14, 1972

If there is one way the President can manage to lose the support of his strongest right arm in the conservative community, Senator Goldwater, it is to "honor" the man Goldwater considers "personally obnoxious" and responsible for the decline of American defense—Robert McNamara. And apparently the President, or the Administration, has done precisely that in raising no objection to his reappointment for five years as President of the World Bank. Here is one of the cushiest jobs on earth, and we appear to have rolled over and allowed reappointment of the "bête noir" of the Senate Republicans, an Eastern Establishment Liberal to his eye teeth. I find it next to impossible to discern any political reason at all why we did not fight to have one of the President's own appointed to this post. With decisions like this, we are making it impossible for a lot of people to be enthusiastic about the re-election of Richard Nixon. [45]

34. Memo to John Mitchell and H. R. Haldeman, February 15, 1972

According to the <u>Washington Post</u> this morning, . . . "The good news is that, at least for the time being, President Nixon has declined to support the growing movement for a constitutional amendment on this subject (bussing) in Congress." That may be good news to the <u>Post</u>—but it is bad news for the President if that word gets out. We are seen, from last week's moves, which have been most helpful, as moving toward a constitutional amendment. Given the crucial nature of this issue, if that is not the case, millions of pro-Nixon people are in for a surprise and shock.

The problem, or one of them, comes from the fact that without the Attorney General's presence on the Cabinet Committee that is to study this constitutional amendment question, it is seemingly stacked against such an amendment. With the Vice President and Attorney General out, to my knowledge, the committee is run by George Shultz with Richardson the second highest figure and Len Garment and Ed Morgan doing the staff work.

If this committee should come down against the constitutional amendment— with [Senator] Scoop Jackson already in favor, and others leaning heavily in that direction—the President will have a grave political problem.

This thing is moving, and moving rapidly, and if we are sliding in the other direction or even standing still—the President could find himself with a number of liberal Democrats supporting a constitutional amendment—and the President thinking the matter over and consulting with his staff.

If the President is flanked on bussing, if he is seen as being dragged reluctantly into supporting an amendment that others have already supported, if he is even late—with other Democrats like Jackson leading him into supporting this—then we may have thrown away one of the major political advantages the President has had—not just in the South, but all over the country where this is the gut issue. These fellows at the <u>Post</u> who are applauding our hesitancy in endorsing a constitutional amendment, I am sure, will be laughing all the way to the Muskie Inaugural. [46]

35. Memo to Richard Nixon, April 3, 1972

Understand the President is giving final consideration to the question of going to the [National Catholic Educational Association] Convention in Philadelphia. Strongly recommend that he do so—and make good on the pledge made six months ago, when RN said, "You can count on our support."

1. We have a commitment, the fulfillment of which means dramatic inroads into that one massive body of Democrats where Republicans can expect to make permanent gains. A backing off, or failure to fulfill this commitment, means disillusionment and disappointment, where we have built up hopes—and inevitable political losses. HHH has already indicated he will make aid to nonpublic schools an issue. This is where we can co-opt the Democratic support with their Catholics, and force them to choose between their lower-income Catholics and their liberal support.

2. It puts the President on the right side of the "tax relief" issue for working-class Americans—an issue being made by every politician in Wisconsin, one that will become a major issue in this campaign. The old GOP argument of cutting taxes instead of increasing spending has now caught the imagination of the entire country—and the Democrats are starting to run away with what was our issue, leaving us with welfare reform, revenue sharing, environment—while they are talking about reducing the tax burden of the working man.

3. A billion and a half in tax credits to Catholic schools is one hell of a lot better investment than another billion and a half into the interior schools. The latter—for whatever reason—are bottomless ratholes—in the last two decades, spending in these schools has probably increased 500 percent, while the quality of education there has gone down. On the other hand, Catholic schools have survived even without public support, even when their continuance means that working-class people have to "double tax" themselves to make them work. When half the public school bond issues are going down the tubes, Catholic parents are still paying through the nose to their schools. Here is an investment in something that works, that succeeds—here is a long-needed break for working people—white—not simply the blacks.

There is a legitimate grievance in my view of white working-class people that every time, on every issue, that the black militants loud-mouth it, we come up with more money, whether for their colleges, for civil rights enforcement, for ghetto schools, for new appointments. The time has come to say—we have done enough for the poor blacks; right now we want to give some relief for working-class ethnics and Catholics—and make an unabashed appeal to these patient working people, who always get the short end of the stick. If we can give fifty Phantoms to the Jews and a multi-billion dollar welfare program for the blacks—neither of whom is ever going to thank this President—why not help the Catholics save their collapsing school system.

4. Strongly recommend the President go to Philly and tell them the un-varnished truth—and that is their fight—they have Richard M. Nixon as an ally—and that this year we are going to Congress to get tax credits to save their school system.

So, HEW opposes this view. HEW's view was not ours when we were elected; it is not representative of the President's philosophy and it is—below the top level—not much interested in his re-election.

Let's do something for our friends and our potential friends this time.[47]

5   The 1972 Campaign
Primary Challengers

Incumbent presidents have structural and institutional advantages during their re-election campaigns, though winning a second term is no guarantee. Richard Nixon's challenge in 1972 was to build on his voting coalition from 1968 when he had narrowly won the popular vote against Hubert Humphrey and George Wallace. Many Nixon advisors, as well as political pundits at the time, believed that a Republican majority was emerging and that "Nixon's reelection strategy depended on increasing his natural constituency," including voters who were "unyoung, unpoor, and unblack."[1] Nixon also worried that since Republicans were the minority party (fewer registered Republicans than Democrats nationally, and Democrats holding the majority in both houses of Congress), and after so many Republican defeats in the 1970 midterm elections, a strong Democratic candidate could lead to his defeat.

Immediately after the 1970 midterm elections, Pat Buchanan thoroughly analyzed for Nixon why Republicans had not performed better in preparation for the 1972 presidential campaign. By early 1971, Buchanan and other White House advisors began assessing several potential Democratic nominees to ascertain who might pose the biggest threat to Nixon's reelection. Specifically, in May 1971, Buchanan was assigned the task of putting together the "opposition research" effort for Democratic candidates.[2] Senator Ted Kennedy of Massachusetts was high on that list, though he announced in 1971 that he would not run (but the possibility of him making an eleventh-hour bid at the 1972 Democratic National Convention remained). According to Buchanan, "The Democratic candidate about whom the White House was most apprehensive as 1972 approached was Ed Muskie."[3] A senator from Maine and Humphrey's running mate in 1968, Muskie's popularity and mainstream Democratic positions gave him an early edge in polling in a crowded primary field of fifteen candidates. Other notable contenders on the White House radar included Humphrey, whose surge in the polls in the final weeks of the 1968 campaign were on the minds of Nixon advisors, as well as Wallace, with whom Nixon had competed for support among conservative voters in 1968. Throughout the prenomination period, Nixon advisors paid little attention to George McGovern, the South Dakota senator who would eventually win the nomination after both Muskie and Humphrey faltered in the primaries, and Wallace withdrew from the campaign after he was shot in May 1972; the incident left him paralyzed from the waist down.[4]

The potential Democratic nominee was not the only concern for Nixon, who also worried about Republican challengers, on both the right and the left, for the nomination. On the right, Rep. John Ashbrook of Ohio ran against Nixon in the New Hampshire, Florida, and California Republican primaries, receiving between 9 and 10 percent in each contest. A prominent conservative, Ashbrook had supported Nixon in 1968, but broke publicly with the president in late 1971 over what he called Nixon's repackaging of New Deal policies such as budget deficits and wage and price controls, as well as foreign policy moves such as Nixon's plan to establish U.S. relations with China. Ashbrook adopted the campaign slogan "No Left Turn" and considered his challenge of Nixon a "rallying point" for conservative Republicans. He would eventually drop out of the race after the California primary and endorse Nixon.[5] On the left, Rep. Pete McCloskey of California also challenged Nixon on an anti–Vietnam War platform. While McCloskey would win nearly 20 percent of the vote in the New Hampshire primary, he would eventually earn only one delegate to the Republican National Convention.[6]

1. Memo to Richard Nixon, November 18, 1970

In 1970, Nixon and Vice President Spiro Agnew campaigned extensively for Republican congressional candidates, urging voters to reject the protest politics on the left. While Republicans gained two seats in the U.S. Senate, along with James L. Buckley winning as a member of the Conservative Party of New York, Democrats gained twelve seats in the U.S. House of Representatives.

(1) The President already has my analysis of the election results. Would reiterate several points.

First, where our operation was far ahead of the field in assessing the impact of the mass media in the 1968 elections—in the length and intensity of the 1970 campaign we did not take into proper account the enormously enhanced power the Vice President, but especially the President have to dominate the media as incumbents. In past years, it took weeks and months to hammer home a single issue. The same can now be accomplished in days. The 1972 campaign should be thought out on the same kind of basis the President thought out his entire 1966–1968 political profile. <u>Now is our time for a "political moratorium." Further, the fall campaign of 1972 should be so constituted as to emphasize various and changing themes</u>, saving the strongest pitch for possibly the last week (or two). We should not underestimate our ability to make a case, our ability to focus national attention on a single theme, or the capacity of the public for being turned off by "overkill."

Second, reexamine the instruments of campaigning. Frankly, to what degree, if any, does campaigning enhance an incumbent's stature in the public mind?

Is a rally with a cheering crowd and an effective cheer line by the President on night TV as good a forum for taking RN's case to the country as a nine p.m. press conference telling the nation why RN needs these men? Will the nation respond in better political terms to Nixon the campaigner or to Nixon the President making his campaign speeches quietly and forcefully in prime time from the Oval Office? Has the day of the front-porch campaign—or its modern counterpart—returned?

If I were to make a shotgun judgment now as to what kind of campaign the President should run in 1972—I would recommend that he wrap himself in the trappings of his office—give once a week major addresses on nationwide television at night—and make not more than a handful of separate campaign appearances at noon to show the nation, via networks, the President has the confidence of the people in the provinces—he is their man.

But the President clearly needs an intensive analysis on the effects of campaigning per se. The team we have put together is by general judgments the best campaign team in history. Even our media adversaries say they wish we could run the government as well as we can run a campaign. The danger that lurks is that we shall become so enamored of our success at managing the techniques of campaigning, 1968 style, that we may lose sight of the fact that they may now be irrelevant—or worse, counter-productive—for a sitting President in 1972.

Third, there are states such as Illinois, Wisconsin, Ohio, and Florida, essential to victory in 1972, where the Party has been mangled. We have to begin now to move to resolve differences and bring these parties together, or else begin almost at once organizing our own political machinery for the elections of 1972. John Sears told me that if the President were interested, he would draft a political memorandum with his thoughts on what should be done now and in the coming year, both on an organization basis and a strategy basis with regard to downgrading Muskie, and perhaps building up Humphrey as our opponent, on countering Wallace and strengthening our political machinery in the swing states. If the President is interested—I will tell him to move on it right away.

(2) Posture of the President through 1970 and into 1971

The immediate necessity is to put politics and the campaign of 1970 behind us. Nothing we can do or say further is going to alter judgments, already made, about whether or not 1970 was a success or a failure. Our case has been presented—the other side has presented its version of the results—and the commentators and columnists have by and large already staked out their positions. Anything more is overkill.

This is consistent with my strong view that the time for Nixon the politician campaigning for his party is over—the time is now for the President to represent himself to the nation as the elected President of the American people—above the political wars now certain to ensue within the Democratic Party.

Through its gross distortion of the kind of campaign the President conducted, the media has driven home the impression of Nixon the partisan of the United States. We must not play into their hands with top-level White House discussions of the campaign of 1970 or the prospects for 1972 in either party. We must get back exclusively to the business of governing and leading the nation.

The election-eve impression left of RN the strident partisan—and Muskie the national conciliator—can be reversed in a matter of weeks. My strong recommendation is that at the President's first press conference, following the election—which will be a bear-baiting exercise—he demonstrate humor, a relaxed attitude, exude confidence—and speak in terms of politics being behind us and now moving forward to work together on the nation's business at hand. Speak of the national need—in calm reasoned terms—for what the President has requested for the defense of friendly nations; speak of the need for action in areas where action has been delayed and people have unnecessarily suffered for that delay. (Unless I hear otherwise, this would be the kind of mood I would try to put into the Q. and A. for the next appearance.)

(With regard to Muskie, he suffers from the fact that he is not considered an outspoken leader by the ideological wing of his party—he is likely, as McGovern is doing now, to begin taking potshots at us, which will be clearly political. We ought to simply dismiss them as political—not engage in head-to-head—and let him go about destroying his media image by himself, which he may well be forced to do to win the hearts of the ideologues that dominate the left wing of his party.)

Looking at further horizons, I see a need for the President to move back toward the role of national reconciliatory—symbolic gestures toward the black majority should be made (not to win votes; we can't) but to indicate to the great middle that the President is attempting to answer the crucial needs of the entire nation—none excluded.

We also need to have something positive and appealing for the working people of this country in the way of tangible major domestic programs. Since in any choice between a counterfeit liberal and the real McCoy, the country will take the real McCoy—we ought to have some domestic initiatives of our own—with the Nixon brand clearly on them. Regrettably, we are now pouring billions into programs like OEO, Model Cities, Urban Renewal, etc. for which we get no credit whatsoever.

My thought would have been to terminate or diminish as many of their programs as possible in order to shift the considerable amount of dollars into Nixon programs—which would have a visible impact by 1972. . . . To put together a new majority in American politics, we are going to have to provide the working men and women, white and blue collar, with more than rhetoric; we have to bring home the bacon, whether in the form of parochaid, or what.

Finally, to counter the impression being pushed by the media that this is an Administration concerned only with cold statistics, an Administration long on public relations gimmickry and short on substance and vision—I feel the President should seek out occasions to demonstrate "humanity" and "heart"—spontaneous occasions, not planned meetings to demonstrate a symbolic affinity with and concern for the unemployed and the less fortunate.

The old Republican nemesis is the national image of the party of the bankers, party of business, the party that doesn't really give a damn about people. The Democrats are going to use this in 1972 as they have in every election since 1932—and we need to consciously consider words, deeds, symbolic acts that will give the lie to this charge before it is made by the National Democratic Party in earnest.

(3) Recommended Changes in Relations with the Media
The networks are not with us. NBC is openly hostile. The national press is in an ugly mood—over both the lack of press conferences, and the feeling that we are B.S.ing them about the election returns. Given their natural affinity for a political fight, given their ideological pre-disposition, given their normal enthusiasm for the challenger, the underdog—our situation here is not good.

On the plus side, it has never really been that good—the hostility of the liberal media was always one element we had to consider. What to do?

We are never going to be loved by the national press corps—that is a given fact. Any transparent attempts to become buddies will fool no one; will succeed nowhere. What our specific focuses should be, I believe, are these:

(a) Go over the heads of the national press to the nation on more televised press conferences. Where we run into a problem of over-exposure, do them in the morning or at noon. Have the national press in for more of the Presidential, non-televised press conferences. These carry risks—but this instrument is among our most effective; we are extremely good at it; invariably the President scores with the people, if not with the press.

(b) While our differences with the national media remain irreconcilable we should take the initiative to ease tensions a bit. While there is much psychologically satisfying in roasting them with regularity, there is not much political profit to this. We have garnered much of that already. If we intend to take them on—and hard—we ought to first re-establish good relations, and wait until the fall of 1972.

Any future attacks on the media should be rifle shots—at NBC for a specific abuse—and not be perceived in such a way as that we are roasting the entire corps. This tends to leave some of them so browned off they make a special effort to gut us at every opportunity.

Our best hope for a fair shake lies now with the Reasoner-Smith team at ABC. We ought to give them our best leaks—provide them with the best breaks. If we have to pick one network to do some major special on—clearly it should be this one.

In attacking and supporting, we should, as mentioned above, be selective—a Herb Kaplow who will do something fair for us on the worst network should not be slighted—while Chancellors and Vanocurs should get nothing. And if we move on the attack, it should similarly be selective.

(4) Use of the Vice President and the Cabinet

Like the President—but to a far greater degree—the Vice President should shift over from the political offensive to the policy offensive. The time for combativeness, for political in-fighting, is clearly over for now. In my view, the Vice President should be given a good slice of the domestic franchise to oversee, an issue or issues, a program or programs, to demonstrate the other side of the man—the capable and competent executive working to get things done. His role as the President's Terrible Swift Sword should be minimized; he should be used in this assignment only when necessary; the President should utilize Cabinet Members and White House Staffers with good liberal credentials to start carrying the fight. They have capital in the bank to do it; the Vice President needs to replenish the capital.

The Vice President makes an effective low-key presentation on television; when he is provided a new franchise, he should take to the networks to argue his case. He should be shown fighting for something—not just against somebody. It would enhance his stature if he were given a foreign assignment of some duration—this would broaden his image with the public; he might well make a campus appearance or appearances; he might well make a surprise visit for a Q. and A. session with black leaders; he should be given the opportunity to demonstrate his abilities other than as simply campaigner; he should be provided the opportunity to show the many other facets to his personality other than fierce partisan.

The Veep is the most loyal of the President's soldiers; he took more wounds and scored more direct hits in the campaign than any other of the President's men—this was his job. But, to continue to do that job effectively, he needs to retire temporarily as a political gladiator to show the nation that he is something other than the War Lover of American Politics.

Whenever there is a new program to be announced that the President is not going to announce—the Vice President should be the one before the cameras. Whenever RN is about ready to let something go of significance in the domestic arena—the Vice President might well be the one who gets the headlines by giving an inkling of the new progressive direction of the Administration.

(The Cabinet)
Unless specifically asked, I would feel it presumptuous to recommend changes in the President's highest appointed body. But my views briefly are these: The President's commitment to clean up the Department of State has manifestly not been carried out by those given the franchise—the career service historically hostile to the President has too many positions of power—and we are going to suffer damaging leaks in the 1972 campaign unless we do something about it. The Secretary of the Interior does this President no good and a great deal of harm with his transparent attempts to ingratiate himself with the liberal media. While I continue to admire Secretary Romney's tenacity and guts, he is a committed believer in the compulsory integration of American society to solve the race problem. My feeling is that this is socially dangerous at this time and politically disastrous—and we spend too damn much time and effort trying to change people's minds to change their policy to accord with the President. We might attempt changing the men rather than the minds. Finally, in the area of the economy, a mortal danger for 1972, we need a man at Treasury who can articulate the President's policies, a staunch loyalist, who has both credentials and capability in the economic and political areas.

(5) Relations with Congress
With regard to the regular Republicans, we are still in good shape. As for the "Baker's dozen," they are going to make their own decisions as to what to do—depending on their own political hides; they care as little about ours as we do about theirs. For example, Hatfield—a True Believer—can be expected to depart little from his former path. Percy, the Opportunist, who is up in 1972, is already making friendly noises. My view is that we ought not to wage war with them—but to treat them in accord with the degree of support they give us—and not

lean upon them. Where we can find areas of agreement, exploit them and see if we can convince them—in their and the party's interests. . . .

As for the Democrats, as one of our aides put it, we are going to be "walking through a vat of acid" for the next two years. In the Senate—half a dozen have their eye on the President—and all their decisions, actions, statements, attacks and support are going to be on that basis. There is nothing at all we are going to be able to do with them. We should have our Cabinet and White House staffers programmed to answer their charges—to deal with them on the political warfare level.

As for our own Congressional Relations—in my view Bill Timmons is not only absolutely loyal—but also the most hardworking of the President's men in the least enviable of Presidential assignments. I think he needs more manpower over there; I think he needs more visible identification as the President's man for Congressional relations; I think he needs more access to the President himself and his inner councils; I think he needs to be given more credibility for his job on the Hill—by the President's visible demonstration that he is our man on Capitol Hill.

Finally, the President should place the onus for starting the political war on the Democratic Party in Congress—by letting them fire the first few shots. Perhaps, when this Congress fails to act, as it will, and goes home for Christmas—the President could, more in sorrow than anger, go on the nation's networks or lead off a press conference with a doleful recounting of its failures to act in the national interest—and the President's hopes that the new Congress will serve the nation a little better.

(6) Presidential Travel
Abroad: The exigencies of foreign policy will dictate if the President must go abroad to advance the national interest. From the standpoint of RN's political posture, I strongly recommend against any "Grand Tour" trips ala the recent sojourn to Europe and the Mediterranean. The President is generally conceded high marks for his handling of foreign policy. The nation via television has already seen the President moving through countless cheering throngs abroad. Repeat performances will be redundant; they will be written off in the media— as the last trip was by some traveling reporters—as politically motivated. We have drawn down our balance in this account—there is not much capital left in foreign visits over the next six months. Lest we be charged, as we have been charged, of going abroad in search of crowds while the gnawing domestic problems remain unsolved, I recommend against. Also, by not going abroad in the

near future, the President will have positioned himself well for a major foreign visit in early or mid-1972—when it would be perceived as something of a far greater interest, and when it could more effectively underscore the President's successes overseas in time for the 1972 elections.

At Home: Consistent with the view that the President must put the partisan image back of himself, reflect the "humanity and heart" of the Administration, reassume the posture of President of all the American people, I would recommend spontaneous visits, stop-offs to areas of social depression in the country— whether of unemployed whites or rural blacks.

Because of the appreciable amount of negative reportage we are receiving for "staging" events—these would necessarily have to be truly spontaneous; symbolic of the President's personal concerns for the people he leads. Democrats have consistently been superior to Republicans with this sort of communication—and given our party's hereditary image as the Party of Big Business—this is a woeful weakness. Such visits will also blunt the inevitable charge of the 1972 elections that Republicans are concerned only with cold statistics like 5.5 percent unemployment—that the President doesn't give a damn about poor people.

Similarly, however, as the nation has seen the President in cheering throngs abroad—so also, from the campaign, has it seen streets lined with cheering people at home. Though the motorcading through the crowds may serve as a rejoinder to any contention the President is not popular with the people—it also would seem redundant in the aftermath of the election.

(7) Final Points

First, we are getting some nasty criticism for having exploited the San Jose incident, and for alleged being an Administration more interested in image than substance—long on P.R. and short on accomplishment.[7] If pressed, this attack could be very damaging and I recommend we consider drawing in our horns on the P.R. operation side of things. The nation is one that is very keen to and very down on P.R.—and the last thing we want in the world is to have the press start picking up the McGinniss theme of hucksterism.[8] We should have a high level review of the effectiveness—or again the word comes to mind, the possible "overkill" of this side of the operation. At all cost we should avoid any tarnishing of the President's image as President in the minds of the people—and these attacks bother me.

Finally, at all costs we must avoid, in the wake of the election, and in the pressure the President is assuredly getting from the left, any kind of transparent public move to the left. This damaged us after Kent State and such would now be tacit admission the Restons and Sideys were right and we were wrong on the campaign. It would be disheartening to the bulk of our support. Rather than any left or right move it should be a forward move away from the partisan role of the campaign toward full-time President again. [9]

2. Memo to Richard Nixon, "The Muskie Watch," March 24, 1971

In March 1971, Nixon directed Buchanan to "do an in-depth analyses of all potential candidates he might face in 1972 and to lay out the strategies for combating each of them."[10]

From the Evans-Novak Newsletter:

"<u>Muskie: He has been deliberately lying low, which is smart politics except when carried too far.</u> Instead of traveling to Nigeria, he might have done better to go to New York, to California, and Texas where HHH has been making inroads with Establishment Democrats. Still, Muskie remains by far the strongest possible candidate against Nixon, according to the Quayle Poll trial heats: Muskie 48%; Nixon 42%; Wallace 10% compared to last month's Muskie 46%; Nixon 44%; Wallace 10%."

Mr. Muskie seems to have recognized the political peril of his high visibility strategy of December and January—and revised it. The highly publicized trips to California and Moscow—with the press pack aboard—have been discontinued. They did little to strengthen him, and exposed not a few weaknesses in personality, in foreign policy. He seems to have arrived separately at the same conclusion, and his profile is now perceptibly lower than it was in the first months of the year.

However, if Muskie does not come out into the open again, <u>if he stays in relative hibernation, it is difficult to see what it is that is going to diminish his standing in the polls on which he now depends.</u> The country has a good impression of him; he presents to millions an attractive alternative; he is not the subject of the kind of attacks which would force a response.

Should he maintain his present posture, more or less, for eight months, he will enter the primaries relatively unscathed, and as Brothers Evans-Novak write:

"If Muskie does win most of the primaries, he will be nominated with ease on the first ballot. If Muskie does not win, he will not even be a factor at the convention."

And if Mr. Muskie is not cut and bleeding before he goes into New Hampshire, he will very likely do massively well there, building up irresistible momentum for the nomination. This scenario is not in our interest—as Muskie today is a figure ideally situated to unite the warring factions of his party, and if they are united that is bad news for us.

Our interests thus dictate smoking him out now and keeping him out in front as long as we can. His performance to date when out front does not argue well for his capacity to survive the kind of pressures and harassments that go with being front runner, pressures and harassments he is not getting today.

One recalls that Nelson Rockefeller had phenomenal ratings in the Gallup and Harris polls by the end of 1967—so long as he stayed in Albany. When he emerged, half the nation said, "Hey, it's him again," and his ineffectual active campaigning actually cost him votes from the time it began until Miami, when we finally surpassed him in the Gallup Poll. The same was true of Goldwater. As Mr. Conservative, unknown to the country, he was an enormous distraction; as Barry Goldwater, campaigning in New Hampshire, he was a disaster. Both he and Rocky dropped in the polls from the beginning to the end of the New Hampshire Primary.

The more specific stands a political figure takes—on divisive issues—the more people he alienates. This is as true for Mr. Muskie as it is for us, and thus he should be forced to take more stands on more controversial issues. The free ride for Big Ed Muskie must be terminated.

It seems not in our interest to let him choose his topics, to wander the land talking about saving our environment, which everyone from Robert Welch to Abby Hoffman supports. It is in our interest—and in the interest of the liberal Democratic challengers for the nomination—to prevent Mr. Muskie's uninterrupted march to the nomination.

The Sears November argument was that we should leave Muskie alone—attack and respond to other Democrats, like HHH, to elevate them. That doesn't seem realistic now, as Muskie is already "elevated." He is already at the top, so far as Gallup and Harris and the Democratic Party are concerned.

There is a danger in going after Muskie, making him the martyr and spokesman of the Democratic Party, and thus insuring his nomination, and even enhancing his chances of election. But the risk should be taken. If we don't do it now, we shall have to play hurry-up football in the two months before election—and people tend to disbelieve political charges made in that kind of partisan environment.

Who should we get to poke the sharp stick into his cave to bring Muskie howling forth? More important, what kind of stick is most effective?

Frankly, Muskie cannot be effectively assaulted from the Right—i.e., he is a Big Spender; he doesn't stand behind the President in time of conflict abroad.

An attack on Muskie from his right, by a Senator Dole or Vice President Agnew, would only rally all Democrats, who are all to the left of us, around him.

The attack then should come between the center and the left of the Democratic Party. It should focus on those issues that divide Democrats, not those that unite Republicans. It should exacerbate and elevate those issues on which Democrats are divided—forcing Muskie to either straddle or come down on one side or the other.

Many such issues come to mind.

THE WAR. Less and less is this an issue dividing Democrats; more and more is it a unifying issue as conservative Democrats begin to adopt a "let's get the hell out" stance. This would explain that it was inexpensive for Muskie and Humphrey to move dovish politically in recent weeks on this issue. The price they are paying for that move is not so great as it once was, and their need to mollify the peacenik Democrats is greater than it has ever been.

THE MUSKIE PERSONALITY. There is fertile ground here. Muskie is short-tempered; he regularly rebuffs reporters who ask hostile questions; he has a reputation, which disturbs him, of being unable to make a decision, to take a stand. Political criticism of Muskie as a Democratic Hamlet with his finger to the wind and his nose in a Gallup Poll would be the kind of attack that would be credited by the Democratic Left. It is their greatest suspicion of Big Ed. Statements by Liberal Republicans such as "At least McGovern has the courage of his convictions, silly though they may be, but who the hell knows where Mr. Muskie stands and what he stands for other than Mrs. Muskie."

THE RACE ISSUE. There are possibilities provided here in that the 1950s Liberal, Abe Ribicoff, has come up with a beautiful "forced integration" program—involving a Federal requirement that every school in the entire metropolitan area have within the student body not more than twice and not less than half the minority population in the entire metropolitan. That of course would necessitate massive bussing of whites into the cities and blacks into the suburbs. We ought to look closely at the details of this legislation, and if it is as radical a piece of "social engineering" as it appears, then the way might be smoothed for its advance; it could be given considerable publicity; and we could denounce it as inconsistent with our principles of freedom of movement—and force Mr. Muskie to take the kind of stand that would either alienate the suburbanites and ethnics who would bear the brunt of this—or appear again as an appeaser of the Right in the eyes of the professional liberals.

REVENUE SHARING. Muskie has stepped in it up to his ankles on this one. His vigorous opposition to RN's program met with silence and disagreement from the mayors and city officials to whom he spoke—most of whom want it and most of whom are Democratic. This ground should be cultivated. Public statements by Democrats, preferably liberal Democrats, calling on Muskie to change his view and lead the Democratic Party in defense of the cities should be made. We can portray this as a "dog-in-the-manger" stance toward urban problems by a Senator, who is playing the reactionary toward a progressive proposal simply because he did not come up with it himself. Moderate and liberal Republicans should be able to find in this matter a political area where they are comfortably supporting the Administration and opposing Muskie, and they should do so publicly.

ABORTION. This is, as we predicted months ago, a rising issue and a gut issue with Catholics. Time this week had a major piece on the rising clerical opposition, not only Catholic. Buckley has called on Catholic Bishops to lead a political offensive up to the point of civil disobedience. It is not unlikely that one of these abortion centers, such as D.C., could be targeted with a bomb—so fiercely do conservative Catholics feel on this matter. The President's stand against the Defense Department should be made public and strong, would be happy to write it. Let us take the far-left losses we would get on this—and then send the ball into Mr. Muskie's Court. After all, he is a Catholic, and one recalls that in liberal, but Catholic, Massachusetts, Senator Edward Kennedy echoes his ultra-liberal Republican opponent on every major issue but one—abortion. He opposed abortion. If the President should publicly take his stand against abortion, as offensive to his own moral principles, while, as President, not interfering with the decision of States; if we should publicly reverse DOD, then we can force Muskie to make the choice between his tens of millions of Catholic supporters and his liberal friends at the New York Times and the Washington Post.

PAROCHAID. Again, this is the big winner for Northeast Republicans, who support it, such as Rockefeller. For while GOPers may be neutral or opposed, it is not life or death to them—while to Democrats, it is a divisive gut issue separating Conservative Catholic Irish and Italians from Do-Gooder, liberal Jewish Democrats who adamantly oppose it. The Supreme Court is moving to decide this issue as it is to decide the abortion issue—and before those decisions come down, we should be on the side of the angels. If the Court decides in favor of liberalized abortion and no Parochaid, then we will have lost two of the gut issues that can make inroads into the Catholic Democrats of the Northeast and Midwest, and Mr. Muskie will have two political problems of some magnitude resolved for him by the Supreme Court. The President has, I understand, the preliminary report of the non-public school task force. Why not make it public with an RN endorsement—let the Catholics know they have a friend in the White House, concerned about their problems. Some Southerners are going to complain, but where will they stand in a showdown between the President and a liberal Democrat. Indeed, should Muskie push too hard against parochaid—to move between us and our Southern friends, he will pay an intolerable political price in loss of support in the Catholic community.

A man is defined by the positions he takes, and Mr. Muskie does well, because his image is fuzzy; people on opposing sides of bitter questions do not know that he is either opposed to one of them or the other. On this matter, we must become the midwives of the people's right to know—if the press does not do the job for us, which it is not doing today.

THE SST. Every worker in Seattle, every union man in the aerospace industry, should be made aware of Mr. Muskie's position on [Supersonic Transport]. He should be targeted as the prime liberal responsible for the cutbacks in defense and space which have cost their jobs. RN should be pictured as the one fighting to save their jobs from Democrats who would put an end to the space program. In the last campaign we took the heat for jobs lost because of cutbacks—cutbacks which the complaining liberal Democrats voted and themselves would have increased.

THE ENVIRONMENT. Mr. Muskie has recognized and moved to solve his political problems here—well before we did. He is traveling the country, holding hearings on the impact of the environment decisions on industry and jobs. He is effectively neutralizing our best issue here—the tactic of telling communities and companies, "if Madman Muskie's environment bill goes through, this industry shuts down and this burg becomes a ghost town." The old scare tactics, on military closings, were used against us to a fare-thee-well last fall—and we should have moved to use this against Muskie. We did not. He seems to be getting well on this—but he remains vulnerable.

A research team should go over what the Muskie original proposal would have required—before any compromises—and then have our party people in the affected areas say publicly that had the Muskie bill gone through, unemployment here would be ten percent. This environmental issue titillates the liberals, but the trade-offs in jobs and income and community recession have not been reckoned and not made public. . . .

THE FORD FOUNDATION. When Whitney Young passed away, one saw a picture of Ed Muskie in the surf with Young, and one learned that they were gathered in Nigeria on a Ford Foundation financed trip. Now, in my research on Ford, this is the third such trip. Muskie was the only Democrat who made both junkets to Japan (some of our Republican friends went also on one) financed by Ford. Certainly some troublesome questions could be raised about Muskie's connection with McGeorge Bundy's giant institution—and are they behind his candidacy. Investigation should be done on this score. This could go hand-in-glove with the Foundation speeches.

THE MUSKIE ADVISERS. Certainly, Harriman and Clifford, two of those responsible for the present situation in Vietnam, have little or no appeal to the young who oppose the war. They are old war horses, who were deeply involved in all the failures of Vietnam. The failures would return to power with Muskie—and Harriman, "who sold Poland down the River," is apparently Muskie's leading candidate for Secretary of State. How would that read on the front page of the Chicago Polish-American?

These are a few of the areas that could be explored. These are some of the issues that can be developed—to the immense discomfort of Mr. Muskie. This has been a hayride for him this far; we cannot rely upon the press to do this work for us. We are going to have to poke Big Ed with some sharp sticks to see how he performs. And from what I have seen, it is not all that remarkable or impressive. He is riding two things right now—his Vice Presidential candidacy in 1968 where an indulgent press slobbered all over him as the great alternative to Spiro T. Agnew—and his televised show the night before the election, which was a good performance but hardly a trial-by-fire.

We ought to go down to the kennels and turn all the dogs loose on Ecology Ed. The President is the only one who should stand clear, while everybody else gets chewed up. The rest of us are expendable commodities, but if the President goes, we all go, and maybe the country with us. My view.

Anyhow, the attacks should not be name-calling—they should be thought out. They should have a specific purpose; they should be designed to injure Mr. Muskie with a specific group where he now has support. They should be framed to force him to howl a bit.

Again, the fellow in his bungled trip to the Soviet Union, in his short temper and testiness, in his botching of revenue sharing—to me he does not seem to have it. The individual who called him the "Romney of the Seventies" may not be too far off the mark.

We will not be, in this enterprise, without allies among the Silent Majority in the Democratic Party in the Senate. Some of them see us as vulnerable; they see the future as the "Democratic Years." I cannot believe they view with any enthusiasm eight years of President Ed Muskie telling them what is good for America. No, I think some of these fellows would not be disappointed to see

Big Ed unhorsed and lying in a ditch by the side of the road. They will shed the same crocodile tears as that splendid little band who put it to his Whipship, Ted Kennedy, in the secret ballot.

My recommendation, then, is for creation of THE MUSKIE WATCH, an operation working perhaps within the Republican National Committee, which may even be a publicized operation, doing constant research on Ed and putting the materials out to the interest groups and to the press. The operation should be tied in with Mort Allin's shop; he can provide a steady stream of all commentary on Muskie. It should be tied in with Colson's shop, which can provide the names of the proper contacts in each community. The group should focus for now exclusively on Muskie and not get bogged down on a dozen other little projects. It seems an interesting idea, one that, if RN approves, the general approach should be tied in with Senator Dole and moved on rapidly.[11]

3. Memo to Richard Nixon, "The Resurrection of Hubert Humphrey," April 19, 1971

In this memo Buchanan analyzes the chances of the 1968 Democratic nominee facing Nixon for a second time in 1972.

One emerges from a perusal of our "Humphrey file" with a grudging regard for Old Hubert. Since November, with but a few notable exceptions, the ex-Veep has conducted himself remarkably well. He receives an excellent press. He has maximized his assets and minimized his deficiencies. The result is that today, unlike six months ago, the man is a serious contender for the Democratic nomination.

Gallup has charted the comeback. The following represents the shift from November to March in <u>Democratic</u> voter sentiment about their preference of nominees.

	1970 November	1971 March
Muskie	33	26
Kennedy	31	25
HHH	16	21

Thus, in four months, Humphrey gained a net of 12 points on Muskie and 11 points on Edward M. Kennedy—a not insignificant advance. One reason is surely that, in this period, it is difficult to find <u>any</u> bad press on Hubert Humphrey. The stories—many of them on women's pages—are invariably straight or favorable.

Following are some reasons for the Humphrey resurgence, which underscore elements of his present strategy, a strategy that appears to be working as well today as that of any man in political life.

Agriculture

First, Humphrey has moved rapidly to fill an issue vacuum—in the farm regions. He had himself named to the Agriculture Committee; has perceived our weakness in this area; has made himself unofficial Democratic champion of rural and farm America—without ignoring the "cities" issue he shares with the Eastern-oriented candidates. Press people tell me HHH promised to stump rural America declaiming that, first, "Mr. Nixon took away your prosperity and now he's trying to take your Department away from you." "I think that'll sell right well out there in farm country." So, HHH has been quoted. Here Humphrey can pick up support in an area others ignore, and is well-positioned to corral rural delegates to the Democratic convention.

The Muskie Decline

Secondly, on analysis, Humphrey's new support is coming directly out of Muskie's hide.

Here is what seems to have happened in four months. McGovern's wild accusations, his far-out positions, have thrilled the Far Left of the Democratic Party, causing McGovern to rise from the infinitesimal two percent to the insignificant five percent. McGovern seems prevented from rising into the teens or twenties at this point, because he <u>is appealing to voters who already have a popular, first-line, left-wing candidate in Edward Kennedy</u>, a candidate who gives them near all the positions McGovern does—at the same time Kennedy offers the realistic hope of winning with those positions—and returning Camelot as well.

But McGovern's candidacy may be having a secondary effect—on the fortunes of Mr. Muskie.

To hold his <u>bridge position</u> in the Democratic Party, Muskie must equivocate on divisive issues; he cannot adopt the Far Left positions and remain viable nationally. McGovern, having no such problem, assumes all these stances and so contrasts himself as decisive and moral and unequivocal. Thus, Muskie fails to "turn people on," and in his glaring publicity as front-runner, this is enervating to this candidacy. And as he goes down in the polls, his supporters, generally centrist Democrats, looking for a winner, drift off to the next best thing—Hubert Humphrey.

<u>Muskie still has broad support among Democrats and Independents, and he</u>

cannot be removed as a factor. But a collapsing Muskie campaign, it seems to me, would lead to an almost inevitable Kennedy-Humphrey, left-center confrontation for the nomination—an altogether satisfactory development.

The Humphrey Positions

Humphrey's attacks on the Administration have been of a scatter-gun nature; he is a single issue man as Kennedy is the health man, and Muskie, the environmentalist. He criticizes the Administration on a much broader front—in essence appealing, with his old politics, to the constituency of the New Deal.

1. As mentioned, he has moved early and hard to become the Democratic champion of the American farmer—a good move, considering there are 37 other candidates contending for champion of the cities, and HHH is among them.

2. He is back on the arms control, missile freeze, "risks for peace" nonsense. While one imagines this would help a bit with the left and the intellectual community, to most people the issue is too complicated to comprehend.

3. He is making prodigious efforts to get well on the Vietnam issue. Having decided there is no more to be gained by a "peace with honor" position, he has all but confessed his sins from the Johnson years, and daily attempts to extricate himself from that record.

4. He is taking a strong pro-Israeli stand, a stand duplicated of course by most Democrats—all of them looking to Jewish money and backing at the convention and, hopefully, in the election.

5. He repeatedly attacks the White House for "public relations gimmickry" and "intimidation of the news media," even though HHH's past quotes show him massively vulnerable on the latter. . . .

6. He is coming down very hard—perhaps hardest of all—on the bread-and-butter issues—the problems in the economy, the unemployed, poor people out of work, etc. This is, again, the old politics, which Mr. Humphrey continues to mix effectively with the new.

The Humphrey Assets

Within the Democratic Party, these are not inconsiderable. He is solid with the blacks, more than acceptable to Big Labor, a friend of the farm bloc; he has party strength in the South and Texas (especially) and California; he remains a "centrist" Democrat; unlike Muskie, he pays his respects to party regulars. Old Democrats from New Deal days have nothing against him. In every publicity encounter with fellow Democrats, he steals the show as he did at the big pie-eating contest on the Hill and the A.S.N.E. session last week. He is ebullient and likeable—very strong with Democratic women. He is a politician of the old hand-shaking, baby-kissing school; not a total disadvantage with many simple people. He came within an eyelash of winning the last time out.

The Humphrey Liabilities

These are very serious. <u>He is a loser, an Old Face</u> whose resurrection has "produced boredom and horror among Democrats, except for some of HHH's big money friends." (Evans and Novak). He is tied up inextricably with LBJ and Vietnam; he remains anathema to the intellectuals and far left of his party, despite his best efforts to heal the wounds. He generates no great excitement of enthusiasm. His nomination would alienate all the "idealistic" McCarthy kids who would have waited four years—and gotten Old Hubert again. His nomination could even produce a fourth party. While he has traveled all over the nation speaking to youth, it is safe to say his nomination would produce ennui among the activist liberal peace groups and disinterest in an RN-HHH election.

<u>By way of a balance sheet then, it seems Humphrey would have a number of the traditional strengths and supports that go automatically to national Democrats—but no more. And he would carry into a general election serious deficiencies—which seem to make him a thoroughly acceptable candidate from our point of view.</u>

The Humphrey Strategy

In December, Humphrey volunteered that Democrats should look over the field in 1971, and by the end of this year, settle upon a candidate, rally about him—and avoid the divisive primaries. This has been, I believe, his sole significant political error since election. Liberal Democrats pounced upon the scheme as wholly out of spirit with the new wide-open convention concept they have been promoting.

But when Humphrey advanced that proposal in December, it would appear that he did not, then, seriously consider himself a potential candidate. For who would have predicted <u>then</u>—including Mr. Humphrey—that HHH could possibly be the national favorite by this next December?

Since then, however, Humphrey's fortunes have risen; he is clearly a potential candidate and sees himself as such.

His strategy seems relatively clear: move about the country, attacking the Nixon Administration on a broad variety of issues; seize all the publicity possible; do the party chores; attack no fellow Democrats; stress one's availability—and wait for events to develop.

Humphrey must, it seems to me, avoid the early primaries. And his derogatory remarks about primaries themselves indicate that he intends just this. Let the other contenders fight it out with one another, the more the merrier, to an indecisive conclusion in the early primaries—and then emerge with broad party acceptance, as the strongest centrist unifying man around, the fellow who came within 500,000 votes, and can now go over the top.

The strategy is working. Humphrey has risen at Muskie's expense; he is now within range of both Kennedy and Muskie—although of the three he continues to run weakest against the President.

Because Muskie is the front-runner, it is Muskie who is up in New Hampshire, being covered by reporters, as he apologizes for his role in Vietnam, and attempts to exonerate himself before the college young. Mr. Humphrey is getting no such intensive, critical coverage from the press. He would be well advised to stay away from the student Q. and A. session—and stick to speeches attacking one shortcoming, speeches which net good coverage and little or no contradiction in the media. Further, so as not to alienate any segment of his party—he should consciously avoid any criticism of other party hopefuls, anticipating in the end that they will thus find him an acceptable if not an exciting alternative. Only if, well down the road, Muskie is running strong out front and needs some chopping would Humphrey have any cause to start laying down policy differences with the front-runner. Right now, he should hang back a bit and let the front-runner Muskie weary himself, setting the pace.

Counter-Strategy

As noted in the "Humphrey Liabilities," his nomination would engender great anguish on the left at a Democratic convention, and might trigger a fourth party—thus, his nomination is not something we should, at this point, look upon with great apprehension. Further, a continued HHH rise in Democratic polls would be helpful—as it would likely come at Muskie's expense, and force Muskie to re-accelerate his timetable, and make the kind of precipitous decisions he is making now—viz., the near unqualified endorsement of the upcoming demonstration.

However, at the same time we want to see Humphrey rise with Democrats, we should be associating him with minority positions that alienate Independent and Conservative Democrats and cannot stand the test of a general election.

The following come to mind:

Catholics. Humphrey does not have the affinity with this primary Democratic bloc that a Muskie or Kennedy might—the latter being co-religionists.

We would thus start with only a minimal handicap with Catholics. Therefore, again, I would argue the President associate himself, publicly, with the report he already has—from his sub-committee on non-public education, headed by Dr. Walton. We have done the abortion thing. But, just today, the Archbishop of Detroit announced the closing of 56 Catholic schools, dropping 23,000 Catholic students into the Michigan public school system. If the President forces this issue with the Democrats, again, it is an issue which divides them down the middle, and only does us minimal damage in my opinion. . . .

Farm Area. Humphrey has the kind of support here, I am confident, that we enjoyed back in 1968—much of it related to a faith in the fellow as one of their own, probably more of it related to an anti-ins feeling among those rural Americans who have not been doing so well as in the past. In any event, these are states on which we depend for our base of support—before even considering the big swing states. If we are hurting in Middle America, we are hurting everywhere. Humphrey obviously feels he has seized a good issue here, both for support at the convention and support in the general, should he win the nomination. This should be a top priority concern of the Administration—yet as Wild Bill Scherle told me, there is really no one in the White House whom farmers and rural America types might conceivably look to as one of their own.

Hard Hats. RN's steps on construction wages, taken for the national interest, were nevertheless politically damaging, according to Scammon who spoke to a conservative group last week. If the demonstrations turn obnoxious this coming weekend and beyond—perhaps we will get back some of these patriotic types. But Buchanan's view is that a meeting between the President and union men connected with aerospace and defense might be highly useful. RN could argue: (a) we have got to end this war honorably and (b) in the present world environment, we cannot let the defense budget go down the tubes. I am doing these things for America. I know you gentlemen feel you can't support me politically, or can't support me on economics in general, but, by God, I am asking for your support on these issues. You have tremendous pull with the Democratic Senators, like Muskie and Humphrey and Kennedy and Jackson. Can you exercise public and private leverage so that they will not cut back on this defense budget and space budget (which incidentally means jobs to union men) and on our commitment to an honorable peace in Vietnam.

A risky venture perhaps.

But it seems there is a natural division between the bell-bottomed ecologists who want to return to nature—and the hard hats whose prosperity depends upon, if you will, the military-industrial complex. Further, if and when the President takes up the defense of his defense budget, he might well argue that it is wrong to indict hundreds of thousands of American workers as a member of some monolithic "military-industrial complex." . . .

Against us, in 1968 and 1970, the Democrats were saying: "If you elect Nixon, you lose your social security; you lose your medicare." Our GOP organizations around the country in the coming campaign ought to be out at McDonnell-Douglas, at Lockheed, at Boeing, with such posters at the plant gate as "If Muskie wins, you lose." "If Humphrey wins, the Defense Budget is lost—start looking for another job election day." In the areas where there is high unemployment, at the Boeing Plant in Seattle, GOP workers should be passing out "Wanted" posters with portraits of Muskie, Kennedy, and HHH, the inscription underneath "Wanted for questioning in connection with the death of the SST." . . .

The Muskie Decline
There is an argument that Muskie is proving himself so ineffectual that we might actually <u>want</u> him as a candidate, and thus ought not to muss him up so badly that he loses the nomination. I can't accept this argument. One recalls that Governor Romney by this point in time was well behind RN among both Republicans and Independents—but he stayed up for fifteen rounds of unexampled punishment. And, though others disagree, I believe that, outside the WH, we should keep the heat on Big Ed. If, then, he does get the nomination, he will be scarred—as to be politically ineffective. If he falls back further, he will yet fight more furiously for it; and the primaries will be no cake walk for anyone and the more brutal the fight within the opposition party, the greater our advantage.

<u>The War</u>
Humphrey is struggling heroically to get well on this issue, to make himself, now, an acceptable alternative to the party's left. The Prodigal Son, however, is not welcome back home—if the New Republic and I. F. Stone are to be believed. A little Machiavelli here might be of use. If the President, who is not revered on the Left, were to publicly express thanks to HHH for the quiet support he has given on Vietnam—HHH is likely to be astonished and stunned, and his left-wing courtship broken off at the spot. Perhaps Dole or the Vice President even might compliment HHH on the "strong support" he has consistently provided for the war in Vietnam.

<u>Integration</u>
True to form, Senator Ribicoff is now maneuvering his compulsory integration plan toward the floor—demanding one and all take a stand on it. <u>We ought</u>

to credit Ribicoff's courage in facing this issue—but come down hard against him—and force Muskie and Humphrey and Kennedy to take a stand on this issue, a forthright stand. Almost certainly they will have to waffle on this one. Again, the issues that divide Democrats must be brought to the public attention, if we are going to prevent the uniting of their party.

Polls

If we could possibly get a poll showing Humphrey taking the lead among Democrats, the "horror" about his re-emergence which E & N detected would rise immediately to the surface, the press would focus on him, and the Democratic Left would start chopping him up, again, advantageous for us in the long run.

LBJ & Riots

Humphrey made a remark about LBJ, "I had a President who was absolutely paranoid about the war," which we should remind him and the country of. Further, Humphrey's statements about possible riots this summer, if some little Federal bureau was shut down, can be used again and twinned with his famous, "I'd lead a mighty good riot" remark. We can depict him as the "Bull Agitator" of the U.S. Senate.

These issues can be aired this weekend in MONDAY [the weekly report from the Republican National Committee], in the sequel to The Muskie Watch. Right now, from our vantage point, it seems to me that "Humphrey's the One."[12]

4. Memo to Richard Nixon, "Primary Strategy," April 29, 1971

Despite some speculation in the news media that a "Dump Nixon" movement would occur in the 1972 Republican primaries, neither Ronald Reagan nor Nelson Rockefeller would challenge Nixon that year for the nomination.

Have given thought to 1972, and preliminary returns indicate to me that RN should:

1. Let Reagan and Rockefeller know early that he, RN, is going after the nomination, that he is not dropping out under any condition, and that RN is going to secure the nomination and run in 1972, and that decision is irrevocable.

WHY: Both Governors are now "positioning" themselves to be the beneficiary of a "Dump Nixon" movement. I don't believe either is promoting or supporting same—but if "Dump Nixon" should succeed, then either Rockefeller or Reagan would become the nominee; and right now, they would be foolish not to alert their staff to the long-shot possibility that in 1972, the nomination may be open.

If, however, the President makes it known to both, in no uncertain terms, that regardless of the left-right division in the party, regardless of the blood spilled—he is going after and taking that nomination—then the interest of both Governors becomes to help make sure the President wins.

In short, for either Governor to have a distant chance at the nomination—the President must voluntarily pull out. If the President goes for it, he has it, regardless of what happens in a few Eastern Primaries. So, if they know for certain RN is going for it—they are more likely to forget any lingering hopes.

2. The President's name should be on the ballot in the early contested primaries—not some stand-in.

WHY: The President would run stronger for himself than any other stand-in, and if a McCloskey ran well against a stand-in or beat him in, say, Rhode Island, or New Hampshire, the press will treat it as if the stand-in had beaten the President anyhow.

Secondly, by using the President's name in the early primaries—there are a good deal more of them—we can blunt any momentum built up in, say, Rhode Island by McCloskey—by whipping him soundly in North Carolina, in Indiana, in Nebraska, in Florida, etc. This way—even if McCloskey gets some initial momentum, we can give the country the appearance that the President has now stepped out, taken this challenge, and then smashed it in one primary state after another.

Further, because we have money, resources and organization, and they do not, we should take on McCloskey in not simply one or two primaries—but whip him in one primary after another by triumphal margins. Force him to spread his limited resources. Thus, we could turn McCloskey's candidacy to our advantage by showing the President—a la 1968—the unmistakable choice of his party for President of the United States and provide us in passing some good media from the string of victories run up.

Third, if we duck the primary challenge, we will open ourselves to all manner of negative media about seeking a "bossed" convention, about refusing to go to the people, etc.

ALTERNATIVE STRATEGY: There might be some merit in—after in-depth polls—using a stand-in only in one or two states where the polls show the President running very weak, and where McCloskey might do very well. If we did that and McCloskey did well, we could point to the other primaries where the President himself was entered and was undefeated, untried and un-scored upon. But this might be too clever by half.

3. The President should not rule out two or three appearances in major primary states—in which he is entered. I am not sure what benefits accrue from

saying, "Well, we never visited that state," as compared with the disadvantages if we do not do well. I do not argue for a stump speech—but an appearance or two, and a Presidential address in New Hampshire I would not rule out. ("He cared enough to come.")

4. The above early primary strategy argues strongly that we send top-flight political operatives <u>now</u> into the early primary states, that we do not wait—especially on states like N.H., where the media is already focusing. If we wait too long, we will have to set our organizational machinery right in the hot light of national publicity.

Others have surely thought this through also. I am not averse to them seeing it and knocking down the arguments—but if they share these views, then we might well be moving on the Primary Road.[13]

5. Memo to Richard Nixon, "EMK—Political Memorandum," June 9, 1971

While he never officially declared his candidacy in 1972, Edward M. "Ted" Kennedy remained a concern for the Nixon White House.

A careful analysis of news clippings of recent weeks, coupled with reports of recent days, removes, I think, vestigial doubts that <u>EMK is running actively for the Presidency</u>.

<u>Items</u>:

Last night on the Elizabeth Drew show, Kennedy pointedly refused to issue any Sherman statements. In April, for the first time, he stated, "I am keeping my mind open" about the nomination. ABC finds that he has written to former top aides indicating he is assessing the situation. Humphrey thinks he is a potential active candidate, as does Muskie. Daley, according to HHH, is "strong for Teddy." Riesel claims nearly all the top AFL-CIO types, excepting Meany, are holding back, waiting for Teddy; the same is true of many political pros around the country, according to Jerry Greene. Andrew Tully said a month or more ago that anyone who doesn't think Teddy is running "suffers from rocks in the head," and Andy Biemiller of AFL-CIO indicates that if a fellow does not think Kennedy is running, he is "nuts."

Buchanan's View: Kennedy is keeping his options open—against the possibility that RN may be so strong by summer '72 that the nomination will not be worth anything. In which event, he can stay out. <u>However, at this point, he and his people have obviously concluded RN can be beaten—and they are not about to sit this one out—risking spending eight years outside the inner circle</u>

of power of a President Humphrey or a President Muskie. If Kennedy believes the Democrats can win—as he quite apparently does now—he will go after the nomination. If he thinks the Democrats by spring of 1972 are sure losers, he can yet stand off.

Hard Evidence:
Mankiewicz, Salinger, Goodwin and Walinsky have all hooked up . . . with sure-loser George McGovern. These are not idealistic school boys willing to spend a year of their lives on an ideological lark. They are interested in power—there is no power to be had by going the route with George McGovern.

It appears they have been given the go-sign by Kennedy to join McGovern, that the purpose is to serve (a) as a "holding operation" for the Kennedy staff, (b) to make top Kennedy personnel familiar with all the levers of state Demo-cratic power when Kennedy makes his move, and (c) to elevate McGovern in the polls and start cutting Humphrey and Muskie down to size where they can't be nominated.

McGovern is now moving in line with this strategy, with his overt violation of O'Brien's 11th Commandment and attack on HHH and Muskie for opposi-tion to the Mansfield Amendment. Last night, Kennedy himself had the needle out for some of the "older" voices locked in the thinking of the past—and he mentioned, specifically, the opposition to Mansfield Amendment as his basis—refusing, however, to name names.

Also, in line with the strengthening of the weak sister, McGovern, is the emergence of candidates Jackson and Mills—both of whom will corral conser-vative Democrat delegates who might otherwise be in the Muskie or Humphrey Camp.

Kennedy Strategy:
Avoid the early primaries in which the left-handers McGovern, Bayh, Hughes, etc. will all be knocked out of the box in the early innings—freeing up their "Kennedyites" for the switch to Teddy. Maneuver to guarantee that neither Muskie nor Humphrey moves into the convention with the nomination locked up. Hold open the option of going into the California Primary itself—if that is necessary to halt the momentum of a Muskie or Humphrey. Nearing conven-tion time—have the left candidates, one-by-one, throw their support to Teddy and Teddy emerge as the single champion of that wing of the party—with good labor backing, with good machine backing, and with young, poor, black unani-mous behind his candidacy.

Muskie versus Kennedy:
Since November Muskie has lost almost 40 percent of his first-choice support among Democrats, dropping from 33–21.

Between March and May, Muskie's 1 point lead among Democrats over Kennedy (26–25) disappeared into an eight point deficit (29–21).

Among Independents—Muskie's long suit—his March lead over Kennedy of 18 points (31–13) was sliced all the way to four points (19–15).

Muskie still has tremendous support among Democratic Party leaders—Kennedy, from the polls, next to nothing—but Kennedy support among the rank-and-file Democrats, his ability to attract publicity and generate excitement, and the support of the ideologically committed give him more than enough to balance off his weakness with the pros.

Impossible for me to believe the Kennedyites, who believe RN is vulnerable, are going to sit by and watch a Muskie or Humphrey take the prize in August—and perhaps the Presidency, thus putting off the "Restoration" for four years, possibly eight, possibly forever.

The Kennedy Assets:
These are well known. Charm, "commitment," affinity with the young, polish, Kennedy looks, mystique, the Myth, charisma along the campaign trail; he generates enormous excitement—as is attested by GOPers traveling with him.

Deficiencies:
1. Even his best friends never accused Kennedy of being an intellectual. On the Drew show, he tended to retreat into the New Left clichés, "we can build a better America," material, which reflects a lack of depth. Further, he tends to react somewhat hotly to attack. (PJB suggestion is that it might be well to hang one or two on him—from the Vice President or Dole—taking some particular excessive statement, and really putting it to him, to ascertain how he handles himself. This would perhaps best be done by a moderate-liberal senator who would unleash a stinging attack on him—away from the Senate floor—before television, about two minutes of good work—then we could see how he reacts.)

2. His far-left foreign policy positions, which win him the plaudits of the New Left journalists and fellow travelers in the media—should be portrayed as shocking, alarming, frightening, dangerous to the peace, inviting war in Europe, "immature," and irresponsible. Not, of course, from here—but in backgrounders with press, he should be portrayed as too reckless, too immature, too irresponsible, at his age, to be President of the United States. This fits hand in glove

with the impression he has left upon much of the country and the center of the Democratic Party in the wake of Chappaquiddick.

It is the quiet constant repetition of private and public comments like, "Sure, Muskie is strong but this 'indecisive' thing is killing him" that is itself inuring Muskie's chances. He has been unable to shake the "indecisive" charge with which we have—with his help—tagged him.

3. His far left social policy positions should be broadcast and re-broadcast. He has the Left and the Radical Kids. We don't and won't get a one. The effort should be to identify him with them, to associate him with them, to tie him to them.

No Matter that EMK is adored by the Party's Left, we have a serious problem only if he gets well with the Party's Center. The more he acts like Brother Bobby the better off we are; the less he acts like brother John, the better off we are.

4. Socially, Kennedy is out of touch with the political moods. The Jet Set, Swinger, See-Through Blouse cum Hot Pants crowd, the Chappaquiddick Hoe-down and Paris highjinks—the more publicity they all get, the better. (The pictures of the Kennedy sisters, in mod attire, at the Kennedy Center, did them no good.)

Chappaquiddick:
This, of course, will be kept in the public mind by the press—speculating on whether it is helping or hurting EMK. We ought to stay miles away from it— indicating even in private, "it's hard to say the effect; we don't know."

Racial Issue:
Kennedy's support of the social-engineering Ribicoff Plan should be emphasized—and a check made to determine how many of his own children go to integrated schools—and then this fact, if relevant, placed in <u>Monday</u> or some publication to get attention. <u>Monday</u> could investigate this—if Kennedy is guilty of hypocrisy on the question—this made known.

The Democratic Right:
EMK openly endorsed the left-wing Mayoral candidate who lost to Rizzo in the primary by a whopping margin. The President might well congratulate Rizzo— if and when he wins the Mayorality—and try to wean some of these tough-line conservative Mayor types to a position of neutrality in a Kennedy-RN contest.

They have no reason to love EMK—and it would appear to me that this effort would be at least as worthwhile as the effort to woo labor chieftains equally locked into the Democratic Party.

JFK:

Since EMK will be trafficking on the JFK myth, it would be well to document JFK's tough line on Defense, foreign policy, Vietnam, Europe, etc. over against EMK's positions—to provide conservative Democrats with some rationale for abandoning the little brother of their hero.

Some of the above are tactical gestures rather than strategic planning. But the main objective, again, is to keep Kennedy out on the Far Left of his Party—to prevent his major inroads into the center—so that if he is the nominee against the President—we have a clear shot at all those conservative Democrats, who make up an integral part of the Nixon Majority. If he is nominated, it should be by the Left Wing of his Party so that LBJ, the South, and the Conservative Democrats will feel they have been run over top of by the unrepresentative radicals and the elite.[14]

6. Memo to Richard Nixon, "The Odds against Henry Jackson," June 25, 1971

Henry M. "Scoop" Jackson, a Democrat from Washington, served in the U.S. House of Representatives from 1941 to 1953 and the U.S. Senate from 1953 to 1983. Known as a hawkish Democrat for his support of the Vietnam War and anti-communist policies, he would do no better than a third-place finish in the Florida Democratic Primary in 1972. Later in the campaign, he made news in his opposition to eventual nominee George McGovern.

That Senator Jackson is a candidate for his party's nomination—there is no question. That he can win it—there appears little hope. But Jackson has some very high cards to play which make him a strong contender for Vice President and a powerful force at the Democratic National Convention.

JACKSON'S STRENGTHS

1. He has almost all the moderate and conservative columnists in the palm of his hand. They like, admire, and respect Scoop Jackson. A cursory review of the last three months finds supportive presidential talk about Jackson from columnists White, both Alsops, Kilpatrick, Alexander, Cuneo, the Drummonds several times, Gould Lincoln, Chamberlain, Wilson—and on and on. (Evans & Novak are solicitous.) They provide him with regular backpage support in most of the papers of the nation. Even columnists who disagree with him (Wicker, Viorst) respect him.

2. A choice, not an echo: He is the single national Democrat who stands as a clear alternative against the crowd of Bayh, Hughes, Muskie, McGovern,

Humphrey, Kennedy. He emerges thus a visible rallying point for conservative Democrats at the '72 convention.

3. Having hired the capable adviser Ben Wattenburg, he is paralleling the Scammon-Wattenburg thesis. His attacks on "environmental extremists," his denunciation of fellow Democrats for paying "homage to the radical fringe," his focus on bread-and-butter issues, the economy and jobs, his call for Democrats to stay on the "Economic Issue," not the war; his rough terminology which is being described in liberal circles as "Agnewian"—in all these instances, Jackson is setting himself up against the trendy, bell-bottomed, elite of the left wing of his party—and with the working man center and right of his party. On issues, he is carving out his own independent sector within the Democratic Party.

4. His super-hawkish anti-Soviet stand in the Middle East, his fight for SST, against the "environmental extremists," for space and defense, not only make him first choice of George Meany—but guarantees a well-financed campaign from Aerospace, from Defense Industries, from the Jewish Community, from Big Labor.

5. He is well respected by his Senate colleagues. A Drummond Poll of the Senate found that 18 percent of Democrats felt Jackson "most qualified to be President" ahead of Humphrey, second only to Muskie (interestingly, EMK got less than anyone, three percent or one vote of those polled).

6. He gets excellent press coverage.

7. His hard line on the Soviets, and on strategic defense, wins him publicity plaudits from the Republican Conservative Community. While such is of little use in a run for the nomination, it might be to any Democrat for his Vice President.

8. On Vietnam he is down-playing his support of the President, leaving it high enough to be visibly opposed to the rest of the pack, but shading it a bit. Domestically, he pays occasional obeisance to such myths as the "repression" by the Administration. Enough to keep his dues up—but not nearly enough to close the sizable gap that exists between him and the liberal left of his party.

9. He is the best vote-getter in the Senate—winning his primary against a Galbraithian type by 85 percent—and beating our candidate in the general by the same margin—85 percent of the vote in a northwestern industrial state. This evidence of massive support across the party lines and throughout the ideological spectrum makes him especially attractive as a Vice Presidential nominee.

10. His strength with press was evident in a poll of editors at ASNE who felt he would probably have nearly the best chance of any Democrat of defeating RN.

DEFICIENCIES

1. He has almost no recognition nationally. This will force him to raise his profile rapidly, to announce fairly early, and probably to go the primary route—and it is doubtful how well he can do against Democrats like Muskie.

2. He is apparently an unexciting speaker who often bores even those audiences who agree with him. One friend called him a "Barry Goldwater without charisma."

3. His nomination would sunder the Democratic Party. And with left-wing strength greater at this convention than the past, difficult to see how his nomination could be swallowed by a Democratic Convention. (However, if a Teddy Kennedy were nominated and Democratic conservatives sufficiently outraged—a Kennedy-Jackson ticket might do for the party what the Kennedy-Johnson ticket did in 1960, bring it together again. Where Johnson had the opposition of Labor and support of the South—Jackson for Veep would have both the South and Labor in his corner.)

4. He is sixty years old, at least will be, when the Democratic Convention is over. This is his last chance to be on a national Democratic ticket, after three decades in the Senate.

JACKSON'S CHANCE

Having carved out an independent Churchillian Position, if you will, on the Soviets, on the Middle East—whence war is likely to come if it comes—Jackson is dependent upon circumstances. If the Vietnam war is raging, and there is calm between East and West—Jackson has next to nothing going for him.

But if Vietnam is removed as an issue, and the Soviets become belligerent in Europe or the Middle East or the Mediterranean or anywhere, then Jackson may very well appear the man for the times. If national focus turns upon American weakness in the face of a rapidly arming Soviet Empire, then Jackson could generate real support among Conservative Democrats, Meany unions, and the South—and even conservative Republicans.

No other Democrat seems today capable of making credible a hard-line policy against the USSR.

But in such times Jackson will have a long shot for the top position and an inside track for the Vice Presidency.

THE FLORIDA PRIMARY

Jackson cannot win in New Hampshire; his lack of public recognition requires him to step out early if he is to have any hope at the Convention. Thus he is forced, it seems, into the primaries. Thus Florida—according to two writers—which is the same day as New Hampshire—becomes crucial to Jackson.

If Jackson wins in Florida, and Muskie is defeated, then the Muskie opening day becomes a flop; Muskie's candidacy is damaged; the Jackson candidacy becomes interesting—and the stage is set for a bitter division at the Convention.

While we may be desirous ourselves of having a massive turnout for RN in Florida—there may be something worthwhile for us in assisting the efforts of Scoop Jackson in that State. Something we ought to keep in mind. [15]

7. Memo to John Mitchell and H. R. Haldeman, September 8, 1971

Muskie's gaffe about the unlikelihood of a black Vice Presidential candidate in 1972 (which we are exploiting) underscores a larger problem for his candidacy for the Democratic Establishment as well—a problem that presents an opportunity for us in 1972.

That opportunity is the escalating alienation between the militant black leadership in Congress and the country—and the Democratic Establishment. Mansfield has refused to see the Black Caucus. Conyers is under pressure from Clay and others to be more strident and demanding. Conyers is openly talking about running for President. Black leaders on the Hill, and beyond, are singing the old conservative refrain, "They're taking us for granted, because they think we have nowhere else to go."

Our opportunity lies not in suddenly signing up disenchanted black Democrats by the thousands into what they call the "Party of Nixon, Mitchell & Agnew." Rather, the opportunity lies in separating that critical bloc from its Democratic base and letting it float.

Here basically is my thought:

Both the student proletariat and the black leadership, which directs much of the black vote, are increasingly militant and ideologically uncompromising. In a straight-on RN-Muskie contest (the growing likelihood) Muskie will get 95% of their votes, but without enthusiasm. Since nine of ten of these votes are not coming to us under any circumstances—let us put aside thoughts of wooing them and focus upon separating them from the Muskie Democratic Party.

How? First, the presidential candidacy of a semi-militant black like Conyers might not only win black support by the tens of thousands, but also drain off from Muskie much of the student left which sees him as compromiser and centrist. Secondly, a Gene McCarthy candidacy on the left would similarly draw thousands of suburban, bell-bottomed liberal votes that would normally go by default to Muskie. Both Gene McCarthy and the Blacks have hinted at Fourth Parties.

<u>We should in my view get the message across to them—through known friends of theirs, and unknown friends of ours—that if a credible black national candidate (Conyers, Julian Bond, Jesse Jackson, Shirley Chisholm, possibly Ronald Dellums) enters the national race—we can guarantee first-rate advertising and funding enough to give them an excellent showing both on the campuses and in the central cities.</u>

As for the McCarthy Fourth Party (The White Liberals) threatened by Gene McCarthy, this would have <u>no</u> appeal in the black community, unless perchance John V. Lindsay were at its head. (A Lindsay-Conyers ticket, as a Fourth Party, seems to me the dream ticket for the Nixon re-election.) But the White Liberals do have appeal in the fashionable communities, in the suburbs, in the peace movement, the environmental movement, etc.—and, again, it should be our policy not simply to encourage such a movement indirectly but to be available to assist it materially—when it comes into existence.

1.) Specially, we should be aware of what is required to get a McCarthy Party and a Liberal (Black) Democrats Party on the ticket in the major states—as Wallace successfully did in all fifty.

2.) We should seriously consider whether from a $50 million (Nixon) media budget, say, $5 million would not be better spent on a Conyers and/or Lindsay in 1972—expanding their vote to its maximum potential, as almost one-for-one those votes will come out of the Muskie hide. (In the Black Community one envisions a massive ad with mugs of the Old Man and Muskie, side by side, and the inscription above, "Racist Wallace is Right! There's not a dime's worth of difference between 'em." Vote Black . . . Vote Conyers.)

3.) If we have a credible and utterly reliable militant black, we should get the word early to the black Democrats that their campaign would lack for neither money nor skills.

4.) We should and can I think get abroad to the left that the old Goldwater argument for the Right is applicable to them as well. (If the Liberal Establishment wins, you lose. The only way to take over this party is to pick up the pieces after a defeat.)

5.) We can and will, from here, <u>start getting across the theme that the blacks are being taken for granted by the Democratic Establishment—that Mansfield refuses to see the Black Caucus, etc.</u> Am going to try to put something together along these lines for this coming issue of <u>Monday</u>.

We are never going to win the blacks and the student/young in 1972, so we ought not to waste effort in that direction, politically, rather start working to see that they slip away from their moorings to the Democratic Party and a Muskie Candidacy. The enemy of our enemy can be our friend on November 7.

What I have in mind then is that we should be on the lookout for a perhaps cynical, but workable alliance of convenience in which we get what we want (re-election) and they get what they want (an unforgettable lesson to the Democratic Establishment that their support is the sine qua non of Democratic Victory). . . .[16]

8. Memo to Richard Nixon, September 25, 1971

Our operations contra Muskie have met, with Muskie's assistance, with considerable success. His slippage is considerable; there is a possibility Wallace could take him in the second major primary; Proxmire in the third (Wisconsin); perhaps even Jackson in Oregon—and EMK is running two-to-one ahead of him in California. We are doing a major analysis of the "gauntlet" Muskie must now run to the nomination for First Tuesday.

However, a problem has arisen and we need a decision:

A) Should we continue to focus upon Edmund Muskie, and do all we can to damage him; or should we turn to Edward M. Kennedy—whom some consider (Nofziger among them) the most difficult candidate the President could face?

B) We think the time has come to do a major <u>Monday</u> piece throwing Jackson into the same bucket with all the rest of the Democrats—and unless we hear otherwise, shall do so.

C) Bob Finch feels very strongly the time has come to lay the groundwork for the "Do Nothing" Congress charge. He recommends a Cabinet meeting, clear of aides, in which RN calls on each member of the Cabinet to begin a round of speeches, taking on the Congress for its failures to pitch the Nixon Programs—and following which each member of the Cabinet goes about the country, both hitting the general Congressional failings—and the specific Congressional failings in their own area. . . .

There should be produced for these Cabinet officers a set-piece speech, in which each Cabinet officer could insert materials in his own area of expertise.

Purpose—To lay the groundwork now, to leave open the President's option in 1972 to put the Democrats on the defensive as negativist Do-Nothing Congress. The schedules should be coordinated through our Cabinet speakers bureau and a major speech drafted which would stand up for a month or so—in order that individual Cabinet officers could make variations on a theme.[17]

9. Memo to John Mitchell and H. R. Haldeman, "Research (As Requested)," October 5, 1971

Because the Old Roosevelt Coalition was composed of numerous parts, there is more than one fissure within the Democratic Party which can today be exploited to the benefit of the President. Some examples:

IDEOLOGICAL FISSURES

The most readily obvious division among Democrats is along ideological lines—the left and the New Left versus moderate and conservative Democrats. Militant blacks, the rebellious on the campus, the radical chic of Eastern liberalism are all within the broad confines of the Democratic Party. So, too, are their most antipathetic adversaries, the blue collar, white collar conservative Democrats.

To exacerbate the ideological division, a few suggestions which surely can be emended and added to:

1) The Platform Plank against Extremism. The Democrats mirror to some extent the Republicans of 1964, and pressure for a plank in both parties denouncing Left-wing extremism and New Left attempts to subvert and overthrow American institutions would be divisive in the Democratic Party. Specific denunciations of the Black Panther Party, SDS, those who have attempted to politicize and destroy the great American universities—these are proposals to deeply divide Democrats. The feat is to focus Democratic attention on this. Could perhaps be done by a Dole speech, calling on both Republicans and Democrats to incorporate such a plank in their party's platform—a speech made after some particularly outrageous campus incident preferably.

2) Republican Praise for Attacks on the Left: Rather than attack the hard left, de rigueur for Republicans, we should shower praise upon Jackson and the Conservative Democrats who denounce the left wing within their own party. A specific example is Jackson's attack on "environmental extremists." We might well go back, dig up Jackson's attacks on his party's left wing, and use them. We did this to some good effect in the early 1970 campaign with the Vice President quoting Meany's and other denunciations of extremism in the Democratic Party.

3) Republican Praise for any Democratic Support on Vietnam. More injurious to HHH and Muskie than an attack on their Vietnam position (which should not be excluded) is "praise" for their support of the President on occasion. This goes far toward making them "Establishment" and driving a wedge between them and the ideological hard core of their party.

4) The McGovern-O'Brien Reform. The Left is counting heavily on these reforms. They may not be carried out to the letter. If they are, they will likely result in one humdinger of a convention; the President's political campaign personnel should be on the watch for violations, which are almost certain to occur—and then elevate those violations in the media as shafting the young, the poor, the black, and the women. We have already had some success with this in the Monday piece, which got national attention, alleging that O'Brien had thrown in with Muskie, they were putting the "fix" in at the convention, and throwing

the blocks to the McCarthy kids and McGovern. Democrats are extremely sensitive about this and concerned about the Convention. . . .

5) <u>Left-Wing Democratic Complaints</u>, i.e., from McGovern and his people should find an echo and an amicus curiae in Republican statements and publications.

6) <u>A Mailing List</u> should be prepared and kept up to date of all Democratic convention delegates as they are named. Anything any major candidate says that is offensive to their fraction should be brought to their attention and the attention of the press in their area.

Example: Humphrey's statement ruling out all signers of the Southern Manifesto should go out, one-page, to Southern delegates and Southern papers—particularly, say, those in Carolina where Sam Erwin was ruled out and Oklahoma where Carl Albert was ruled out by HHH.

7) We have to develop several covert outlets within the national press, who will ask the hard questions that only a political adversary can think up. In addition, and perhaps as a substitute for this, we should have several divisive questions worked up and distributed at major press conferences of the leading Democrats. Also, direct mail to questioners of major Democrats—in short, little briefing papers to newsmen—should go to those who interrogate them on ABC, NBC, and CBS Sunday shows.

REGIONAL FISSURES

South versus North. Here the dividing line is essentially that of the race issue, but it goes further into the "liberalism" of the national Democratic Party leaders and major candidates, which does not sit well with the essential "suburban conservativism" and even "Wallaceism" of Democrats in the South. To force a choice here, we need more than just rhetoric and mailings. Actions taken by the President and Administration are decisive here:

1) <u>The Supreme Court nomination of a Southern Constructionist</u> will force Democratic Northern liberals, and major candidates, to anger either the South with a veto vote, or the blacks and the labor movement and the Northern liberals. A highly qualified Southern Conservative nominee to the Supreme Court is de facto a divisive issue in the Democratic Party.

2) Elevation of the issue of compulsory school integration and neighborhood integration, via such as "bussing" and the Ribicoff Plan. Clearly, this puts Northern liberals like Muskie on an untenable hook. And with the Detroit horror show shaping up, this is going to be even more a national "voting" issue. Mr. Wallace has recognized this.

The serious problem here is that while Muskie may be in favor of compulsory integration by his votes—the Administration is the one that is seen as in power, while various odious rulings and policies are being enforced.

Many of my sources tell me that it is the President—since he is visible in office and has made strong statements—who is today being hurt worst by the bussing fiasco. That is not as it should be, as I understand that the President's political and moral position is that it is wrong and contra-productive to forcibly integrate the races.

However, if we are to draw a line between us and the Democratic liberals, which leaves the Democratic conservatives on our side of the line—then action will be required, in my judgment, on the President's party.

Frankly, this requires the kind of historic decision, bringing a constitutional end to the national pressure to integrate races in housing and schooling—which requires a decision on the part of the President. This would really tear up the pea patch, and our current policy is one of accommodation with the courts, not confrontation.

In conclusion, this is a potential throw of the dice that could bring the media on our heads and cut the Democratic Party and country in half; my view is that we would have far the larger half. But that is not my decision.

3) <u>A Wallace Candidacy in the Primaries</u>. This is an excellent vehicle for surfacing and hardening the divisions within the Democratic Party in the South. Regrettably, such a primary run is likely to hone his organization for a pass at the general. And if Muskie is the Democratic choice, "There's not a dime's worth of difference between them" is an effective slogan. But Wallace victories in Florida, North Carolina, and Tennessee—if they are in the cards—could create some truly serious problems for the Democratic Convention.

4) <u>The Defense Issue</u>: Though less so than before, defense is an issue on which the majority of Republicans and conservative and Southern Democrats unite on one side—with the liberal Democrats on the other. Again, this involves Presidential decision. Should the President elevate this issue, it is one which would divide the opposition party straight down the middle with Meany, Jackson, and the Southerners on one side—and Kennedy, McGovern, and Lindsay on the other.

Again, however, the accomplishment of such a division requires a Presidential elevation of an issue where we have sought to mute differences via our thrust: "We have <u>already</u> re-ordered our priorities," the Defense Budget is the "lowest percent of GNP since the Fillmore Administration," etc.

5) The elitism and quasi-anti-Americanism of the National Democratic

Party have little appeal below the Mason-Dixon Line, and we should contrast the Party of Roosevelt, Truman, and JFK—with the party of Ramsey Clark, Ronald Dellums, and George McGovern.

ETHNIC/RELIGIOUS

The great Northern cities see a clear dividing line between the liberal, academic, intellectual Democratic elite in the Party—and the working-class Roman Catholic, Polish, Irish, Italian Democrats from the Bronx, Queens, and Cook County.

1) My view has been that these minorities, Poles, Irish, Italian Catholics, are larger minorities and easier to win than the "media minorities"—i.e., Blacks, Puerto Ricans, Mexican Americans, Indians, etc., the darlings of the mass media.

Conspicuous appointments of the larger minorities, the more available minorities (Irish, Italian, Poles, Slovaks, etc.) would reap us greater dividends and wean away from the Democratic Party a more significant base than the play being given today, say, to blacks.

2) Aid to Catholic Schools. Clearly this divides the Democrats who run the New York Times from the Democrats who run for office in Queens and the North Bronx. The President's strong stand on abortion, a gut issue with Catholics, is another divisive factor within the Democratic Party—if we can force Democrats to come down on one side or the other.

Again, however, these issues which have been shown by Governors like Rockefeller to be deeply divisive to Democrats on the State level have to be elevated on the National level in order to do us any good. There is another drawback. They are also divisive to Republicans. The Ripon Society liberals will be anti-aid to Catholic schools, pro-abortion, and more concerned with "censorship" and "repression" than porno.

But the favoritism toward things Catholic is good politics; there is a trade-off, but it leaves us with the larger share of the pie. If we want to throw the dice on this divisive issue, the way to do it is via a specific, tangible program of Federal assistance to non-public schools to save them.

Here, too, we have to force Democrats to choose among their vital voting blocs—where the interests of those blocs directly collide.

3) Fourth Party Candidacies. Top-level consideration should be given to ways and means to promote, assist, and fund a Fourth Party candidacy of the Left Democrats and/or the Black Democrats. There is nothing that can so advance the President's chances for re-election—not a trip to China, not four-and-a-half percent unemployment—as a realistic black Presidential campaign.

4) <u>Black Complaints</u>: As we did with Muskie, we should continue to champion the cause of the Blacks within the Democratic Party; elevate their complaints of "being taken for granted."

ECONOMIC FISSURES

Where before, the economic interests of the Roosevelt Coalition were complimentary of harmonious, today that is not the case. This, fissure, too, can be exploited:

One could divide it between the loafing classes (welfare, students) and the working classes.

A cutback in welfare, a hard line on welfare would force Democrats to choose between the working class outraged by the excesses in that program and the welfare class, which is becoming a cohesive voting bloc.

A specific political position of stating that while the Democratic Left is constantly speaking up for the welfare class in this country, "the time has come for someone to represent the working class" might well be considered philistine or worse by the media, but would seem to be good politics. Tax relief, for example, is of a good deal more interest and concern for the working men of this country than the massive welfare scheme we have proposed—and the President is more likely to get working-class support, Wiley's Welfare Mommas behind him.

Note: Since taking office, the President has increased by 500 percent—from $400 million to $2 billion—the food stamp and food assistance funds, and he still gets it in the neck for "starving the poor." Methinks there would have been more gratitude and greater rewards if those funds had been directed to the President's potential friends in the working class and their interests.

If the President would become the visible and outspoken champion of the Forgotten American, the working people of this country—and assert that the welfare types have been taken care of for years, it would force a division within the Democratic Party, would align the media against us—but methinks it both divides them and assists us.

Like other proposals, the above calls for what the Vice President has termed "positive polarization" and requires really the kind of go-for-broke decision that we may not feel is either necessary or justified by our comparatively good field position.

<u>The Black Vice President</u> bumper stickers calling for black Presidential and especially Vice Presidential candidates should be spread out in the ghettoes of the country. Also, anti-Muskie stickers. We should do what is within our power to have a black nominated for Number Two at least at the Democratic National Convention.

INSTRUMENTS

The President—Used to the Absolute Minimum. His Muskie comment was most helpful (on the Black V.P.) but the President and the Presidency are the quintessential political assets we have and should be used in a partisan situation, only in extremis.

The Vice President: We need a decision as to whether he can be used or should be—both from him and from higher authority within the campaign. Of course, he has incomparable visibility; he can make political issues in a way that few others can.

MONDAY—Excellent credibility in the media; has already been used to good effect; will continue to utilize it along lines suggested in above memorandum.

MAILING OPERATION—There should be set up a Mailing Operation to Democrats, on the Hill, and in the Party and Delegates, which will make sure that none of them misses a majority candidate position that is against his interests. Example, pro-abortion statements might be mailed to all Catholic newspapers and wire services. Cut-the-Budget-to-the-bone statements should be mailed to military and conservative publications, etc.

This operation would serve as midwife of the Democrats' Right to Know. We ought to consider how to set this up, with perhaps the least possible "Republican" credentials, or perhaps if that cannot be avoided, set up some "Kremlinologist" operation for the Democratic Party, acknowledge it, and play it straight. Would require a full-time operation, and what should be avoided at all cost is the "excessive" mailings that really turn off editorial writers and the like.

GOVERNORS/CABINET OFFICERS/HILL PEOPLE—When and how these types are to be used is a decision that needs to be made; also, what of Dole's use. Not much in a major way can be accomplished, absent a political operation which can "produce" for them what needs to be said. It is hard to visualize this being done on a part-time basis.

WHITE HOUSE POLITICAL AIDES—Should they take the risk of "feeding" these kinds of materials from the WH?

Above are some thoughts on Dividing the Democrats that need honing and discussion. [18]

10. Memo to John Mitchell and H. R. Haldeman, December 14, 1971

From our own analysis, from recent news reports, from sources within the Democratic Party—our judgment is that Ed Muskie is a good deal closer today to a first ballot nomination in Miami Beach than most people suppose him to be. Here is some of the recent supporting evidence:

1. First, Tunney's endorsement plus the decision of Ted Kennedy's legislative assistant to help run the Muskie Massachusetts campaign are unmistakable signals that Edward Kennedy will not even take his own Massachusetts delegation with him to the Convention; further, that Edward Kennedy, the most formidable potential Muskie opponent in the most crucial primary, California, will not even be on the ballot in California.

2. Sources very high up in the McGovern Camp tell me that Gilligan in Ohio, Sargent Shriver, and even left-winger Joe Duffy in Connecticut are on the verge of endorsing Muskie.

3. The most recent polls, including the Broder article, have now become arguments _for_ rather than _against_ the nomination of Ed Muskie; in these measures of Democratic standing—Muskie seems to be again Numero Uno among Democrats.

4. Other Democratic sources tell me that the Party, especially O'Brien, were truly demoralized by the President's defeat of their tax check-off plan. Today, there is a growing feeling among them that—unless they can get together before the Convention—the primaries may drain off so much Democratic money, that they will not be able to run a respectable campaign in the fall. In short, the defeat of the check-off has created new Democratic pressures to avoid a costly and divisive primary fight. Muskie is clearly the beneficiary of this sentiment.

5. Looking at the primaries, _in sequence_, they seem to be structured now to create a snow-balling effect for Ed Muskie. In New Hampshire, Muskie will surely win, and win well, and thus, one week before the critical Florida primary, Muskie—already the admitted national front-runner—will be riding a wave of publicity as victor in the nation's first. With so many others now scheduled in Florida—Lindsay, Chisholm, McGovern, Yorty, Humphrey, McCarthy, Jackson and Wallace—only Wallace who has an independent base seems to have both the separate base, the recognition, and the attraction to defeat Muskie, as of now. But should Muskie win here—as one would have to bet today—then he would pick up delegates in the Illinois Primary, where he is conceded to be strongest—and roll into the most critical early primary, Wisconsin, where he is _already_ a strong favorite.

Unless the Muskie bandwagon, which is gaining momentum, is upset early, as stated, we could have a) a united Democratic Party b) an attractive "new" candidate, who has the backing of both Democratic Left and Right, and who has strong personality references in a political campaign against us. In my view, a Muskie nomination with a united party is as of now possibly the _strongest_ opposition the President could face—and we ought to do all we can to prevent it. How?

Clearly, if Muskie is to be stopped, he must be defeated in Florida or Wisconsin—or his victory in New Hampshire must be of such a nature as to appear a defeat. What's to be done?

a) In New Hampshire we should have polls telling us precisely what percentage of the vote Muskie will probably receive, and then set a percentage hurdle that he cannot surpass—and provide what aid and comfort we can to the candidacies of both McGovern and Yorty, his only opposition there.

b) Get a precise poll in Florida to determine which of the menagerie can best defeat Muskie. My view is that we can probably count only on two possibilities. The more likely and less desirable is a Wallace victory; less likely, but far more desirable would be a Humphrey victory.

If HHH can beat Muskie in Florida, he will have the momentum going into Wisconsin and a possibility of knocking Muskie off in the Dairy State—which would be a crippling blow to ESM.

Note: Every candidate who ran in Florida will be on the ballot in Wisconsin—like it or not—because of the mandatory nature of that primary. That makes it all the more difficult for one of the eight opponents of Muskie to put together a majority to match that of the then acknowledged front-runner and likely candidate.

Looking further down the road—there are 13 primaries whose filing deadline has already passed by the time the Florida primary takes place. As for now, Muskie would have to be rated the favorite in very nearly every one of those primaries; his opponents will, in each of these primaries—especially the later ones—already be tarnished perhaps by more than half a dozen defeats.

One reporter who talks with him tells me that Larry O'Brien is said to agree with the above assessment and to feel that if Muskie wins the early primaries, he will roll through the later primaries almost without opposition, and the nomination could thus have been decided before the 15th of March—and put on ice on the 4th of April—two months before California takes place.

In my judgment, this prospect, increasingly likely with each passing day, is not in the President's interest. First, some Democrats tell me that Kennedy, should Muskie win in N.H., Florida, and Wisconsin, might himself step up and endorse Muskie. That would guarantee a united party behind Muskie—putting the President in the political fight of his life.

Again, we need the polls first to see if it is realistic to help HHH. I think it may be, as HHH is sort of the Nixon of his party, having built up years if not decades of I.O.U.s and friendships—and having yet his own independent base of True Believers.

The way we could help him up would be specific responses and answers to all of his criticism, maximum publicity for HHH, comments about his strengths, etc. Anything to give him publicity and credibility with his own electorate. We could devise a program of this nature—if the decision to build HHH were made. Again, that depends on whether the polls tell us he has a chance.

If not, HHH, then a Muskie defeat by Wallace in Florida, Tennessee, and North Carolina is the next best thing. . . .

A Muskie sweep of the primaries, with a first ballot nomination and a united Democratic Party, is increasingly probable right now. As it is not in our interest, we ought to take whatever steps possible to prevent it. The most effective way we can prevent it is through some kind of assistance to his opponents in the early primaries. But to decide who has the best shot, who we should assist, we need some accurate poll information on the Democrats in both New Hampshire and Florida—as soon as possible.[19]

11. Memo to John Mitchell and H. R. Haldeman, December 15, 1971

Rep. Pete McCloskey (R-CA), a liberal, and Rep. John Ashbrook (R-OH), a conserva-
tive, were the only two candidates to officially challenge Nixon for the Republican
nomination in 1972.

Following are Ken Khachigian's and my brief ideas on the outlines of an anti-McCloskey campaign in New Hampshire.

Our best hope for a tiny McCloskey turnout lies in an open, active, hard-fought, interesting, increasingly evenly matched battle on the other side of the ballot—in the Democratic Primary. If McGovern appears to have a chance, if Muskie is forced to go all-out, if Yorty-cum-Loeb are pulling upward in the polls, all national and New Hampshire media will focus on this crucial race—and McCloskey's seemingly ineffectual run against the President will be relegated to back pages.

Thus, to advance our dual purpose—to diminish both the size of the Muskie victory and the size of the McCloskey vote—our interests dictate that George McGovern and Sam Yorty be given as much assistance, publicity-wise, on background and off the record, that McGovern's organization may surprise everyone, that Muskie may be in trouble, etc.—in addition to heated in-fighting among Democrats—are to be encouraged in any way possible.

Our public posture from this theory would be to a) Set a hurdle publicly so high that Muskie can't possibly reach it and b) Put out the word that a hell-for-leather run by McGovern and Yorty seems on the verge of denying Muskie the margin he needs to impress the polls and press and nation.

Specific Posture toward McCloskey Candidacy:

1. Publicly, it should be ignored, by all top Administration officials, WH officials, and no statements should be made which would enter us into media debates with the Congressman himself. In our official view, he has a "right" to run in the Republican primary—and we are content to leave it to the New Hampshire voters to assess both the wisdom and efficacy of that kind of approach by a Republican politician.

The worst thing we could do would be to go after him in such a fashion as to enable him to don the garb of the "martyr for principle," the David of the Republican Party, fighting Goliath of the White House and all the Philistine host of media experts and advance men.

2. An intelligence operation should be conducted to determine a) all the Democrats supporting him publicly and privately, b) all the Democratic money he is receiving, c) all the connections he has with the peace wing of the Democratic Party, i.e., Lowenstein & Co., d) the party affiliation of all his workers, and e) where his dough comes from.

If McCloskey's campaign can be portrayed—with any legitimacy, as the covert effort of Democrats, attempting to use a Republican to damage or destroy the Republican President in a Republican Primary—then we have a tremendous case to use with every Republican who leans to McCloskey.

If every speaker we have programmed for New Hampshire can lead off his speech thus:

"I know Pete McCloskey; he is a nice guy; but he is being used as a cat's paw by the big money of the Democratic Party; he is simply being exploited to do the dirty work of Larry O'Brien, he is getting secret big money from left-wing Democrats who don't give a damn about our party, only about destroying our Republican President." . . .

A simple listing of all the big names back of the peace money, New York Jewish money, and California fat cat money—in a lead piece in the Union-Leader—might throw McCloskey on the defensive for much of the campaign. . . .

The Purpose: To paint McCloskey as a Democratic tool, and destroy his credibility as a legitimate Republican.

3. Rule out at this point face-to-face debates with McCloskey by such as Jack Kemp. McCloskey is unknown, attractive, articulate—and the greater exposure he gets, the more likely his vote is to rise at least to a presentable figure.

4. Have RNC/Khachigian gather the <u>Most Extreme</u> and least popular of McCloskey positions—say, ten of them—and then provide pro-President rebuttal material for each of these points; provide this ten-page Briefing Book to every Republican who goes to New Hampshire on behalf of the President, every Republican working in New Hampshire for the President.

Likely, all McCloskey's unpopular views on issues of importance to students should be provided to our students for his campaign appearances at the schools and universities where, surely, he will focus attention.

All his extreme statements should be gathered as well for Mr. Loeb of the Union Leader and perhaps run in an advertisement in that paper. Our people should publicize and comment upon these, but really, more in sorrow than anger, "Poor Pete, he's gone off the deep end, etc." . . .

5. Have a brief study done of which national columnists have the widest circulation in N.H. (In 1968, Drew Pearson was in all papers but Loeb's, and big columnists were the <u>Times</u> boys, Reston, Wicker, et al.) and feed from Washington to <u>these</u> columnists the materials which paint McCloskey as the dupe of the left-wing Svengalis of the Democratic Party.

6. Perhaps the Gay Liberation and/or Black Panthers and/or Students for a Democratic Society at Dartmouth could be prevailed upon to contribute a grand or so to the McCloskey campaign. And when the check is cashed, that fact [could be] brought to the attention of the voters of New Hampshire by the <u>Union-Leader</u>, who might be skeptical of the source of the funds.

7. The three New Hampshire Congressmen, who are Republicans, should be programmed for an early Enthusiastic Endorsement of the President. When asked about Pete McCloskey, the "Pete's a nice guy, but he's just being used by the Democratic Party; he hasn't a snowball's chance in hell; they're just exploiting and using a naïve nice guy . . ." might be an approach that could be taken.

8. A Congressional Truth Squad should be hand-picked and briefed with background on McCloskey positions and readied—but not sent, until the need for heavier artillery becomes clearer than it is today. These Congressmen should be briefed on our line; they should be young, articulate, attractive, the Buckleys and Brocks and the moderate, articulate Republicans in the House. Perhaps a group of us can get together and pick these fellows out. Youth, attractive, articulateness should be the criterion—as no one is going to know their ideology.

9. We should be exceedingly wary of any kind of slick, commercialized approach to this campaign—as I'm sure that McCloskey is waiting to use the charge that the President's PR men and media experts and advance crew are not

substitutes for simple honesty and truth, "Pay no attention to their slick commercials, etc."

10. If Ashbrook can be prevailed upon to stand down, contact should be made with the <u>Union-Leader</u> management so that a working relationship can be constructed—for the campaign against McCloskey. Buchanan can undertake this, if desired. Mr. Loeb controls perhaps the most powerful political weapon in the State, and he has no hesitancy or qualms about wheeling it out at every biennial juncture.

11. The RNC, working with Ken Khachigian, should go over the McCloskey record and find those issues where McCloskey has taken positions unpopular with the GOP centrist-conservative philosophy of the New Hampshire Republican Party—and literature should be prepared for speakers and voters with this material contained. Brochures might be prepared and tailored for the various audiences in New Hampshire, students, regular Republicans, Catholics, etc.

12. If McCloskey does get Guggenheim, as is being bruited about, we should turn this to our advantage by charging that Mr. McCloskey has gotten the biggest merchandiser of Democratic candidates to sell to the people of New Hampshire, by slick commercial, a McCloskey candidacy, which could not get a vote on its own merits. In short, if they go in for slick advertising, we should charge them first with what they are surely going to charge us. Pictures of Guggenheim—the Master Merchant of Image—should be prominent throughout the State and in its media, should he get aboard.

13. Questions should be drawn up by analysts of the McCloskey record and provided, as stated, for press and students—whenever McCloskey's schedules allow for a Q. and A. environment. Again, Khachigian/RNC to handle.

14. As McCloskey is zeroing in on Truth in Government, anything to catch him waffling or hiding something—whether on issues or about support in his campaign—should be publicized and the "Truth in McCloskey" charge hurled back at him.

15. On the four issues where McCloskey is running, i.e., Truth in Government, Judicial Respect, Vietnam, Civil Rights, a short, strong briefing of the RN record—taking the offensive—should be provided our New Hampshire organization and all our speakers, with other above-mentioned materials.

16. Lastly, let's keep our options open. If McCloskey begins to move in the polls, the President may <u>have</u> to go in. If we are going to use television, my idea would be to put in the can something straight from the President, and straight from the Heart. . . . [20]

12. Memo to John Mitchell and H. R. Haldeman, January 11, 1972

As noted in the memoranda of December 14 and January 2, "the Florida Primary is shaping up as the first good opportunity and perhaps the last good opportunity to derail the Muskie candidacy."

According to Evans-Novak (January 9) Humphrey has arrived at the same conclusion, stepped up his campaign schedule, and placed all his chips, very nearly, on a Florida victory. Given Muskie's present momentum and broad national support, even a defeat in Florida may be insufficient to stop him at this late date—but there is no question but that a Muskie defeat in Florida is in the President's interest.

The worst of all possible worlds for us right now would be for Muskie to handily dispatch his dozen adversaries, to sweep the primaries, to undercut any arguments of the Left that they did not get a "fair chance," to go into a united convention and emerge the unanimous choice with Kennedy and Jackson and Humphrey and Lindsay all lined up behind him.

Muskie's defeat in Florida might befoul that scenario; it would surely tarnish the Muskie candidacy in the general election. There is an outside possibility that it might be the first of a series of dominoes which convinces the Democratic leadership that its prospective horse cannot carry his weight.

According to both Muskie and Humphrey polls made public, there is a real possibility that Wallace may finish first with Humphrey a close second in Florida, which would very nearly be ideal for us. It would guarantee that a) George shows up in Miami Beach with a bag of delegates and itching to make trouble and b) a credible centrist challenger to Muskie in the Wisconsin primary, i.e., HHH.

To help bring this about, there are many options open to us:

1. The President could, prior to China or perhaps better, hard upon the China trip, call in Hubert as a "personal friend" and "titular leader" of the Democratic Party for an hour talk on the up-coming summits and a briefing for HHH. The Press Secretary could simply put out the word that given Humphrey's experience and background in government, his record of standing with any President in a crisis, his position as "titular leader" of the Democratic Party, the President felt he, above others, should be briefed. The other candidates do not have HHH's knowledge or background in foreign policy.

An RN-HHH meeting in Key Biscayne or at the White House could give Hubert considerable credibility, though there would be enormous howling.

2. If Ashbrook can be gotten out of the Florida race, we can turn our orga-

nization to the task of drumming up votes for Wallace and/or Humphrey—depending on what our polls are showing as to who needs to defeat Muskie.

Had Ashbrook not entered, we could surely have worked with Loeb to canonize Yorty the way he is beatifying Ashbrook, and we would not face the problem of needing our GOP voters in our own primary in Florida.

3. Maybe the word should be passed through our political people to the press, especially the Florida press, that HHH would be our toughest opponent, the one who would make the strongest case against the President.

4. We ought to have an analysis done of the Florida media, find out which of them are friendly to us, and have them trumpet Humphrey—not Jackson or any of the others in Florida.

5. Though we have no line to Jackson, if we could get him to drop out—if the polls show him doing nothing a few days before the election—and favor Humphrey, it might be decisive.

6. We yet need that poll information from Florida to deem whether or not their polls are "phonies" and whether or not it is feasible to help Wallace and/or Humphrey to run, both of them, ahead of Muskie.

Finally, if Muskie wins Florida, our best hope of a Chicago repeat is gone; if there are going to be any divisive "late primaries" for the Democrats, he has to be slowed down in this one. Maybe there is a need to dispatch some resources into both Florida and New Hampshire to work on this specific objective: cutting Muskie's lead in the Granite State, and insuring his defeat in the Sunshine State. Methinks the fellow who achieves that will be doing the President as much good as anyone else this election year.[21]

13. Memo to Chuck Colson, January 12, 1972

We have some areas of genuine issue vulnerability at the present time, but they are not being exploited to the full by our adversaries, and they are hardly being exploited at all by the President's Democratic and Republican opposition.

THE DEMOCRATS

Muskie is making some inroads with his emphasis on the "trust" and "credibility" issues, but much of his energy is diverted in fending off his own Democratic opponents. Thus, he has moved hard left on the war, and opposed the shuttle, and spends time answering his "No Blacks for Vice President" charges—none of which is of real concern to us. Humphrey is fighting for his life, focusing on Florida, moving rightward on bussing, supporting the shuttle, attempting to re-establish his own credibility as a man for these times, and as a man who is not over the hill. Jackson is spending all his time pointing up the differences between himself and the other Democrats. Lindsay is attempting to create a "new coalition" of young, poor, and black; he is trying to raise himself with TV and charisma; and attacking the "centrists" in his own party responsible for the policy of 1968.

(NOTE: This fact—that the Democrats are too busy focusing upon each other to concert their attacks on the President in his areas of vulnerability—points up anew the need to keep the Democratic nomination open for as long as we can. If Muskie emerges the sure nominee, by winning Florida the Democratic Party can get behind him and focus on their primary adversary—who is us. But as long as we can keep a 1968 situation going, where more than one Democrat has a chance, they will focus upon getting a leg up on one another, as opposed to focusing upon getting the upper hand on us.)

THE REPUBLICANS
Ashbrook is getting considerable press, but he is not zeroing in, not canalizing the attack enough, on the President. Most of the media he gets is based on his contention that the President has moved too far left; he has not captured an "issue" like the "war issue" in 1969, which he needs to make a strong showing. McCloskey continues along the same vein he has been working for a year—nothing new, nothing dramatic, that is anti-RN. At the same time, the President gets good support from across the GOP spectrum from the regular optimistic statements from Republican Left, Right, and Center about the President being a sure winner in 1972 as the economy shapes up.

ISSUE AREAS OF VULNERABILITY
The Economy—This is an issue where we have great trouble right now across the spectrum. The statistics simply do not confirm the "good year" that was promised. In particular, the 6.1% unemployment is being zeroed in upon by the press and everyone in the other party. The AFL-CIO is running a daily assault upon the Pay Board and Phase II. The impression being left with the public about Phase II is a cloudy one at best. And the conservatives are becoming increasingly "ideological" about the controls condemning them because of their constrictions of American freedom. This issue contains the seeds of all our problems. There is the "credibility" issue with the President's pledges in 1968 which the Left will take up, and the "credibility" issue in 1972, which the conservatives are using now—the RN promise not to take us down "that road"—to controls. Further, there is this AFL-CIO obstructionism which seems part of an organized campaign to bring down Phase II—and then, surely, the general

public, as the year goes on is inevitably going to be less, not more enthusiastic about controls as more and more are adversely affected by them. Clearly, this is the best issue the opposition has today—as they can make a case against us on one or another aspect of the economic issue which can appeal to voters, left, right and center.

Credibility & Trust—If the economy turns around, this is the single area of greatest vulnerability that can defeat us. Muskie obviously has polls to this effect; he used the theme "trust" in his kick-off; Adlai III said that what this election is coming down to—as he came out for Big Ed—is who can you "trust." In the New Year, we have taken a very bad beating in this area. The media has expressed shock and horror at the revelations that the Administration, in the person of Kissinger, "lied" to the American people. The issue is still being chewed over the back pages. Nearly every press adversary we have, and we have not a few, went into a head-shaking, deploring posture at the revelations in the "Anderson Papers." Anderson himself is being lionized in the national press; he is on television, nationally, more than any other figure; he has become a great personage in his own right; and charges of lying and deception are the daily fare of the editorial and op-ed pages of the nation's press. Further, this is an issue where we have serious problems on the Right. The most effective anti-Nixon segment of the 90-minute conservative show with Buckley hosting was the RN footage a) ruling out China's entry into the UN, b) demanding of Congress a "balanced federal budget" so that Americans can balance the family budget, and c) a June 1971 all-out indictment of economic controls, "I am not going to take America down that road."

On this issue, we can be hoisted by an unscrupulous campaigner with a bit of imagination.

RN's '68 pledges (conservative) in nature, which were reversed in 1972, would be one facet. Every "credibility gap" issue on Vietnam could be used. The economic forecasts that came out wrong would be a segment. And wrapping it all up would be the Anderson Papers, where the charge would be made that the Administration is consistently lying to and deceiving the American people.

This is a real area of vulnerability for us—given, quite candidly, what the polls show the American people as believing and given the President's past problems in this area (i.e., Tricky Dick). A Democratic campaign with all guns firing in this direction, that did not cross the line of vicious slander of the President, but which did the kind of job we used to do on LBJ, could be critical. Clearly, the dominant national media would act as a voice box for this kind of campaign— the Democrats would not lack for an echo chamber in the national media.

Vietnam—An area of vulnerability with the center and left—not right here. Basically, the President, in my judgment, is not hurt politically when the bombers fly north—the peaceniks are never going to be ours. Where we have a problem in our own heartland is in a) military reversals in Laos and Cambodia, or a possible real setback, which could convince most Americans that the whole thing is unraveling, and the three years of dying have been a total waste, b) the prisoners thing. The networks are giving broad play to the families of prisoners, and very probably a majority of Americans would go for the prisoners-for-pullout deal, and let Mr. Thieu "hack it" on his own. We ourselves made the "POWs" into an issue of tremendous national emotional concern, and now they are being used by the national media against us. Further, the press focuses on every casualty and where are the wounded of this war adds to the general war weariness in the country.

However, my judgment is that Muskie's moves farther left—i.e., let's let them fight it out and accept the outcome even if we don't like it—is not a threat to the President's more center position. Further, as in 1970 with RN's October speech, we have the "ball" and a Presidential announcement of a) a deadline, b) more withdrawals, and c) no more draftees could cut the ground out from under the opposition. So, my view is that the great danger here lies in grave military reserves for the United States and the Vietnamese which show the enemy as holding the whip hand.

Politics over Principle—and Too Much P.R.—The President has always had a problem in being identified as "too political." And polls given us some months ago found that everyone, but everyone thought we were too P.R. oriented.

We face a potential danger that the President's "summits" will come under attack as gigantic P.R. gimmicks to win the President's re-election at the expense of the nation's interest. This is an allegation that could be sold, again, across the spectrum.

Reston is pushing the idea; Rather raised it on television in a very political year, in the primary season, with Peking, Moscow, and SALT coming up—the charge is certain to be iterated and aired by the Democrats. The right is already prepared to believe that the President ignored and bypassed the interest of Taiwan, Japan, and Korea so he could spend seven days in Peking. The liberal community following the Anderson Papers now has its own "case" that the President sided with dictator Pakistan against Democratic India so as not to jeopardize the President's televised visit to the Gate of Heavenly Peace. Even liberal papers are now raising conservative questions, i.e., "What is the price America has to pay for this visit to Peking?" In this regard, George Meany has been making this same case for months—charging the President with "gimmickry" and performances for their P.R. benefit.

This is, like the credibility issue, tied to the character of the President, and surely if Muskie is the nominee as appears likely, this, too will be a focus of political attack. Even Mr. McCloskey and Ripon on the left as well as Kevin Phillips and the right chide us for the "P.R. and advertising" types around the President. We should not underestimate the damage that could be done to the Administration and President with all shades of opinion—even Middle America—with a well thought out and concerted campaign on us as men without principle, men who change policies like some people change clothes, men who will do anything to get back in the White House.

Were I in the Muskie camp, these are the long-range themes I would be developing, and would have the leaders of my party develop—when the primaries were concluded.

COMING ISSUE AREAS

--The Richmond School decision, which means compulsory integration of suburbs and city schools is surely an issue which we and the Democrats are going to have to face.

--If there are more incidents like Forest Hills, the issue of scatter site housing and suburban forced integration will become as cutting a one as bussing.

--Defense. Though only the right is really elevating this issue, it is getting more and more attention, especially after the India-Pak war and the Soviet advances in the Subcontinent. Talk of relative fleet strength is one area of focus; the charges that the Southern U.S. is wide open to air attack; the American Security Council report and all the attendant publicity; and the certainty that Ashbrook and Wallace will zero in on this eventually make this another issue area where the President is vulnerable—however only from the right.

One thing should be noted before closing. George Wallace is keeping his own counsel right now. He has not begun to open up—but with the above three issues—housing, school integration, and defense, we can expect some hard times from the right on this. [22]

14. Memo to John Mitchell, "Attack Organization & Strategy," March 14, 1972
We have been called upon to compose a memorandum delineating the division of responsibility and the formations of the "attack" strategy for the fall campaign. Herewith, our views and recommendations.

PRESENT SITUATION
"In my Father's house there are many mansions."
John 14:2

There are currently several quasi-independent attack operations running. There is Dole and the RNC, not infrequently orchestrated by C. Colson with Koch on drums. There is the "Speakers Bureau" run by Pat O'Donnell again, out of Colson's shop, co-ordinating with Parker for the President and Damgard for the Vice President. Further, O'Donnell serves as conduit for the Administration "fact sheets." There is a Hill operation with Koch placing the materials at Colson's intermittent direction. There are political "surrogates" scheduled out of 1701 by Bart Porter, who moves Hill and Administration types into Re-Elect settings in the Primary States and beyond.[23] And there is Van Shumway, who moves the political "line" out of 1701 to reporters and columnists.

CAMPAIGN
For the campaign, in our judgment, to canalize the attack to focus our resources, to avoid any embarrassing "gaffes," we need more co-ordination of attack materials being used, we need greater central direction of the scheduling of speakers, we need a central point of authority and direction over the attack—holding veto power over what goes and what does not.

The one positioned to exercise this authority is the Campaign Manager, the Attorney General.

1. We recommend that no new controversial printed or media attack be made upon the Opposition Candidate without the concurrence of the Attorney General or his designated Deputy for this purpose.

2. There should be a marriage of the scheduling operations of 1701 and the White House; speakers should be placed under the one or other operation for the campaign's duration, and the scheduling of the two groups should be regularly and closely co-ordinated so we can avoid both over-kill in one area and the neglect of another.

The attack materials for both "surrogates" (who will be the majority) and "Speakers Bureau" should be provided from the same source.

The "schedulers," both at 1701 and the White House, should leave their clients with open dates in October to move them into swing states, and they should receive regular guidance from the highest level of the campaign as to where our manpower should be directed.

THE ANSWER DESK

This operation was most useful in 1968; it can be made more effective in 1972. We recommend that:

1. An Answer Desk be set up and running in the RNC by the first of August, with a report by the 15th of May to 1701 and Buchanan/Khachigian as to how it is to be staffed.

2. That the Answer Desk contain an "expert" on the Democratic candidate, as familiar with his positions and statements and record as the candidate's own staff. That this expert, from the end of the Democratic convention to the first of August, review and glean the entire research file on the candidate—so that we can have available only what we will need to use.

3. That by the 1st of August, the Answer Desk have prepared an Attack Briefing Book on the Democratic candidate that has been gleaned and cut to usable portions, containing voting records, position on top ten major issues of the day, etc., etc. The book should be put together in such a way as to emphasize the negative and the vulnerable; it should contain only the best items and quotes, etc.; it should be brief enough so that it will not by its very size prohibit inspection. Buchanan/Khachigian operation will look it over, attempt to glean it further, and provide paragraphs and pages which can be inserted into speakers' kits.

This attack Briefing Book should be updated every several weeks of the campaign; it should be provided to all surrogates, Cabinet Officers, the Vice President, Dole, Klein, etc.

4. Names, functions, home and office phone numbers of members of the Answer Desk should be in hand at Campaign Headquarters and contained in Attack Briefing Books of all speakers by August 1.

5. Answer Desk will provide daily a report of the Democratic candidate's attacks (also Vice President and major opposition speakers, if possible) plus a response—to 1701, to the Vice President, White House, etc., throughout the campaign.

6. The Answer Desk should be provided with direct lines into all Administration research centers—so they can get immediate access and first call on needed information to develop the answer to opposition attacks.

NIXON STATE CHAIRMEN

These individuals should be provided as well with Attack Briefing Books on the Democrats for their own use; they should be phoned on a regular basis as to what issues and what aspect of the opposition they should hit; they should be contacted immediately prior to a visit to their state by the Democratic candidate.

We cannot keep a daily watch on the Nixon Chairmen; they will be "left to their own devices" most of the time. But when a Democratic candidate, Presidential or Vice Presidential, arrives, the National HQ, 1701, should have something available for the State Chairman that is consistent with the present line of attack being pushed at the national level.

LETTERS OPERATION

We already have had great success in this area. Ken Khachigian should be responsible for determining, prior to August 1, that we have a) a beefed up operation at the national level, b) "letter operations" at the local level in each of the major swing states. This is an excellent way to put volunteers to work. The "letters" people at both the State and national level should be given the political attack line and regularly, and much of their work should be on the attack basis, getting guidance from the campaign leadership. Khachigian will get together with those in 1701 to determine that this operation is organizationally set—by August 1st at the latest.

TRUTH SQUAD

Occasionally, these have been effective; too often, they are a waste of time and money. We propose making an effort to make it work this year. Basically, we envision the Squad as small, divided between the "tough cop" and the "nice cop." The former handles the gutting of the Democratic candidate; the latter the achievements of the President.

General to this is the advanceman. He need not know how to build a crowd, but he must know how to attract media, both television and press. The advanceman further should be responsible for getting to the Truth Squad, before they touch down, the "lead" story the Democratic candidate has left in the headlines of that day—and the "lead" story of the day in an issue context.

Reason for above is that the Truth Squad may want to focus on a local crime—pointing up RN's record and statement—or a local strike—point up an RN proposal—rather than the Democratic candidate's attack if it has been of a pro forma character.

Our ideal of a typical first rate Truth Squad would be Hatchet Man Dole with Good Guy Rumsfeld; young, tough, aggressive, attractive—and willing to mix it up with the Democratic candidate.

The value of a Truth Squad is not in the faithful it attracts, but the media it receives. We ought to take a long second look at how our Truth Squad is doing—three weeks into the campaign—to determine if it is a cost-effective operation.

THE AX MAN

In 1968, Humphrey made extremely effective use of George Ball, who had independent, excellent foreign policy credentials of his own. Ball was willing, without prodding or even mention, to gut either the President or Vice President. He attracted tremendous national media simply on his own standing and expertise. Bob Ellsworth performed something of this function for us on the Primary Trail—where he, as "Campaign Director," could attract press in his own right and say those things the rest of us would have to go to confession for.

In any event, with the Attorney General as Campaign Manager, we should have a similar "heavyweight" with a similar title, but no organization responsibility, solely a duty to get national press, to get on national television shows, and to hammer the opposition candidates. This would be an added weapon in our arsenal; he could play the role that Ray Bliss was constitutionally ill-designed to play in 1968. The title would not cost a dime; it would give us an added voice; he should be a man of stature, of Cabinet weight if not rank—someone who on his own is worthy news. We need someone, however, with an instinct for the jugular; he should be provided the Attack Briefing Book, all the attack materials, and programmed solely for the national media—not GOP rallies.

A Nelson Rockefeller—if he would turn over New York management to his aides—and handle this national attack job, would be the kind of individual to whom I am referring.

SURROGATES, HILL & ADMINISTRATION SPOKESMEN

By September, after the GOP convention, our scheduling operations should be married, or co-ordinated totally at the least. We should inventory our people— from the Hill, Cabinet, White House, etc.—and top Campaign Management should determine what states we heavy up in—then the "schedulers" from WH and 1701 should co-ordinate the scheduling of our people into these states.

Running two separate and equal operations is foolish; the needs of the campaign should dictate where our people go, and those needs are best determined by Campaign hierarchy.

THE VICE PRESIDENT

On the assumption Vice President Agnew is our man, the following should be done. His plane should carry at least two top speechwriters, the full attack updated briefing book, a telex for direct communication, telecopiers, phones from 1701, etc. Election of 1970 demonstrated that V.P. Agnew can get more coverage than any Vice President in history; that he makes tremendous copy; he will be the bayonet of the Administration in 1972.

The error in 1970 was not the "Law and Order" issue; it was in not realizing how the Vice President could overwhelm the national media in three weeks to the point where the issue had already been "made" nationally, to the point where by October 1, the Democrats had been thrown on the defensive, had re-directed their media to defense the issue, had started talking law and order, and were seen climbing in and out of police cars. By the time September was over we had played our "attack" trump and we had no other effective "attack" issues to make.

All our gains of September were thus lost in the attrition of October, when the pendulum swung back.

Again, the Vice President will have a planeload of reporters with him; he will get more media than any other "attack" resource we have; our best writers should be aboard his aircraft.

In the 1972 campaign, we should keep before us some of the lessons for an attacking candidate—from 1968 and 1970:

1. The old situation where it took months or weeks to "make" an issue and bring it before the public no longer obtains. The President and the Vice President—with the kilowatts of their office—can "make" an issue in a matter of days, by repeated hammering.

2. Correspondingly, issues come and go more rapidly. The Democrats got well on "law and order" in October of 1970. This argues strongly for a) flexibility on our part, a flexibility we did not show in the last two campaigns in shifting either gears or issues, and b) an inventory or bank of campaign attack issues so that we can switch off one and onto another as the need appears, and c) a phased attack plan which can provide us ahead of time—what issue the Administration "attack" people will focus upon that week. Instead of shooting our bolt in the first speech—we should in 1972 be able to shift easily off of one "attack" issue and onto another and then a third, d) We may need to demonstrate ammunition until a later point in the campaign.

Eisenhower once indicated that while plans were worthless, planning was essential. We ought to have by September 1 a planned schedule of "attack" on the opposition candidate, which moves from one issue to another, in ascending order, until the major attack is not launched until October 10th at the earliest and see if that schedule works out in the early days of the campaign.

Again, what we are suggesting is that a) we have four or five issues ready to surface at any time, b) we not put all our eggs in a single basket and start swinging that basket in September, and c) despite pressure to go "all out" in September, due to bad polls or the like, we "hold back some powder" for October.

SENATOR DOLE & THE RNC
In our view, Bob Dole should be brought in on strategy meetings, provided with all the attack materials, plus a writer, and he should be kept focused upon the shortcomings of the Democratic candidates—rather than respond to O'Brien, who will be attacking the President and Vice President.

His scheduling should likewise be co-ordinated with our surrogates; he has a position giving him national stature and access to national media. Like the Vice President, but to a lesser degree, he should be heavied up.

ACCURACY IN MEDIA
We did not need Edith Efron to inform us of what the national networks did to RN in 1968; this has to be prevented in 1972. Suggest establishment of a "Fair Coverage Committee" or "Equal Time Committee," which might be located in the RNC, which would "clock" precisely the positive and negative coverage of presidential and vice presidential candidates on the networks. If we are getting anything more than "equal time," this committee can remain silent; if we get anything less than equal time, it should confirm same with Mort Allin's news monitors—and then send a memorandum to John Mitchell who should get on the horn to the network President and point this out, indicating that if it is not corrected and equal time not provided—this will be made an issue in the campaign and the subject of legislation in the coming Congress. The newspapers can do what they want, but we cannot allow NBC to start "making" the economic issue for the Democrats the way they sought to do it in 1970.

COPE'S COUNTERPART
The most effective instrumentality of the Humphrey campaign was alleged to be, not without justification, the AFL-CIO Committee on Political Education (COPE).

COPE's Herculean efforts in 1968 putting out millions of pamphlets, attacking specifically the anti-union record of George Wallace, won back millions of union voters to the Humphrey banner by election day—and very nearly carried the day for the former Vice President. We have nothing to rival COPE—AMPAC and BIPAC do not have the tens of thousands of volunteers that COPE can muster in a particular campaign.

But we have the necessary volunteers in our citizens' groups, GOP and youth groups, etc., in the various states, and we do have the needed expertise and writing capacity here in D.C. to emulate their effort.

Recommend that soon after the Democratic convention there be established one General Committee, with a high-sounding name, and other committees tailored to specific issues, i.e., "United States Security Council," which can issue effective attack releases, which can then be mailed in bulk to GOP and Citizens Groups for distribution in target states. Chuck Colson's shop could have such, one imagines, established in a matter of hours.

The specific committees should zero in on issues—depending on the Democratic candidate—where the opposition is especially vulnerable. For example, were Muskie the nominee, we would have a Committee on Defense of the United States, one on Space, one on Aid to Non-Public Schools, etc.

Again, these committees would issue hard-hitting, targeted material, which we would then have distributed by regular GOP troops, outside churches, plant gates, ball parks, etc.

MEDIA ATTACK

In our view, the Democrats in 1968 were more successful than we in using "attack" commercials. They focused on the Vice President, with some nasty materials, but also on Social Security and Medicare—suggesting that a vote for Nixon was a vote to diminish both. These were effective, selected targeted media attacks—using commercials. We recommend a program of something similar for this year. Here are some ideas.

1. In areas where bussing is a gut issue, which is likely to be half the metropolitan areas in the United States and all the South in September of 1972, we run straight one-minute commercials using Muskie or Humphrey or Kennedy statements in support of bussing. They should be tough, airtight, and make their point. . . .

2. In areas where space is a concern, like Houston, Florida, and Southern California, we should spot ads against the Democratic votes to cut the space program.

3. Same with defense. The Democrats have voted against almost every weapons system proposed by the Administration. Muskie's and Kennedy's records are atrocious. We should have a one-minute spot on television and radio in conservative areas which documents these votes against and concludes, "Senator Muskie voted to strip America's defenses below the danger point; President

Nixon believes that peace requires American strength. Re-elect the President—Vote for Richard Nixon."

Further on this issue. We should have the VFW, at their conventions, mail the Muskie Defense record to their entire membership. We should do a direct mailing to the American Security Council list, if we can get it. And take out ads on defense, contrasting RN and Democratic positions in all four conservative publications.

4. On all black radio stations in Swing States, we should run ads on Muskie's statement about no blacks for Vice President. "If he doesn't think the time has come for one of us to be even considered for Vice President, then the time has come for Black America to tell Ed Muskie we don't think it is time for him to be considered for President. Write in Shirley Chisholm."

5. The SST vote alone, where the Democrats were against us, should be used on radio and television and at plant gates throughout the State of Washington. Again, a television ad or a radio spot—just stating the Democrat votes, what it did to Seattle and the State of Washington, how RN fought for it—and vote for Richard Nixon. In some cases in these ads, it may be sufficient to attack the Democratic position, simply to turn off the voter—where we have no possibility to winning that particular voting bloc.

6. In the farm belt, we should be able to contrast Butz "fighting for the farmer" with statements by the various Democrats that the prices of farm products are too high—again, targeted commercials to specific groups. Every individual has contradictions in his position—we ought to be sure that every concerned group is aware of those of our opposition—and media attack advertising is the way to do it. . . .

The Attorney General should clear the media ads—and draw off the poison if there is any—but we should not hesitate to use them. Most of the best pro-media we get will be the President himself, live as President, and we ought not overlook this effective mechanism.

Just as the Democrats ran that ad of the Vice President—with the heart thumping to indicate a heartbeat away in 1968—so we ought to have the capacity to put together spot ads in a matter of days and have them on the air as the campaign develops. In any event, we need a budget for this—small pre-convention and much larger post-convention.

Were Humphrey the candidate, for example, we could run the horror clippings of 1968, war, riots, coffins, urban violence, crime, and say this is the result of what Hubert Humphrey called the "politics of joy" in 1968. Let's not go back to that horrible year, 1968—let's move forward with President Nixon.

THE REPUBLICAN CONVENTION

Just as the largest audience the President had in 1968 was at his August convention, so the largest audience the Republican "attack" surrogates will have in 1972 is in San Diego. We need a Walter Judd or several of them out there—doing the job in 1972 on the Democrats that Judd did in 1960.

Following the Democratic convention, we should consider who our speakers will be, at what hour and time in San Diego, and guarantee that some of the most hard-hitting and tightly drafted attacks on the Democratic candidates come out of that convention.

The attack speeches should be orchestrated and advanced, with an audience cheering at the right lines—the way the President did it himself in 1968 in his acceptance speech. We will get no better chance to focus the nation's attention on the weakness of the Democratic candidates and the Democratic Party than in 1972, and we ought not blow all that national television.

BUCHANAN-KHACHIGIAN

Our primary role, given the small size, is oversight and assistance.

1. Provide checks on various "attack" operations to determine their effectiveness in terms of media.

2. Take a direct hand in creating radio, TV spots on the "attack" and the pamphlets and help direct where they are to be distributed.

3. Monitor operations through news summary staff.

4. Recommend to Attorney General shifts in strategy—point up when we feel one line of attack is being exhausted, and another might be better pursued. In campaign we anticipate regular, if not daily, communication with the top campaign staff on how well things go and where there needs to be a new attack or improvement.

5. Help draft the speeches and the attacks on the Democrats for the Republican convention.

6. Have a seat on the board where the attack strategy on the Democrats is being considered and where states are being selected. Further, we will need to have direct access to the poll data of the campaign, so that we can know where the attacks should be directed, against whom and how in what states.

7. Produce, with a small group, some of the covert materials—i.e., matter we would not want to be identified with, but nothing that would be wholly destructive, if uncovered.

8. Oversee update of the briefing books.

GENERAL THOUGHTS

1. In the turmoil of a campaign, it is likely that centralism will break down; that is not unexpected nor necessarily bad; however, it is important that we attempt to impose some kind of strategy upon our surrogates who are making the attack and the other instruments we have.

2. After the August convention, for certain, we ought to go at once on the attack—as we did in 1970. We have the forums to command the media, and we ought to throw the Democrats on the defensive and keep them there—so that they have no choice to make their issues, in particular the "economic issue." There is no reason—given our superior media position—that we can't dominate the news.

3. Avoid at all costs the kind of attack by individuals or media or ad that opens us to the "Tricky Dick" charge or the "Old Gutfighter" allegation. . . .

4. Keep in mind that there are only two deadlines every day and one evening news show. If an attack has captured the media, no need to top it with a new one; let it ride.

5. Start the attacks early in the campaign as the number of undecided is then largest. Again, however, we should show the kind of flexibility we did not in 1968 by being able to open up an entirely new front in mid-October, if some other attack is being countered or stalled. The old military adage—always commit your reserves from a new direction—should here apply.

6. The last five days of the campaign, we should close up shop—and everyone who is not tongue-tied should be out in the boonies on as many radio, television, speech appearances as he can fill. The last voice heard in the campaign may be the one to which some swing voter hearkens. About one week before the end of the campaign, we can no longer rely on Red Blount's fellows to deliver our message to the outlanders; we have to start using the phone—and everybody who can skate should be out on the ice.

7. When the candidates are determined, there should be a strategy meeting of sorts to determine what "<u>personal</u>" aspects of the Democratic candidate are vulnerable, and while these may not be the grist for attack ads, we should get them out to our speakers. For Muskie, for example, "instability," his outburst of temper, his breaking down completely after criticism from a publisher. For Kennedy, "immaturity," "playboy," etc.

8. The Congressmen who will be running, especially those who are safe, should be given—via phone—the line to hit for the President, the attack line, in a boiler room operation, plus last mailed materials—one week prior to election, with phone calls for any late update.

9. Finally, the attack strategy, as stated, should be flexible; it may be that after making attacks early in the campaign, we want to go over to promise what we are going to do for America in the second term, to ignore the opposition. Perhaps the polls will tell us that is the approach to take. If so, no problem; we would as soon walk to victory as run.[24]

15. Memo to John Mitchell and H. R. Haldeman, April 12, 1972

Our primary objective, to prevent Senator Muskie from sweeping the early primaries, locking up the convention in April, and uniting the Democratic Party behind him for the fall, has been achieved. The likelihood—great three months ago—that the Democratic Convention could become a dignified coronation ceremony for a centrist candidate who could lead a united party into the election is now remote.

The purpose of this memo is to suggest new goals and to elicit advice from the campaign leadership on how to proceed and against whom. Had we our druthers, we would at this point choose as opponents McGovern, Humphrey, Muskie, and Kennedy in that order. Here is the way the primaries shape up at present, in both our judgment and that of the more respected politicians about, in the media, and Democratic Party.

WISCONSIN—April 4: The Wisconsin returns made McGovern a credible candidate and whipped up a Goldwaterlike enthusiasm for him throughout the country, from which he will benefit from now until July. He has inherited the media enthusiasm Big Ed retained with the Cape St. Elizabeth Show 18 months ago. Humphrey lost a golden opportunity to assume the mantle of front-runner; he was injured in terms of November; he lost the publicity and momentum that went to McGovern and could have been his. But he is still very viable. Muskie was crippled, but not killed. Wallace was strengthened for the merry month of May, which we anticipate he will demonstrate.

MASSACHUSETTS & PENNSYLVANIA—April 25: Both states have personality as well as delegate contests. HHH, McGovern, Muskie, and Wallace are on the ballot in both. However, Humphrey is concentrating on Pennsylvania to the exclusion of Massachusetts, and McGovern is focusing upon Massachusetts with only targeted districts in Pennsylvania. Muskie, who is in danger of being whipsawed in the two primaries, seems to have opted to make his major effort in Pennsylvania. The 182 delegates in Pa., compared to 102 in Mass., is clearly one reason. Another is that Muskie seems to believe now that he stands a better chance of becoming the Regulars' candidate acceptable to the Left than the Left's candidate acceptable to the Regulars.

At this point Humphrey looks like the winner in Pennsylvania, which will give him a leg up in Ohio a week later. And Muskie, who two months ago was a 4-1 favorite in Massachusetts, could conceivably lose both primaries on April 25. If he does, he has another bullet hole in him, though he may still not be completely dead.

INDIANA, OHIO, ALABAMA, AND THE DISTRICT OF COLUMBIA—May 2: In D.C. Walter Fauntroy is favorite son, about whom no more need be said. Alabama is inconsequential. In Indiana, all the major candidates seem to be abandoning this primary to George Wallace, and at this point Wallace will win the Indiana Primary and the headlines that go with it—setting himself up for Michigan, and other good things to come. Muskie has just about pulled up stakes, Hubert is focusing on Ohio, and McGovern is simply not a statewide winner—give this one to Wallace.

Ohio, however, is another story. The winner of Pennsylvania a week before—we believe HHH will take it for the first primary win in his political lifetime—will have the whip hand here. Muskie will contest this with all he has; if he loses here as well as Pennsylvania, it becomes difficult to see how he can last another month till California. McGovern is here—as everywhere—targeting on delegates to pick up a few even if he loses the primary by a major margin. It's HHH or Muskie in Ohio. We pick Humphrey here as well.

WALLACE MONTH

TENNESSEE—May 4: Everybody's abandoning this one to Wallace, who should sweep it—along with 40–45 of the delegates.

NORTH CAROLINA—May 6: Everyone is abandoning North Carolina as well—everyone that is except Terry Sanford. We give North Carolina to George Wallace also. (If Sanford should upset Wallace here, highly unlikely, he will be Tom Wicker's "New South" here for next month.)

NEBRASKA & WEST VIRGINIA—May 9: West Virginia will feature a head-on between Wallace and Hubert Humphrey, the only two candidates on the popular ballot. If Humphrey whips Wallace, he will get immense favorable publicity—good both in Maryland and Michigan. He will look more and more to the Regulars as the Regular to support all the way. If Wallace beats Humphrey here, it will be a humiliation for Hubert and the Democratic Party nationally—exposing just how far away the national leadership of the Party has gotten from its base. Wallace's momentum for North Carolina and Tennessee will be working in his favor here. (Any way to help Mr. Wallace would help in November.)

Nebraska—everyone is on the ballot. It is a McGovern target state; he could do well here. We have no real reading.

MARYLAND & MICHIGAN—May 16: If Humphrey has defeated Muskie in both Pennsylvania and Ohio, then both these states shape up as Humphrey versus Wallace contests, and either man could win both of them or one of them.

Maryland has 53 delegates and Michigan 132. The latter is the major northern industrial state most suited to a Wallace campaign, as bussing is "the" issue.

Yet, there is no way to predict the outcome here—as much will depend on what has gone before. If Wallace and Humphrey do as we predict in the previous primaries, then the Maryland and Michigan contests should be showdowns between the two, with McGovern picking up his customary handful of delegates to both. Muskie has formal UAW support, but if he loses Pennsylvania and Ohio and does not win Massachusetts, that UAW endorsement will be more an embarrassment to Woodcock than an advantage to Big Ed.

Note: Cross-over voting is allowed in Michigan. Again, our people should go for Wallace and McGovern.

OREGON & RHODE ISLAND—May 16: Rhode Island with 22 delegates is Muskie country, and if Big Ed is still alive, if not well, these delegates could be his. Oregon, with 34 delegates, is symbolically important—given the nature of the state, and the media attention it invariably receives. Everyone is on the ballot in Oregon—including Teddy. In the wake of Wisconsin, some have already conceded Oregon to McGovern, but whether he carries the state will depend greatly on how well he does in the intervening six weeks between then and now.

Jackson's support is not strong in Oregon, and it is difficult to see how he can last until then. More likely, this will be a McGovern, Humphrey, and Muskie contest—again, depending on whether or not Muskie is still alive.

Muskie's polls, which showed him leading in Oregon, are now as out of date as all his other polls. No projections here—but this is central to McGovern's planning.

CALIFORNIA, NEW MEXICO, SOUTH DAKOTA & NEW JERSEY—June 6: Despite Wallace's challenge, South Dakota's 17 have to go to McGovern. New Mexico's 18—who knows—likely a split between Humphrey and Muskie, and perhaps Wallace, who says he may work the state.

New Jersey is one of the two crucial primaries of the day—though it will be overshadowed by California, which is Big Casino. In Jersey there are 109 delegates; Muskie had the upper hand here, but appears to have lost it as both former Governor Hughes and Senator Williams are backing away from him. This rebounds to Humphrey's benefit. He is probably the favorite here, with McGovern again targeting on districts where he can pick up delegates. (Wallace has not decided yet on a major push here, though he has two weeks left to file.)

California is where it is at for the Democrats, with 271 votes—winner take all. This is nearly a fifth of what is needed for the nomination. This prize, the possibility of seizing it for bargaining leverage and prestige, is what may keep a bedraggled Ed Muskie in the race.

Wallace could not get on the ballot; McCarthy will not campaign and Jackson will have pulled out by then—in our estimate. This leaves it between Humphrey and George McGovern. If Muskie stays in and has any appreciable support, then what he draws from Humphrey could well give the Golden State to George McGovern. McGovern has organization here, enthusiasm, and money; it could pay off.

Further, he is the lone candidate on the Left for the balance of the primaries, and thus the more "centrists" left in the primaries—Jackson, HHH, Muskie, or Wallace—the merrier for George McGovern.

NEW YORK—June 20: New York's 278 delegates is the largest, but this will be split up considerably by the time it gets to Miami. New York does not have a statewide vote; moreover, the delegate slates do not have the candidates' names appended. So you vote for delegate John Jones, and that is that. Candidates tend to get popular figures pledged to them to run for delegate; strong grass roots effort is essential here, so McGovern should do extremely well in the Empire State, probably more delegates than anyone else, but not more than 100.

THE NON-PRIMARY STATES
Several points need to be made.

A) Regular Democrats are not doing as well as they have in the past.

B) A lot of liberals are getting into the convention who weren't there in 1968.

C) Unions are not doing as well.

D) There are sizable numbers of "undecided" delegates winning, and we do not know precisely to whom they will go.

E) McGovern is doing extremely well in non-primary states, maximizing his potential—when George is winning them in Georgia and Virginia and picking off two-thirds of the Kansas delegation, it means they have a Goldwater type operation going and going well.

THE SCENARIOS
SCOOP JACKSON—No way we can see him winning the nomination, and no reason for his continuing much further. Wallace has eclipsed him on the party's social conservative right. We predict Jackson will either be out after Ohio or after Oregon—the longer he stays in, however, the better for us, as he draws votes that would otherwise be Humphrey's or Muskie's—and so he aids George McGovern.

HUBERT HUMPHREY—Victory for Hubert lies in knocking Muskie out of the race in Pennsylvania and Ohio, in taking West Virginia and Michigan and Maryland from George Wallace, and winning California. Humphrey, in our view, is the odds-on favorite to become the Last Best Hope of the party Regulars against the McGovern insurgents. By and large, he does not contest any more major primary races with McGovern, directly, head-on—before the decisive California primary. His competition in Pennsylvania and Ohio is Muskie, and if he takes Muskie out of the play there—he contests Wallace in West Virginia, Maryland, and Michigan.

Clearly, once Muskie is eliminated—if he is—Humphrey's approach in California is to paint George McGovern to the Regulars as the death-knell of the Democratic Party they have known. Even should Hubert lose California narrowly, he will likely carry New Jersey and pull some delegates out of New York.

Our problem with HHH is that he has <u>never</u> won a contested Democratic Presidential primary.

ED MUSKIE—It is truly ten minutes to midnight for Big Ed. If he loses both Massachusetts and Pennsylvania on April 25—which he could—it is hard to see how he can regain his momentum to become the Candidate of the Party Regulars. McGovern has already locked up the Left.

Muskie's chance to rehabilitate himself comes April 25 in Pennsylvania and then a week later in Ohio. If he wins the first, he can conceivably win the second, and become himself the Candidate of the Regulars—the last man who can prevent a McGovern nomination. The problem for the Regulars is that unless they settle on a single candidate before California, they are going to lose California—to McGovern. From our standpoint, then, it would be good to have Muskie win something, good to have him and Jackson stay around for the California primary.

Muskie is today in a position not dissimilar from RN in 1968—had RN not swept the primaries. Had Miami come down to a three-way contest between RR, NR, and RN—then as soon as it appeared, the left or right candidate would win—RN in the center would become the beneficiary of the opposite wing's support. In other words, had Nixon not won on the first ballot, he could still have won on a later ballot by getting the panicked Rockefeller support should Reagan rise, and the panicked Reagan support should Rockefeller approach the nomination.

Ed's second chance lies in the fact that he is more acceptable to the Left than Humphrey and to the Regulars than McGovern.

Absenting only Teddy Kennedy, he still has the best chance of uniting the Democratic Party today.

One final note: Muskie could come alive and well if he should two weeks from now win <u>both</u> Pennsylvania and Massachusetts. That could bring him to life in an instant—and though highly unlikely, it is not altogether outside the realm of possibility.

GEORGE MCGOVERN—McGovern has these assets going for him:

A) He is maximizing his support in the non-primary states, with a hustling team maximizing his support and winning him, nickel and dime, delegates in some of the damndest places.

B) Even in the primary states where he is very nearly conceding defeat, such as New Jersey, Maryland, Michigan—he will be picking up small pockets of delegates.

C) He has momentum after Wisconsin; he has generated tremendous enthusiasm on the Left; he has convinced the True Believers that they can take over the party; and their challenge now has a "credibility" it has never previously had.

D) He is targeting well. The states he says he can win—he can conceivably win, i.e., Massachusetts, Nebraska, Oregon, South Dakota, California, and New York.

E) He will go to Miami with support in every section of the country if not damn near every state.

F) The convention he goes to will be more liberal and conscience oriented than any previous convention since the GOP in 1964. If Kennedy stays out and the convention goes more than two ballots, a lot of delegates are going to vote their hearts instead of their heads—and the Democratic Party could wind up with this fellow as nominee.

McGovern's problems are apparent; he is of course anathema to conservative Democrats; but also, after Massachusetts, he is going to have a dry spell in terms of publicity for a few weeks—and this could hurt him if Humphrey is dominating the news and building momentum with headline victories.

GEORGE WALLACE—As someone put it, if Wallace were nominated, the Democratic Party would self-destruct on his way to the rostrum. There is <u>no</u> scenario for a Wallace nomination. However, he could take 300 delegates into the convention; his delegates will be challenged; anything is likely to happen; there is no way to predict what he will do or what will be done to him—the Democrats themselves will have to decide that.

OUR NEXT GOAL

<u>What we need now is a decision on whom we want to run against.</u> We believe that McGovern is our candidate for dozens of reasons. He could be painted as a

left-radical candidate, the Goldwater of the Democratic Party; and at this point in time we would inundate him. The Wallace Democrats, South and North, as well as the Daley and Meany Democrats, would have to take hemlock to support a fellow whose major plan is to chop $32 billion out of defense. Also, he is weak with the blacks and would have to cater to that vote—to his great disadvantage. Humphrey can take the blacks for granted in a contest with the President.

If we want McGovern—and we believe we should—then what we want is a showdown in Miami between the Regulars and the Left—between Humphrey and McGovern with McGovern winning. And if McGovern loses that show-down—then by all means, we want Humphrey. The Left would never take him again; he would guarantee a horror show in Miami Beach and a walkout of the Left following.

Muskie is our third choice—the reason being that Muskie, despite his weaknesses, is still a potentially unifying candidate for the Democrats after a Humphrey-McGovern deadlock.

EDWARD MOORE KENNEDY

Evans-Novak, in a column that looks to have come from the horse's mouth, say that Kennedy would accept a genuine draft. He is on the catbird's seat today. Though there will be pressure to endorse McGovern—if McGovern carries Massachusetts two weeks from today—he can sit back and observe until July.

If the convention deadlocks on the first ballot, and if there is a deep division within the Democratic Party—he is the major unifying figure on the national scene today. Though he would be unacceptable to the South, in a national election, he would bring to his candidacy all the McGovern support, plus the Kennedy charisma, plus the support of the Meanys and Daleys. A Democratic Party deeply divided, thirsting for unity and victory, would welcome a Kennedy.

For this reason, we do not believe our strategy should be to flush Kennedy out. As Kennedy is elevated, McGovern recedes—and We Want McGovern.

Just as it would have been foolish for LBJ—who wanted Goldwater in April—to flush out and elevate the more formidable RN—so it is foolish for us we believe to flush out and elevate EMK—when he is far stronger and more dangerous than McGovern. We should elevate and assist McGovern in every way conceivable.

Nor can we surface Kennedy—if he doesn't want to be surfaced. If we indicate we are apprehensive about his candidacy, that makes his candidacy more likely. Right now, Kennedy is still in the background. There is a liberal media love affair going on with George McGovern; they will help George against Humphrey and we should help him as well. Every notch we move Kennedy up, we move McGovern down a peg. What we should do is begin publicly to take George McGovern seriously, and any pressure we could place upon EMK to endorse McGovern as the leader of the Left should be exerted. We might even attack McGovern to elevate him—also, to get the record on him into the media.

McGovern has a long shot at the nomination, a very long shot. But if he wins, we win. Let's let him have his run at the nomination and assist him in every way we can. Today, he gets 5 percent of a Democratic vote nationally, and RN swamps him in the polls—and people do not yet know what a wild man he is. McGovern's The One.[25]

6 The 1972 Campaign
Nixon v. McGovern

Since late 1970, Pat Buchanan and other advisors had been analyzing the Democratic presidential hopefuls and strategizing how Richard Nixon would match up against each in his 1972 bid for reelection. Much to the delight of the Nixon White House, the Democratic Party nominated Senator George McGovern of South Dakota. McGovern, initially a dark horse candidate, would only emerge as a viable contender after other Democratic heavyweights did not officially enter the contest (Senator Edward Kennedy) or faltered during the primaries (Senators Edmund Muskie, Hubert Humphrey, and Scoop Jackson). With little national name recognition and liberal policy positions, the Nixon White House considered McGovern to be "the weakest of all the Democratic challengers."[1] McGovern also enjoyed a strategic advantage during the primaries due to reforms from the 1968 contest that he had helped to enact. The McGovern-Fraser Commission reformed the party's nominating process, including more delegates to the convention being selected from primaries as opposed to caucuses or state conventions. These new rules provided for greater delegate representation at the Democratic National Convention from women, young voters, and African Americans, with fewer politicians, party bosses, and union leaders able to cast votes or make deals on the convention floor. While McGovern's top issue was ending the war in Vietnam, the Democratic Party platform represented a more liberal agenda on some domestic issues than their nominee espoused, including amnesty for draft evaders, public school busing to achieve racial integration, banning the sale of handguns, ending capital punishment, and promoting women's equality and gay rights. Less than three weeks after the convention, McGovern would have to replace his initial vice presidential pick, Senator Tom Eagleton of Missouri, with R. Sargent Shriver, former director of the Peace Corps, when it was revealed that Eagleton had undergone electric shock therapy for depression.[2]

The shift to the left allowed the Nixon campaign to effectively paint McGovern as a radical out of step with mainstream Americans. Conservative columnist Robert Novak wrote that according to an unnamed Democratic senator, McGovern was "for amnesty, abortion, and legalization of pot," and that once "middle America—Catholic middle America, in particular," learn that, "he's dead." The attack morphed into McGovern being the candidate of "amnesty, abortion, and acid," and the original quote would be attributed years later to none other than Eagleton a few months prior to McGovern winning the nomination.[3] This allowed Nixon to have an "easy campaign," staying mostly "out of the battle, nourishing his image as a bold world leader and utilizing people on his staff, congressmen, and cabinet members as 'presidential surrogates' to push his cause."[4] Yet the "Assault Strategy" against McGovern, fortified by the "Attack Book" of opposition research developed by Buchanan and Ken Khachigian, animated Nixon's campaign strategy through Election Day despite the obvious advantage he enjoyed in the polls. Never wanting to completely discount McGovern's potential, Buchanan and Khachigian urged Nixon to be the leader of Middle America while painting McGovern as an extremist.

This strategy became even more compelling after news of the break-in at the DNC headquarters at the Watergate Complex in June 1972. According to Buchanan, whose views were at odds with others in the White House: "Ken and I argued vehemently that attacks on McGovern for his far-left ideology, statements, and stands on issues must be paramount. People could believe Nixon was a good president and still vote for McGovern. But if they were convinced McGovern was a radical and an extremist—the way LBJ's crowd portrayed Goldwater—moderate Democrats would say that we just can't take a chance with this guy, we have to vote for the President. . . . The way to create a landslide for Nixon was not to celebrate Nixon, but, in Truman's phrase, to 'scare the hell' out of the American people about George McGovern."[5]

The strategy worked, as Nixon won the 1972 election with 520 Electoral College votes (McGovern would win only Massachusetts and the District of Columbia) and a popular vote margin of 60.7 percent to McGovern's 37.5 percent. Despite the overwhelming majority in both the Electoral College and popular vote tallies, Nixon did not earn a governing mandate as Democrats maintained control of both houses of Congress. Buchanan's successful "assault" and "attack" strategies, as outlined in his numerous memos, would become a focus of the Watergate investigation, as Buchanan testified before the Senate Watergate Committee in September 1973. Numerous news organizations reported days before the testimony that Buchanan's memos, obtained by the Committee, showed that he was the "architect" of political sabotage and "dirty tricks" against Democratic candidates in 1972. In his testimony, Buchanan chastised committee staffers for leaking "false and derogatory" information about him, defended his opposition research work on Democrats in the primaries (particularly Muskie) and McGovern during the general election, and stated that Muskie lost, and McGovern won, on their own accord.[6] Despite the attention paid to his campaign strategy memos during the Watergate hearings (many of which are included here and in the previous chapter), Buchanan, unlike numerous other White House staffers, was not involved in criminal misconduct related to Watergate.

1. Memo to John Mitchell, June 6, 1972

We agree with virtually everyone that post-California, the McGovern Record must begin to become part of the public record. The national perception of McGovern as a moderate and even a conservative must begin to change—before McGovern begins changing his positions from left toward center. We have all the necessary materials in our judgment—in an Assault Book to be ready tomorrow possibly—to tar McGovern as an extremist. Not in our memory has there been such a wealth of material with which to tag a national candidate as an extremist; and if we fail here, the price will be significant as McGovern could then conceivably march into November as the "Citizens Candidate" with the cleanest national image since Mr. Eisenhower. Booting our opportunity would be a tragedy—the important questions are not whether we get our materials on the public record, but timing and tone and degree and emphasis.

In our judgment Humphrey's effort to tar McGovern as an extremist was a gross failure because a) Humphrey came off as a politician in panic, making wild accusations against a calm, conservative appearing fellow; b) his tone of attack was negative and bitchy and strident; c) it came too late in the game.

In our efforts, which we feel can begin with the Re-elect campaign statement, following McGovern's smashing victories—we can avoid these pitfalls.

First, McGovern will be in his pinnacle of glory—he will have a sympathetic press, even an indulgent one—and the Nixon Campaign Statement should not go hard against the grain of this national sentiment, should not be immediately "rough and tough." Some congratulations, generosity and whimsy in that statement might well fit the occasion. But at least one crucial part of our message—perhaps iteration of his welfare reform proposals and awe at the cost to taxpayers—should be reflected in the statement by John Mitchell.

The next occasion we understand will be the appearance by Mr. Mitchell on Sunday. For that, we think we either ought to prepare a briefing paper, plus a book—or make some sort of joint determination as to what points we wish to get across in this national forum. The ex-AG will be able to make headlines on this—we can determine ourselves which of the materials we have we want dropped here, and iterated by our speakers around the country.

Our tone should at all costs avoid any sense of being embattled; we should be generous to George, if you will, but looking forward with enthusiasm to the contest. Any talk of McGovern being an easy mark should be eschewed. We probably have on record right now ninety percent of the outrageous or idiotic positions or statements Mr. McGovern will take—and we have five months in which to get those to the American people.

There is no need now to shoot it all out of the cannon. We should feed it out to the public in materials—one at a time—and wait until the public has digested one outrageous position, and McGovern has been forced to answer—before moving onto another. Here, rather than a sudden massive attack—a very gradual escalation, it seems to me, is in order—husbanding our resources and dealing them out bit by bit.

We will proceed—unless told otherwise—to draft a statement for Mr. Mitchell post-California, and have it ready for him by noon on Wednesday.

1. There is a strong feeling on our part that the term "radical" was overused in 1970; that it lost much of its electric charge; that the term "extremist" is a far more difficult one to defend against; and that in our on-going effort against McGovern—his positions and he himself should be characterized as "extremist" in character, not "radical."

2. A portion of this Assault Book—perhaps the segments dealing with the au courant and controversial issues—should be moved out to columnists and editorial writers. Some portion of the Assault Book should be put into the hands of surrogates, for their use, in coming weeks, before the Democratic Convention. The segments should be chosen by the Attorney General. Again, we would recommend that right now, we restrict ourselves to "seconding" the allegations of Humphrey and Jackson, not using too much of the unused material immediately—and quoting Democratic attacks on McGovern as much as initiating new ones.

3. There are already some press appalled at McGovern's potential candidacy—and there is no certainty the regular Democrats—after their shellacking today—are going to roll over and play dead. Far better if they do the preliminary hatchet work. They are a good deal more credible than we at this game. Before we move on, we should know what, if anything, Daley, Meany and LBJ, etc., plan to do.

4. There is an interesting development shaping up. McGovern's ambitious children seem to be busy "stealing" Wallace delegates—and playing false, by "ripping off" the Wallace delegations in Tennessee and elsewhere, places like Michigan. This is excellent. We should hold back commenting upon the process, which Governor Carter is raising hell about, until it is accomplished—and then accuse the Democratic Convention of shafting the legitimate popular winner, and stealing the delegates of a bed-ridden martyr.

5. Quietly, and right now, we should put to work—as far away from us as possible—an in-depth of the background, character, financial deals, land transaction, loans, business associations of George McGovern. Was he associated with Billy Sol Estes or Bobby Baker; who are his sugar daddies in the Dakotas? In short, a thorough, intensive investigation of the kind that the liberal press did on Vice President Agnew in 1968.

6. Post-California, let's proceed along these lines for the next week. But, in our view, there should be more input, and we should await more reactions—from the four primaries Tuesday—before "locking in" to any strategy all the way to the Convention.

Again, our immediate recommendation is a "gracious" response to McGovern's win—a response which at the same time moves onto the public record McGovern's welfare proposals—and raises the question of where the tax monies will be coming from to put all these millions of Americans on welfare.[7]

2. "Assault Strategy," June 8, 1972

This lengthy memo on strategy accompanied the "Assault Book" of research that Buchanan and Ken Khachigian had compiled on George McGovern, the presumptive Democratic nominee.

Herewith the Assault Book on which Ken Khachigian and I have been working the past week. Within are enough McGovern statements, positions, votes, not only to defeat the South Dakota Radical—but to have him indicted by a Grand Jury. If we can get these positions before the public and if the election hinges upon issues—only with enormous effort could we boot this election away.

However, in addition to the statements, issues and positions of George McGovern there are "perceptions" which we must address as well—"perceptions" that, unless dramatically altered, could give us considerable difficulty in the fall.

1. In a country where the "politician" is in increasing disrepute, George McGovern is perceived as a candid, honest straight-forward, citizen non-politician.

2. In a nation where the "Establishment" is viewed with a mixture of frustration and contempt by the left, right and the angry Wallace center—George McGovern is perceived by many as an anti–status quo, anti-Establishment figure—the candidate of the common man.

3. In a political year when the mood, we are told, is "throw the rascals out," we are the "ins" and Mr. McGovern is perceived clearly as one of the "outs." He is outside the power elite of the Democratic Party; he is perceived as outside the power elite of the American Government.

4. George McGovern has been and remains the "underdog" in a nation that has always had a warm spot for the "underdog."

5. In an era when the public yearns constantly for a "new face," George Mc-Govern is the newest, freshest face on the national scene, and the face of Richard Nixon is the most familiar of any political figure in the United States.

Before addressing how I feel we should deal generally with each of these "perceptions," and specifically with the assault materials provided, let me add these concerns:

1. The Republican Party is sleek and fat and incumbent. Our Conservative foot soldiers who out-marched the Democrats' union troops in 1968 are sullen, bitchy, angry. Our little old ladies in tennis shoes are not all enamored of H.R. 1, wage and price controls, and $100 billion in deficits—while George McGovern has an organization the likes of which the U.S. has not seen since the Goldwater Legions.

He has tens of thousands of True Believers, working night and day for him—spurred on by unanticipated triumphs and the anticipation of running the "Old Politics" right out of the White House.

As of now, in a seat of the pants judgment, I would say that if we are running 50–50 with George McGovern in the polls election day—he could conceivably beat us by four to six points, on the basis of his first-rate get-out-the-vote machinery.

2. The hard-fought Democratic primaries have resulted sharply in increased registration—especially by McGovern types—and any lopsided registration figures in the primaries will be lopsided anti-Nixon votes in the fall.

3. While McGovern's positions are wooly-headed, he is an ambitious and pragmatic politician—who will not hesitate to move crab-wise to the center to win this election. Some of the more garish of his positions will surely be shed by the fall. Further, my understanding is that his campaign film biography is an excellent piece of work—designed to portray him as the antithesis of the "radical," indeed, as the bomber pilot who won the war against Nazi Germany. We can anticipate that his commercials will be equally designed to hit the Democratic center.

Clearly, in addition to the problems listed, we have tremendous advantages—the Presidency, the view of millions that McGovern is some sort of wild radical, the split within the Democratic Party, the tendency of McGovern's red hots to "stick it" to the Daleys and Meanys when the opportunity arises, etc. But this memorandum is directed toward both general and specific suggestions to resolve our problems, to get the radical record of McGovern into the public record, to change the national perceptions of the two.

GENERAL RECOMMENDATIONS

1. We should move to re-capture the anti-Establishment tradition or theme in American politics. Incumbent Presidents <u>can</u> do this; RN did it in November 1969, when, as President of U.S., he called on the common man to stand with him against the elitist-backed mobs in the streets. That, coupled with the Vice President's standing up to the Establishment media, and slugging it out, raised RN to the highest point of his Presidency—69 percent approval. Why did we reach that level? Because, even though <u>Newsweek</u> led "Nixon in Trouble," even though Broder was writing of the "Breaking of the President," RN held both the Presidency position and the anti-Establishment position. How do we enhance our anti-Establishment credentials—and take Mr. McGovern's away—without surrendering the political asset of Incumbent President?

a) We need to shed the "in bed with Big Business" image. PJB believes we should seek out the opportunity to "take on" some egregious giant, preferably, but not necessarily Democratic, corporation publicly—as Kennedy did with Big Steel in 1962. Business will be with us in 1972—but one of our problems is a too close identification in the public mind with Corporate Powers. ITT reinforced that. Public presidential anger at the price-gouging of some Big Business firm would be, in my judgment, a good thing.

b) If we have abandoned the idea of introducing or supporting "tax reform"— I trust we have not—I would recommend RN publicly veto one, two, or three huge spending bills—on national television. Two minutes would be sufficient. The focus of the veto is that the taxpayer is already burdened enough by massive liberal spending programs that accomplish nothing, but break the back of the taxpayer. And RN believes the time has come in this country for less massive federal spending, not more, for lower taxes, not new inflation, and not new taxes. Most likely, McGovern will be voting for all these spending bills.

Our objective: Move him visibly into the posture of more and more govern-ment spending—and get ourselves on the "tax cut," working-man side of the issue. In my political judgment—what the nation wants is not more spending or the taxes or inflation required to pay for it—but less spending and lower taxes. Government takes too damn much of the earnings dollar in everyone's view, and we should be anti-tax in 1972.

(Indeed, in my opinion, this would apply to the so-called added value tax as well—since the average fellow is not likely to make the distinction between good and bad taxes.) One recalls that some years back, the President, in a quite effective television piece, vetoed, with a sweep of the pen, a major spending bill. Suppose we knocked off three in a row—calling for holding the line on spending and holding the line on taxes.

c) As the campaign progresses, we should increasingly portray McGovern as the pet radical of Eastern Liberalism, the darling of the <u>New York Times</u>, the hero of the Berkeley Hill Jet Set, Mr. Radical Chic. The liberal elitists are his— we have to get back the working people; and the better we portray McGovern as an elitist radical, the smaller his political base. By November, he should be postured as the Establishment's fair-haired boy, and RN postured as the Candidate of the Common Man, the working man. . . .

Just as Goldwater ended up 1964 portrayed <u>both</u> as a 100% Conservative— and a radical; so George McGovern must end up in 1972 portrayed <u>both</u> as an extremist and as the pet of the national liberal Establishment. Both are, after all, true.

d) The individual nationally who has done the best job on the above is Kevin Phillips—who writes of George hobnobbing with Schlesinger, Ford Foundation liberals, the radical chic, prancing around his $100,000 Japanese palace in $15 Pucci ties. My recommendation is that PJB—using our Radical Chic materials, as well as the Assault Book materials, write not a full-length book but a 5,000-word piece, using full color, good paper, like <u>First Monday</u>, with pictures of Hiss and Hoffman and other endorsees, and that this be printed and distributed by the millions. A quality, brightly written, colorful, pictures biography of McGovern of 5,000 words would be infinitely superior to those old full-length hatchet biographies that are never read.

e) "The clammy hand of consistency should never rest for long upon the shoulder of a statesman." –Senator Ashurst.

In addition to portraying McGovern as radical—we should, at the same time, never let the public forget he was part and parcel of the Democratic liberal establishment that passed all the huge spending programs of the fifties and sixties that failed. McGovern's high spending, high tax proposals have been tried. They failed to help the poor; they bankrupted the working man; they are taxing to death the middle class.

2. We cannot allow McGovern to succeed in this fraudulent effort to portray himself as Mr. Honest Citizen—rather than Mr. Politician. He can and should be nailed as a waffling, deceptive, crafty politician. In this, I disagree with the President. We should not only nail him with his radical positions, <u>but also</u> hold up a mirror to his shifts of position—which are certain to come. There are any number of sticks to beat him with—including that of the waffler who doesn't know where he stands. <u>The use of one does not exclude use of the other as well</u>.

Further, though a bit outrageous, McGovern can be charged, among Democrats, with "packing" caucuses, with "stealing" the nomination from the more popular candidate, with not representing the average man in the Democratic Party—but rather the left-wing organizers. As stated in an earlier memo, we should also wait until his people take delegates from Wallace—and then charge him with "stealing" delegates from a man in a hospital bed—discrediting his "reforms" and his "new politics," as no more than the old Gut Politics of the past. Also, anything that shows the McGovern people making deals, softening positions, backing off, waffling—should be spotlighted—not downplayed.

3. To reverse the "underdog" image of Mr. McGovern—we should, upon his nomination, cease speaking of any easy win. We should, in public, both to rally our troops and to remove this "underdog George" label—argue that the Democrats have the largest party. We should leak polls showing us worse off than we are. We should attempt as well and often as possible, again, to show McGovern as the Candidate of the <u>New York Times</u>, the Ford Foundation, Harvard, elitist left-wing professors, snot-nosed demonstrators, black radicals, and the whole elitist gang. This contest must wind up not as they envision with McGovern, Honest Man from South Dakota against Tricky Dick and his advertising budget—it should be Richard Nixon, candidate of Middle America, against the radical darling of the Liberal Establishment.

When Harriman and Clifford and the old gang assemble around him—that will be the moment to strike.

4. About the "new face" thing—little we can do. Except to use the attack materials herein to fill in all the blanks in the McGovern image, fill them in with some of these materials, in working-class neighborhoods, and we cannot but turn them off of George McGovern. The man has not been known well at all nationally—except for two weeks or two months at most. Impressions of McGovern may be favorable, but they are not fixed. They can be changed. And we should be moving this material into the public record. How?

a) Not bitterly or stridently. To do so gives the appearance of arrogance and power which we want desperately to avoid. Thus, when our "heavies," if you will—the Vice President, Bob Dole, etc.—use this material they should for the present be scrupulously exact and precise, and avoid for the present—the blistering attack. There will be "time enough."

b) The material should be targeted—not shot-gun. For example, abortion, amnesty, pot, the removal of the personal tax exemption (a killer for large Catholic families) these should be targeted for speakers and for pamphlets and for ads in Catholic and ethnic areas, Catholic and ethnic papers, Catholic and ethnic forums.

c) We should focus <u>at once</u> on the welfare schemes here—and on the military budget. They hurt George in California. McGovern is clearly moving on these proposals even his friends, at the <u>Post</u> and <u>Times</u>, are signaling him to get off them, and he is indicating that he might. They ought to be hung permanently around his neck as the first order of business.

d) We must not blow all of this assault material out of the cannon now; in 1970, we shot our wad in two weeks. There are five months between now and the election, and we should hang these one at a time around McGovern for the rest of the year.

SPECIFIC RECOMMENDATIONS
CATHOLICS
The abortion, ZPG, statements, aid to parochial schools, and marijuana statement—as well as the removal of the personal tax exemptions which would be devastating to large Catholic and ethnic families—should be used in a campaign flyer (contrasted with McGovern positions) to be distributed at Catholic churches in key states on Sundays—and should be used as the basis of targeted ads in the Catholic and ethnic press. (Once after the Convention—and last 2 Sundays of campaign.)

2. Volpe could take up McGovern propositions and before a national Knights of Columbus group—indicate that unintentionally, some are "anti-Catholic" in character, which Catholics concerned about Catholic values and the preservation of the Catholic family should fight. (If we could get Volpe to do this—PJB could write the two-page speech insert, for release, all media.)

JEWISH VOTERS
3. No reason why, with McGovern, we cannot make strong inroads here. Suggest that Secretary Laird devote a single speech to the impact of McGovern's Navy cuts on the American Sixth Fleet—with the conclusion, not unjustified, that the future of Israel, the survival of Israel—with McGovern's naval cuts—would be the decision of the Soviet Politburo. Again, the lead should be that—with George's defense cuts, without building the F-14 and F-15 to combat the MIG—"U.S. Navy could not intervene to save Israel."

4. The gist of the attack materials here on Israel—the HHH, the [Scoop] Jackson quotes about Israel being endangered by McGovern's position included—and McGovern's voting record—should be used in speeches before Jewish groups, in soliciting funds of Jewish groups. (Needless to say, above should be surfaced on television stations in N.Y.C., Chicago, Los Angeles.)

5. Again, targeted material here. Florida, Texas, Southern California. We

should get a list of the top ten defense plants in the country, the top ten aero-space plants, as well as the five NASA centers. And leaflets should be prepared and distributed at each of these entrances—at least twice this coming fall.

Lines: <u>If McGovern wins, Los Angeles will have an unemployment rate that will match Seattle's and Southern California will be the West Virginia of the seventies</u>.

The SST votes, as well as Jackson's quotes, should be used in media ads all over the State of Washington. (We lost it in 1960.) McGovern should be blamed for not only threatening future unemployment in Seattle—but for the existing unemployment in aerospace. But, again, the pamphlets should be targeted—and the statements should be made on regional television, primarily.

DEFENSE

6. As stated, Laird is doing an excellent political job. But we ought to go down this list of military cutbacks of McGovern—determine what firms (such as McDonnell in St. Louis) build these various weapons. And all these firms and their employees should be notified by campaign workers, by ads and the like—<u>just what plants will have to be shut down</u>.

7. We have Defense already busy at work on a major speech or statement by Laird which will name all the bases that will have to be shut down by McGov-ern's defense cuts. This information should be also provided to both Demo-cratic or Republican Congressmen in that district and to the local press there. And the Democrats should be called upon to support or repudiate McGovern's cuts.

8. In every "conservative" district—our people should be provided with the McGovern book; and Republican candidates should be encouraged to call upon their Democrats to repudiate this or that particular stand of their national can-didate. This will require distribution eventually of hundreds of copies of our completed book.

9. We believe sections of this attack book should be sent out, piecemeal, to all pro-Nixon columnists and newspapers in the country. We can have it printed in sections by the Republican National Committee—condensed even further than it is in a tight handy book for newsmen and editorial writers. But this should be done—only after the specifics in each section have been used to make front-page attacks.

10. All military publications, Navy League, etc., including the conservative publications . . . should be induced to run in brief, but full, the McGovern De-fense Programs, ASAP.

11. We yet believe that the focus of attack on defense should be—at the national level—scare the hell out of the public first; and then follow on and say that incidentally, this would also mean a loss of X million jobs. McGovern will want us to focus on jobs first—but we should not lose the Defense Argument—we are stronger here, frankly, than on the jobs argument. (For if we don't need those planes and ships and missiles, hell, everyone would want to switch over, as at the end of WWII.)

WELFARE

12. McGovern has two proposals. He has tried to get away from the $6,500 per family one—but he can be hung with both. Our speakers, our people on the tube should be conversant with each.

One good line: "Under George McGovern, two dozen and one hippies could get together and set up a commune in Taos, New Mexico, and not do a lick of work all year—and McGovern would send them every year a check for $25,000. No wonder Jerry Rubin and Abby Hoffman enthusiastically support his candidacy."

PROGRAM FOR BUSINESS

13. Again, these two pages should be double-checked, then used for fundraising and for possible ads in the WSJ and for scaring the living hell out of the business community.

14. At appropriate time, Shultz and/or John Connally should give a hair-raising speech on what the McGovern proposals would mean to American society and the American economy and the stock market.

15. From the way the market is reacting, it is apparent that McGovern's nomination should bring about a sharp drop. We should do nothing to prevent this from happening. Indeed, if Shultz or Connally or one of them can predict that McGovern's election would mean a depression or panic on Wall Street, and do it credibly, then they might well do so.

16. Specific business groups—such as real estate firms and brokers and the like—should be the target of direct mail, with a brief outline for each of what the McGovern proposals mean to them. To other business groups—direct mail, in this case, is the best means of alerting the businessman without alerting the liberals—the mailings might well be done (these and others) by independent groups. (Needless to say, the McGovern plan to phase out the oil depletion allowance should not go unnoticed in the Lone Star State.)

INTEGRATION & RACE

17. This has to be handled gingerly—but on digging up that Ribicoff proposal, we find it legitimate to charge McGovern with wanting to use federal coercion to integrate the suburbs, with favoring "racial balance" in this nation's public schools, with believing that bussing is an "essential" tool to accomplish the job.

On this, our speakers should say, we know George is sincere, but we think that compulsory integration of neighborhoods and schools would lead to racial tensions and disorders, not racial peace and harmony; we oppose him on all three.

18. Southern Senators and Congressmen should be shown the specifics of the Black Caucus program which McGovern has endorsed "in toto," even before we use these publicly. The Southerners will have to repudiate McGovern or force McGovern to repudiate these proposals—or take hemlock. Our candidates in the South—Senate and House—should be provided all this material by Harry Dent. As should our State Chairmen in the South. We can put it into form.

19. When McGovern backs off some of these Black radical schemes, as back off he must—we should continue to hang them around his neck—and then mail his recantation to the black media.

20. In Forest Hill, Missouri, and Warren, Michigan—and in blue-collar neighborhoods, frankly, speakers should argue against the McGovern integration proposals—and in favor of retaining the integrity and value of ethnic neighborhoods.

CHICAGO & DEMONSTRATORS

21. McGovern has said that the May Day demonstrators would not be on the streets but "having dinner at the White House" if he were elected. In this section—we have an idea for a commercial—juxtaposing RN and McGovern on the May Day demonstrators and indicating a vote for McGovern is a vote to have Rubin and Hoffman ("Guess Who's Coming to Dinner") at the White House.

22. McGovern's comments about the Chicago police ("those sons of bitches . . . those bastards") should be used—not prudishly, not condemning him for bad language. He can be excused for that—but condemned for the attitude his statement represents, a lynch mob attitude toward the nation's peace officers, a knee-jerk tendency to exonerate hell-raisers and condemn the policy. This should be done also in letters to the editor to all Chicago papers.

(Indeed, our letters operation—as well as speakers—should be using these materials to target in on sections of the country.)

23. Resurrecting McGovern's comments on Hoover would be most effectively done by the ex-AG and Pat Gray and the Vice President.

24. MONDAY can do an effective job for us—by back-paging each week one of a numbered series of effectively written and documented attacks on McGovern—giving readers materials for use themselves in the boonies. (For example, suppose MONDAY one week simply ran the McGovern Defense Program as outlined in our package for the locals.)

ELLSBERG

25. McGovern's personal encouragement of Ellsberg to violate Federal law is a matter which we should wait to exploit . . . say two months after the Democratic Convention—it should serve as a centerpiece of a national speech—perhaps by the Vice President. (Again, our concern is that we not "mix up" our attack.) One specific area per speech. . . .

VIETNAM

26. Two points should be hammered here: a) McGovern has been constantly wrong in his predictions about what Hanoi would do; he has even been duped by Xuan Thuy and b) the SOB would leave our prisoners in Hanoi—and count on the good will of that barbarous regime to get them back. Any attack on his Vietnam position should be prefaced by saying, "We do not question his patriotism."

27. McGovern's Right from the Start can be countered—but this is a defensive maneuver for us since presumably we think his position wrong now and wrong then. Rather, the approach to be taken here is to charge that he is a) Old Sour Grapes in harassing and stabbing in the back the President who is ending a war his President could not win or end and b) McGovern waffled all over the lot on the War, like every other Democratic politician, and we have the quotes here to prove it.

RHETORIC

28. We have dug up a 1964 quote where McGovern called Goldwater the most "unstable radical and extremist" ever to run for the Presidency, which can be used against him. Also, his rhetoric, which we have documented, should be used to make either a pre-emptive or retaliatory strike for his certain charge that we are "polarizing" while he is attempting to "bring us together."

29. In terming McGovern as an extremist—we should begin by quoting

Democrats like Carter, Yorty, Humphrey, and Jackson, of course—just as the Rockefeller quotes were more devastating against Goldwater than the LBJ attacks.

MCGOVERN'S FRIENDS

30. This fellow Mott, who bankrolls McGovern, is I understand a screaming fairy who makes $800,000 a year and pays no taxes—we are trying to interest MONDAY in doing a take-out on him in the near future.

SPEAKERS

31. To make the case against McGovern most credible, we not only need our heavy hitters—but we need the Democrats mentioned—and especially our liberals. Neal Freeman suggests the following be commissioned to do some of the rough work on "George McGovern extremism."

1. Rockefeller
2. Javits
3. Aiken
4. J. S. Cooper
5. Douglas Dillon
6. Scranton

If, of course, we could get Meany, Wallace, or Jackson—that would be outstanding.

32. Ken Khachigian and I will monitor McGovern's appearances and hopefully be mailing and phoning questions to any panels or interviewers. If we have an advanceman traveling ahead of the McGovern campaign—he should be providing the questions, which we can provide him.

33. Some on the media are slobbering all over George; they may have to be charged publicly with being pro-McGovern—to force them to back off a bit. In this light, Godfrey Sperling had an excellent piece today, we understand, which perhaps our people should be quoting. (Incidentally, given his performance the other night, [Sander] Vanocur is a positive disaster for us—and McGovern's most effective campaigner. He may have to be fired or discredited—if we are to get anything approaching an even shake out of that left-wing taxpayer subsidized network.)

34. Again, we have to be on guard against any too harsh or strident an attack. With a hostile media out there—they will pounce on the first allegation of "Tricky Dick" or "smear" campaign. Perhaps an early address—attacking some

of the smear books around already about the President, and some of McGovern's comments might be used to pre-empt or mitigate this certainty.

35. Mr. Dent can make the argument that George McGovern "said he would be delighted to run with a black man, but not George Wallace."

36. We need to dig up film of McGovern at some of these demonstrations with the VC flag in the background, and with demonstrators chanting and shouting, etc.

37. From McGovern's statements, it is fair to say he would cut off all assistance to our NATO ally Greece, but consider giving military aid to the black guerillas in Southern Africa.

38. McGovern favors giving away (Black Caucus) 1% of U.S. GNP to foreign aid, with priority on Africa—which amounts to $11 billion—about a 400 percent increase in foreign aid.

39. McGovern's old statements about Henry Wallace, about the U.S. starting the Cold War, etc., should be moved into all the ethnic language publications. And all his far left background should be disseminated to the far right in the U.S for them to publish as it is too complicated for us to handle.

NIXON'S THRU IN '72

40. This is a slogan we can turn to our own advantage. For example, if Daley is booted out of the Democratic convention—on his arrival at his Mayor's office in Chicago—some bearded types can be out front with signs—"DALEY'S THRU IN '72—VOTE MCGOVERN"—or some such. Other combinations—about Meany, for an example, comes to mind. Or at Defense Plants "The M-I-C IS THRU IN '72" [Military Industrial Complex] VOTE MCGOVERN.

We have some other thoughts and ideas—but we are sending these along for immediate consideration.[8]

3. Memo to H. R. Haldeman, "Response to HRH Memo of June 12, 1972," June 18, 1972

A response from Buchanan and Khachigian to critiques of the "Assault Strategy" memo from Haldeman and others.

Many of the points HRH mentions were omitted in our original Assault Strategy memo for the basic reason that we were focusing exclusively upon the "negative" rather than the positive. Some recommendations in the HRH memo we would concur with—others we do not. Let's take them point by point:

1. "The Buchanan memorandum fails to recognize the necessity to keep our

strength up front and center. In other words, all of our attack lines on the opposition should end up emphasizing our strengths."

We don't agree with this. For the following reasons. First, millions of Americans vote not _for_, but _against_—their hostility toward one candidate is _the_ compelling motive at the voting booth, not their enthusiasm _for_. And a "negative" campaign—largely directed from the positive one on RN—would in our judgment be much more convincing to those swing voters who have never been pro-RN, but who can be "terrified" by this new phenomenon. LBJ could not conceivably have gotten his sixty percent against RN—he got it against Goldwater, not because of the positive LBJ "ad," but because Goldwater was portrayed as a threat to the Republic. We should, in our judgment, recognize that potentially millions of knee-jerk Democratic voters are going to come our way, if they come—because though they are not enthusiastic about RN, they are anti-radicalism.

Secondly, when one observes that McGovern apparently lost 15 points in one week in California—among Democrats, it is clear that there is tremendous room for movement downward by McGovern—from a relatively small investment. On the other hand, we see that RN—from the unprecedented China trip and attendant publicity, and from the historic Moscow visit and SALT agreement—has only risen seven or eight points.

The lesson is clear. The potential for movement by McGovern—downward—is far easier and less costly than the potential for additional upward RN movement. In short, if it takes a Peking and Moscow summit and a SALT agreement—and reams of hours of heroic copy to move up seven points—while George can be dropped fifteen in a week by some hard-nosed Humphrey attacks—dollar-for-dollar—when it comes to McGovern this argues we ought to put our campaigning dollars into attacking him, rather than boosting ourselves.

Third, and related: RN is _known_ to the nation; impressions of RN have hardened over a period of twenty-five years. There are not likely to be any sudden new perceptions of RN by the masses in five months. On the other hand, the perceptions about McGovern have not even begun to harden with the nation as a whole. We have a far better chance of affecting a change in the present image of McGovern than we do in the present image of the President.

Fourth, let's look at it this way. RN cannot possibly get below 40% of the vote, and cannot probably exceed 60%. Those swing voters are more than likely Democrats, or independents somewhat lukewarm toward the President (a group that would probably split half for RN and half for JFK in 1960). What is most likely to convince them to vote 95% for RN: Is it a major campaign convincing them of what they already know fairly well—that RN is competent, experienced and innovative in foreign affairs? (Even many of RN's opponents would concede this.) Or is it more likely to result in greater returns if we convince them rather that the "alternative" is an utter disaster for the country. In short, anyone who can be convinced that McGovern is a disaster is automatically a vote for RN. While someone who can be persuaded that RN is an imaginative foreign policy leader is not necessarily a vote for RN—and he can still vote for McGovern. My view is that the negative McGovern campaign needs not be—and should not necessarily be—tied to a pro-RN pitch at the end. If there were five people in the race, I would subscribe wholly to point one—but there are only two and anyone whom we can convince that McGovern is a wild man is ours—for certain—even if he at the same time thinks RN is a conservative square.

Fifth, and finally—not only does the pro-RN approach tend to dilute an anti-McGovern message; the President should not be twinned with McGovern on these issues where our disagreements are of degree rather than kind. For example, if we are going to say McGovern is toying with the security of our country—whereas we, too, have cut back, but only responsibly on defense—then we are weakening our case. Where the President can be contrasted with McGovern is where the breach is clean as a whistle, i.e., McGovern favors abortion on demand—RN thinks this is morally wrong; i.e., McGovern favors legalization of marijuana; RN thinks this is wrong and a threat to the American family. We should keep in mind that what we have is a President and a statesman and what they have is a light-weight and a wild man—and we ought not to be comparing them too much in speeches, just as we don't want any debates which would have the effect of putting them on the same plane.

Lastly, look at it this way. During the fall campaign the pro-RN news footage of RN as President will probably amount to seven times the pro-RN advertising footage. Thus, the pro-RN ad materials will only be a minor reinforcement of the RN national image—a minor fraction of the time RN is seen. On the other hand, given the pro-McGovern disposition of the liberal media, the anti-McGovern material from our campaign is likely to be a major and crucial segment of the entire anti-McGovern materials that go out to the nation.

2. "We must not get trapped into McGovern's bog of peddling himself as a new face. If people want new ideas, this Administration has the boldest initiatives in history."

We agree with the first sentence, but not necessarily with the second. The reason is this: We have spent countless hours and unrecorded effort selling the bold dynamic "New American Revolution,"—more effort probably than we can duplicate between now and November—and the returns are, in my judgment, not encouraging. If we took a national poll dealing with RN's <u>domestic</u> proposals—and asked how many considered them bold, new, imaginative and then further, how many were going to go with RN because of them—the returns, one assumes, would not be particularly heartened. Dollar-for-dollar, again, it is not a cost-effective investment of PR time, money, or effort to attempt to portray the Nixon Administration domestic programs as "exciting." We would be going against a public perception; we would be attempting to convince millions of the attractiveness of "programs" when increasing numbers have about had it with government "programs" in general.

The first sentence—about knocking down the "new face"—is right on the money. McGovern has been part and parcel of the Congress which has sat on its duff for two years; he has been a member of the Democratic majority which has controlled both houses of Congress since McGovern came to Washington.

Who wrote the loopholes in the law; who raised the taxes; who failed to provide relief; who is now sitting on its can doing nothing for the average man—but waste his dollars. Why who, other than the Congress of which George McGovern has been an integral part since 1956, the Congress he and the left-wing liberals have been in control of, absolutely, ever since McGovern came to Washington. Wallace hit them on this, and so can we. McGovern should rightly be portrayed as not something with new ideas, but someone with a plan to dump new billions in tax dollars down the old ratholes he and his friends constructed over the last 16 years. . . .

3. "The Buchanan memorandum deals almost entirely with domestic matters and totally misses our big issues which are foreign policy. Who is the bold leader? Who is the fresh leader? Who is the dramatic leader in foreign policy?"

Basically, we agree that foreign policy will be a long suit for the President—and we mentioned specifically attacks on McGovern on Israel, Europe, defense, and Vietnam. But, again, the same question arises. The entire nation has seen RN in China, seen RN in Moscow, seen RN sign SALT—the coverage has been sweeping and massive. Can we really advance that appreciably with speeches and verbal references to what the nation already knows and already believes—that RN is an imaginative statesman?

We should—in our positive advertising, and in RN's posture during the campaign, publicly, emphasize the Somber Statesman, the imaginative statesman, who has mastery over the issues of peace and war. But we don't need to constantly draw explicit comparisons. The implicit one is satisfactory. If we can get individuals like Rockefeller, liberals and moderates, saying that McGovern is

naïve and a madman, if he thinks we can gut the Sixth Fleet, without Israel going down the tubes. If George can be portrayed as something totally out of his
element in questions of foreign policy, a man who is both too soft and too much
of a light-weight, a foolish man whom Brezhnev would eat for breakfast—then
anyone who is convinced of that is <u>automatically</u> an RN voter. There is no other
choice.

There are two foreign policy problems we see. One—Vietnam. Polls show
McGovern's support is tied inextricably to the desire to get out of Vietnam. In
our view, the "wrong from the start" materials in the Assault Book, portraying McGovern as repeatedly duped, and misled by Communist profession of
good intentions, and his "abandoning" of our prisoners should help neutralize
his potential strength here. Also, if RN pulls the rug out on McGovern with a
settlement—we should lace into him as a "squalid nuisance" who only harassed
and nit-picked and back-stabbed the President who brought America out of
the war—while McGovern and company got us into a war they could not win
or could not end.

The second serious problem is that McGovern is milking the old right and
the new left isolationism both. Frankly, foreign aid truly has no constituents
left—and McGovern recognized this. The argument against spending our
money for exotic weapons, when we need to re-build here at home; the argument that maybe our allies should do more for themselves—these arguments hit
home far beyond the McGovern constituency. (The McGovern endorsement of
that 1% of CNP foreign aid [$11 billion] with "priority on Africa" ought thus to
be hung around his neck. Like Mr. Wallace used to say, "Those fellows want to
give more billions of dollars away to Hottentots.")

Given the necessity for foreign military assistance and its growing unpopu-
larity, we may have to out-demagogue George on this one, cast him in that role,
and use the arguments that the only way to prevent Americans from fighting
future wars is to provide the natives with the guns to defend themselves. If
we don't, we'll have American Marines rather than South Vietnamese Marines
defending South Vietnam, as we did when McGovern's men sat in the White
House.

4. "We should attack McGovern in a way that surfaces our point, not just hit
his points. We should not get trapped into putting out the enemy line."

We concur. We think this is covered in our earlier points.

5. "We have to build the foreign policy issue in terms of the question of
changing horses in mid-stream. In other words, President Nixon has launched
some very major, far-far-reaching foreign policy initiatives. We can't afford to let

an inexperienced novice come in and pick up the reins at this point. We cannot afford to have McGovern in the White House in terms of foreign policy. His inexperience and naivety in the foreign policy field would be disastrous. Do we really want 'White Flag McGovern' in the White House?"

Excellent here. This is one area where we can contradict No. 3—especially in a possible RN speech. How should we build RN up while tearing McGovern down. Here are several ideas:

The theme that RN has brought 500,000 boys out of Vietnam, has saved that little nation from collapse, has opened the door to China, has negotiated a truce in the Cold War, has brought into bearing the most historic arms agreement in history—and, for God's sake, let's not throw this away by putting into the White House, some rank amateur and clown who doesn't know his fanny from first base about foreign policy.

We can build up this theme, and should. The United States today stands on the threshold of building a structure of peace that can last for the remainder of this century. There is a chance, a good chance, but not a certain chance, that if RN can finish the structure which is now half built—that for the remainder of this century no more American boys will be dying in places like Vietnam. But for God's sake, to fire the architect when the cathedral is half finished, and replace him with an engineering student is insane. This is like firing the research physicians at NIH right at the point at which they may have a cure for cancer—and replacing them with some hippie medical students.

This could serve as a counter to the McGovern argument that RN's initiatives in foreign policy are good—but that job is done. We must now turn to the home front. Our argument has to be the job is not done—and anyone who thinks it is and acts on that belief is likely to bring down the entire structure just before it is completed. The concrete is still soft—it has not yet hardened; now is not the time to change builders.

Further, along these lines, we should emphasize the incredible naiveté of McGovern who thinks that the way you negotiate with the Soviets is to cut your fleet in half, reduce your army to pre–Pearl Harbor level, mothball half your bombers, scrap much of your nuclear deterrent—and then negotiate. RN and the people high up around him can say—"We have been there in Peking and Moscow and candidly, they will not be impressed by a nation which strips itself naked to show its good will."

They will not treat an America that abandons its strength with respect, but with contempt. They will not then be convinced that the path of peace is best, but the path of hostility and testing. My friends, a weakened and softened and beseeching America is not the kind of America that can keep the peace. Only a strong and resolute and tough nation will be respected, and be treated with respect. If we throw our arms into the sea—the enemy response will not be to love us, but to laugh at us—and to treat our friends and allies as totalitarians and bullies have always treated the weak. . . .[9]

4. Memo to H. R. Haldeman, June 18, 1972

In response to your memo of June 12 re: RN Posture—

A) Have no hard feelings about what RN should be doing between Conventions. He should of course maintain the Presidential pedestal, eschew partisan activity, if not political. On this, however, we should be flexible, pending the outcome of the Democratic Convention. That is the event off which the President's activity should be keyed. If the dominant theme coming out of that convention is, say, pro-marijuana, abortion—or pro-welfare—then in our substantive actions, taken by the President, there might well be the drawing of the issues. Again, however, we will have to await the Democratic convention to determine this.

B) Post-convention to election, again, we should hold now to a posture of flexibility. If RN is running a lead following the GOP Convention, a good lead, his surrogates should handle the campaigning for him—and he should only do enough to defeat the charge of the "front-porch" campaign. Since our strength is foreign policy in a world where there is a deep desire for peace—RN should not rule out major foreign policy meetings, high visibility, which cast him in the role of Statesman, in unspoken contrast to McGovern, who one imagines will be waging a partisan argumentative campaign.

C) RN should hold off vigorous campaigning for as late as possible. Perhaps a couple of days early in the campaign—then a testing of the effectiveness of his personal campaigning. I have a real question whether RN on the stump tends to add uncommitted votes, or whether the benefit is largely in terms of rallying troops, with the uncommitted tuned out. Even the drawing of differences between us and them should be on a high level.

D) Would not rule out of consideration a half-hour televised address by the President, or V.P. stating the "differences" between the candidates, in nonpartisan, but ideological ways. We have so much on McGovern; we may want to take it directly to the people in a single message—even while our surrogates are hitting the individual messages on the stump.

E) Suggest consideration be given to a series of Oval Office fifteen minute addresses, with the President using the sounding board of the White House to make his campaign appeal to the American people. Foreign policy, Social policy and more Government vs. less Government (and less taxes) could be the Nixon appeal. They should be candid, straightforward, and give the clear-cut differences between the two of us, rather than a blurred type thing. (This corresponds with my view that while many elections find both candidates ending up saying the same thing—this time we want to put some air between us and McGovern, and paint him as honest, sincere, and way, way out.)

F) Let's keep his travel schedule flexible. However, the President in campaigning should not restrict himself to GOP audiences at all. The idea of a giant Catholic or ethnic audience—a kick-off address in Cadillac Square—something symbolic to indicate the new GOP should be actively considered. It would be wrong to rule out GOP audiences—but we have to assume that they are going to be ninety percent with us. The President should seek out massive audiences of the swing voters in this election—who will not unlikely be the Northern Democrats who cannot abide the elitist, permissive liberalism of George McGovern.

G) One thought. Why not have the V.P. candidate, assuming that it is Mr. Agnew, and John Volpe, right at the head of the Columbus Day Parade down Fifth Avenue. From our polls, one understands that what we risk losing to McGovern are upper income moderate GOP WASPs (we have to scare them back with the "socialist" issue) and what we stand to gain are the lower and middle income ethnics and working class, many of them of immigrant origins, and many of them Catholic.

(One thing we could do for the President is to put that crazy Forest Hills integration scheme over the side; it would help us immensely with Jewish and ethnics, who don't want their neighborhood busted up by liberal bureaucrats.)

H) On strategy for attack—my thoughts are already largely in hand. However, just some reminders:

1. Don't shoot it all out of a canon at once; dribble it out so that as soon as McGovern has spent four days answering one charge, the next one is moved from the front burner onto the serving board.

2. Avoid stridency and nastiness and partisanship—some of this is certain to creep in late in the campaign, but the press here is intolerant of our attacks where it is indulgent of the opposition's. Keep our cool for as long as possible.

3. A late start in the campaign—unless we are behind in the polls, would be my recommendation. I recall well how all our people and some press were saying, "Get the hell up to New Hampshire; Romney is starting to make enormous gains." We waited to the last minute, and then campaigned sparingly and rolled up an eight-to-one margin. We ought to again hold our fire until they are right in front of the trenches.

4. We ought to have a formal reassessment of the strategy midway in the

campaign. And have what I do not feel we had in the general election of 1968 or 1970—the flexibility to shift gears rapidly and move off one theme or one approach onto another.

OPPOSITION LINE OF ATTACK
Already, they are signaling what it is. They are going to use the "trust" thing, McGovern is a candid, honest man whom you can believe, while Nixon is shifty, and crafty and has a credibility gap—and the character of our leader is important. (This partially explains their reluctance to move off their "tinkertoy proposals." They don't want their man to be in the position of being portrayed as another shifty politician. Some of them fear that worse than the radical charge.)

Our response. Wait a piece until they start up this attack; it will get harsh. And then our top surrogates should go over on the attack—accuse McGovern and his people of using a campaign of character assassination against the President of the United States—and demand that if they are going to whisper at rallies that the President is dishonest and untruthful, by God they should have the courage to come out and say it publicly. Accuse them of using "code words" to call the President an evil man; accuse them of a gutless refusal to debate us on the issues, and of a retreat into the politics of slander and smear. If they confront us on the issues, I don't see how—if they are clearly and politely and consistently made—we can lose this one.

Random thoughts of a summer afternoon. The important thing is to keep our flexibility, not lock into a Schlieffen Plan at this particular point in time. The old Eisenhower adage here is apposite. Planning is essential; plans are worthless.[10]

5. Memo to John Mitchell and H. R. Haldeman, June 25, 1972
The manner of McGovern's response to our attacks upon his rhetoric, and positions, has emerged. Responding to a rather mild critique of his welfare plan and new politics—by Herb Stein—McGovern responded thus:

"He called the attack 'the opening shot of this year's campaign against me' and said, 'Nixon obviously realizes that this year's campaign is going to be waged primarily over the rampant unemployment, inflation, economic uncertainty and favoritism, which now burden this country.'

"The attack (Stein's) tipped his (Nixon's) hand that he is going to try to cover up with the kind of political hatchet work which has characterized every campaign he has ever run."

Thus even a mild criticism of McGovern's record will likely produce charges of "Tricky Dick," "Smear Tactics," the old "Low Road" so familiar to Nixon and his hatchet men. This is, it appears, the McGovern strategy for answering all of the material we have piled up on Georgie; and it is a strategy which McGovern will be counting upon the press to assist in its implementation.

What this means for us, I think, is that we must

A) Be scrupulously accurate in our allegations, and calm and reasoned in quoting his wild statements and positions.

B) Get the jump on McGovern by using his Adolph Hitler quotes, and other blood-curdling charges on the record, before he starts charging us with vicious attacks. We have four or five of McGovern's statements which justify a demand for an apology to the President, which justify further our moving them into the public press—with the expressed hope that George McGovern will not do this kind of vicious name-calling and comparing of the President with Hitler in this campaign. Our hope is that George McGovern will get his campaign out of the smear stage, right off the bat. "We intend to confront Mr. McGovern on his issues and his position, but he has an obligation to clear the record of the slanderous libels he has made against the President of the United States; I refer specifically to ….etc., etc. etc."

Each time McGovern raises this charge of "smear" we ought to have those quotes to stuff right down his throat.

In the last analysis, if the need appears, we should be ready to have the President go, late campaign, with "more in sorrow than anger" speech, detailing the McGovern positions and denying the "Hitler" charges.[11]

6. Memo to Richard Nixon, June 25, 1972

Cronkite is right. The McGovern camp is divided between True Believers and Pragmatists; the former of whom would be distraught with a McGovern "deal" to save the Daley delegation, for example. The True Believers are not unlike the Goldwaterites in the galleries at the Cow Palace, who gave Rocky the treatment before a national audience, while Cliff White and the others on the floor were holding their people to a respectful silence.

The Pragmatists in McGovern's camp, however, are themselves divided, essentially over the question of what courses to follow:

A) Stay on his positions, with little fudging, thus running against the President as a truthful, honest, candid, far-reaching reformer, who does not back off what he believes. (By doing this, he will force some Democrats to bolt.)

B) Or move to the center, right in the public glare, by "embracing" a Democratic Platform more moderate than his own on welfare, taxes, defense, etc.

Manckiewicz and some of the others who are pragmatists apparently feel that the pragmatic thing to do is to stand fast—to try to win not on coalition politics, but win on the undiluted Prairie Populism approach, which keeps the True Believers happy.

On the challenge at the convention, however, all of McGovern's pragmatists wish they could go away. They don't want Dick Daley kicked out of the Convention; they are not supporting the challenges openly, though it is inevitably their people (Jesse Jackson & Co.) who are carrying out purges.

The point of the matter is that right now, McGovern does not control his delegates the way Cliff White and the others could control the Goldwater delegates. They are "issues" people, many of them, who are women's lib, pro-abortion, antiwar, etc. types first and McGovern delegates second. They are for McGovern because of his stand on these issues, not for the issues—because McGovern is for them. Their first loyalty is, in many cases, not to form a coalition that can win—but to guarantee the success of the particular and independent causes in which they are working. Some of them are using McGovern as a vehicle for the advancement of their own objectives, which McGovern's best interest may or may not dictate at this point in time.

And if McGovern tries to turn them off, they will raise hell publicly; and if he does not—and lets the purges and challenges run amok—he risks the outrage and alienation of the party regulars, because it is his animals raising hell in the cage.

Buchanan will be astonished, and we will be in for some difficulty, if these Gay Lib, Women's Lib, black militant, etc. types—all of them camera hogs—do not raise hell if they do get their way at Miami Beach. At this point, it seems to be impossible for the Democrats to quietly reconcile the basic differences they have—and highly improbable that the resulting internecine war can be kept off the television cameras.

Some of the preliminary caucuses promise exciting events for Miami.[12]

7. Memo to Richard Nixon, July 5, 1972

At HRH's request, some thoughts on 1968 and 1960.

First, it is imprecise to say that "in 1968 there was a substantial decline during the campaign." (If there is a single hallmark of RN's runs against both JFK and HHH, it is the remarkable stability of the Nixon vote from August through November.) The President did not so much lose votes from August to November of 1968—as we lost a historic opportunity, the "lost landslide" as someone has referred to it. While we failed to edge upwards in the slightest, Humphrey closed a 13 point gap. What were the reasons for this?

A) Some of the HHH gains were inevitable; the Democratic candidate, if he performed reasonably well, was simply going to win back some of the traditional Democratic vote, horrified at the Chicago convention, but not a Nixon voter at heart.

B) We failed utterly to pick up the Wallace defectors in the North, who slipped away from Wallace through Nixon, back to HHH. This return to HHH is partly due to the efforts of the AFL-CIO, probably partly due to RN's "anti-union" image from the fifties, partly due to our own short-comings. (Incidentally, we are in better and the Democratic Left in worse shape with these voters than in 1968; our opportunity is renewed.)

. . . But, in my judgment, our own campaign had serious short-comings in 1968. Basically, they were these:

a) A lack of flexibility. We established a game plan, and followed it through, although in early October, it should have been evident that we were losing the interest of the press and the country as well. The hoopla campaign—to demonstrate RN had the kind of enthusiasm and unity HHH did not, was ideal for September. It was not for October.

Once Humphrey made his Salt Lake City speech, the President should have, in my judgment, attacked him directly and vigorously, to force back the split in the Democratic Party between the pro-bombing and the anti-bombing forces who had fought at the convention and who were yet at sword's point. We let HHH off the hook on this. By so doing, he got off of that petard and went over onto the attack.

On the attack, he began to move, to make new and different charges, to attract interest.

b) The President in the fall campaign of 1968 was plagued by the identical problem he had in the fall campaign of 1960. A Hostile Press. Teddy White testifies to this in 1960 and Miss Efron in 1968. In addition, I have on personal knowledge that a group of 19 Washington press types who had divided 10–9 pro-RN in September, were 18–1 pro-HHH at election time.

What explains the bad press? We are partly at fault, I believe. We shut down communication with them—compared with the primaries where we got good press. We also, because of circumstances, were maneuvered into the upper-dog position. We were the more conservative of the two leading candidates. We did not deviate from the set-speech-Man-in-the-Arena-handout routine sufficiently to attract their on-going attention or interest. They were more concerned with reporting a breaking story, The Humphrey Comeback, which was exciting news, than the RN Radio Speeches, which with few exceptions only got a stick of type or two. Our personal relations with the traveling press deteriorated from the campaign, partly due to the "size" of the corps, the natural hostility of liberals, and our natural antipathy toward them which was coming through late in the game.

c) But, rather than strict comparison of 1960 and 1968, which may or may not be useful, and rather than belabor the shortcomings of the various campaign, which are many—but which are as well counter-balanced by the right decisions, let me rather enumerate those dangers which lurk for us, in my view, in 1972—based on the campaigns presidential of the last 12 years. What we face in my view is:

THE DANGERS OF 1968 & THE OPPORTUNITY OF 1964

1) We must place him on the defensive from the outset, and not let him off of it until November. In our 1968 and 1970 campaign, we did this for the first three weeks—then either HHH "got well" on Vietnam or the liberals "got well" on "law and order," and our issue hand had been played. Again, we have enough on McGovern to keep him on the defensive throughout the fall—we ought not to blast it out of the cannon at once; our speakers should be on the attack.

2) We have to maintain a flexibility that I do not believe existed in 1968 and from what I read did not exist in 1960. As Ike said, "planning is essential; plans are worthless." We should have a mapped-out game plan before the campaign starts—both for attack on the Opposition and for presentation of the candidate, but there should be a "Review Committee" to look over that plan and over our media at least once a week.

3) While we should rule out the President—for the time being—on the Attack Role, I would not rule out a Presidential address to the country, splitting RN off from McGovern on the issues, right now.

4) We should have ourselves a strategy meeting on dealing with the press and media between now and November. In my view, we have discredited them for the bias of which they are guilty for three years—indeed, public confidence in their performance is on the decline. . . .

5) We should keep in mind that it was not LBJ's performance and personality which won him 60% of the vote—it was the portrayal of Goldwater as an extremist, which frightened even Republicans.

In my view, given the antipathy of the national media and the smallness of the GOP, there is no way we could conceivably do better than a 54–46 victory over a centrist, popular Democrat with a united party. Against a divided Democratic Party, however, with a candidate who is far out on the issues, with a press that is less concerned with their antipathy toward RN than with the wild schemes of his opponent, we could go up to 58 to 60 percent.

Thus—it will not be how wonderful we are, but how terrible McGovern is—that will make the difference this fall between a respectable clear victory and a Nixon landslide. Seems to me vital that we keep this in mind.

To get that good media, we should confront McGovern on the "issues" clearly; we should be almost generous to him personally; we should deliberately avoid any nasty smear attacks. We have enough on the record to hang the guy—what we have to avoid at all costs are such media-negatives as the 1970 "ads" and the 1972 Watergate Caper, which they are trying to hang around our necks. We should hammer the issues and his positions—and let McGovern come off as the "name-caller."

6) One great concern of mine is the "Humphrey Phenomenon"—of McGovern, if nominated, being cast into the role of "under-dog" "anti-Establishment," "come-from-behind" candidate—whose campaign will provide one hell of a good deal more media interest and human interest than ours.

We should have some real-life "drama" in store for this fall—to attract national attention. We should, in a pleasant enough way, but unmistakably make this the campaign of Richard Nixon and the Average Man against the Establishment and the Radical Chic. . . .

7) As for the suggestion that RN go out and do more, a la 1960, I would say, no—if that means "political campaigning." However Richard Nixon on the move as President, yes; and Richard Nixon in action in the White House, as President, yes, and Richard Nixon addressing the nation—for fifteen minutes as President, to strike a contrast with McGovern, yes. But not the stump-speaking. RN as President is a far more effective campaigner than RN as campaigner.

8) Scheduling. This campaign, unlike 1968, we should schedule RN into the "undecided" arenas, union halls, Columbus Day activities, Knights of Columbus meetings, etc. We should keep in mind that there is only—at most—20 percent of the electorate that will decide this, not who wins, but whether or not it is a landslide, and quite frankly, that 20 percent is not a principally Republican vote. Perhaps RN has to make appearance at GOP rallies—but when he does, he is not going where the ducks are. In a McGovern race the ducks are suddenly in city areas of the North we never carried before.

9) Perhaps this has been repeated before—but again, of maximum importance is that we not convince the media to make McGovern a picked-on under-dog by name-calling. We have to massively confront him with his positions, and if we need any characterization—we can take that from the Democrats.

Regrettably, the media does not allow us the same latitude in name-calling it will give McGovern, who has already charged the Administration with "racism," Hitler-like conduct, and war-mongering.[13]

8. Memo to H. R. Haldeman and Clark MacGregor, "Thoughts on the Post-Convention (Democratic)," July 7, 1972

This memo deals with strategy thoughts strictly for the period between the conventions.

DISENCHANTED DEMOCRATS

This is the first priority. No sooner should the dust have settled from the Democratic Convention (a few days following, perhaps) than a National Democrats for Nixon should be formed publicly to serve as an "umbrella" for all of the less bold fence-straddlers to join. We should move fast on the Democrats, post Miami Beach, as they will be most vulnerable immediately following the convention. If we have a number of Democrats already locked in, to either abandon their ticket, or bolt the party—we should trickle these out, state-by-state—not drop them all at once.

In our judgment, if we have a choice it is far better for Democrats to stay in their party and denounce McGovern than to switch parties now.

Elitism and extremism in the Democratic Party should form the basis of the abandonment of McGovern—followed by support and endorsement of RN. But, in my view, the former is the more important news story. . . .

In addition, we should focus upon and publish not simply the major names but the minor ones—state legislators and the like—and publish those names in ads in the "swing states" especially. The purpose is to leave the impression of massive defections, not just major ones, from the Democratic Ticket. We should be working on these people right now—all over the various swing states.

Sometime during the campaign this fall, we need a national press conference and a national mailing to all political writers etc. listing the hundreds of Democratic party officials who have publicly abandoned the McGovern ticket. The idea, of course, is to create a stampede so that the fence-straddlers and others who might want to hang in there will at the least be publicly disassociating themselves from McGovern.

Also, in this time, GOPers running for State Legislature, Governor, Senator, Congressman, should be instructed to force their opponents to take a stand for or against McGovern and his positions. (This might well involve mailing a copy of the McGovern Assault Book to every GOP candidate, with instructions on how to use it.)

THE SHAFTING OF WALLACE

If this is a credible argument, it should be made intensively by our people. That Wallace who had more votes than any other candidate, before California, was stripped of delegates and dignity by the radicals at Miami. That the convention which was supposed to be "democratic" ended up stealing his delegates and denying him the rightful claim to a voice in the platform. The Party is highly unlikely to buy the Wallace positions as announced today on national TV; we should go directly to these voters—and the GOP Platform should mirror some of the Governor's concerns. On matters of defense, bussing, welfare, responsiveness of government, etc., this should not be difficult.

1701 (RNC) should be collecting assiduously all of the negative statements by Wallace people about their treatment at Miami and about the Democratic Platform; we already have some excellent ones that will go into the Briefing Book.

CONVENTION

The theme, "If they can't unite their party, how can they unite the country; if they can't even run an orderly convention, how can they run the United States," the same one used in 1968 is a natural.

THE MCGOVERN SMEAR

Again, clearly the McGovern answer to any and all attacks will be to charge the "Old Nixon" with his "smear" tactics. The response of Stein demonstrated this. We will have five or six of the most egregious McGovern attacks listed—and out to all speakers, with a short memo by convention's end—if McGovern is nominated. At that point we ought to elevate all of these horrible statements and demand to know if McGovern intends to campaign on the issues—or to continue in this vein of comparing RN with Hitler, calling his Administration "racist" etc. McGovern is still being allowed to get away with being "the most decent man in the Senate" and his rhetoric has been the wildest of any man in recent political history.

THE ESTABLISHMENT THEME

We ought to set this early that McGovern is not the candidate of the people, but of a small elite, of New Leftists, the elitist children, etc. Again, this impression should be made early in the campaign, before many voters have made their minds up. McGovern theme is certain to be to make himself the "candidate of the people" against the "candidate of the politicians," i.e., us. We have to get in early with this elitist idea; we have to capture the anti-Establishment theme early.

Again, my great concern is that McGovern may successfully establish himself as underdog, anti-Establishment, "out" candidate. Our speaking resources, early, should be directed to thrusting us into the position of the candidate of the common man, in the titanic struggle with the power of the Eastern Establishment.

THE WAFFLER
Again, another strength of McGovern's which will necessarily be weakened post-convention is his reputation for "candor, honesty," "you know where he stands" nonsense. He will start moving, he already is moving on the issues right now—and there is no contradiction between nailing him with his $1,000 give-away program one day, and denouncing him for "trimming" by abandoning it the next. For McGovern, movement in and of itself can be damaging—because his whole campaign program is "Right from the Start." We should nail every shift, every movement—and nail that "Right from the Start" right from the start. . . .[14]

9. Memo to Richard Nixon, July 12, 1972
Observations from a study of the McGovern primary ads, TV, radio and press— and the interesting McGovern biography. Points worth noting:

1. Despite the ideological liberalism of Mr. McGovern, there is a clear conservative thrust to many of his issue ads—particularly those for "cleaning up the welfare mess," and relieving the property tax burden on the average citizen. The McGovern proposals to increase the welfare payments and roll, and the manifest inconsistency in proposing $150 billion in new spending—while appearing to be for a reduction in and redistribution of the tax burden are not present in these ads. Further, late in the primaries, his new "hard line" on Israel was a major topic of his advertising. Could find nothing in the way of elitist, new left ad themes in McGovern's primary campaign. Amnesty, abortion, pot, soak-the-rich, slash defense, $1,000-a-person were clearly not major themes. There are, however, several old-liberal approaches which he has pushed in his advertising. These include:

a) Social Security benefits beginning at 62 years of age—a straight shot appeal to old folks, along traditional Democratic lines.

b) An interesting emphasis on "occupational health and safety." For example, a number of TV spots focusing on how workers were losing life and limb in unsafe plants, and this was a serious problem. Imagine this approach to be one with great appeal where McGovern is weak—among production workers.

c) Medical care for everyone. This is one of the positive "liberal" programs, which McGovern emphasized in the primaries. Again, it is traditional Scammon-Wattenberg economic liberalism. Again, there is hardly a trace of what one might call social liberalism or "radical chic" politics in the McGovern advertising campaign. And, clearly, our people should never cease making references to his "elitist" "radical chic" positions—and focus on them, rather than leaving the debate to resolve around his more traditional "liberal" approaches.

d) A relatively hard-nosed approach on drugs.

OTHER APPROACHES

The KENNEDYS—Mr. McGovern is clearly running on the coattails of two dead men, John and Robert Kennedy; his documentary is almost a Kennedy documentary; his TV and radio spots make extensive use of the Kennedy endorsements of George McGovern as the "most decent man in the Senate." We can expect much of this in the fall.

PERSONALITY—McGovern's campaign consistently contrasts Mr. McGovern as an honest, open, straight-forward, candid, consistent candidate with Mr. Nixon's Administration, which is portrayed as deceitful, closed, secretive, distrustful. This is clearly in the McGovern campaign judgment a winner for them—and a loser for us. They focus upon the "personality" of the two candidates and the two campaigns, as much as upon any two issues. The need for us, again, in my judgment, is to move early to get out the record of both the McGovern waffles on positions, that McGovern compromises on principles, McGovern's nasty and vindictive attacks upon the President and his political adversaries. The press, which nails Mr. Agnew to the mast for his rugged rhetoric, has allowed Mr. McGovern to get away with some of the more incredible statements in American politics. We have Mr. McGovern's cruel and nasty statements recorded, but these, along with his waffles and back-downs, have to be moved into the public record. As with Mr. Muskie, one of our problems is to contradict this idea that, whether you agree or disagree with McGovern, you "know where he stands," and you know he can be trusted.

Other attributes the McGovern camp is playing up are such as "warmth, humanity, sympathy, compassion," and they are attempting to contrast them with a cold-blooded, super-efficient, rather heartless White House and President. Such as RN's visit to the flood-stricken areas of the country is most helpful as an antidote to this kind of approach. We could do more of the last.

Also, an openness and a new accessibility to the press and public on the part of the President might, in my view, be helpful in working against this "inaccessibility" allegation that is part of the McGovern mode.

ISRAEL—McGovern's extraordinary sensitivity on this issue is manifest in the 180-degree turnabout on the issue and the astonishing hawkishness of his latest ads. He is vulnerable here, and the lesson is obvious that we ought to continue to focus upon his opposition to the Eisenhower Doctrine, to measures to promote Israeli security, etc. He is vulnerable here and aware of it.

POPULISM—While "Professor McGovern" is a representative of the "outs" against the "ins," the fighter against the "interests" for the common man who bears too much of the burden, while powerful corporations and institutions get off without paying their fair share. The clear need is, as stated in previous memos, to portray McGovern as a candidate of the Elite, "Professor McGovern," the leader of the party of the PhDs and limousine liberals, whose elitist shock troops took over the party of the people, the "noise-makers" and the "exotic," the tiny minority who are imposing an asinine social policy of bussing on a country, eighty-five percent of whose people do not want bussing.

There are few larger imperatives in our campaign than to move McGovern into the position of the Establishment Candidate—running against the candidate of Middle America. Crucial to our success this fall is to put McGovern in the bag with the "radical chic" and this message, it seems to me, has to be impressed upon our speakers. If we allow him to be perceived as his ads and previous campaigns portray him, we could have a serious problem.

VIETNAM—McGovern's approach is that he is the one man in the country who has been "right from the start" about this miserable, horrible war. This should be confronted, not ignored, and surely not conceded. These are three basic approaches, some of them not complementary, if not consistent:

a) McGovern has been a waffler on the war; he voted for the Gulf of Tonkin in 1964, against its repeal in 1966, for appropriations for the conflict throughout the early and mid-sixties, and only voted to get out—after a Republican had come in to clean up the mess McGovern's Presidential choices (JFK, LBJ, HHH) had made of the situation. His bitter attacks on RN thus come not from principle but from the effort to pick up partisan dividends from under-cutting an American President trying to get us out of a war into which he voted us.

b) McGovern has repeatedly made predictions as to what the enemy would do if we made concession—and every single McGovern promise and prediction has been wrong. Nobody had a worse record on Vietnam in terms of understanding the enemy than McGovern.

c) McGovern's attacks on the President who is now honorably ending American involvement in this war are not something to be proud of—they rank among the most shameful episodes in American history. While President Nixon sought courageously to extricate America from this conflict—with his two objectives, American honor intact, and our commitment not defaulted—McGovern badgered and sabotaged this courageous effort every step of the way.

Again, our people should <u>not</u> concede the war is immoral, should <u>not</u> concede that McGovern was right, but we are right too, and we are trying to end it as best we can. We should challenge him on this issue on many grounds. We should confront his claim—<u>not</u> co-opt it, by saying: "Well, we are against the war, too, and we are trying to do our best to end it."

McGovern should be conceded nothing on Vietnam. He is a back-stabber who would go "begging" to Hanoi—and abandon our prisoners to the enemy, without any guarantee we would ever get them back. We should view his positions, not with disagreement, but with contempt.

THE STRENGTH & WEAKNESS OF GEORGE MCGOVERN THE MAN—From reading <u>McGovern</u>, a most interesting and sympathetic biography, and observing the man, the following becomes clear. McGovern's great strength and great weakness lies in his personality; he is a minister in his own right and a minister's son; he is a True Believer, his is the "Passionate State of Mind"; he sees issues in moral terms, not simply mistakes versus wise, but evil versus good. At the same time he is extraordinarily ambitious—unlike Goldwater. Frankly, he bears striking similarities to our present Secretary of Housing and Urban Development, Mr. Romney. That it is that McGovern can both shift positions and express a righteous faith in his new position to match his faith and fanaticism in expressing his old.

This, it is that McGovern can compare RN with Hitler and his bombing policy with extermination of the Jews—and still believe in his own mind that Mr. Agnew is the "demagogue" who says horrible things. McGovern's self-righteousness can be a great strength—he has a preacher's appeal; against us his is the appeal of a man who believes deeply in a "faith" against the man who is the quintessence of the pragmatist.

His weakness is, again, the weakness of Romney—he is not unlikely to state and re-state his convictions about RN being like Hitler when pressed on the question, rather than backing off. In a pressure situation, he will fall back upon the "Gospel" of the left, rather than frame some non-committal neutral response. Very probably, he will be more sensitive, more likely to move to outrage with the suggestion that he is a waffler, a hypocrite, than against the blanket charge he is a radical. <u>Indeed, his campaigns have shown that he is extremely effective in com-</u>

bating the charge that he is a "radical"; he has been at his most effective against the straight-on smear attack and his worst defeat—to Karl Mundt—came when his zealotry and hatred of Karl Mundt got the better of him.

This analysis of McGovern's character reinforces my belief that our best attack against him is not the heavy-handed direct charge that he is a radical and extremist, not a shouting denunciatory approach—but repeatedly elevating his wild positions, his slanderous statements about the President, suggesting and pointing to his radicalism and extremism without raging against it. No meat ax; the scalpel is to be preferred.

Keep his positions and statements in front of the public, but a posture of humor, an incredulity about the wildness of his positions, of indignation and justified anger at the character of his slanders of the President and other decent, good men will, in my view, be far more effective than for us to think up another new way to call McGovern a jackass every morning. What McGovern the radical has going for him is something which Jim Buckley had going for him—when you look at the guy on the tube and listen to him, it is hard to accept him as a radical. We have the media which will be helping him clean up his past for this election; and our job is to consistently, and insistently, get that past on the public record—and make McGovern defend or talk about that record and, hopefully, hysterically denounce us as SOBs, which his sense of moral worth and righteousness is fully capable of leading him to do.

WAR HERO—Look for Guggenheim, his documentary man, and his ad campaign, and his statement, to appeal to his lost constituency by focusing heavily upon his war record as a bomber pilot, and one will find, I would think, that the national media will help out with regular reminders that George McGovern was a medal-winning bomber pilot in the war against Nazi Germany, and thus can hardly be considered a woolly-headed peacenik. McGovern has expressed consternation that the press was constantly referring to "War Hero McCloskey" and not to "War Hero McGovern." Their documentary also focused heavily on his war record.[15]

10. Memo to Richard Nixon, "The Jewish Vote and the President's Opportunity," July 23, 1972

No need to read the attached, but good reason to make note of the points contained. . . .

The upshot of this piece is that RN, Bête Noire of all good Jewish liberals since the days of Alger Hiss, has an opportunity today to make inroads into the Jewish vote, none of us would have dreamed possible two years back. Secondly, it is not RN's actions in the Middle East alone that afford us this genuinely historic opportunity. It is McGovern, his views and the men around him.

1. American Jews have traditionally benefited from a "meritocratic" situation—where advancement was based on education, brains, performance. Yet today the Democratic Party is returning to the evil old days of "quotas"—which quotas when used for blacks, Chicanos, Indians and women are leading to the exclusion of not only Catholics, farmers, old folks, but Jews as well.

2. The same "quotas" are being imposed in those occupations—education, for example—where Jews have dominated. Our own HEW with its idiotic "affirmative action" program is forcing universities to hire blacks and women (usually militant and incompetent) not on the basis of merit, but on the basis of race and sex. The same trend is working against Jewish teachers in the New York public schools, and Jews, who long suffered under "quota" systems in the Ivy League, are deeply concerned.

3. As this piece points out . . . Jews who used to be ridiculed racially for being "rootless cosmopolitans" by anti-Semites are increasingly in the United States setting down roots in the cities and are behaving less like political liberals than like ethnic communities. Jews are coming increasingly to defend and protect their ethnic identity. Thus, the "Forest Hills project"—perhaps the most outrageous example of "scatter site" which would set down hundreds of blacks inside a Jewish community, has become a fighting issue among New York Jews in particular, and American Jews in general.

4. The radicals in the country have become anti-Israel; and the black militants—anxious to displace Jewish liberals in positions of power in the civil rights movement—have become anti-Semitic, many of them. In self-defense Jewish intellectuals are not actively fighting against the radicalism and militancy among black and white young, that their own children are on occasion actively supporting.

5. Despite their liberalism, American Jews, doctors, lawyers, publishers, writers, etc., have prospered economically, and have prospered greatly, in a capitalistic society where the greatest economic rewards go to those who work hardest and do best—regardless of race, creed, or color. There is not a small amount of economic fear of the McGovern socialistic and egalitarian proposals, which would take from the successful to give to the unsuccessful.

6. In conclusion, McGovern and his people are the driving force behind the new "isolationism" of the Democratic Party which threatens Israel; they are the movers and shakers behind the "quota" system which can be imposed on occupations, parties, and government at the expense of Jews. They are sympathetic to

the militants, black and white, who are all too often anti-Semitic. They are true
believers in the kind of socialism that represent a distinct threat to the primacy
of the Jewish economic position in American society.

The President's Opportunity

Working with Len Garment, we are getting together a blue-chip list of Jewish
and other intellectuals—the heavy-weights—to take out a full-page Times ad,
not endorsing us but expressing great concern about the ideas and programs of
George McGovern. Some of the names have been the leading lights of liberal
intellectualism for the last decade.

For our part we should in my judgment:

1. Immediately clamp down on the "quota systems" and "affirmative action"
programs being imposed upon university faculties by the Nixon Department of
HEW, the last bastion of coercive integration in the American Government.

2. Put the Forest Hills project over the side publicly—with a simple statement to the effect that the President believes that the "integrity of neighborhoods," and their "ethnic composition" should be primary considerations—and
that RN as a matter of principle opposed the kind of scatter site housing which
radically alters the character of neighborhoods.

Assuredly, in the 1970s the coercive integration of neighborhoods is going to
be an even more bitter issue than the enforced integration of schools was in the
sixties. We saw what the latter has done to the National Democratic Party in
the sixties—do we want the former to do the same to the GOP in the seventies?
In point of fact, coercive racial integration is not only morally wrong, it doesn't
work; it is politically idiotic; it divides and embitters communities and cities the
way it has when we tried to force it down the throat of Warren, Michigan.

3. Instruct HUD to undertake—between now and the election—no more of
these "scatter site" projects, which try to force "medium and low-income" housing into communities which do not want such housing. These policies win us
nothing but enemies.

4. What is needed, however, is a Presidential affirmation of his own personal
philosophy which has always been consistent with Jewish belief in a meritocratic, democratic society, where opportunity is blind to race, creed and color. . . .

Lastly, to the new elite, to the new "radical chic," the American Jewish community has become part of the Establishment, not one of the "victims" of society—and the Jewish community is reacting naturally to this treatment as one
of the haves rather than the havenots. The opportunity is great—the President
philosophically and politically is on the right side of all these issues.

RECOMMENDATION

Find an opportunity for RN to address a prestigious Jewish community, where we can go and touch all the bases, all the concerns: a) the Middle East, b) Soviet Jews, c) the Sixth Fleet, d) quotas in universities, e) anti-Semitic radicals, f) forced integration of traditional Jewish communities, g) discrimination against Jews—in favor of women and blacks in Jewish communities, h) economic fear of the McGovern shaft-the-successful economic programs, i) urban crime and welfare waste. A first-rate RN speech—just one—could be a tremendous winner in the Jewish community across the nation; we could contrast RN's view with McGovern on every issue of importance and come off a winner on all of them. The opportunity for RN here is one I did not think would even come in our lifetimes—as of three years ago.[16]

11. Memo to Richard Nixon, "The Vice President and the Campaign," July 23, 1972

Because the Vice President remains, outside RN, the biggest gun we have, the Veep should be staffed up—at least on the level of the 1970 campaign. Full plane, and gear and constant contact and communication with the White House and Re-Election Committee.

1. He will have to visit those states the President cannot visit, as of course the first responsibility.

2. However, as often as possible, the Vice President should be scheduled into those areas and among those groups—that are the battleground in 1972. And that is not Republicans. We, by and large, have the South now. In the North, it is Catholic, ethnic, urban, Jewish, middle-income, working-class Democrats who are the swing votes, the ones who will decide by how large a margin we will win this one, if we do win it.

Therefore, schedulers should look to Pulaski Day Parades, Columbus Day Parades (What about a WH function, along the lines of the St. Pat's Party), union halls, Knights of Columbus, Queens, PBA, and the ethnic community meetings.

This is vital, in my judgment—and we should schedule Dole and MacGregor into the GOP functions, using the Veep for those areas where he can do us the most good—among the Wallace Democrats in the North, in places like Michigan and elsewhere.

3. The Vice President should have a set-piece speech, as the President had, and instead of an entire new text every day—as in 1970—we should have a new "Ten Graphs" in each speech. This is one hell of a lot easier on speech writers, and gives us greater control of the material that the press runs.

4. The Vice President should carry the fight to the opposition ticket, by and large ignoring Eagleton—and zeroing in on McGovern. The Veep has the Assault Book. What is needed now more than anything is co-ordination of the attack strategy so that we don't pee away everything in the first weeks, and so that our strategies can be co-ordinated.

5. Frankly, we need better press relations between the Vice President and the national and local press; this might well require a more conciliatory attitude on the part of the Veep's staff toward the traveling press. (We had good relations we thought, by and large, in the 1970 election.) Certainly, the Vice President should do something for the locals at each stop. And we ought, of course, to shelve for the campaign the broad anti-media attacks unless it proves politically necessary in light of their shafting. We have the political dividends out of this—our target is McGovern.

6. Contact on a regular basis between the President and the Vice President would be especially helpful—not simply for morale purposes, but to review the success or failure of a given strategy and to maintain campaign flexibility.

7. We should, on the campaign trail, avoid I think the epithet and make our charges—based strictly on the record. So that McGovern is forced to respond to what he himself said—not to what we called him. However, the extremism of the McGovern positions and statements, and the "elitism" of the New Left controllers of the Democratic Party remain an effective theme appealing to Democrats.

8. We should remember that the swing voters in this election are Democrats—and strictly Republican appeals this fall are only useful for rallying the troops, nothing more. The "McGovernites" is right on the mark.

9. The situation of 1970 where the President's people were on board the Veep's plane—at the Veep's invitation—was a good one. Since the President is not going to be stumping, his top writing talent, or much of it, should be with the Vice President.

10. I recognize the need to defend the President and his Administration, but what the press considers "news" is usually negative news, i.e., an "attack" rather than a defense. And we must not allow McGovern to swing over onto the offensive—i.e., I would argue that the Vice President should be carrying the struggle to their ticket, rather than waiting for them to attack, and defending the President.

In my view, whereas in 1968 it was relatively easy to scare the voters with attacks on RN's economics and position on medicare, etc.—that tactic on the part of the other side won't work today. Whether they agree with RN or not, very few Americans are "frightened" by the prospect of another RN term. The same cannot be said of McGovern, and this is the factor which opens up the possibility of a landslide. Thus, a campaign which continually raises specters about McGovern's extremism, and the craziness of his ideas, is the only kind of campaign I think that can win us a major landslide. A defensive strategy, thus, does not commend itself to me—especially for our biggest gun outside of the President. We ought to have other views on this.

11. We have to be wary of making George a Martyr. Mean-spiritedness has no place in this campaign; thus, it is important that the campaign staff not be tired and bitchy as the campaign heats up. The humor used should be light and needling—not mean in character.

Again, on this score, though unfair, it is true that we have a smaller margin for error than the Democrats. The Veep can call McGovern a "fraud" and be excoriated for it—McGovern can compare RN to Hitler and his policy in Vietnam to the "extermination of the Jews" and get away with it, without comment. Without tearing into our friends in the media, we have got to keep pointing this up.

12. Vitally important that we not allow a situation to develop, as in 1960 with RN or 1968 with the Veep, when the candidate and his traveling press were at sword's point. Even if the press is shafting us, it is not to our advantage to conduct a Cold War with them—when they are reporting what we say and do. In the fall, on the Vice President's plane, there should be some who will bring that "can of oil" when necessary, and will, in a good cause, eat a little crow and humble pie.

13. Essential that the Vice President, this fall, feel that he has the full confidence and support of the President and regular backing. My view is that in 1968, when the Vice President was under attack, we would have done better by bringing him on to answer the charges against him. In 1972, we can be sure that the Vice President will be an issue—the answer to this is to put him on the air, on national television, and to let him in his own calm way, with his own accents, answer the allegations that will be made against him. To show he does not have horns. We might even consider a visit to some campus—or a youth confrontation on the tube—for the campaign. As in 1952, a harsh and strident and unfair attack on a Vice President can be made to back-fire against its perpetrators.

Considering that one of the advantages of McGovern is that he may be perceived as the underdog, the anti-Establishment candidate, it might be good to get the Vice President into this role, and come fighting back fairly, against all these elements and institutions that are out to get him.

14. Lastly, the major appearance the Vice President—the major national im-

pression—will come from his acceptance speech. This speech can do a tremendous job for him, and for us, in laying out the record of the Democratic ticket, in appealing to those Democrats who have bolted, and in leaving an impression of the Vice President before the country. . . .

15. Recognizing that there are many within the White House and the Hill who are not exactly enthusiasts of the Vice President, word should go forth that this is a "team" effort, there should be no "background" knocking the Number Two man, who will be shouldering, as RN did, much of the nasty workload of the party and the campaign. Nothing is more embittering than to pull off the wire some holier-than-thou statement from a fellow Republican. . . . Even a word from RN to all involved that this is a team effort, that no good is served us or the Party by background back-stabbing, and that this is an all-for-one, one-for-all operation would be beneficial in the campaign, I would think—from the 1970 experience.[17]

12. Memo to H. R. Haldeman, August 7, 1972

Were I counseling McGovern on the attack phase of the campaign, I would stress primarily these four issues:

A) The traditional bread-and-butter attack. Economic Issue. Under the Nixon Administration your food bills have shot up; unemployment has hovered at five million out of work; we have had inflation, stagnation, unemployment—all at once. Nixonomics has shafted the economic well-being of the common man and his family.

B) Vietnam. Nixon failed to keep his promise to end American involvement in that bloody endless conflict; we have him four years; that's enough, no more American dead—get our men out, our ships out, our prisoners out and let the North and South Vietnamese decide their own future. We have enough troubles at home here—to worry about wasting away blood and treasure and prestige and honor in an idiotic military adventure ten thousand miles away, an adventure all but the wildest hawks have written off as a gross mistake. Let's get our prisoners and go, man, go. (This is the leading issue for McGovern to keep his troops fired up.)

C) The incestuous relationship between the Nixon Administration and the Corporate power brokers. Nixon & the Big Guys vs. McGovern & the Little Guys. Examples: ITT and the $10 million slush fund from fatcats (unknown) buying future favors from a government whose door is open to the corporate heavies, but which cannot find time to hear out concerns of common men. A Wallace-type "tax reform" thrust here—arguing that RN is the defender of the loopholes, and McGovern is the friend of the Common Man, a redistribution of income downward to "working people."

D) The flawed morality and flawed integrity of the Nixon Administration using the "credibility gap," the Watergate incident especially and the PR-oriented White House. Would contrast the "candor, sincerity, honesty and openness" of my candidate with the secrecy, trickiness, deceptiveness of the Nixon White House, which is hostile to first amendment rights, to civil liberties, to a free press.

These above, I think, would be the best avenues of McGovern attack, at this point in time—they are all issues that move him into the middle, into the traditional Democratic vote, which is the McGovern necessity at this point. As for the opposition's four weakest issues, where our attack should focus, they are:

1) <u>McGovern, in his positions, statement, character is an extremist, outside the mainstream of American politics</u>, outside the center of his party. He is a fringe candidate; he represents not the great Democratic Party, but a hard-core ideological elite of zealots who have hijacked the great Democratic Party—and driven out liberals and moderates. He is the most radical candidate ever proposed for President; and his philosophy would overturn much of what we know as the American way of life.

2) His positions on economics, income distribution, defense, and foreign policy are just this side of insane. His economic proposals would bring a collapse in the stock market and a national depression, the end of the free enterprise system as we know it. His defense policies would leave America naked in a dangerous world, tempt aggression, and leave our closest friends in the most perilous condition since the rise of Hitler in the 1930s. His welfare proposals and income proposals are a declaration of economic war against the American middle class. His drastic unilateral cutbacks would not make this a safe but more dangerous world than we have ever known.

3) He is a permissive pro-pot, pro-abortion-on-demand ultra-leftist wooly head, Ramsey Clark type whose lifestyle and beliefs are part of the problem of America, not part of the solution.

His campaign has attracted elitists and kooks and ultra-leftists and radicals; and a victory for him would be a victory for the radical chic and militant leftists—over the values and traditions of Middle America and the common man.

4) In a time when ice of the cold war is breaking up, and a great new cathedral of peace is being built, George McGovern and the men around him simply do not have the capacity or experience or understanding to lead the United States in the days ahead. They are not qualified by temper or capacity to hold the job.

OUR FOUR BEST ISSUES—My view would be to dramatize and underscore our "differences" with McGovern on issues, ability, etc. Thus:

a) The President's effort to bring peace to the world and Vietnam. What RN has done to end the war, bring troops home, bring the casualties down, the China opening, the Moscow summit, the SALT agreement, etc. When this is portrayed, it should be contrasted with McGovern who has simply dogged RN's tracks every step of the way; who clearly is no match for RN in knowledge or experience or ability to keep America safe in a dangerous world, to lead America into the future.

b) The "moderation" of RN's proposals on welfare and domestic spending as opposed to the wildness of McGovern. We ought to make sure that in this campaign, he comes off as the "Super Spender" and we come off as concerned about reduced taxes and the size of Government.

c) RN's strong stands on crime, drugs, porno, bussing, permissiveness, etc.—the man who represents and defends what is right about America and the best in its values and culture. Again, we should draw the line with McGovern here as permissive, etc. We ought to have the strong side of the social issue—up and down the line—with McGovern's soft permissive side. Though we need not be strident, we need to be right on these.

Lastly, we should be certain that when the voters enter the booth, they know who represents the common man and who the elite, who speaks for American strength and who for national weakness, who would be permissive on social issues and who would be tough, who is interested in more government "programs" and who wants tax cuts, who is the darling of the purple sunglasses set and who represents Middle America, who is a moderate centrist and who is an exotic extremist, who is a man of the middle and who is a man of the far left, who would disgrace us in Vietnam and who would bring the prisoners home in honor, who would save Israel and who would lose it, who prefers J. Edgar Hoover and who prefers Ramsey Clark.[18]

13. Memo to H. R. Haldeman, August 7, 1972

The President's acceptance speech should be directed to the whole nation, of course, but politically to the voters between RN's rock bottom 40 percent and his top of 65 percent. That 25 percent of the electorate is our target. It is not Republican at all; Independent and Democratic, conservative socially, moderate politically; middle income, working income economically; Northern Catholic and ethnic largely but Southern Protestant also; in addition, there are several million young people who are largely apolitical, one would guess—they are probably not the brightest or best students; they are more likely from Ohio State, SMU, Notre Dame, NYU, than from Harvard and Yale.

This is the segment of the population which is the "swing vote" this fall, where the opportunity is great, where our appeal can and should be made— without alienation of the 40 percent base, which is essentially Conservative and Republican.

STRUCTURE

The speech in my view should be essentially of three parts:

1. What the President has accomplished. Foreign policy, Vietnam should dominate here, but the Supreme Court, the efforts against crime and pollution, the new approach to the cities, etc., can all be included.

The purpose of this section simply would be to remind the voters of tremendous accomplishments of RN and to set the stage for the last crucial part of the speech—which deals with RN's Vision of where we should be going. Would argue that RN detail briefly and toughly what was the situation in the nation when we took over the helm in 1968—what was it at home; what was it abroad and how all that has changed dramatically.

2. The middle part of the speech should strongly contrast the President's positions and views with those of McGovern—on Defense, Amnesty, Permissiveness, Welfare, Foreign Policy, Isolationism, Taxes, and Spending. We should draw McGovern's position without naming here in stark terms on one side— and RN's views on another. This should be interspersed with the strong political material, making clear they are dreadfully wrong in their approach and options, and we should be fairly tough here.

3. The third section is the Vision. RN's view of where we are going if you choose to join us. My view is that this section goes into two parts—the evils we will continue to halt, and combat, in the society—but more important the concrete dream of what we and our gathering here intend to do. We are to be the instrument of a new elite or a new order in American society, where the sons and daughters of working men and middle class are going to assume the helm of the nation, at every level from that elite which has dominated so long.

We should portray the President and his people as the instrument who are pushing open the door—not to affluence for these people—they are fairly well off—but to leadership, to bringing into Government the successor generation to the New Deal types who did their thing, but who now must give way as the Hoover business types did. We should be concrete here.

And what are the accomplishments of this new generation of leaders to be?

The ending of the agony in Vietnam, the building of a new enduring structure of international relations that can preserve for our children the peace this generation of war veterans has never known. The remaking of American society so that not just the sons of Harvard and Yale, but of SMU, Notre Dame, of NYU and Whittier move into the decision-making positions in American life. They chart the destiny of the nation henceforth. The President is the John the Baptist of a new leadership emerging in all aspects of national life. The Old Establishment must give way to these new blood, new men, with new ideas and old values.

At home, their jobs are to preserve and protect the environment that has been destroyed, to provide new guarantees for the rights of the victims in society. In any event, this will be spelled out in much more detail in subsequent memoranda and paragraphs. These will be coming up today and tomorrow.[19]

14. Memo to Richard Nixon, September 6, 1972

McGovern, as anticipated and predicted, has moved off the left and is making for the center with all deliberate speed. No more do we hear of pot, amnesty, abortion, etc.—as the attached column by McGovern indicates, the name of the game is the white working class. Thus, we hear now of jobs, of welfare rolls and crime rising under RN, of unemployment, of inflation—all primary concerns of working men and women. O'Brien and others are talking of which party, Democrats or Republicans—not which man—can best handle the economy and the needs of working people. McGovern's campaign has become a traditional HHH-style bread-and-butter attack on the "Republicans" with the Big Business–Watergate–$10 Million issue thrown in to demonstrate our coziness with corporate power, etc.

THOUGHTS:

We should recognize that the operative reality is not that <u>President Nixon is 34 points ahead—but that George McGovern is 34 points behind</u>.

He is there because the American people perceive him to be an ultra-liberal, incompetent and somewhat radical character, surrounded by the types whom they dislike and even despise. As argued some months ago, given the Republican minority in the nation, the only way for us to get in the neighborhood of 64–30 is not only an excellent performance on our side—but a disastrous performance on the other side which we have been given.

McGovern's present efforts to play the centrist is probably the best way to guarantee at least a partial "Return of the Natives."

RECOMMENDATIONS:

A) There is nothing we can do about McGovern's emphasis on issues, on the offensive. However, we can:

1. Make him pay a price with blacks and the left and the True Believers, and even voters generally, by portraying him as a cynical, opportunistic politician—willing to sell out his principles for a precinct. In short, some Republican attacks should focus on the waffly, shifty character of McGovern, while we do our best to stir up trouble for him on the left, on the campuses, etc., by portraying him as a sell-out artist.

While this will not likely lose him too many votes, it can destroy the McGovern enthusiasm which has been one of his lone suits.

2. At the identical time, McGovern is portrayed as a waffler, who abandons principles at the drop of a hat—he should <u>also</u> be hung and re-hung with all his radical positions. This is the Big Winner for us—it is the reason, in my judgment, that we are, or were, 34 points ahead. While some are writing in the back pages and for the children and blacks that McGovern is selling them out for the hard hats—the hard hats, if you will, should be reminded of McGovern's ultra-leftism, his general incompetence, the radical character of his supporters, etc. Again, there is no inconsistency in hitting McGovern both as a Far Leftist and an Opportunist.

3. The attack operation should continue, using the surrogates and others, to keep attempting to get McGovern to answer and explain and defend—so that he does not build up the momentum he is now working on so far as the "workingman" pitch goes. This does not argue that the President should be the one to jam the stick in McGovern's spokes—but that it should be done continually between now and election day. We are managing currently both an answering and tactical attack operation—and a regular offensive strategy—at lower levels that should continue despite complaints about negativism at the level.

4. Just as McGovern had hoped and predicted that "Richard Nixon is the issue this fall"—so we have succeeded in making "George McGovern the issue," and if McGovern ceases to be "the" issue this fall—then we will do less well than we are now. Thus, again, the attack on McGovern positions rather than discussing economics and unemployment and statistics, etc., appears to me the stronger strategy.

OUR PROBLEMS:

5. Value-Added Tax. I don't know whether we are locked in yet to this proposal—but politically, I think it is a mistake. Any new tax, in my view, is a

mistake—even if it is one tax to relieve another, for all the folks will see or understand or hear about from McGovern is "Nixon's new tax" while we spend several weeks explaining the concept, and several weeks after that explaining that yes, it is a new tax, but it is a trade-off.

Our strongest suit, or one of them has been the charge that McGovern will increase taxes, while we are interested in less taxes and less government. Now McGovern is starting to focus on our new tax.

6. Watergate. This cannot help but hurting somewhat right now, in light of the truly incredible publicity being accorded the matter. Though this has been passed along verbally, it suggests that the moment the indictments come down, the President make a strong statement, condemning the operation, etc., putting this into perspective, demanding fair and just trial and punishment, and then moving it into background by stating it is not the issue---the great issues. Something public and forthright on this. Then when McGovern continues to carp—that is the precise and ideal time to unload on him for his role in a far more serious crime, the leaking of top secret documents, wherein he personally encouraged Ellsberg, now on trial, to take them to the Times. The Vice President would be the one, at that point, to make the charge—and I could put together three pages on short notice. But, if possible, we should wait for the Grand Jury to hand down its indictments.

7. Media Analysis. For the first time, our own media analysis is showing some McGovern consistency and pickup. Their political lines a) Labor Day is the beginning of the campaign (i.e., we have a clean slate); b) the bread-and-butter issues are our big issues; and c) McGovern's appearance at Wall Street must be compared to JFK at the Houston Ministers—have all been picked up and moved along in varying degrees by the national media.

8. McGovern has bottomed out. This is beginning to become the big theme of some political writers, and if McGovern moves up in the Gallup Polls or Harris Polls in several weeks, it will likely be picked up by the media, and moved.[20]

15. Memo to H. R. Haldeman, John Ehrlichman, and Charles Colson, September 13, 1972

Beginning Monday, there are but seven weeks left in the Presidential campaign. Our two operative principles on the tack in those seven weeks should be a) the issues of 1972 have long ago been decided and made and b) we should re-cycle those issues, points and positions which resulted in the collapse of the McGovern campaign. There seems to be a tendency on our part at times to seek out some new indiscretion on the part of the Opposition and attack that simply because it is "new." When we have an airtight case of forcible rape—this is like saying, "And yeah, we can get him for jaywalking, too."

In the last few days, in my judgment, we have allowed McGovern to "lead" the national debate; our major political statements have focused (i.e., Butz counter-charges, and MacGregor) precisely on those issues McGovern thinks are the only winners he has. In addition, we have sought to counter the charges of campaign financing finagling with the old discredited "tu quoque" argument ("you're another")—which is the weakest of all arguments.

Meanwhile, little has gone into the public record in the last several days— from us—which focused on and advances the major personal and political issues which are ours. This is partly our fault; but partly the reason is that we now need heavier guns than the ones we have been using.

There may be a point to muddying up the matter, but we have other fish to fry this fall; and we ought to be about that business.

THE FIRST WEEK. I would open up with two barrels this week. The first is Foreign Policy. And the Vice President is the man. High-level defense of RN's brilliant foreign policy is first third—and then into McGovern's Asian and European policies as enunciated by him and Chayes. Filled in with McGovern quotes; McGovern on the POWs; McGovern on the Middle East. Conclusion and lead—George McGovern is a well-intentioned but naïve bungler whose foreign policy views are fooling and would be dangerous to the peace and security of the United States and the world. Call for a national debate on two opposing views of America's role in the world. The second barrel would be a John B. Connally, highly publicized response to McGovern, hammering on the title Confidence and Credibility. All of the McGovern waffles would be rolled into this one on the credibility side—the McGovern flip-flops—then also, in a peroration, the worst of the McGovern radical rhetoric. Why John Connally broke with McGovern could include Hoover remark, Hitler remarks, etc. Extremist rhetoric unbefitting a presidential candidate—least of all these charges is what he says about me. If we could get that peroration on the air, "the language of an extremist," we could resurrect our big winner. Also, to be included here is the Humphrey, Jackson, Muskie and Meany statements—the more brutal ones on McGovern. Why Democrats are staying away in droves. . . .

What we ought to remember in both these speeches is that the press is less interested in writing about a pro-speech than they are about attack material— whether the attack is high level or low level. Both speeches should be built up—and we should make our television on them those nights.

Note: The attack group should be aware of what the President is doing that day also for media—he can knock us off the front pages and the networks quicker than anyone else.

THE SECOND WEEK. Economics and Welfare. Connally and/or the Veep would be excellent on Economics. Reagan, if he would do one of our speeches, would be ideal on Welfare at the National Press Club.

The economic speech would give the voters a choice between the present prosperity and radical change—radical change that would mean a busted stock market (capital gains tax), a destroyed aerospace industry, and an undeclared economic war in the American middle class. The McGovern previous proposals should be regurgitated; his simplistic and naïve approach should be laid out. His $100 billion increase in budget and thousand in taxes the lead. The language in an economic speech is vital. We could work on this one as well. The Welfare speech should focus on McGovern, of course, as in favor of pouring millions more in, putting millions more into the rolls.

These items should serve as the key for surrogate speakers as well. However, the letters operation need not be geared in to this—in our judgment that should be moving the negative, radical material on McGovern into the key states at full blast. We can be much more direct in letters than in rhetoric.

THE THIRD WEEK. The Social Issue. In this week a major address should be written, again preferably with the Veep in the lead-off contrasting the President and McGovern on social issues. Marijuana and drugs. McGovern's endorsement of the Black Caucus and what it contains. Bussing, bussing, bussing. RN versus McGovern on the use of scatter-site housing; amnesty. While the Vice President can high level this—laying out the deep differences between the two—others can really start hitting hard on the issue. Also, law and order, the Hoover quote—etc. This can all be drawn into this question. This is 1970 politics, but the issues are ours this time, and if we can get McGovern talking on them, they are winners. No name-calling—just point out here the radical record.

THE FOURTH WEEK. Defense. This is one area McGovern has held fast. We could lay out his defense budget at the top level and portray it as an invitation to disaster in Europe, the Mideast, the world, the future. Again, here we have quotes from Jackson and Humphrey to back us up. And two days after the defense speech—there is released the "ECONOMIC CONSEQUENCES OF THE McGOVERN DEFENSE BUDGET" from Laird to Capitol Hill, giving state by state the number of jobs lost by McGovern Defense Budget and aerospace cuts, also the number of bases shut down and exactly which ones and where. All laid out, special mailing to every newspaper in every state in the country. Something he will never catch up with.

Within this week as well, we ought to have some real tough speeches in the aerospace communities, the "Ghost Town" stuff. Also, the same thing they did to us around military bases in 1970. Included in the military stuff would be McGovern's attack on the Military Industrial Complex whereas what he is talking about is the workers of GE, McDonnell, etc.

If we go this route, we are at the Middle of October—there is no need now to decide what we will do those last three weeks. This includes our basic inventory of large, overall issues. Other sub-themes include:

A) The Ellsberg connection, tying McGovern to him and his crime—as soon as the indictment comes down, if McGovern insists on charging people, uncharged by the Grand Jury. This would be a separate tough attack, and it should be echoed all over the country.

B) Space and defense should of course be on-going issues for any speaker in a community near an aerospace plant or military bases. Perhaps our Nixon people ought to be doing what they did to us in 1970—put out the rumor around every big base in the country that if McGovern is elected this base will shut down, this plant will close.

C) The McGovern Quotes need to be gotten out. We will do another mailing on the Best Twenty-five—and maybe the time has come to move them and our Attack Book (truncated) to the National Press, or at least the most friendly of the national columnists.

D) The Democratic Party and its rescue. This is an ideal Connally Big Speech some time, urging Democrats to take back the party of their fathers, by repudiating the extremists who have seized it in November. In the speech, he could lay out cold all the radical leftism and extremism of McGovern's positions, a real blistering speech on McGovern, the kind that the President and the Vice President cannot make—but hitting him on the twenty-odd issues where he has been so vulnerable. The kind of thing that Human Events would publish—genuinely hard, which we could then get out into the hands of our entire speakers list from top to bottom to use as their basic text.

E) We have to start back to getting the Democratic anti-McGovern quotes into the record again—the Meany, Humphrey, Jackson quotes. Also, the "elitism" and "extremism" themes need to be renewed to the average voter.

F) The attack group should continue—making sure that these themes are moved week-by-week—still meeting day-by-day to key off something McGovern has said, to fire at targets of opportunity, to program our people on the media to keep moving all these good materials we have back into the public record again and again. The Hoover quotes and the quotes on the Chicago Police are two examples. Our objective should be to either move McGovern off of his Watergate issue onto our issues or kill him on our issues; secondly, to continually break any momentum he develops by changing the subject in a week.

FINAL NOTE: Again, the critical point is that just as McGovern ought to make "Nixon" the issue—so the issue this fall is McGovern. Will he and the hard-core left-winger radicals who took over the party take over America? That's the bottom line. If the country goes to the polls in November, scared to death of McGovern, thinking him vaguely anti-America and radical and pro the left-wingers and militants, then they will vote against him—which means _for_ us. What we have done thus far, and fairly well, is not put the President thirty-four points ahead—but McGovern thirty-four points behind.

The best tribute to what we have done, I think, came from McGovern, I believe, just after the convention when he said—"They've got fifteen guys shooting at me from all sides while the President's acting like he's not even in a campaign." If we can continue that, we're golden.[21]

16. Memo to H. R. Haldeman, September 19, 1972

In my judgment, it would be a serious mistake to start setting any "targets" for what we expect to do—other than win. Predictions never help when you are right; and they are murder when you are wrong.

What we should do is what we did in New Hampshire and the other primary states. a) Keep quiet as mice while the election is on; and b) Start crowing the instant the returns are in.

Note from below that the "landslide" (a victory of 10% or more) is damn near the "rule" in the twentieth century, rather than the exception.

Also, while Eisenhower won by 15 points in 1956—Harding won by 26 in 1920, Coolidge by more than 25, Hoover by 18, and TR in 1904 by 19 points—all greater margins than Ike (Coolidge of course had LaFollette drawing liberal votes).

For the Democrats, LBJ won by 22 points, FDR by 17 in 1932, by 23 points in 1936, and by 13 points in 1940.

Also, Harding won by damn near two-to-one, and Coolidge actually did (although Coolidge had a third-party candidate in the race, lending a hand).

Buchanan's Suggestion:

Let's wait until the election is over; and then if RN meets Eisenhower's margin, this is what we say:

1) Richard Nixon got the largest percentage of votes of any minority party candidate in American presidential history. (Note: TR, Harding, Coolidge, Hoover were majority party candidates.)

2) Despite the fact that Republicans are a smaller minority than 1956, and RN is not the beloved war hero, like Ike—he swept a higher percentage of votes than Dwight David Eisenhower.

3) Conceivably we could say <u>RN swept more states than any other Presidential candidate since the incredible Roosevelt landslide of 1936—or more states than any Republican candidate in the history of this nation</u>. (All RN needs is 42 States to accomplish this.)

4) Not since the Civil War has a Republican won more states, or won a higher percentage of Southern votes than Richard Nixon—who has achieved the historic feat of, at one stroke, changing the solid Democratic South into the solid Republican South—and thereby building the framework of a new majority in American politics.

5) We should have in hand, by election night, also the Catholic vote totals from previous years, so we can show that vote and the Jewish vote totals.

Finally, what we should do is as in New Hampshire—that night and the next morning have all our spokesmen and interpreters putting out these lines so that they go into all the interpretive pieces and into the history books. But, for God's sake, let's not be setting any "targets" at this point in time.[22]

17. Memo to Richard Nixon, "Political Memorandum," October 9, 1972

With four weeks to go the political situation seems to have stabilized. With McGovern not moving as dramatically as necessary; indeed hardly moving at all, according to Harris.

The following are what I see as potential problem areas for us politically, which could cause a rapid dissipation of the present lead.

1) Sam Ervin & the Watergate. Should a Congressional hearing be called the focus of the campaign could be turned off of the "negatives" of McGovern onto our "negatives." Given the present disposition of the national media—the major demos are disappointed in the lack of a contest and enraged and frustrated by RN's above-the-battle tactics—the hearings would be the most celebrated since Army-McCarthy.

2) The McGovern anti-Nixon Commercials. McGovern's people seem finally to have come to the conclusion that their best hope lies not so much in resurrecting their candidate's image—they don't have the time—but in tearing down our man. My guess is that they will be extremely rough, and if they are not overdone, fairly effective.

My personal view is that we ought to now go on a crash program for some more anti-McGovern commercials to keep in stock.

Beyond that, the latest poll is certain to put pressure on McGovern, and given the fact that his three most sensitive points seem to be Vietnam (he is proud of his "consistency"), Eagleton, and "credibility," maybe we ought to begin moving, with some of our surrogates, in a more direct way.

If we can get him talking and arguing about these—we do well. Frankly, I would like to see the entire Eagleton business, which is such a loser for McGovern, re-elevated by some of our people.

Back to the commercials momentarily—HHH's anti-Nixon commercials were brutal in my judgment, but effective—and we should expect that McGovern's will go after the "scandal," "corrupt" issues—and if they are smart they will not use their principal, McGovern, as they have mistakenly in the past, to act as the Prosecutor.

3) A sharp McGovern movement upward in the polls could conceivably cause a reverse leverage on the "analyses" and "polls" and "local statements" which are right now so damaging to him. Every time a newspaper or survey goes out they come in with startling negative returns for McGovern. And every time a local pol speaks off the record it seems, he raps George. This has to hurt in community after community—if McGovern starts up, however, this will reverse and one will find poll after poll saying, "McGovern closing the gap." While the possibility recedes with each week, the possibility remains of the "comeback" theme catching with the press and public.

4) The apathetic electorate and the low turnout. Though the liberal press has egg on its face now, for its earlier discussion of aroused and alienated electorate looking for McGovern's kind of politics, there seems to be some truth in the possibility of a low turnout, over-confident Republicans, and a McGovern-hard-core maximizing his vote, while we minimize ours. We ought to be giving this problem serious consideration—although I do not believe it at all calls for RN to hit the stump at this point in time.

5) The media hostility. One has to have seen Agronsky & Co. to visualize it. Since the Broder column there has been piece after piece, taking up the theme that RN has "outwitted" the press, that he is using the enormous resources of the White House to such effect that it is no contest; that McGovern is at an unfair disadvantage; that the President is ignoring the issues, playing above-the-battle, refusing to "engage" in campaign debate, even by long distance, and—to top it all—appears headed for a landslide which the press can do nothing about. If one took a poll of the press corps, I would guess that ninety-five to one hundred percent want to see the gap closed.

Recognizing that they are negatively disposed to our campaign at this point, and anxious to leap on any embarrassment—perhaps we should give consideration to an offensive media strategy to feed the animals, so they aren't chewing on us the rest of the campaign.

Don't know what we have of substance coming down the pike—but the more of that the better. One notes that RN's Texas visit which had some substance to it was played extremely well—and the NY to LA jaunt was played equally badly. We should be thinking of something to give these fellows to write and talk about—rather than bemoaning our "lack" of a campaign.

THOUGHTS & SUGGESTIONS:

A) We ought to have adopted in advance a strategy for the McGovern ads, whether to ignore them—or attack them as "smear"—hopefully they will be so bad that they will indict themselves. But it would be serious for us, I think, if McGovern's ads succeeded in moving the focus off of McGovern's screw-ups and incompetence and his radicalism—which should be the last four weeks of this campaign.

B) We should be planning now—not locking in, however—some election eve, Saturday, Sunday, Monday type drills, which are certain to create massive national interest and participation in the election—by our folks. We do need to have our troops excited more out there—they do need to get stirred up—and given the Presidential podium, one can get the national attention with relative ease.

C) In two weeks or perhaps three, the time may be ripe to be calling—not for a mandate for RN—but for a repudiation of McGovern by Democrats. On these grounds, we should move out the line that the McGovernites have given up; they are interested only in a large vote to control the party machinery—and a Connally and Meany and Fitzsimmons and other Democrats can all call for a national "repudiation of extremism"—so that the Great Democratic Party can be restored to its rightful owners, the American people. Cast a Vote Against Extremism kind of theme—something that will convince Democrats that if McGovern even comes close their part is gone from them forever.

D) If we can contain McGovern for twenty more days even, or two more weeks, assuredly there is a fail-safe point at which local Democrats have to jump off and start pushing out their split-ticket sample ballots, with sort of an every-man-for-himself philosophy taking over. That almost but did not happen with Humphrey—as the unions never deserted him. But if McGovern is hanging where he was last—two or three weeks from now it could start with him.

E) The President should stay out of the attack business altogether, as of now. This still looks good. Also, the President of the People, standing up for America, is something disgruntled and even anti-Nixon Democrats can vote for—if the rest of us can keep McGovern painted as an incompetent and opportunistic radical—who would do or say anything to win. With McGovern's recent horrible charges he has diminished the possibility of his becoming a sympathetic figure, a martyr, which leaves us some room for toughening the attacks on him.[23]

18. Memo to H. R. Haldeman, John Ehrlichman, and Charles Colson, "Administratively Confidential/Political Memorandum," October 13, 1972

McGovern appears to have but one card left to turn over—the "corruption" issue. And it is not a bad one. There is a theme abuilding in the media, which runs like this: What has happened that America and Americans are sympathetic that they will not become enraged at the atmosphere of scandal and chicanery that now exists in Nixon's Washington. . . .

The Times has put its top Mafia guy on the Watergate-Espionage-Sabotage issue—and the Washington Post may very well have a few more trumps to play.

My concern is that we not "freeze the ball" with our twenty-odd point lead, and three and a half weeks to go—as we did in 1968. We have two possible lines of attack as I see it, and I would prefer the latter.

First, is to attack the Post head-on along these lines. "Just as in 1968, the leftist press is digging up all the dirt it can print between now and the election to salvage the collapsed McGovern campaign. In 1968 it was the Times with their smear on Agnew; in 1972 it is the Post's desperate last-ditch effort to smear the President on Watergate. Innuendo and unproven charges are being given the kind of ride they have not gotten since the days of Joe McCarthy. Where Dick Tuck's screw-ball antics were applauded and laughed off—pranks performed by some over-zealous types a) have not even been tied to the President's organizations; and b) are condemned as though we were running a concentration camp."

Something along these lines—taking the attack to the Post. However, before proceeding up this avenue, we had best know exactly how much more the Post has than the stuff it is running right now.

However, my preferred line would be for us to use the above only as an "answer" and to respond to the Washington Post's vendetta, and the others who are fortifying McGovern's charges, with their venom and outrage—by stepping up the attack on McGovern on our issues. To this end, I believe that:

A) The earlier we use Connally, the broader the audience, the better. This speech not only creams McGovern—it turns the focus of national debate back onto our issues—foreign policy, defense cuts, amnesty, bipartisan tradition—and hits McGovern hard for his radicalism.

B) We need new and more attack ads, in my view; and a crash program should be initiated to provide them. What are the issues hurting McGovern most? When we find these, we ought to have one-minute reminder ads—for massive use on a state-by-state basis in the waning days of the campaign.

C) We ought to consider the possibility of placing print ads in black papers all over the country condemning McGovern for not placing such ads and "taking blacks for granted." An ad which says in effect—you won't see McGovern taking an ad in this paper because he thinks you're already in his pocket.

D) While we have hit McGovern some on his Vietnam speech, it is not enough, and not hard enough—his speech disappointed and concerned even Kraft and Reston—we should be hitting him hard and repeatedly, and at high levels on Vietnam.

E) We have several "bombs" lined up like the Defense Budget Analysis, the Welfare Analysis, the Connally Speech—we need more major "events" or "attacks" at high levels, which can frame the debate in our terms, not theirs. We must keep the country thinking of McGovern and his idiotic schemes, his ineptitude and his radicalism—if we are going to hold onto our existing lead.

F) The time is approaching, I would think, when we would want to move the issue further by calling for a "vote against extremism" and get prominent Democrats and Union Leaders to start talking publicly and calling for the "repudiation" of the Radical Left that has seized our party.

G) Perhaps we need once again to go back through all our anti-McGovern material—pick out only the harshest and toughest material we have—and feed that to the press for one more round.

In brief conclusion, the next ten days are crucial to breaking the back of the McGovern campaign; we ought not to be holding back material now—but pouring out everything we have. We should be getting as much of this anti-material into the record as possible; if McGovern has made no progress by two weeks before the election, the stampede might begin, and that may be it.[24]

19. Memo to Richard Nixon, "Political Memorandum," October 23, 1972

Coming out of the backturn and into the homestretch—two weeks to go—we are in an enviable position, some 25 points ahead by Harris. This memorandum is essentially an argument against any policy of pulling back on the accelerator and coasting home.

In 1968, at this point in time, Humphrey was pouring on the coal, making his harshest attacks on RN, and the Democrats were returning to the fold by the millions. The only way for us to prevent this is to keep the McGovern negatives front and center—before the Democrats.

Currently, RN is rated between 59 and 62 points by some national polls. In my judgment, everything we get above 55—from 4 to 7 points, from 3 million to 5.5 million voters—is less pro-Nixon than anti-McGovern. This group of voters is the "softest" in the electorate; it has probably voted Democratic all its life; it is anti-McGovern, not pro-RN; and it is holding for us, just about solely because it is holding its nose over George McGovern.

If McGovern can focus national debate and attention the last two weeks upon the Watergate and our handling of the economy; and we fight it out the final two weeks on those fronts—he can diminish our margins appreciably. Thus, I think we should in this week continue to go all out—at the entire surrogate level, below the President—to keep before these Democrats the reasons why they should vote against George McGovern.

IDEAS & RECOMMENDATIONS

McGovernites to focus away from RN and the campaign and onto other matters—it is the idea that the Democratic defectors and deserters are going to take back over the party in December they took a walk on in the fall.

We have a letter along these lines prepared for Connally—we believe it should be signed by as many Democrats for Nixon as possible, and should make these two points only: a) McGovern must be repudiated by Democrats in November, else he will control the party of Roosevelt, etc., for years to come—and b) after crushing McGovern at the polls in November, let's take the party away from him and his radicals in December.

A bitter internecine war over the future of the Democratic Party—one week before election—can only benefit the unified Republican Party and the President.

2) Remembering that our "soft" vote—from 55% to 60% is more anti-McGovern than pro-Nixon—this week we should continue our anti-McGovern attacks by surrogates and anti-McGovern ads on the national media—as well as the non-partisan pro-RN, presidential material. We need both—not simply one or the other. As stated many times, a Democrat can believe RN is doing a good job and feel no qualms about voting for McGovern. But a Democrat who thinks McGovern is a crazy, incompetent radical will not vote for McGovern—even if he thinks RN is a lousy Republican.

3) In addition to Connally who has a strong appeal to some Democrats, we need to re-surface and re-publicize the northern, ethnic, Catholic, labor, blue collar types for RN—publicly again. Why? So that their types—working-class stiffs—can be aware that voting for Nixon is not betraying their party and their

traditions—because their leaders are doing it openly. We need to broaden the Democrats for Nixon appeal—which is right now a heavy Connally for Nixon appeal.

4) Perhaps the President himself should communicate with the surrogates to urge them to keep on the pressure, and not let it off now. Perhaps RN can be seen again with the Democrats for Nixon who have national recognition, and are Northern—as opposed to merely Southern Conservative Democrats.

5) The issues that should be focused upon in our attacks are those issues appealing to Democratic defectors—i.e., radicalism, loss of jobs through weakening America's defense, welfare giveaways, amnesty for deserters. We have prepared radio ads on exactly what bases in which states will be shut down and exactly how many jobs will be lost—perhaps in the final Sunday of the campaign, we can go with full page ads in major papers in swing states, headed up—"If McGovern Wins, You Lose," and hitting hard the three or four negatives on McGovern in those states, in terms of social issues—and job losses and welfare costs.

6) The President should remain in the Presidential level—the purpose being to give the partisan anti-McGovern Democrats, who are probably not pro-Nixon, some reason for pulling the switch for their old adversary.

7) Our get-out-the-vote effort should really be going full-blast, of course, especially with any Republicans anywhere where RN is pulling better than 95% of the vote—but remembering this is not where the swing votes are, this is not where or to whom we should be directing our anti-McGovern appeals.

8) While Ehrlichman did a good job, my own view is that it is a serious mistake to attempt to defend our economic record when McGovern attacks it. We only re-elevate the issue which is our weakest at best. Our approach should be essentially a) McGovern has nothing good to say about anybody and anything in this country; b) we have the highest rate of growth and lowest rate of inflation in the Western World; and c) McGovern's welfare boondoggle and $150 billion budget increase would put half the nation on welfare, raise taxes for the working man, raise prices for the working man—and do for U.S. economy what General Sherman did for the economy of Georgia.[25]

20. Memo to H. R. Haldeman, John Ehrlichman, and Charles Colson, October 26, 1972

With a dozen days to go, suggest the following—even in light of the Vietnam events today:

A) Creation of new "attack" television ads, along the lines of McGovern's, using straight copy if we can't get visuals—though I think we should get visuals. Purpose of the attack ads is to "re-cycle" on national television all of the worst McGovern positions of the campaign. PJB willing to draft several of these this weekend—to be run, as one-minute spots, simply as test—we could go with amnesty, abortion, pot, surrender, etc., the same way McGovern is doing with us.

B) Strongly recommend that we not fall back on our attack ads in any event— McGovern's stuff is now late—but it is straight anti-RN—his best approach.

C) The Democrats for Nixon start calling for civil war in their party—to win our party back November 8 from the Extremists—after we all repudiate McGovern. (This seems on the track as of Thursday afternoon.)

D) Consideration be given to asking the Vice President to deliver a Connally-like speech—only this one defending the integrity of the President. . . .

In short, the essential thing now is to 1) not let ourselves be driven on the defensive the last two weeks; 2) get back in front of the public every crazy or radical or incompetent thing McGovern did or stands for—so all those undecided Democrats and RN Democrats realize why it is that they just can't go for George McGovern.[26]

7 Watergate and the Second Term

Despite the now infamous break-in at the Watergate Complex in June 1972, Richard Nixon achieved an overwhelming reelection victory just five months later. Watergate gained little traction during the campaign, but as the congressional investigation into White House connections to the break-in and other "dirty tricks" against Democrats intensified, Nixon began to lose political advantage over the policy agenda. The loss of key White House advisors also struck a blow to the strategic operation of Nixon's inner circle when, after firing White House counsel John Dean in April 1973, Nixon accepted the resignations of his chief of staff, H. R. Haldeman, and his chief domestic policy advisor, John Ehrlichman. Dean, who was deeply involved with the White House cover-up of various illegal activities, would cut a plea deal and become a key witness in the investigations. After Alexander Butterfield, an aide who had no involvement in the Watergate scandal, revealed the secret White House taping system in Senate testimony, Dean's testimony during the summer of 1973 was most damaging to Nixon's credibility as it directly linked the president to the cover-up operation. Dean, Haldeman, and Ehrlichman were among several White House aides convicted of various Watergate-related crimes. Haldeman would be replaced by Alexander Haig as chief of staff; Haig would serve in that position until Nixon resigned. In addition to the Watergate scandal, Spiro Agnew would resign after pleading guilty to felony tax evasion in October 1973. Gerald Ford, the Republican minority leader in the House of Representatives, would replace Agnew as vice president (via selection and confirmation as outlined in the 25th Amendment), ultimately succeeding to the office of the presidency ten months later upon Nixon's resignation on August 8, 1974.

According to Pat Buchanan, Nixon's first term in office had been one of "extraordinary accomplishment."[1] Opening relations with China, an emerging détente with the Soviet Union, successful negotiations of the SALT and ABM treaties, and bringing most of the U.S. troops home from Vietnam were among Nixon's foreign policy achievements. On the domestic side, Nixon had ended the draft, created the Environmental Protection Agency and the Occupational Safety and Health Administration, elevated the National Cancer Institute to wage a "war on cancer," enacted federal revenue sharing with state governments, and signed into law Title IX to ban discrimination against women in education, among other legislative accomplishments. Optimism among White House staffers was high that a second term would be as successful. Buchanan, who was not involved with the Watergate scandal, wrote of Nixon becoming a "Republican Roosevelt" in a memo just days after the 1972 election. Instead, the next nineteen months would include congressional investigations, the appointment of a Watergate special prosecutor, revelations of an internal White House taping system, the "Saturday Night Massacre" with Nixon ordering the firing of the special prosecutor, legal battles over subpoenas for tapes, a unanimous decision by the Supreme Court ordering Nixon to turn over the tapes to the special prosecutor, and Nixon's resignation.[2] Buchanan would remain in his White House position until October 1974, serving briefly in the Ford administration, having been an integral part of the Nixon presidency from the first day until its last.

1. Memo to Richard Nixon, November 10, 1972

In the wake of Nixon's reelection, Buchanan outlined how Nixon could secure his presidential legacy, as well as what he wanted his role to be during the second term.

My own "plans and preferences" for the second Nixon Administration cannot be divorced from my own ideas and hopes for that Administration. Thus, the extended recommendations—prior to my personal suggestions for PJB. First, a bit of history.

In a historical context, the President's victory in 1968, narrow though it was, was the first major defeat inflicted in ten years upon the political and intellectual regime that dominated life in the United States throughout the past decade. Consider what the Left controlled in 1968—before the President's November victory.

Their candidate, though anti-Left, was in the White House, a landslide victory over Mr. Conservative. Their political instruments, the Kennedys and the liberals, were the dominant forces in both Houses of Congress. Their philosophy and appointees held a conclusive majority of the United States Supreme Court. Their voices dominated the major networks and newspapers and news magazines. They controlled all the major socially active and intellectual foundations and think tanks across the country. Liberalism, and the Left, was master of all it surveyed on the great campuses of the country. They controlled the best publishing houses—and the most significant intellectual journals and reviews without exception. In a sentence, the American Liberal Left dominated the cultural, social, intellectual, and political life of the United States to an unprecedented degree—and their hegemony left us a nation in social chaos and endless war.

THE NIXON COUNTER-REVOLUTION

But what has happened in four years?

First, the White House has now gone, for a second time and in an incredible landslide, to a political figure who the American Left views as an archenemy.

Second, the Congress, however, still rests in the control of the Left; little has changed in its composition in four years; this has been one of our shortfalls.

Third, the Supreme Court is another story. The President has all but recaptured the institution from the Left; his four appointments have halted much of its social experimentation; and the next four years should see this second branch of government become an ally and defender of the values and principles in which the President and his constituency believe.

Fourth, while we failed to move decisively to exercise control of the bureaucracy in the first crucial months of 1969—that error seems to be on the way to correction, if one is to believe news reports from the first days after the election of 1972.

Fifth, with the Vice President's pre-emptive strike at Des Moines, the elite and liberal media has been driven onto the defensive and has suffered an unprecedented and justified loss in the confidence and esteem of their fellow citizens.

Sixth, because of their manifest cowardice in the face of the depredations of student mobs, the elite colleges and universities have suffered a loss of confidence with the American people—even exceeding that of the liberal journalists. They caved under pressure—and in front of the whole country, and the fact that Harvard went overwhelmingly for McGovern shows how much further the academic elite is from the views and values of the American majority.

Seventh, as for their foundations and think tanks, we have done little or nothing either to expose their inter-connections and anti-Administration bias or toward developing competing institutions of our own.

THE REPUBLICAN ROOSEVELT

Our primary objective in the second term should be making of the President the Republican FDR, founder and first magistrate of a political dynasty, to dominate American politics long after the President has retired from office.

In 1932, the nation went to the polls and repudiated Hoover and the Depression; in 1964, they repudiated Goldwater and the "radical right." They did not vote for the "100 Days" or the "Great Society," but that is what they got because strong leaders grabbed an ambitious mandate and translated it into sweeping social reform. In 1972, the nation has repudiated McGovern and McGovernism, and the President should use the mandate to impose upon the nation his own political and social philosophy.

THE SUPREME COURT

The President's four appointments to the Supreme Court were among the most significant and far-reaching of the first term. Fifty years from now, liberals will say: "what we have to do is turn the Supreme Court in our direction—the way President Nixon did." In my judgment, the President should a) begin quietly now the selection process for the next two seats on the Supreme Court; b) ascertain who in the Federal and State Judiciary are the most brilliant strict constructionists; and c) select from among these men ethnics and Catholics so that the next appointment will not simply further the President's convictions about the judiciary, but help to cement the New American Majority.

Beyond this, a study should be made of the most outstanding jurists and attorneys in every sector of the country who are strict constructionists—and through their on-going appointments to the Federal Bench, the President can re-make not only the Supreme Court, but the entire Federal Judiciary.

But the "search" should be undertaken now—so that problems associated with a public search, i.e., when a member of the High Court dies or steps down, are avoided. One of the most serious problems the nation faces is the assumption by Federal jurists of the broader role of judicial legislators and agents of social reform and social change.

THE MEDIA

The President will be the beneficiary of considerable advice to "try to get along" with the media in the second term. It will be argued, we have to live with them—so let us follow a policy of live-and-let-live.

With regard to the major networks, that situation in the national media is not simply occasionally hostile to the President and his purposes—but endemically hostile. The Nixon White House and the national liberal media are as cobra and mongoose—the situation extends beyond the traditional conflict between democratic government and free press. For what it obtains is this:

A small, ideological clique has managed to acquire monopoly control of the most powerful medium on communication known to man; and they regularly use threat unrivaled and untrammeled power to politically assault the President and his Administration. This is not a question of free speech or free press—it is a basic question of power.

Shall we acquiesce forever in left-wing control of a communications media from which 50-70% of the American people derive their information and ideas about their national government? The interest of this country and the further-ance of the policies and ideas in which we believe demand that this monopoly, this ideological cartel, be broken up. Already the Sevareids, before their captive audience of this world, are doing dirt on the President's victory. We are being told "racism" played a major role in the landslide, that "backlash" was a dominant factor.

Before these characters are finished they will be having us apologize for the tremendous victory the President won. And anyone who thinks that any temporary "détente"—which was to our tactical advantage—represents perma-nent co-existence does not understand the nature of their dislike and distrust and hostility toward this Administration, and its philosophical point of view is rooted in their guts.

Again, this must be viewed as a question of "power"—there are strong ar-guments that can be made—and made publicly—against their monopoly. We should move against it the way TR moved against the financial monopolies. Our timing should be right, but we should be unapologetic about what we are doing.

What I would like to do in this area is work with those of a similar cast of mind to develop, quietly, a media strategy for dealing with the Left combination of the networks—and other powerful organs of opinion. It would include our defenses against the network, a strategy against their monopoly control, and a thought-out program for cleaning out public television of that clique of Nixon-haters who have managed to nest there at taxpayer expense.

THE NEW AMERICAN MAJORITY

If the President is not to enter the history books as a second political Eisen-hower—a Republican Regent between Democratic Magistrates—then we have to begin to make permanent the New Majority that returned the President to office. That new majority essentially consists of the Republican base nationally; the Nixon South; the ethnic, blue-collar, Catholic, working-class Americans of the North, Midwest, and West.

The danger I see is that the silent majority—which spoke out loud and clear November 7th, fell silent again on November 8th. And whose voices are again dominant? Those of the liberal media. And the pressure they will place upon us will be the same as in the past, to advance the political and social interests of the "fashionable minorities"—principally blacks, women—and to ignore the ethnics and working-class Americans who voted Republican for the first time. If we accede to these pressures—for example, for a higher percentage of blacks and women in top-level positions, etc., we will be wasting our energies on a politically sterile and foolish game. Our future is the Democratic working man, Southern Protestant, and Northern Catholic—and ethnic. And people whose primary interest in political plums and patronage for these Democrats should be structured directly into the personnel shops of every department of Government, including the White House. We already have a "women's department" in our personnel shop—we need an "ethnic" man in there, who will be on the lookout for Italians and Poles and Irish Democrats who stood with the President and who are the backbone of this new majority. The same principle should apply to the handout programs of HEW, OEO, and other giveaway agencies. If we are going to continue to give away tax dollars at bureaucratic discretion, then the dough should start going as well to those who are our friends.

Fordham and Whittier and Brigham Young and Kansas State should be getting the swag from OEO—Harvard, Yale, Princeton, and the other Left institutions should be cut back. If we do not dis-establish OEO—which I recommend—then OEO poverty grants should be shifted from exclusively black and Spanish-speaking and Puerto Rican communities to poor Jewish and Italian neighborhoods.

But the central point is that the "fashionable minorities" didn't give the President the greatest landslide in history. We did our worst with Women's Libbers and black activists and Mexican American poverty concessionaires.

We owe them justice—but we owe our friends more. My fear is that media pressure will become so intense that we will return to the discredited political game of spending the resources of Nixon taxpayers to benefit McGovern bureaucrats.

THE GREAT SOCIETY R.I.P.

Our pressing domestic need is stabilization of the American economy and an end to inflation. Perhaps the greatest on-going threat to that stability is the pressure of the burgeoning Great Society programs upon the federal budget. As many of these programs as politically possible should be eliminated—even the agencies abandoned—and it should be done almost immediately.

The President's landslide of November will have evaporated on Capitol Hill by June, if not before. If we do not eliminate these programs now, they will never be eliminated, and President Nixon and all his successors will be wasting the annual increment of Federal revenues, funding inefficacious programs for the greater honor and glory of Lyndon Johnson.

This would be a tragedy. If RN has to pay the political price of raising taxes to pay for LBJ's schemes—it would be an act of political generosity, unmatched in history, one we should not make. On the other hand—if the Great Society programs are cut and dropped, it may mean an avoided tax increase this year—and possibly tax cuts in the next few years—or programs that have upon them nothing but the RN brand.

And the country is ready and waiting for the ax to fall upon these programs. In the sophisticated sociology circles, it is recognized that these programs have always created greater problems than anticipated—and never matches the promise of their inception. Invariably, while they have been paid for in either inflated prices or working people or the taxes of Nixon voters, their principal beneficiaries have been poverty concessionaires, liberal bureaucrats, social workers, university professors and teachers—and other assorted anti-Nixonites. The Great Society can be looked at many ways. One of them is that it represented an enormous increase in power and influence and income for the "public sector" at the expense of the private sector. Another is that it represented a national rip-off of the working class that brought enormous prestige, power, and money to the upper-middle-income professional class. The Moynihan article on this development is brilliant.

My specific recommendation here would be to employ at once the services of Edward Banfield—the best man in the field—of Harvard, have him identify what programs and agencies to drop over the side—and to get on with it—before our political adversaries have time to dig out from under the avalanche.

As with the removal of recalcitrant bureaucrats, the elimination of wasteful and unsuccessful programs should be done all at once—in a brief span of time. Otherwise, the dropping of each program or each bureaucrat has its own special set of headlines—creating its own separate political and journalistic backlash. If they all go at once, and soon, they will be forgotten before they can be adequately protested.

THE BUREAUCRACY

The call for resignations from all political appointees has likely, in a stroke, regained a measure of discipline over the bureaucracy that had badly dissipated over four years. Frankly, conspicuous removal, first of all appointees who resisted the philosophical direction of the Administration, would be perhaps the single most beneficial act we could perform—to guarantee a successful four years in domestic policy. With the names Toby Moffit, Leon Panetta, Wally Hickel, and Bussing Jim Allen, one recalls that it was our own appointees and indeed some of our own agency shops—that inflicted upon the President some of the most serious damage in the first four years. A house-cleaning of the bureaucracy, coupled with the massive transfer of politically disloyal civil servants, it seems to me, are essential for a successful second Administration.

Beyond the purging of the disloyal and recalcitrant and the infusing of new blood, there is an over-riding need for this Nixon Administration to create a new "cadre" of Republican governmental professionals who can survive this Administration and be prepared to take over future ones. One of the recurring problems of the first term, in my judgment, was "credentialitis," the insistence that our appointees have credentials and extensive experience in respective fields. Whenever we start at credentials, however, we find that people politically sympathetic and loyal to the President can rarely match professional bureaucrats and liberals—because they won their credentials in Democratic years.

Political and philosophical loyalty to the President and Administration should be the first criteria of appointments. Very few of these types of appointments have embarrassed the Administration. However, of those with credentials who were never with us in heart, we have had many embarrassments.

Again, one of the valid criticisms of our first assumption of office was that we gave away the franchise to Cabinet officers who in cases such as the Department of State did not "clean house" as we had promised, but were in effect captured by the bureaucracy.

This mistake should not be repeated—we should clean house in every Department; we should bring in new blood; we should seek out leaders of the New Majority and bring them into positions of influence and power. Instead of being an Ivy League Paradise, the State Department might do with a few more FSOs from the middle class that gave the President this victory.

FOUNDATIONS & INSTITUTES

Among these lines, if we are to build an enduring Republican Majority, then we need to construct institutes that will serve as the repository of its political beliefs. The Left has the Brookings Institute, tax-exempt, well-financed and funded— sort of a permanent political government-in-exile for liberal bureaucrats and Democratic professionals.

Conservative thinkers and Republican professionals need the same kind of institution here in Washington. The AEI is not the answer. What is needed is something new, initiated in the coming year sometime, and funded both by Government contracts and contributions from American business—and other pro-Republican foundations. This could serve many purposes: a) a talent bank for Republicans in office; b) a tax-exempt refuge for Republicans out of office to stay at work and stay together; c) a communications center for Republican thinkers the nation over.

An institution of this character—with an imaginative leadership—could provide Republican Administrations for decades with policy ideas and programs that would present a realistic and principled alternative to those now issuing forth from an essentially liberal-left bureaucracy and places like the Brookings Institute.

We should not leave office without such an Institute in being.

With regard to other Foundations—our political interests dictate public exposure of the ideological bias of the Ford Foundation—and circumscription of its manifold efforts to fund the political activism of the American left.

With its $3.5 billion in assets and its hundreds of millions in annual allocation, the Ford Foundation has become both Exchequer and Command Post for the entire American Left. Groups as diverse as Brookings, the Fund for the Republic, NPACT TV, and the Southern Christian Leadership Conference—all depend for survival upon the financing of Bundy and his friends.

A public exposure of Ford's record and repeated political attacks could sensitize the nation to what they are doing, frighten Ford to back away from "social activism," and perhaps produce a cornucopia of Ford funds for Republican and Conservative causes—to spare Ford from being taken apart by the Congress at some future tax reform hearings. Despite the appearance of power and solidity and confidence, the Ford Foundation like the American Left is a paper tiger.

This is another area in which I have some knowledge and understanding and in which I would like, with others of a similar kind, to develop and create a strategy of neutralizing their institutions and power centers and helping to build our own.

CULTURAL LEADER

One of the findings of a recent poll was that President Nixon, unlike President Kennedy, was not viewed as a "cultural leader" by most Americans. Yet, in modern politics, the meshing of culture and politics is taking place on the Left—and the political clash of 1972 was mirrored in the cultural clash between, for lack of better terms—Middle America and the "adversary culture" written by Lionel Trilling.

My strong belief is that one of the functions of the President is the celebration—through the use of the powers and honors at his disposal—of traditional American values and their exponents and defenders.

The President should have put together on his behalf an ad hoc White House staff group to generate and sift ideas—for this kind of association of the President's name and office with men and women who are the reflections of traditional values and adornments of American culture. A splendid example here would have been a Freedom Medal for the late and great American writer John Dos Passos, a giant of our time, who was wholly out of favor with the liberal left.

Beyond this, the idea of White House dinners with distinguished academicians, journalists, and artists in attendance—from which the paragons of the Left are conspicuously absent—is an example of what we have in mind.

There is a deep fissure in American society that goes beyond the political into the realm of the social and cultural. As the President was clearly Middle America and McGovern the candidate of the counter-culture—we should pay tribute and honor to those who carry the body of our traditions—just as McGovern would have celebrated the Robert Lowells and Arthur Millers.

RACIAL AND SOCIAL ACTIVISM

Though the nation is more at peace with itself than four years ago, there are still bitter and rancorous social and racial troubles—as manifest in the bussing situation in Detroit, the Forest Hills and Canarsie situation in New York.

Social peace, the basis of any progress, seems to me to dictate that the Government at the national level get out altogether of the business of mandating the racial composition of either neighborhoods or schools.

While there is no indication that forced integration has advanced the cause of education—there are manifest signs that it has injured the cause of racial harmony and social peace. The integrationist philosophy of the fifties is providing a prescription for social chaos in the seventies. The moral capital of the U.S. Government is being expended in a fruitless endeavor. HEW, an agency that gives away fifty billion dollars a year, is a hated term in many American communities.

To me it would be a tragedy for the President to fritter away his present high support in the nation for an ill-advised governmental effort to forcibly integrate races.

Far better, it seems to me, for the President to preach the positive thrust of an open society that contains both integrated communities and ethnic communities—and indicate the unwisdom of Government's massive intrusion to change the racial topography of the nation. Such a speech could be done—it would be one as well that goes directly against the philosophical under-pinnings of the "quota" system, which needs not only to be condemned, but removed from Government policy in its present "affirmative action" manifestation.

Those people including Mr. Pottinger and other similarly well-intentioned souls in the Government should be removed. For four years the Administration was plagued by zealots at Justice and HEW who took their policy cues not from the President—but from a rejected ideology.

Beyond this, the President should move to get political control of IRS—in particular the tax-exempt division. Today, social activism, outside the purview of the code, is being financed with tax exemptions; and the elimination of tax exemption from some conspicuous offenders would have a decidedly cooling effect upon the other organizations which utilize their tax-exempt status for political raids and assaults upon the larger community.

CONCLUSION & BUCHANAN INTERESTS

From the President's interview and actions of the past three days, the coming year promises to be one of the most crucial in the political history of the last two decades. The issue of reduced government and reduced taxes versus more government and higher taxes is a re-aligning issue—one on which, if the President draws the sword and holds his ground, the nation will be politically divided, and on which we can cement a New Majority.

As this is what the President has in mind in the next six months, I would want to remain here in the White House to assist in the undertaking and the defense of the decision.

My principal complaint of the last four years is not that I have been required to do too much, but that I have been asked to do too little, and have been involved too late in decisions which I feel could have been influenced for the better. In the next Administration I would like to be structured into the decision-making process in such a fashion as to influence the direction of domestic and political and social policy—as well as the defense of it once made. If the President is going to move after the ineffectual programs and recalcitrant bureaucrats, there are few in here with greater aptitude and enthusiasm for the talks, or willingness to help research and carry it out than yours truly.

In terms of specific area of assignment, this is difficult to say, as I do not know who will stay or who will leave, what is going to be structured in and what structured out.

But if, as reported, Herb Klein is leaving, I would want to be considered for the position.

First, it would provide regular access to the decision-making process where I think I can help the Administration; the job would require the kind of knowledge and information of the news which we already have in my shop because of the news summary. Third, it would provide me with the opportunity to articulate and defend Administration positions against attack, with some spirit, and too, in turn, better carry out the attack assignments which the President has from time to time some of which I could then undertake myself, rather than persuading some recalcitrant Cabinet or sub-Cabinet officer to deliver what we have written. Beyond that, the office could be re-structured, and re-staffed, to bring in individuals who were editorial writer types who could by-line pieces, articulating or defending Administration positions.

If the President is moving hard in the direction of the <u>Star-News</u> interview, then that is the kind of direction, kinds of directions, that I am uniquely qualified to support and defend.

Briefly, that position would but enhance my present assignment of presidential press conferences; it would enable me to continue overall supervision of the news summary operation; it would not inhibit my writing the major addresses which the President from time to time requests. Beyond that, it would provide that access to information a measure of influence in policy decisions that I think would benefit the White House, and also an opportunity to defend and articulate the President's decision, which I feel qualified to defend.

If that is not open or not a possibility, I would still want as first choice to remain inside to help with what I have outlined above and what the President is doing. Greater involvement in the decision process does not preclude, but would enhance, my ability to do what we are already doing in this shop. If the President is interested in my staying on in the White House and lending a hand with what he is doing, I am at his disposal and would happily settle for a title and amenities commensurate with others of like ability, contributions, and responsibilities.

Finally, if the President does not see a significant role for me in any new staff structure, I would then like his consideration for the USIA Directorship—if Frank Shakespeare is vacating it. That is in the world of communication; at this juncture in time, I would imagine no great difficulty in confirmation; the appointment of an individual of 34, a presidential loyalist, to the job should reflect well, not badly, on the Administration.

Above are but a few thoughts, which are difficult in the absence of knowledge of what staff structure is now being put into place.[3]

2. Memo to H. R. Haldeman, December 11, 1972

Despite Nixon's landslide reelection victory, the Watergate scandal began to unfold rapidly in the months that followed. In October 1972, the Washington Post *ran a story about Donald Segretti, who had been hired by Dwight Chapin and*

paid with CREEP funds, to direct the "dirty tricks" campaign against Democratic
candidates. He would eventually plead guilty to three misdemeanor counts
of distributing illegal campaign literature and spend four months in prison.
Those involved in the break-in of the DNC headquarters at the Watergate
Complex went on trial in January 1973, and the U.S. Senate voted in February
1973 to create the Select Committee on Presidential Campaign Activities, to be
chaired by Senator Sam Ervin (D-NC), with Senator Howard Baker (R-TN) serving
as deputy chair.

As I don't know the degree of involvement, if any, at the White House level in either the Watergate or the Segretti-espionage operation, it is next to impossible to recommend a specific strategy for handling it. But the following considerations should be noted:

First, on the matter of Watergate, for us to say something now would be a) belated and b) unsuccessful in terms of squelching the controversy, as the matter will be before the public again, assuredly, when the trial comes up in January. Nixon campaigners will be testifying for both the prosecution and defense, one imagines. Nothing that the President or anyone else says between now and then can prevent that being a major news story which makes moot any previous announcements or comments of ours. So I see no advantage in going public with anything on Watergate per se—in which, as I understand it, there was no White House involvement.

On the Segretti-espionage matter, that is quiescent for the moment, and whether it remains so will depend perhaps primarily on what Kennedy does. If the Hill has an investigation, or is about to have one—there would be an advantage to moving ahead of time, to make it seem that we were not dragged into cleaning our house, so to speak, but did so at our own initiative. . . .

Again, these statements are made on the basis of the fact that I do not know the degree, if any, of the involvement of the President's people or the CREEP people in the Watergate or the Segretti matters. While the immediate post-election period saw a near unanimous call for the President to clean house, this has died down appreciably in recent weeks—and only the trial or the Kennedy investigation or some similar investigation is likely to raise it again.

Another point to keep foremost in mind. The President himself should not go "public" on this matter—except as the clean-up hitter. In short, if the President makes the statement, it should be either a "last word" on the matter or the "whole story." The very worst error we could make at this point is to have the President's credibility laid on the line in this matter—and then have some subsequent story or development make it appear that he either did not know the whole story or did not tell the country the entire story.

Therefore, I would surely argue against the President's going public now with any sort of statement—pre-trial and pre-investigation. If pressed in a media forum, he could indicate that in the wake of the trial of the gentlemen charged, he will have a full statement on the matter, the entire matter—and how it has been treated; but will not at this time make a public statement upon it.

What about a White House White Paper of sorts—to a friendly press source? This I couldn't answer, again, not knowing the degree or involvement or absence of involvement of our people alleged to be connected in one way or another. But before any White Paper goes, we should know that the other side has fired its last round—and doesn't have another one left in the chamber.

Unless I hear some strong arguments otherwise, and unless someone knows something coming that I don't at this point in time—I think the best thing to do at this point is to do nothing.

The time for the President to address the question publicly—at this point—is when it is concluded or when circumstances dictate a Presidential response. I don't see that point as of now.[4]

3. Memo to Ron Ziegler, December 14, 1972

Per our conversation—some thoughts.

Media Strategy should not cover more than a 3-month period—so as to determine results—the three months post-Inauguration.

POSITIVE THOUGHTS AND RECOMMENDATIONS

1. Feed not only the Star, but other pro or neutral papers in conflict with anti; such as NYDN over Times, Globe-Democrat over Post-Dispatch, Chicago Tribune over Daily News, Star over Post, ABC over CBS, etc., in addition to such as the Richmond News Leader, Columbus Dispatch, etc. (Buchanan/Allin Shop to draw up list of ten for review by RZ.)

2. Invitation to White House dinners, worship services, entertainment should go to list of 100 reporters, columnists, editorial writers, TV types, etc., drawn up initially by Buchanan/Allin, appended by Klein/Clawson and RZ. The list should cover both Washington-based and national press in all lines of media work, including magazines, cartoonists, etc.

3. Letters-of-commendation operation, currently running from Herb's shop, should be continued.

4. Top White House Assistants, including Kissinger, should be briefed by RZ

on "press relations" in candid terms—indicating what publications we should assist, and what we should ignore. Perhaps this could be done by indicating that any <u>Washington Post</u> call, for example, should not be answered without "clearance" from Ziegler's shop. With Inauguration and new Congress, there is much hard news to come from the White House, and we should guide the flow to friends and neutrals.

5. President should be persuaded to consider small working dinners with most distinguished pro-Administration and neutral media. Dinners at the White House, or even perhaps on the boat in the spring, which can be of use to the President—and of interest. This should go in as proposal—which, if approved—will bring several specific recommendations.

6. President should be asked if he will consider more Burger-type sessions, or more Horner-type situations—with friendly columnists and the like. Perhaps one hour, one day, can be set aside for three columnists to talk with the President for twenty minutes each. Again, if the President indicates a willingness—then we can work out a situation where they can be invited.

7. Presidential backgrounders of the kind done for the <u>New York Daily News</u> might be done for the <u>Richmond News Leader</u> or the <u>Wall Street Journal</u>—both of which are strong intellectually and pro-Nixon. Or their editorial crews could be invited up here for a dinner with the President and some top staff.

The above are some positive ideas to which I hope you will add some thought. Will be in touch with Clawson on these, from Herb's shop, when you get back with your thoughts. Will do a final draft then.

ATTACK OPERATION

Vitally important for the credibility of this Administration that neither the <u>Post</u> nor CBS get away scot-free with what they did in the campaign. Should they do so, then any hostile media institution can consider us a paper tiger, and the word will go forth for networks to carve up the more conservative candidate—two weeks before an election—and nothing will happen.

8. We need a strategy of options on how to deal with CBS, and that should go into the final product.

9. We need a strategy for dealing with the problems raised by the PBS situation and public broadcasting in general. PJB will get this included also as a separate item.

10. We need a listing—not extended—of perhaps the 10–20 most serious media problems we face—in terms of hostile TV reporters, commentators, columnists and their counterparts in the writing press. And this memorandum

should name them—and include specific measures which the White House staff can and will take to deny these individuals materials to use against us. A blackout is one tactic and could be enforced in the present environment, for example, by firing the guy in the bureaucracy found talking to Daniel Schorr.

But, unless there is a campaign to specifically deny privileged access to our adversaries, then any strategy is something of a joke.

In any event, give me your dictated thoughts on these matters. I will contact Clawson and Colson and put together the draft memorandum. It will be comprehensive and hopefully confidential.[5]

4. Memo to H. R. Haldeman, December 21, 1972

In the 1972 congressional elections, Republicans gained twelve seats in the U.S. House of Representatives, while Democrats gained two seats in the U.S. Senate. Democrats maintained control of both houses.

As requested:

With several of the points in that PR memorandum I concur. As we predicted over here, the President is getting negative treatment for not "helping" GOP candidates enough. That was to be expected given our strategy of running as the President in the White House. Our strategy, frankly, was the right one; the criticism was bound to come up; but the criticism is unfair, in my judgment, inevitable though it may be. If RN sweeps a state by 60% or 65% of the vote, and the incumbent—whether an Allott or a Miller—goes down the tubes, that is their <u>fault</u>, not his <u>fault</u>. Though you will not convince them of that.

Second, we live in the age of the ticket-splitter, and when RN carries Alabama by some incredible total, and then Sparkman does the same against an RN Republican, what the hell are we supposed to do to save Red Blount?

In my view, the President's strategy was right for himself and the party; what his political assignment was was to win in a landslide and he did. We should do the best we can to heal any wounds; we could probably have done better in turning over some dough to our people; and perhaps some calls for "a Congress to work with" would have helped. But—candidly—I don't think the charges are justified.

One recalls that in 1970 RN and the VP barnstormed across the country for them—and then when they didn't win—they bitched their heads off, too. Let's face facts. When we win huge, and they don't win at all, there are going to be recriminations, and we just have to live with them.

The second point is one that the history books <u>will</u> get across but the media does not today. Where we can make an effort—that is to point up repeatedly the enormous odds against which the President has been battling for a quarter century—and which he has survived to mount a political record matched only by that of FDR, if anyone. This is something we should work on.

As for the dominant point of the memorandum, I simply don't accept it. True, we are not given great credit for having "heart"—for being warm and human—but the author of this memo betrays a lack of knowledge of the world we live in or the past 25 years. A thousand PR men have broken their picks trying to make Richard Nixon appear "warm and human," a man of "heart." One thanks the Lord that this school of thought did not prevail in the advertising campaign of 1972.

Second, we have to remember that it is the liberal press that says "yes" or "no" on the warmth and humanity bit. They did it for Roosevelt and JFK—they didn't do it for LBJ or RN. But if we want to get some grades for warmth and heart—I can tell you how to do it. First, we can get RN to give an impassioned pro-Civil Rights speech, tearing into Southern and Northern reaction, and with tears streaming down his cheeks, sing "We Shall Overcome." But that is not RN's style, that is not the man—and the first thing one learns on joining Her Majesty's Secret Service is that it is utter folly to attempt to change the man.

The President is not a heartless, cold SOB, and public exposure to him and his performance in office has shown the Nation he is not. We know that once the country saw him themselves without filter of the media, we could accomplish that and we did. And we should be satisfied with it.

Third, there is a contradiction in the article handed me. He says that RN should not do anything more himself to portray his "heart," and that his top briefers are incapable of doing so. How, in the hell, then does he propose we accomplish the goal?

My own view is that the country ought to see more of the President in the second term—he ought to be out and around more socially, in unstructured events, spontaneous events—see more of the man. Only the President, not his flacks, can make appreciable changes in his image before the country. To hire a new army of PR types to devise ways and means would, I agree, be folly.

Fourth, some of the "image" of this administration is not altogether inaccurate. Let's face it. Haldeman, Ehrlichman, Shultz, and Kissinger do not exactly come across as the lovable Lavender Hill Mob. But, so what? If we have a reputation for being a little tough and mean at times—maybe we deserve a portion of it.

Consider this: Post-election, ten hours after it was over—the President called for resignations of the entire government. He then proceeded to the mountains, while here in Washington, terrified bureaucrats are being carted off in tumbrils—and all that is absent is the sound of the guillotine. That is what we are doing—it has to be done—I concur with the necessity to do it. But, damned if I can think of a way to make the process "warm" and "human," to show "heart" while chopping up this hostile bureaucracy, bombing the North Vietnamese into submission, and attempting to induce a sense of responsibility in the networks.

Frankly, it does not bother me in the least that the President does not have Hubert Humphrey's reputation for "heart" and apparently it does not bother the American people a great deal either. It would be nice to have "heart" too, but we ain't going to convince the media to write about it, and we might just as well face up to that.[6]

5. Memo to Richard Nixon, May 3, 1973

On April 30, 1937, Nixon appeared on national television to announce the resignations of his chief of staff, H. R. Haldeman, and his domestic affairs advisor, John Ehrlichman, as well as the firing of White House counsel John Dean. Attorney General Richard Kleindienst would also resign, replaced by Elliot Richardson.

The other day, the President publicly amputated his right arm; the senior White House Staff has been decimated; our political adversaries have the scent of blood; and the public is becoming somewhat numb from revelations of the daily press about what Liddy-Hunt did and what the top White House Staff knew.

Where do we go from here?

The first necessity is to knock down the widespread impression of a paralysis of government, of a White House lying dead in the water. There needs to be movement and decision.

Thoughts:

1. There are a number of sub-Cabinet posts currently open; we should be moving rapidly to fill those with the kind of visible public appointment made yesterday—Bo Calloway.

2. While any sudden flurry of phony activity should be avoided, the President can and should identify with domestic and foreign policy issues with regularity.

Some of those can't-lose programs like mass transit, simplified tax structures and forms, should be promoted. Ken Cole's shop can provide a list of these.

3. A Presidential schedule that involves a measure of movement and action—even outside of Washington—should be drawn up.

4. While the Administration has taken some crippling blows in the last few

weeks—the central necessity to avoid is any lurch, any sudden shift in policy in a vain effort to accommodate our critics. The President will be under tremendous pressure within and without to throw in the sponge on all controversial issues, to avoid at all costs a hard political fight.

Let me expand briefly. The current effort to discredit Bob Haldeman and John Ehrlichman is also an effort to discredit the "new" directions of the second Nixon Presidency and Mr. Nixon himself. Despite Watergate, what must be kept in mind is that, unlike 1960, the election of 1972 was not stolen. The policies and candidacy of the Democrat left were repudiated by the nation—and the politics and positions and person of the President were overwhelmingly endorsed by the American people.

Nothing has happened since November to demonstrate that the country wants to go the way the networks and major news organizations want it to go. As of only 6 weeks ago, the Nixon White House was master of all it surveyed; the nation was behind the President's tough line in Southeast Asia and tough line on domestic spending. Nothing in this Watergate mess changes that basic truth—and we ought not to allow our adversaries to use this Watergate mess to repudiate and divert the course and destination of the second Nixon Administration.

In terms of policy then—the President's course should be "steady as she goes." And those who counsel the President to make dramatic and sweeping gestures to accommodate our opponents understand neither the character nor the true objectives of those opponents.

THE MEDIA—the President—and Ron Ziegler—were both gracious and correct in conceding the point to Bernstein, Woodward, and the Washington Post. But let us not delude ourselves, nor concede what it would be wrong and foolish to concede.

They were right and we were wrong on Watergate—but we have been right and they have been wrong on Vietnam and social policy. We have been with the country and they have not. And simply because Bernstein and Woodward were correct on Watergate and we minimized it does not mean that in the larger collision between the national media and the Nixon Administration, we have been wrong and they have been right. One hell of an investigative success by the Washington Post against the Nixon Administration does not in my judgment exonerate the Washington Post Company from 25 years of remorseless malice against the person and Presidency of Richard Nixon.

Clearly, we need a détente with our adversaries in the national press. Clearly, our case with regard to the media—despite its validity—cannot now be effectively pursued. But we ought not to abandon our positions, or retract everything we have said—because we were right. Currently, the Washington press corps is indulging itself in an orgy of self-congratulations which in my judgment will in six months have the nation about ready to throw up.

For the time being, we have to keep a low profile; we have to concede where we were wrong—but we do not have to retract everything we have said; and we would be making a terrible mistake if we thought that by donning the sackcloth and ashes preferred us by our adversaries in the press, we will thereby win their forgiveness and indulgence. We should look upon this current period for the next six months as the aftermath of a serious defeat, during which we ought not to provoke our adversaries—but we ought not to surrender all claim to the positions we have held in the past. This is a time for a low profile and quiet rearmament in this worthwhile struggle.

One of the great tragedies of Watergate is that it has enabled the likes of Catherine Graham and Daniel Ellsberg to pose as victimized moral heroes of the day. This indeed is a painful purgatory for our sins.

APPOINTMENTS—There are some general and specific recommendations which seem to me wise to follow in the present circumstances.

1. The loss of the top White House staff should be taken as an opportunity to broaden and strengthen that staff by bringing in new and outside talent. A mistake would be made if we indulged ourselves in a game of musical chairs, with present staff members simply filling the vacuum left by the departing staff.

2. Some of the criticisms of the White House Staff in the past have not been without justification. They are (a) too PR oriented; (b) not substantive enough or heavy enough on the domestic side, and (c) too callous and indifferent to the President's friends in Congress and the country.

3. The President should move slowly and deliberately in filling the large gaps that have opened up on his staff. The crisis of the loss of Bob and John also has another side—and that is an opportunity to present a strong and fresh new approach to the last 44 months.

SPECIFICS—The domestic side. In this area, in candor, we have never been nearly so strong as the Nixon-Kissinger team, with its tremendous background and knowledge in foreign affairs.

Essentially, since 1969, the domestic side of the White House has been John Ehrlichman and the veteran advance men—few if any of whom ever had any knowledge of or even interest in domestic policy. Some of them have proved to be excellent mechanics and administrators—but in the final four years of this Administration, that side should be beefed up with men of knowledge and experience in domestic affairs from the Hill, from the academic, from perhaps the upper reaches of the bureaucracy, from the Republican foundations.

While Cap Weinberger has his own major franchise at HEW and in here, he is the kind of heavyweight we should have in mind for honchoing the domestic side. George Shultz, of course, is another. From the academic community, Banfield and others might be brought in as consultants on policy—men who have studied and lived with government programs for years, who share the President's philosophy, and know what needs to be done to carry it out.

THE HALDEMAN POSITION—What the President needs as a chief of staff is a man of weight, authority, and experience—who can command the respect of every member of the White House staff—someone with the stature and reputation of a George Shultz. Someone like that who has the President's trust and at the same time he enjoys tremendous standing in the intellectual community and the national press. While I do not know Roy Ash, my own view is that he simply does not command the kind of widespread respect and authority—for his achievement and ability—as does a George Shultz. What is needed here in my view is a new more accessible structure and a strong and authoritative new man to head it.

DEPARTMENT OF DEFENSE—In major positions like this, I lean now to men of established reputations and prominence, whose arrival will attract the klieg lights and take them off of those who have departed. Either John Connally or Nelson Rockefeller would be a tremendous asset in this post.

FBI—Now that the Matt Byrne thing is dead (in light of his record on the Scranton Commission this is not an altogether bad thing) we need in this position an individual of visible integrity, of background and experience in law enforcement or criminal justice—and, frankly, someone who will be warmly received by Nixon Democrats and seen as an independent man, with stature in his own right.

THE WHITE HOUSE STAFF—In structuring the senior staff of advisers to the President, consideration should be given to guaranteeing that all decision-making bodies have the full spectrum of opinion represented. With the departure of Colson and Haldeman it is clear that the harder line—on a variety of policies—is a good deal weaker than in the past—and the current danger that I see is not a sudden lurch to a hard line, but rather inexorable and almost exclusive pressure on the President to move in the other direction. Again, the course set by the President in the beginning of 1973 has not been discredited; it is not wrong; it is in tune with the nation's needs and desires; and nothing will be gained by abandoning our position.

THE ERVIN HEARINGS—Perhaps it is not possible to devise, but what the White House needs most of all is to see light at the end of the tunnel, a day in the foreseeable future when all revelations will have been revealed, when "Watergate" is a thing of the past, when we can pull out of the dive and start the climb again. What we stare in the face this morning is the possibility of (a) indictments of some of our people; (b) their trial and conviction; (c) the granting to them of immunity; (d) new indictments; (e) new trials with their attendant publicity, and (f) when this is all over, the Great Constitutionalist putting on his daily television show. Now, we can probably do nothing about speeding up the judicial process—is there anything that can be done to abort the hearings? I would even think that we ought to give consideration to self-revelation of all the "dirty tricks" ourselves, if we know them all—as well as all of McGovern's that we are aware of—to draw off the publicity value of the daily revelations of a trick-a-day.

What does seem to me to be unacceptable is to simply sit here and take this daily dribbling of stories—where the picayune is equated with the monumental in headlines in the <u>Times</u> and <u>Post</u>—and where we suffer the death of a thousand cuts. Patience has never been one of my stronger virtues—and I am unsure that patience is today justified. Perhaps the President's senior staff should give some consideration to a counter-attack, at the least in the "dirty tricks"—although it would be more effective if we could get the "major" revelations behind us by then.

Perhaps the moment is not now, but somewhere along the line we have to stop taking it and go over to the offensive. In the political "dirty tricks" department we are probably as much sinned against as sinning—from some of the research that was done.

COUNTERMEASURES—With the President's painful decision of Monday, he has demonstrated he will do what has to be done. Perhaps there is an advantage in staying ahead of the matter by having the President endorse legislation on campaign financing, on directing Justice to move to devise such legislation.

Thoughts from the foxhole.[7]

6. Memo to Richard Nixon, May 16, 1973

The President must move, again and soon, to push himself away and clear from Watergate and all involved—and this requires some painful and risky decisions.

Three clouds yet hang over the Administration. First: Suspicion of the President, if he knew nothing of the break-in, must have known of the cover-up. Second is the question of how possibly RN's Commerce Secretary, AG, Counsel, Special Counsel, Chief of Staff, Appointments Secretary, and Domestic Assistant could have been involved in improper, unethical, or illegal activities without the President's knowledge—and even if RN did not know, still, what does all this say about his choice of men and the atmosphere of the Oval Office. Third, the suspicion of cover-up lingers, fed by White House silence and refusal to comment substantively, by new "executive privilege guidelines," by Richardson statements about pressure re: the Krogh revelations, by alleged WH recommendations for special prosecutor, by reports that FBI guard on files of H & E was a sham, etc.

A FORWARD POSTURE

A persuasive case can be made that the time is at hand for the President to move his position forward—thus:

1) Eight weeks of revelations and independent investigation have led RN painfully to the inescapable conclusion that illegal, improper, unethical conduct was engaged in by his men—and extensive efforts made to cover this activity up. And regardless of the motives of these men, their actions must be condemned and all involved exposed and punished.

2) While RN was uninvolved in the activity or the cover-up, clearly, in retrospect, hand signals and warnings should have been heeded, should have been taken more seriously. (If RN says that no one alerted him whatsoever, then we are open to retaliation by departed, stung, and vengeful aides.)

Risks and consequences of this position: A) Retaliation by stung aides who will feel abandoned. B) RN will be casting adrift old friends and allies and diminishing perceptibly their chances of rehabilitation in the public eye. C) Another personal wrench for the President. D) We will be required to state the President was, in effect, misserved, misled, and deceived—and the finger of suspicion must inevitably then point to H and E or Dean, etc., as the ones who misled, misserved, and deceived the President.

There have been eight weeks of revelations since March 21; eight weeks for us to investigate allegations of misconduct. If our conclusion is what it was two weeks ago, that Bob and John are two splendid public servants who deserve their day in Court, then we are no longer in a credible posture so far as the nation is concerned.

In short, we have had more than enough time to ascertain if the grave but pointed allegations against John and Bob are true or false. If false, we should denounce the charges publicly. If true, as they increasingly appear to be, then the imperative being forced upon us is that—to survive—the President must join his enemies in denouncing his friends—or, at the least, deeds alleged against his friends.

To be brutally frank, the choice is now between the President and his friends. Haldeman, Ehrlichman, Dean, Mitchell, Stans, Kalmbach appear headed, perhaps with Colson in tow, for the political abyss. If they are to survive, they have to do it on their own. The only question extant now, it seems, is whether we are going down as well. If we are not culpable, then there is no moral obligation upon the President to share the fate of those who deceived the President.

Once the President states that inexcusable acts were committed in his name, by his men; once the President concedes that he received conflicting counsel, and that the warnings rather than the assurances should have been heeded; once the President states that he, too, was deceived—then the President, too, becomes a victim, and not as is widely believed today, a party to the matter.

Having taken that posture, we <u>may</u> perhaps have at last found a ground upon which to turn, stand, and fight. We <u>may</u> be able then to bring some perspective to the Star Chamber proceedings.

ON THE BUGGING—On this, we can condemn the electronic surveillance, even as we chastise for pious hypocrisy those who ignored the bugging of Adlai at Chicago in 1960, of Barry Goldwater in 1964, of RN-Agnew in 1968. While we can denounce the bugging in RN's name, we can also, for our own followers, show that CREEP may have practiced surveillance; certainly it was not we who introduced the wiretap to politics.

COVER-UP—Here the President should follow up upon his August statement that the cover-up is indeed worse than the crime; that those who sought to draw innocent parties into the obstruction of justice are more culpable than the Watergate Seven.

DIRTY TRICKS—Here again the matter is suffused with hypocrisy, and a sense of perspective is needed. We can only deplore those individuals who laughed at Dick Tuck, and then become appalled when someone sends 200 pizzas to a Muskie rally. There are traditional pranks and illegitimate pranks—the latter include the letter ascribing sexual misconduct to Senators Jackson and HHH; if anyone did this in RN's employ, they were acting without his guidance and against his wishes. "Dirty tricks," however, are not new to U.S. politics. Both parties have engaged in them. And when Teddy White writes in praise of LBJ's "Five O'Clock Group," which had Goldwater's speeches long before they were delivered, let us not now recommend jail terms for young Nixon workers attempting to get McGovern's schedule before it, too, was made public. Of all the "dirty tricks," however, perhaps the most pervasive and least excusable is the use of mobs to shout down speakers—as happened to HHH in '68 and RN and Veep in 1970 and 1972.

VESCO—(This is the softest ground.) These men served RN with great loyalty; he has confidence they will be vindicated; they have a right to a presumption of innocence.

ELLSBERG CAPER—While Krogh was guilty of inexcusable excess (end does not justify means), let us consider the climate of the times: the national security leaks that were taking place; the investigation was both justifiable and defensible; and Mr. Ellsberg does not merit the national lionization he is receiving.

Having made these points, the President is on more certain terrain to move to the offensive.

1) Let us be on guard against the emergent spirit of vigilantism, where the reputations of innocent men are being damaged in the frenzied search for the guilty.

2) Individuals are seeking to use Watergate to repeal the democratic verdict of 1972—to discredit with headlines not only the men who may have been involved but the "movement" they were unable to defeat at the polls.

3) The election of 1972 was not stolen; it was vindication of the political beliefs of a New Majority in this nation, and the course they set for America at the polls in November is a course which we intend to follow.

TIMING—When should we move? Quite soon in my estimation. In light of May's astonishing revelations, the posture of April 30 is insufficient. Movement has to come.

FORUM—Presidential address or press conference? Have not made any judgment on this. Perhaps the President should call in a spectrum of friendly, neutral and one or two hostile columnists, seniors, and lay it out to them.

STRUCTURES—Suggest a daily senior staff meeting focused upon this and related questions. Further, a small group of loyalists with Timmons as liaison be set up on Hill, and group of GOP heavyweights, with Vice President as liaison around the country—to focus solely upon this.

TONE—While nothing is gained by a "mea culpa" apologetic posture, we are simply in no position to take the all-out offensive. Nor, when one considers the character of the Court sitting in judgment upon us, should we consider throwing ourselves upon the mercy of the Court. What is needed is sorrow mixed with Presidential anger at what has been done to him, to his cause, and to his Presidency.[8]

7. Memo to Alexander Haig, July 31, 1973

Talked with Kevin Phillips; you may have seen this. In a poll of 2,250 persons, taken July 20–27, the question was asked, which concerns you most: Chappaquiddick or Watergate?

Chappaquiddick 40%

Watergate 37%

Which is more morally reprehensible?

Chappaquiddick 44%

Watergate 34%

Also, reportedly in the early returns, John Ehrlichman's emphasis on "national security" was favorably received, and apparently his fighting posture was also favorably received with hard-hat and Middle American types.[9]

8. Memo to Alexander Haig, October 23, 1973

The Saturday Night Massacre occurred on October 20, 1973, which resulted in the firing of Watergate special prosecutor Archibald Cox. Cox had subpoenaed Nixon to obtain secret White House tape recordings. Nixon refused to comply, offering instead a compromise that would provide Cox with a written summary of the tapes. When Cox refused to accept the compromise, Nixon ordered Attorney General Elliot Richardson to fire Cox, but Richardson refused and resigned in protest. Nixon then ordered Deputy Attorney General William Ruckelshaus to fire Cox, and upon his refusal, was fired. Ultimately, Solicitor General Robert Bork, serving as acting Attorney General, would fire Cox. Within three days, under intense pressure, Nixon reversed course to comply with the subpoena and release some of the tapes. He would hold a press conference on October 26, where he was questioned extensively about several Watergate-related issues.

For God's sake, don't let the Old Man get bogged down in legalese . . . —few of us, let alone the average man, understand the complexity of the constitutional issues involved. Clear, unapologetic, "tough-it-out" in segments, brief, using none (repeat, none) of the customary clichés about "generation of peace" or "put Watergate behind us" or "I could have taken the easy course . . . " lines.

None of that. Straight forward, and forget the "let us dwell together in unity" routine.

Also, Ken Khachigian strongly recommends and I concur that the President give consideration to the possibility of breaking away from the text and speaking directly into the camera as he has done before, with great effect, in foreign policy speeches.[10]

9. Memo to Alexander Haig, October 23, 1973

Ken Cole noted this morning in the mess, and I concur, we have got to get our people on television and on the attack. We are being creamed on that medium. We should have, even if we hate the phrase, a "game plan" for every television show dealing with this issue, where we demand and get half the time.

Secondly, given the rage and hostility on the other side, maybe our posture of sweet reasonableness is not the right one. Perhaps we should be hammering these people and Cox, publicly, in statements and the like—to rally some of our people out there, all of whom seem to be hiding in mountain cabins or lying in the weeds. We are doing a fairly good job of getting many of our points in the press—we are not getting our share of TV time, and the absence is killing us. [11]

10. Memo to Richard Nixon, October 25, 1973

Herman Kahn has been in to see me, urging upon the President the following points, several of which I am sure the President will find unacceptable; but you ought to have them:

1) Do not under any circumstances mention "national security" reasons for having done this or that with reference to Watergate; the old adage "Patriotism is the last refuge of a scoundrel" will be applied. People believe it is a "cover."

2) An excellent idea. At the end of the Conference, the President might say something like this: "I would like both the people of this country, and the people of the world, and our friends and adversaries, both to know, that you will be making a serious mistake if you attempt to use this occasion of our political crisis, to seek advantage at the expense of the United States or the expense of our friends. We will not be distracted from doing our duty."

3) RN can note in passing that he recognizes that 40% of the American people voted against him; while RN is President of all the people, he is under no obligation to get along with or follow the directions recommended by his opponents.

RN might throw in this comment: "I know there are some people who would like to change the results of the last election; well they can't do it."

4) This one is for Ziegler or Buchanan, not RN. Using the call to the <u>Herald Tribune</u> not to investigate vote fraud in 1960, we should say, "President Nixon is not in the business of reversing elections; and we are not going to allow those elections to be reversed."

5) On the San Clemente house, Herman thinks that the President should state that he had always intended to turn it over to the American Government, after he and his wife have lived out their years there. Herman argues that by the

Year 2000 such homes will be "white elephants" anyway; no one will be able to provide servants; and the tax deductions of contributing it to the U.S. would be well worth it. Pass this along, at his request.

6) On the Rebozo question, Kahn says the President should take a hard line; he said to tell you that "President has no right to have friends," and RN should say that "I can't defend the $100,000."[12] I told Herman that this is simply not possible. At the least Herman argued, President should say I knew nothing about it; I cannot defend it; Mr. Rebozo will have to explain it. Told Herman several times this was inconsistent with President's way of acting in past; he said please convey my thoughts anyway.

7) He contends that an excellent point is to state simply that "We cannot do business here if 400 Federal Judges have the right to look at my confidential papers."

8) On the tapes, he thinks the President might do well to say that he made the decision in the emotion of the moment, and RN still thinks it may have been the wrong thing to have done. That RN is not sure he did the right thing in giving them up.

Told him I would pass these along.[13]

11. Memo to Alexander Haig, October 31, 1973

Herb Klein called with an excellent idea: a dinner for some twenty of our heaviest and best friends in the print media, perhaps one or two in television; the President sitting down in the White House and talking with them—to get some of the folks back aboard who hung in there even during Cambodia and Carswell. I think it is a good idea; it is one Herb could put together and he indicated a willingness, if given the go-ahead.

What do you think: would the President go for this?[14]

12. Memo to Richard Nixon, November 5, 1973

The immediate need is to stop the hemorrhaging, to prevent the falling rocks from cascading into a landslide of defections. . . . What's to be done:

A) Tough Presidential statement that he will not resign 1) Because that would be an admission of wrong-doing; 2) Because despite the most massive investigation and probing of his Administration and private life in history, no sign of wrong-doing shown; 3) That RN alone is uniquely qualified by experience, capacity and judgment to deal with the nation's problems in this world and 4) Because RN indicates [that he intends] to vindicate himself as President.

A fighting three-minute statement to the National Press Corps, calm, clear, and concise for openers—tomorrow.

B) The promise of "White Papers" dealing with each and every allegation, separately, against the President. Not only the legitimate serious charges, but the lies, falsehoods, the insinuation, etc. One by one they will be answered.

C) A Presidential interview with three of the network's top—HKS, Cronkite, and Brinkley. In one hour the President should show the country, by demeanor and determination, he remains cool and remains in charge.

D) The current necessity is that the President himself get out front and center on this issue and on every other major issue before the country. Aides, surrogates, Cabinet can and must be enlisted, but they are no substitute for the Commander-in-Chief in front of his troops.

THE WHITE PAPERS

Having considered the matter, I do not know what good would be accomplished by further disclosures of confidential documents. The appetite for documents and papers and tapes is insatiable, and even if no wrong-doing is shown, the more sensitive and controversial the documents we release, the greater the demand, the lower we drop in public support and esteem. We are dying by inches, being "nibbled to death by ducks" as someone put it. None of our concessions has proved successful.

However, we can and must use our own materials to prepare defense on each of the many, many grounds on which we are being charged, all the way from wiretaps to the Presidential tax returns. If we can get these prepared and clear the air on at least a number of these issues, we can perhaps rally back some support, and focus the question on the unresolved questions.

On many issues, such as the Cambodian bombing, the Huston paper, and the Ellsberg break-in—we can make a strong defensible case with the public, even when we are wrong. The White Paper should be drafted, delivered in five hundred words to the country on television—and then we should be prepared to answer questions on the subject. Our side of the story.

Our margin for error has disappeared; our reservoir of credibility with the American people is dried up. Even if we have made mistakes—such as bugging Safire and Sears—we should come forward and admit that in the context of the legitimacy of the other wiretaps. But Norman Mailer's campaign slogan, though uncouth, has to be our watchword henceforth, "No More B---s--t." Otherwise, we are down the tubes. The American people will forgive the blunders, excesses, wrongs—they will not forgive us attempting to deceive them about same.

TAPES

If there is no cost to it, perhaps we should consider doing that summary for the Ervin Committee, since Sirica has the tapes anyhow, and this will get the word out sooner rather than later in a less purple form. Also, on the milk deal thing, certainly if they are going to look at us, perhaps the Department of Justice should look into all the contributions to Congressmen by the milk producers, or promises of same, prior to that arrangement.

ISSUES

Surely, on the "white paper" issues, there are examples—such as the alleged campaign funds to buy San Clemente, the charge that Tricia evaded her capital gains tax, the allegation about the $1 million investment portfolio, the charge of influence peddling against Bebe in connection with the competing bank's charter, etc., where we can come off strong by a hard, tough, straight denial and a demand that the press cease printing as fact what is proven false.

WHAT'S AHEAD

There is no other alternative to our taking the lead, rallying the remnants of our army, and going over on the offensive. If we wait, if we hold back, we are going to be destroyed—simply because the public is hearing the allegations and no rebuttal. And the rebuttals must now come frequently, and they must come also from the top—or be backed up from the top.

The White House briefing room is the place to present these White Papers.

But the immediate necessity is to stanch the bleeding by alerting the American people to the fact that the answers are going to be forthcoming; they will not have to be dragged out of us by a Congressional Committee or by a Special Prosecutor; we will be providing them in detail ourselves. And while we have no choice but to protect the confidentiality of the Presidential papers and tapes, we must be complete and thorough and truthful in the exercise and the President's assistants must have access to the papers if they are to make the case.

Coupled with the above, there needs also to be an on-going co-ordinated attack strategy on these issues, joined to a regular on-going mailing operation to the nation's editorial writers as well as supporters in the press, and the President's list of friends.

If we intend to resist Rodino's subpoenas, or more Congressional demands for documents and papers, etc., the only way to prevent that from appearing as a cover-up is to get out the truth ourselves.[15]

13. Memo to Richard Nixon, November 10, 1973

This idea from Shultz is the best one I have seen; it recommends the kind of effort that is needed if we are to compete on any kind of an equal basis with our legal and political adversaries. Because of a deficiency of resources, because the President's defenders are at an "informational disadvantage," our adversaries are getting away with murder. There have been things done wrong; there have been in addition blunders and errors but some of the charges now extant against the President and the President's men are out of whole cloth; and the New McCarthyism is rampant in this city. Backing up the Shultz Memorandum, I would recommend the following:

1) Creation of a Presidential Defense Office, headed by a first-rate trial lawyer of tremendous experience and reputation. Under him would be task forces structured precisely along the lines of the Watergate task forces, so that we are not at a terrible disadvantage in terms of both information and the quality of the legal defense of the President.

2) A strengthening of the "Research Operation" in the White House, so that here, too, we can have researchers assigned to particular facets of Watergate, who could be in charge of the "file" on each of the allegations, and who could provide the materials both for the lawyers defending and for speeches in defense of the President and his Administration. Our resources here are good, but they are not sufficient in my judgment. This research operation could be placed under the general jurisdiction of Buchanan, and we could make sure that the relevant researcher and relevant lawyer were routed any new clippings or press information on each charge. We would need to hire some more people here.

3) In my judgment, the November-December reduction in manpower in the President's staff, especially in the response and public relations area, if you will, was a mistake. We are too damned thin here in terms of personnel; we do not have sufficient resources to fight our battles in the national media, given that the media itself here in Washington is wholly unsympathetic. We need to strengthen this operation; we need to do more mailings; we need to get more materials out—from the Research Operation, mailing the distortions, and beyond that, fighting the Administration's fight against some of these charges—especially those that are utterly without foundation.

There is one problem with what I would recommend here and what Shultz is recommending. It implies that we recognize the Congressional Investigation Committee and the Cox/Jaworski staff as political hostiles and fight them publicly, up and down the line. Further, it could tie us back in with the defense of some of our own recent departed in the public mind.

These are matters that have to be taken into consideration in making this judgment. But the Shultz Memorandum, if the President has not already seen it, is must reading. The recommended strategy there is to fight them up and down the line, on one issue after another, to concede wrong-doing where that exists, without having something dragged out of it, and then presented to the nation by our adversaries, in their perspective rather than ours. In any event, these ideas merit consideration.[16]

14. Memo to Richard Nixon, November 11, 1973

Talked with Jesse Helms, N.C. Senator, the other day. He asked me to convey the following:

1) His mail is two-to-one pro-RN, post the Cox firing, and in recent days. So is Carl Curtis'.

2) His statement of support for RN and Curtis produced the only prolonged ovations of the N.C. GOP State Convention of 5600.

3) He urged RN to "relax" at the press conferences, to use humor and laughter rather than the attack on the national press, to get together with a few friends, media experts like his and RN's friend Charlie Crutchfield and Bob Coe of ABC, both friends, so that RN will laugh at the press in a lighter manner, rather than bang them in a direct manner.

4) The essence of his argument was that RN should use levity, humor, and banter with the press—in a relaxed fashion—in making the case against the press, as the public is aware of press bias, and is receptive to President's arguments, and the former case is more effective than the frontal assault.

Promised him I would pass these thoughts along.[17]

15. Memo to Richard Nixon, November 13, 1973

Here is a general breakdown, off the top of the head, of the charges against the President, his friends and associates, and his Administration—that range from rumor, to allegation, to report, to charge.

A. WIRETAPS (1969)—While generally conceding RN's right to tap for national security purposes, the NSC, and even the press—though this is a sore point—Cox himself admitted that his Committee wanted to know the genesis and reason for the taps on John Sears and William Safire. Also, some of the NSC taps were said to have been continued after the individuals left the NSC and joined, for example, the staff of Ed Muskie. Further, the tap on Don Nixon is a dormant issue as is the question—mentioned last week in the New York Times—as to whether or not there were other, yet unreported taps of either

WH staff, NSC, or press or other individuals. The Times last week was working on a story to ferret this out, Ruckelshaus being the key man on this issue, but nothing came of it.

B. 1970 HUSTON PLAN—This is one of the charges left-wing Congressmen contend to be an impeachable offense: specifically, that in the Huston Plan of July 1970, the President approved use of clearly identified "illegal" covert activities against domestic radicals. This matter touched upon, of course, on May 22.

C. CAMBODIAN BOMBING—My own view is that this issue is a strong one for us; but the New York Times, in its bill of particulars against the President, used the so-called illegal bombing of Cambodia, a neutral country, and the falsification of bombing reports to conceal it as a major issue—as have other opponents of the Administration. Though not a "Watergate" issue, our adversaries, especially on the Far Left, consider it among the most serious of allegations. As Exhibit A in this case is RN's statement of May 1970 that, heretofore, we had rigorously respected the "neutrality" of that country.

D. PLUMBERS—One of the most serious charges revolved around the break-in at Dr. Fielding's office. Krogh and Ehrlichman and Young and Hunt and Liddy, I believe, have all been indicted in California. Krogh has been indicted not for perjury but for "lying" to a Federal Grand Jury here in D.C. We have dealt with the Ellsberg break-in repeatedly in statements in the past.

However, under "Plumbers" should be placed the "Odessa" operation and the "M-1 Operation" which continue to crop up on some news reports as a result of leaks. Nothing I know of has been made public about what these operations entailed, but the terms are used occasionally in the press, and they were apparently doings of the Plumbers. On the Plumbers, one of the outstanding charges against the President is the Dean testimony to the effect that Krogh had told him orders to do the Fielding break-in had come "right out of the Oval Office."

E. THE MILK DEAL—This involved two government actions, one the raising of support prices in 1971, after Hardin had indicated he opposed it; and the cutback of imports of ice cream, etc. There is the Hillings letter to RN, which indicates that the milk industry is ready to fork over $2 million in campaign contributions for 1972 and that now (I paraphrase) is the time, politically and economically, to act on RN's authority on imports. There is the entire "milk case," the thrust of which, anti-administration, is that the milk lobbyists promised to chip in hundreds of thousands in campaign contributions for 1972, in return for favorable consideration on the support price, which meant to them hundreds of millions of dollars. On this question, apparently OMB, Treasury, Agriculture and just about everyone else opposed the support price increase, but were reversed. And about that time the milk money started rolling in in huge dollops to the GOP.

The basic arguments being used in the milk deal against this allegation are that a) the Democrats had been and were getting chunks of dough from the milk producers, and that b) the Democrats on the Hill were beating the drums for an even higher increase in support prices, and they would have voted it in in any event, so all we were doing was moving to forestall and somewhat diminish the otherwise inevitable.

Ralph Nader has been pursuing a civil suit on this which I believe has successfully unearthed any number of memoranda, but there has been no conclusive proof that the milk price support increase was a quid pro quo for the campaign contributions—which basically is the case that our adversaries are attempting to prove. In recent days, November 5 in the Wall Street Journal to be exact, there are reports that the Ervin Committee staff members are giddy with excitement over what they have found out, and that JBC may have some problems with the milk deal, though I have not seen any of this spelled out in great detail. But the November 5 Wall Street Journal article is the best recent piece on the "milk deal," I believe.

F. ITT—This has been hanging fire for a couple of years now. Basically, the thrust of the allegation here is that, also, the ITT settlement—their keeping Hartford Fire—was a consequence of illicit political dealings, the gravamen of the charge being that ITT got a "favorable" settlement in exchange for a pledge of $400,000 to the GOP Convention in San Diego.

There are numerous problems here. One is did Mitchell commit perjury; did Kleindienst commit perjury in his confirmation hearings when he said that [there had been] no White House influence of any kind in his decision. This came up after Cox revealed he may have been the source of leak that Kleindienst had told him that RN had said in effect, "You son of a bitch, don't you understand English?"—when RN called, allegedly to tell Kleindienst not to appeal the ITT decision to the Supreme Court.

But the heart of the charge, so far as we are concerned, is that ITT influence peddling within the White House and Administration, and ITT's promise of $400,000 to the GOP Convention, were major criteria upon which the Justice Department made the decision not to take its appeal from the Appellate Court to the U.S. Supreme Court.

Our arguments, boiled down, are basically that everyone, including Cox, felt the ITT divestiture, the largest in history, to be an equitable and just solution. That ITT grew huge under the Democrats, and was broken up under us. That

RN has a perfect right to contact Justice and give them orders about the "Bigness" policy, that the contribution promised, the figure for which is in doubt, was not that large—and had nothing to do with the final decision.

The matter is quite complex, involving Dita Beard, what her memo says, the spiriting of Dita out of town, any number of individuals who were alleged to have been contacted and to have put in an ear at some point in time.

But the thrust of the charges is, I think, above.

G. CAMPAIGN FINANCES—A number of charges here. Some partially proven by virtue of the fact that at least four corporations have pleaded guilty to contributing corporate funds to RN's campaign. (They got Andreas on doing something similar for HHH in 1968.) Under this category there should appear also repeated press reports that our campaign was guilty of quasi-extortion, in hitting up big companies and the like for a percentage (I think it was one percent of income or some such in the reports) of their income. There are reports—no formal charges yet—that our fund-raisers would offer favors to companies in trouble with the government, in exchange for their contribution. Again, no formal charges have been placed; but this is the sort of allegation floating about, which has appeared from time to time in the press. One hard news item came this last weekend when it was reported in the <u>Times</u> that an investigation (a House Committee, I believe) had turned up evidence of kickbacks and the like in the OMBE program. This is an on-going story right now. The charges, I believe, are that officials at the OMBE promised federal loans, etc., to some small business in exchange for considerations; that, first and foremost, and secondly, that funds were channeled to political supporters of the Administration, in the minority committees, although little of substance on that has surfaced.

<u>Townhouse Project</u>: As a sub-category under Campaign Finances, it should be noted that the 1970 so-called Townhouse Project is again the subject of some investigation, according to press reports. This is alleged to be an operation in 1970, run by WH or Administration aides, to channel funds to Republican candidates. Again, nothing hard, no evidence of wrong-doing demonstrated, but these reports are flourishing that this was being looked into.

<u>Vesco</u>: This, too, should come under Campaign Finances. As is known, both Mitchell and Stans have been indicted here; John Dean is scheduled to testify and perhaps the President's brother, Ed Nixon. My understanding of that is briefly this: The charge is not only perjury against both the principals, but that they—in exchange for a campaign contribution in amount of some $200,000—conspired to help out Vesco who was having serious SEC problems, while Casey was Chairman. They have, I believe, a good bit of circumstantial evidence in

terms of the timing of phone calls around the time of the contributions, phone calls from Mitchell to Casey, etc. No charge has been made, of any kind against the President's brother; his knowledge extending only to the fact that he was called in New York, brought to Vesco's firm, and given the suitcase in which $200,000 in cash contributions was made. Believe he called Mr. Stans and asked him if this was according to Hoyle and was told yes, and he, I think, brought in the money.

The Vesco trial has been held up, I think, until January. Tapes have been requested. Vesco, who himself was in Central America, successfully fighting extradition, made the mistake of going to the Bahamas where apparently they have captured him, and are holding him pending an extradition proceeding. The President's nephew is in Vesco's employ, a fact that has not gone unnoted in the national press, especially with investigative reporters.

H. PRESIDENTIAL FINANCES—Here the public charges are numerous; some of them being less charges than political smoke. And several have already been handled. First, there is the allegation that RN used campaign finances to purchase San Clemente; second, the political charge that the property at San Clemente is under-valued for tax purposes. Third, there is the allegation in the <u>Providence Journal</u> that RN paid no more than several hundred dollars in Federal taxes in 1970 and 1971, as a consequence of legitimate deductions. Fourth, there is the charge that RN's "deduction" for Vice Presidential papers was improperly handled, and should be disallowed, retroactively. There is a private left-wing tax-exempt foundation looking into this and pushing this demand. The allegation on the papers is specifically that the Archives did not have constructive receipt of RN's designated papers at the proper time; the necessary forms were not done until months after the deadline, etc. Fifth, there is the ABC report, based on suggestion that Cox staff was looking into a "Second Checkers Fund" which was supposed to be a $1 million investment portfolio; RN knocked this one in the head at his last press conference. Sixth, there is the allegation, conveyed to the nation via <u>Newsweek</u>, that the capital gains on RN's two lots down in Florida were taken by him—and offset by his deductions—rather than taken by Tricia, who allegedly did not have deductions to cover the large gain, and thereby would have had to pay the tax. Apparently, this last is made out of whole cloth in its entirety. Seventh, I would place the allegations about unnecessary and excessive government expenditures in San Clemente and Key Biscayne. This, too, has been covered in a presidential statement, but that does not prevent the charge from being repeated in the public or by opposition politicians.

I. DIRTY TRICKS—Segretti went into Lompoc for six months on these; there appears little more of interest here, other than prosecution efforts to tie this one around Dwight Chapin's neck.

J. BEBE REBOZO—Bebe has been the subject of a full-court press by the press and Ervin Committee. The charges against Bebe are a) He took a $100,000 contribution from Howard Hughes in either 1969 or 1970 and returned it under suspicious circumstances in 1973, never having gotten interest on the money or reported it to any political committee. RN dealt with this at last press conference. b) That Bebe, knowingly, cashed in stolen stock, which was being used as collateral for a loan. This seems to have been disproven fairly well. c) That Bebe was guilty of "influence peddling" in preventing a competing bank from being established and in having his friend set up an S&L on his own premises. This, too, has been knocked down very much by the evidence, though the charge lingers. d) That Bebe laundered campaign contributions through the Bahamas and his bank, an ABC charge of some weeks past, which has not surfaced recently. Very recently, an officer of Bebe's bank was discharged, I believe, at the behest of the FDIC; the fellow's name is Frank De Boer.

K. CIVIL RIGHTS VIOLATIONS—HRH, Ron Walker, and Bill Henkel have been charged, I believe, with civil rights violations in connection with the Charlotte appearance of RN, when they allegedly violated the civil rights of demonstrators by preventing them from getting into the Hall. (This is a civil suit.)

Confidentially, this is something that the Cox Committee people have been working on, attempting to charge our advance men with civil rights violations, criminal violations, as a result of their handling of demonstrators at numerous appearances of the President in the past two years.

Also, there is an effort underway to charge, I believe, Chuck Colson with the disorders attendant at the Hoover funeral, where Barker, I believe, and some of our people punched out Daniel Ellsberg. Again, this one is hazy, but I get reports that there is an effort afoot over at Cox's outfit to try to nail some sort of crime to Charles Colson, their having failed to gather sufficient evidence to indict him in either the Ellsberg break-in or the Watergate. What seems to be being attempted over there is to bring conspiracy to violate civil rights charges—rather than simply break-in charges—which would enable them to cast a broader net.

L. MIS-USE OF GOVERNMENT AGENCIES—Investigations on the Hill, I believe, as well as in the Cox crowd, have been looking into possible mis-use of IRS to hassle our political "enemies" and of the FBI to investigate Dan Schorr, although the latter is dormant and I believe a Hill committee looking into the matter has concluded no wrong-doing on our part in the IRS matter. (Will have to check this.)

The IRS focus is not only on those, for whom audits were allegedly demanded by the White House, but also those like J[ohn] Wayne and Billy Graham (Jack Anderson) on whose behalf the White House is said to have allegedly intervened.

In the FBI matter, I know of no specific charge, although the FBI was said to have had Joseph Kraft tailed in Paris back in 1969.

Also, under this category, perhaps there should be put the breaking story on the SBA, or OMBE—which is being looked into for allegations a) of kickbacks and b) of political influence in the decision as to where the grants would go. The Ervin Committee rushed over this last week, I believe, in their hearings.

M. THE HOFFA PARDON—No investigating on-going, but there have been some published contentions that Hoffa's release was done for political reasons, in connection with union-labor support. This is something of a throw-away charge that is heard.

N. HATCH ACT VIOLATIONS—On a rumor basis, I hear that the Cox Committee may be looking into political activities of White House "hatched" aides in the 1972 campaign—to see if they involved themselves wrongly in political activities in 1972. But this is, again, in "rumor" stage.

O. WATERGATE & COVER-UP—This is of course Subject A, so far as the Cox Committee is concerned; no indictments have been handed up this far; they are waiting upon the tapes and other subpoenaed material. Dean, Magruder, LaRue have already pleaded guilty to a single count. Indictments here are expected, I would guess, in December or January. Have no idea how sweeping or extensive they will be.

As stated, some of these charges are out of whole cloth, others are political in character and involve no wrong-doing. They can and should be broken down and broken out—and when definitive, in some case aggressive and tough answers provided and then conveyed to the country.[18]

16. Memo to Alexander Haig, November 26, 1973

Buchanan testified before the Senate Watergate Committee in September 1973, where he answered questions stemming from numerous campaign strategy memos he had written in 1972. On how the Committee obtained the memos, according to Buchanan: "[The Committee to Reelect the President], after being sent

them, sent a passel to the Archives, where the Ervin Committee retrieved them."[19]
Two months after testifying, Buchanan was still waiting for the materials to be
returned to him.

Am uncertain if I conveyed the measure of my concern at not having my own
papers restored to my files, and I hope this memo will do so.

A) No other loyal active senior staff member has been placed in this position,
and few others would have tolerated it this long.

B) Those are my papers, from my files, surrendered over temporarily and
voluntarily, and the refusal of the lawyers to return them constitutes, in my judgment, a breach of faith.

C) If the lawyers' refusal is based on some fear of what will happen to the
lawyers should they give them back, that fear is certain to enlarge rather than
diminish as the crunch comes—so the time for resolution is now.

D) If our own team is unwilling to take even the miniscule risk of minor embarrassment involved in turning my own papers back over to me, then the hell
with it, we can pack it in right now.

Let me repeat the situation. Jaworski has not subpoenaed my files; we have already beaten Ervin in Court; I have already testified; the most flamboyant of my
political papers, which Ervin had subpoenaed, are already in the public sector.

Cannot believe the President would endorse this dog-in-the-manger posture,
given his own willingness to go to the brink on this question. In any event, if
the "lawyers" refuse the return of those papers, when asked, I want to take the
matter up in my next conversation with the President.

Realize the lawyers are busy, they have other great concerns—but what is of
insignificance to them has assumed great importance to me. All I want is those
five boxes out of the Bomb Shelter and back where they belong.[20]

17. Memo to Richard Nixon, February 20, 1974

Herewith the Briefing Book, as requested. As of now, here, in my judgment are
the Top Ten. All are covered:

1. Oil Embargo. Will it be lifted; and are the Arabs holding us hostage to get
it lifted by demanding progress on Syrian-Israeli negotiations?

2. Solzhenitsyn. Here the President will likely be pressed on what is being
judged to be Kissinger's tepid U.S. response to the plight of one of the great
moral heroes of the 20th century. Kissinger and Administration were hit hard
by press on response.

3. Special Prosecutor. Certain question is how RN equates his pledge of co-

operation with refusal to turn over tapes. Also, they will be zeroing in on potential confrontation—if Jaworski goes to Court, will President abide by a Court
decision? They will be hungering after some indication of a second Saturday
Night Massacre.

4. Judiciary Committee. Again, what will we give him; will we accept a subpoena; will RN appear type question should be expected.

5. Politics. What is RN's interpretation of defeat of Ford's protégé in Michigan, etc.? Political impact of Gate would be a certain question this morning, less
certain Thursday night; but likely—if we are on the tube, they will want to let
country know the race was lost.

6. Press. If this were an in-office conference, RN would be pressed on (a) "vicious, distorted reporting" (who?) and (b) on RN's latest comments on the <u>Post</u>,
etc. They may be somewhat reticent to take up their own parochial concerns on
network television.

From here on out, it is more difficult, but these would, I think, be the Second
Six:

7. Opening to Havana. Are we planning "détente" with Havana; and is RN's
personal animosity toward Mr. Castro the reason why our two countries have
been unable to get together and be friends?

8. Vietnam & Cambodia. One year after "peace with honor," 50,000 are dead,
and Phnom Penh is being shelled. Very likely something on this situation.

9. Presidential Travel Plans. Europe? Moscow? Even if impeachment proceedings are moving forward?

10. Military Spying. How serious; what did Plumbers uncover? Was this the
super-secret matter to which RN referred; why not punitive action?

11. Energy. Emergency Bill, will RN veto? Include here possible question
on rationing, with reporter raising spectre of lines outside of gas stations, etc.
Note Simon's response: National rationing system not necessary to deal with a
problem that is serious only in a number of states. Why impose federal rationing
on states where it is unneeded?

12. Mitchell-Stans. President may be asked a philosophical question about
his feelings about his old friends, etc., upcoming indictments; what he thinks.
Especially in view of the fact that they will be on the news tonight and tomorrow, as they were last night.

13. The Eighteen Minute Gap. Despite Sirica warning, RN may be asked
this on national television; has he spoken with Rose Mary Woods; has he conducted his own investigation?[21]

18. Memo to Alexander Haig, May 10, 1974

On May 9, 1974, the House Judiciary Committee began impeachment proceedings against Nixon.

This thing is hemorrhaging terribly. The Old Man cannot resign; that would be an admission of guilt. But he has to get out front and center, as there is no sign that the bleeding on the Hill, and among our residual supporters in the national press, is going to stop. If he doesn't move soon, there is a possibility that, politically, he could wind up in the middle of next week with a handful of Congressional supporters at best, and his Swiss Guard here in the White House. Is there any possibility that he would step out into the press room this afternoon, show himself to the nation, and make these strong points, which I would be pleased to draft:

1) No hard evidence of wrong-doing on those tapes, no criminal conduct.

2) Those who have seized upon and exploited the unelevating passages are some of the great hypocrites of our time.

3) Regret that, in this crisis of my Presidency, some of my oldest and best friends have chosen to absent themselves from the battlefield.

4) But I am not guilty; I will not resign; I intend to stand up and defend this office; and if the members of the House and Senate believe that I am going to provide them with the easy road of abandoning my Presidency, they are mistaken. They will have to stand up and be counted—on the basis of evidence.

Surrogates cannot do the job for the President now. He has to get out there himself; let the nation see him fighting the uphill fight. Let the country see his determination to maintain his office.

Let him lay it back into the court of Scott and John Anderson and friends, directly.

But, whatever is done, we ought not to let this fire storm stampede us into anything foolish or precipitate.[22]

Notes

Chapter 1. Introduction

1. Patrick J. Buchanan, *Nixon's White House Wars: The Battles That Made and Broke a President and Divided America Forever* (New York: Crown Forum, 2017), 19.

2. Thomas J. McInerney and Fred L. Israel, eds., *Presidential Documents: Words That Shaped a Nation from Washington to Obama*, 2nd ed. (New York: Routledge, 2013), xvi.

3. Email correspondence between Lori Cox Han and Patrick J. Buchanan, November 28, 2018.

4. "Biography," official website of Patrick J. Buchanan, http://buchanan.org/blog/biography.

5. For a full discussion of Buchanan's role in the 1968 presidential campaign, see Patrick J. Buchanan, *The Greatest Comeback: How Richard Nixon Rose from Defeat to Create the New Majority* (New York: Crown Forum, 2014).

6. Laura Byrne, "Pat Buchanan: Romney Will Win Florida," *Daily Caller*, October 16, 2012, dailycaller.com/2012/10/16/pat-buchanan-romney-will-win-florida/.

7. C. Brant Short, "Patrick J. Buchanan," in *American Voices: An Encyclopedia of Contemporary Orators*, ed. Bernard K. Duffy and Richard W. Leeman (Westport, CT: Greenwood Press, 2005), 16–22.

8. George Grant, *Buchanan: Caught in the Crossfire* (Nashville: Thomas Nelson, 1996), 3–4.

9. Quoted in Grant, *Buchanan*, 3.

10. Dean E. Alger, *The Media and Politics*, 2nd ed. (Belmont, CA: Wadsworth, 1996), 340. On Buchanan's 1992 convention speech, see also Stephen J. Wayne, *The Road to the White House 1996: The Politics of Presidential Elections* (New York: St. Martin's Press, 1997), 185.

11. Timothy Stanley, *The Crusader: The Life and Tumultuous Times of Pat Buchanan* (New York: Thomas Dunne, 2012), 6.

12. S. Thomas Colfax, ed., *"Deng Xiaoping Is a Chain-Smoking Communist Dwarf": The Sayings of Pat Buchanan* (New York: Ballantine Books, 1996), v, x.

13. Patrick J. Buchanan, *Right from the Beginning* (Boston: Little, Brown, 1988), 325.

14. Stanley, *The Crusader*, 6.

15. Email correspondence between the author and Buchanan, November 28, 2018.

16. Benjamin Hufbauer, *Presidential Temples: How Memorials and Libraries Shape Public Memory* (Lawrence: University Press of Kansas, 2005), 188.

17. "Presidential Libraries," National Archives and Records Administration, http://www.archives.gov/presidential-libraries/.

18. Buchanan, *Nixon's White House Wars*, 19.

19. Buchanan to Haldeman, Assignments Book, November 29, 1972, Buchanan Files, box 3, Richard Nixon Presidential Library (hereafter RNPL).

Chapter 2. The 1968 Campaign

1. Interview of Richard Nixon on *The Merv Griffin Show*, December 20, 1967, "The Merv Griffin Show, 1962–1986," DVD (Chicago: MPI Home Video, 2014).

2. Warren E. Miller and J. Merrill Shanks, *The New American Voter* (Cambridge: Harvard University Press, 1996), 153–154.

3. Buchanan, *Greatest Comeback*, 5.

4. Buchanan to H. R. Haldeman, November 15, 1967, "On the Uses of Television," White House Special Files, Returned, box 35, folder 19, Richard Nixon Presidential Library, Yorba Linda, CA (hereafter RNPL).

5. Buchanan to Nixon, "Research," April 17, 1968, White House Special Files, Returned, box 35, folder 12, RNPL.

6. Buchanan to Nixon, July 13, 1968, White House Special Files, Returned, box 33, folder 13, RNPL.

7. Buchanan to Nixon, July 28, 1968, White House Special Files, Returned, box 26, folder 7, RNPL.

8. Buchanan to Nixon, August 1968, White House Special Files, Returned, box 35, folder 12, RNPL.

9. The Reverend Ralph Abernathy was a Christian minister, civil rights activist, and a friend and mentor to the Rev. Martin Luther King Jr.

10. Buchanan to Nixon, August 15, 1968, "Strategy, Some Thoughts On," White House Special Files, Returned, box 33, folder 12, RNPL.

11. Buchanan to Nixon, September 1968, White House Special Files, Returned, box 35, folder 13, RNPL.

12. Buchanan to Haldeman, September 25, 1968, White House Special Files, Returned, box 36, folder 8, RNPL.

13. Buchanan to Haldeman, September/October 1968, White House Special Files, Returned, box 23, folder 1, RNPL.

14. Buchanan to Nixon, October 5, 1968, White House Special Files, Returned, box 35, folder 14, RNPL.

15. Buchanan to Haldeman and John Mitchell, October 13, 1968, White House Special Files, Returned, box 36, folder 9, RNPL.

16. Buchanan and Ron Ziegler to Dwight Chapin, October 18, 1968, White House Special Files, Returned, box 35, folder 15, RNPL.

17. Buchanan to Nixon, October 22, 1968, White House Special Files, Returned, box 35, folder 15, RNPL.

18. Buchanan to Nixon (via Haldeman), November 13, 1968, White House Special Files, Returned, box 41, folder 7, RNPL.

19. Buchanan to Haldeman, December 20, 1968, White House Special Files, Returned, box 42, folder 1, RNPL.

Chapter 3. White House Communication Strategies

1. See Lori Cox Han, *Governing from Center Stage: White House Communication Strategies during the Television Age of Politics* (Cresskill, NJ: Hampton Press, 2001).

2. Richard Nixon, *In the Arena: A Memoir of Victory, Defeat, and Renewal* (New York: Pocket Books, 1990), 293.

3. Lou Cannon, "The Press and the Nixon Presidency," in *The Nixon Presidency: Twenty-Two Intimate Perspectives of Richard M. Nixon*, ed. Kenneth Thompson (Lanham, MD: University Press of America, 1987), 196.

4. William Safire, *Before the Fall: An Inside View of the Pre-Watergate White House* (New York: Da Capo Press, 1975), 104, 342.

5. Buchanan, *Nixon's White House Wars*, 69–70.

6. George C. Edwards III, *The Public Presidency: The Pursuit of Popular Support* (New York: St. Martin's Press, 1983), 128–132.

7. Mort Allin to Haldeman, July 22, 1970, White House Special Files, Staff Member and Office Files of H. R. Haldeman, box 124, Richard Nixon Presidential Library, Yorba Linda, CA (hereafter RNPL).

8. Michael Emery and Edwin Emery, *The Press and America: An Interpretive History of the Mass Media*, 8th ed. (Boston: Allyn and Bacon, 1996), 441–443.

9. For a discussion on the Nixon White House communication strategy, see Han, *Governing from Center Stage*, chap. 3.

10. John Tebbel and Sarah Miles Watts, *The Press and the Presidency: From George Washington to Ronald Reagan* (New York: Oxford University Press, 1985), 506.

11. Jon Marshall, "Nixon Is Gone, but His Media Strategy Lives On," *Atlantic*, August 4, 2014, available at https://www.theatlantic.com/politics/archive/2014/08/nixons-revenge-his-media-strategy-triumphs-40-years-after-resignation/375274/.

12. Buchanan to Nixon and Haldeman, January 5, 1969, "President's News Summary," White House Special Files, Returned, box 42, folder 2, RNPL.

13. Buchanan to Nixon, March 4, 1969, President's Office Files, Memos, box 77, RNPL.

14. Richard Nixon, "Address at the Air Force Academy Commencement Exercises in Colorado Springs, Colorado," June 4, 1969, *The American Presidency Project*, https://www.presidency.ucsb.edu/node/239334.

15. Buchanan to Nixon, June 6, 1969, President's Office Files, Handwriting, box 2, RNPL.

16. Haldeman to Buchanan, June 24, 1969, Haldeman Files, box 49, RNPL.

17. Buchanan to Jim Allison, July 2, 1969, Haldeman Files, box 49, RNPL.

18. Buchanan to Nixon (cc: Bill Safire), July 14, 1969, President's Office Files, Handwriting, box 2, RNPL.

19. Buchanan to Nixon, September 2, 1969, President's Office Files, Handwriting, box 3, RNPL.

20. Buchanan to Nixon (per Haldeman), September 28, 1969, News Summaries, box 3, RNPL.

21. Buchanan to Nixon, September 28, 1969, President's Office Files, box 3, RNPL.

22. Buchanan to Ken Cole, October 10, 1969, President's Office Files, Handwriting, box 3, RNPL.

23. Richard Nixon, "Address to the Nation on the War in Vietnam," November 3, 1969, *The American Presidency Project*, https://www.presidency.ucsb.edu/node/240027.

24. Buchanan, *Nixon's White House Wars*, 69–75.

25. Buchanan to Nixon (per Haldeman), November 5, 1969, Haldeman Files, box 54, RNPL. See Buchanan, *Nixon's White House Wars*, 69.

26. Buchanan to Haldeman, November 11, 1969, Haldeman Files, box 54, RNPL.

27. Buchanan to Nixon, May 21, 1970, Dwight Chapin Files, box 20, RNPL.

28. Buchanan to Haldeman, June 27, 1970, Haldeman Files, box 156, RNPL.

29. Buchanan to Nixon, June 29, 1970, "Chancellor, Smith, and Sevareid," Haldeman Files, box 64, RNPL.

30. Buchanan to Haldeman, September 8, 1970, Haldeman Files, box 68, RNPL.

31. Buchanan to Nixon, November 4, 1970, "Special Report, Media Coverage, Predominantly TV, during Last 10 Days of Campaign," Haldeman Files, box 72, RNPL.

32. Buchanan for the Staff Secretary, January 13, 1971, "Press Conference Responses," Buchanan Files, box 1, RNPL.

33. Buchanan to Haldeman, January 14, 1971, "Neither Fish nor Fowl," President's Office Files, Handwriting, box 9, RNPL.

34. Buchanan to Chuck Colson, February 4, 1971, "The 'Isolated President,'" Buchanan Files, box 1, RNPL.

35. Buchanan to Haldeman, March 2, 1971, Buchanan Files, box 1, RNPL.

36. Buchanan to Nixon, April 23, 1971, "Press Conference," Buchanan Files, box 1, RNPL.

37. Buchanan to Nixon, May 3, 1971, "Political Memorandum: The PR Campaign," Buchanan Files, box 1, RNPL.

38. Buchanan to Nixon, July 1, 1971, "Pentagon Papers," Buchanan Files, box 1, RNPL.

39. Buchanan to John Ehrlichman, July 8, 1971, Buchanan Files, box 1, RNPL.

40. Buchanan to, July 23, 1971, Buchanan Files, box 1, RNPL.

41. Buchanan to Nixon, September 17, 1971, Buchanan Files, box 1, RNPL.

42. Buchanan to Haldeman, November 30, 1971, Buchanan Files, box 2, RNPL.

43. Buchanan to Nixon, January 13, 1972, Buchanan Files, box 11, RNPL.

44. Buchanan and Raymond K. Price to Haldeman, February 15, 1972, Buchanan Files, box 2, RNPL.

45. Buchanan to Nixon, June 19, 1972, President's Personal File, box 166, RNPL.

46. Buchanan to Haldeman, August 3, 1972, Buchanan Files, box 3, RNPL.

47. Buchanan to Haldeman, August 14, 1972, Buchanan Files, box 3, RNPL.

Chapter 4. Governing, Policy, and Politics

1. For a discussion of Nixon's domestic policy agenda, see Michael A. Genovese, Todd L. Belt, and William W. Lammers, *The Presidency and Domestic Policy: Comparing Leadership Styles, FDR to Obama*, 2nd ed. (Boulder: Paradigm, 2014), chap. 10.

2. Larry Berman, *The New American Presidency* (Boston: Little, Brown, 1987), 259–261.

3. Sidney M. Milkis and Michael Nelson, *The American Presidency: Origins and Development, 1776–2014*, 7th ed. (Thousand Oaks, CA: CQ Press, 2016), 369–377.

4. Melvin Small, *The Presidency of Richard Nixon* (Lawrence: University Press of Kansas, 1999), 309.

5. Buchanan, *Nixon's White House Wars*, 19.

6. In March 1969, Nixon appointed Otto Otepka, a conservative, to a position on the Subversive Activities Control Board.

7. The Rev. Theodore Hesburgh, an ordained priest and president of the University of Notre Dame, wrote an eight-page letter to the student body, reprinted in major newspapers, stating that any anti-Vietnam protesters on the Notre Dame campus had fifteen minutes to "cease and desist" before facing suspension or expulsion.

8. Buchanan to Nixon, March 7, 1969, President's Office File, Handwriting, box 1, RNPL.

9. Buchanan to Nixon, March 13, 1969, President's Office File, Annotated News Summaries, box 30, RNPL.

10. Buchanan to Nixon, April 11, 1969, President's Office File, Handwriting, box 1, RNPL.

11. Buchanan to Nixon, April 29, 1969, "Committee of Six," President's Office File, Handwriting, box 1, RNPL.

12. Memo Pat Buchanan to Nixon, September 12, 1969, President's Office File, Annotated News Summaries, box 30, RNPL.

13. Pat Buchanan to Richard Nixon, 12/5/69, "My Lai Incident," President's Office File, Handwriting, box 4, RNPL.

14. Richard Nixon, "Address to the Nation on the War in Vietnam," November 3, 1969, *The American Presidency Project*, https://www.presidency.ucsb.edu/node/240027.

15. Buchanan to Nixon, December 18, 1969, Haldeman Files, box 57, RNPL.

16. Evan Vassar, "Nixon, the Supreme Court, and Busing," April 2, 2015, Richard Nixon Foundation, https://www.nixonfoundation.org/2015/04/nixon-the-supreme-court-and-busing/.

17. Buchanan to Nixon, January 30, 1970, President's Office Files, Handwriting, box 5, RNPL.

18. Buchanan to Nixon, March 9, 1970, President's Office File, Handwriting, box 5, RNPL.

19. Pat Buchanan to H. R. Haldeman, March 10, 1970, Haldeman Files, box 59, RNPL.

20. Buchanan to Haldeman, June 16, 1970, Haldeman Files, box 62, RNPL.

21. "Background Press Briefing by the President's Assistant for National Security Affairs (Kissinger)," August 14, 1970, *Foreign Relations of the United States, 1969–1976, Volume 1, Foundations of Foreign Policy, 1969–1972*, Document 69, https://history.state.gov/historicaldocuments/frus1969-76v01/d69.

22. Buchanan to Nixon, August 21, 1970, President's Office Files, Handwriting, box 7, RNPL.

23. Buchanan to Nixon, August 24, 1970, Contested, box 50, folder 19, RNPL.

24. Buchanan to Nixon, January 6, 1971, Buchanan Files, box 1, RNPL.

25. Pat Buchanan to John Ehrlichman, February 3, 1971, Buchanan Files, box 1, RNPL.

26. Buchanan to Haldeman, March 5, 1971, Buchanan Files, box 1, RNPL.

27. Buchanan to Nixon, February 12, 1971, "J. Edgar Hoover," Buchanan Files, box 1, RNPL.

28. Pat Buchanan to Henry Kissinger and H. R. Haldeman, March 12, 1971, "Full Generation of Peace," Buchanan Files, box 1, RNPL.

29. Buchanan to Nixon, May 7, 1971, "Political Memorandum," Buchanan Files, box 1, RNPL.

30. Richard Nixon, "Remarks to the Nation Announcing Acceptance of an Invitation to Visit the People's Republic of China," July 15, 1971, *The American Presidency Project*, https://www.presidency.ucsb.edu/node/240410.

31. Buchanan to Nixon (per Haldeman), July 16, 1971, Buchanan Files, box 7, RNPL.

32. Buchanan to Haldeman, July 28, 1971, Buchanan Files, box 1, RNPL.

33. Buchanan to Nixon, August 4, 1971, Buchanan Files, box 7, RNPL.

34. Buchanan to Haldeman and Colson, September 13, 1971, Buchanan Files, box 1, RNPL.

35. Buchanan to Nixon, September 20, 1971, Buchanan Files, box 1, RNPL.

36. Buchanan to Nixon, September 29, 1971, "Supreme Court," Buchanan Files, box 1, RNPL.

37. Buchanan to Haldeman, October 1, 1971, Buchanan Files, box 2, RNPL.

38. Buchanan to Nixon (through John Ehrlichman), October 26, 1971, Buchanan Files, box 2, RNPL.

39. See Buchanan, *Nixon's White House Wars*, 226–267.

40. Buchanan to Haldeman and Colson, October 26, 1971, Buchanan Files, box 2, RNPL.

41. Buchanan to Haldeman, December 1, 1971, Buchanan Files, box 2, RNPL.

42. Buchanan to Mitchell and Haldeman, December 3, 1971, Buchanan Files, box 2, RNPL.

43. Buchanan to Mitchell and Haldeman, December 13, 1971, "The Manhattan Twelve," Contested, box 7, folder 23, RNPL.

44. Buchanan to Nixon (per Ehrlichman), December 15, 1971, John Ehrlichman Files, box 38, RNPL.

45. Buchanan to Haldeman and Colson, January 14, 1972, Buchanan Files, box 8, RNPL.

46. Buchanan to Mitchell and Haldeman, February 15, 1972, Buchanan Files, box 2, RNPL.

47. Buchanan to Nixon (per Haldeman), April 3, 1972, Buchanan Files, box 2, RNPL.

Chapter 5. The 1972 Campaign: Primary Challenges

1. Melvin Small, *The Presidency of Richard Nixon* (Lawrence: University Press of Kansas, 1999), 245. Small is quoting Richard M. Scammon and Ben J. Wattenberg, *The Real Majority: An Extraordinary Examination of the American Electorate* (New York: Coward-McCann, 1970).

2. Buchanan to Haldeman, May 27, 1971, Buchanan Files, box 1, RNPL.

3. Buchanan, *Nixon's White House Wars*, 250.

4. Paul F. Boller Jr., *Presidential Campaigns: From George Washington to George W. Bush* (New York: Oxford University Press, 2004), 334.

5. "Who Was John Ashbrook?" Ashland University, http://ashbrook.org/about/john
-ashbrook/.

6. Max Frankel, "Nixon Renominated," *New York Times*, August 23, 1972, available at
https://archive.nytimes.com/www.nytimes.com/library/politics/camp/720823convention
-gop-ra.html.

7. On October 29, 1970, Nixon gave a speech in San Jose, California, with hundreds
of protesters gathered outside. When he exited the auditorium, his motorcade was hit
with rocks, eggs, and tomatoes. Rumors spread that the Nixon team had helped to initiate
the protest in an effort to provide the President with a photo opportunity in line with his
promise to restore "law and order" in the United States. See David Greenberg, "The Time
a President Stoked a Protest So He Could Play the 'Law and Order' Card," *Politico*, October 28, 2918, available at https://www.politico.com/magazine/story/2018/10/28/nixon
-protest-law-and-order-221920.

8. See Joe McGinniss, *The Selling of the President 1968* (New York: Trident Press,
1969).

9. Buchanan to Nixon, November 18, 1970, Contested, box 49, folder 41, RNPL.

10. Buchanan, *Nixon's White House Wars*, 251.

11. Buchanan to Nixon, March 24, 1971, "The Muskie Watch," Buchanan Files, box
1, RNPL.

12. Buchanan to Nixon, April 19, 1971, "The Resurrection of Hubert Humphrey," Buchanan Files, box 1, RNPL.

13. Buchanan to Nixon, April 29, 1971, "Primary Strategy," Returned Files, White
House Special Files, box 21, folder 24, RNPL.

14. Buchanan to Nixon, June 9, 1971, "EMK—Political Memorandum," Buchanan
Files, box 1, RNPL.

15. Buchanan to Nixon, June 25, 1971, "The Odds against Henry Jackson," Contested,
box 24, folder 2, RNPL.

16. Buchanan to Mitchell and Haldeman, September 8, 1971, Buchanan Files, box 1,
RNPL.

17. Buchanan to Nixon, September 25, 1971, Buchanan Files, box 1, RNPL.

18. Buchanan to Mitchell and H. R. Haldeman, October 5, 1971, "Research (As Requested)," Buchanan Files, box 2, RNPL.

19. Buchanan to Mitchell and Haldeman, December 14, 1971, Buchanan Files, box 2,
RNPL.

20. Buchanan to Mitchell and H. R. Haldeman, December 15, 1971, Buchanan Files,
box 5, RNPL.

21. Buchanan to Mitchell and Haldeman, January 11, 1972, Charles Colson Files, box
6, RNPL.

22. Buchanan to Colson, January 12, 1972, Buchanan Files, box 2, RNPL.

23. The headquarters of the Committee to Re-Elect the President is located at 1701
Pennsylvania Ave. NW, Washington, D.C.

24. Buchanan and Ken Khachigian to Mitchell, March 14, 1972, "Attack Organization
& Strategy," *Hearings before the Select Committee on Presidential Campaign Activities of the*

United States Senate, Ninety-Third Congress, First Session, book 10, exhibit no. 181 (Washington, D.C.: Government Printing Office, 1973).

25. Buchanan and Khachigian to Mitchell and Haldeman, April 12, 1972, Contested, box 16, folder 19, RNPL.

Chapter 6. The 1972 Campaign: Nixon v. McGovern

1. Paul F. Boller Jr., *Presidential Campaigns: From George Washington to George W. Bush* (New York: Oxford University Press, 2004), 334.

2. Boller, *Presidential Campaigns*, 334–336.

3. Timothy Noah, "'Acid, Amnesty, and Abortion': The Unlikely Source of a Legendary Smear," *New Republic*, October 21, 2012, available at https://newrepublic.com/article/108977/acid-amnesty-and-abortion-unlikely-source-legendary-smear.

4. Boller, *Presidential Campaigns*, 337.

5. Buchanan, *Nixon's White House Wars*, 274–275.

6. Buchanan, *Nixon's White House Wars*, 334–337.

7. Memo from Pat Buchanan to John Mitchell, *Hearings before the Select Committee on Presidential Campaign Activities of the United States Senate, Ninety-Third Congress, First Session*, June 6, 1972, book 10, exhibit no. 186 (Washington, D.C.: Government Printing Office, 1973).

8. Memorandum by Pat Buchanan and Ken Khachigian, "Assault Strategy," June 8, 1972, Buchanan Files, box 2, Richard Nixon Presidential Library, Yorba Linda, Calif. (hereafter RNPL).

9. Buchanan and Khachigian to Haldeman, "Response to HRH Memo of June 12, 1972," June 18, 1972, Buchanan Files, box 2, RNPL.

10. Buchanan to Haldeman, June 18, 1972, Buchanan Files, box 2, RNPL.

11. Buchanan to Mitchell and Haldeman, *Hearings before the Select Committee on Presidential Campaign Activities of the United States Senate, Ninety-Third Congress, First Session*, June 25, 1972, book 10, exhibit no. 189 (Washington, D.C.: Government Printing Office, 1973).

12. Buchanan to Nixon, June 25, 1972, Buchanan Files, box 2, RNPL.

13. Buchanan to Nixon (per Haldeman), July 5, 1972, Buchanan Files, box 3, RNPL.

14. Buchanan and Khachigian to Haldeman and MacGregor, "Thoughts on the Post-Convention (Democratic)," July 7, 1972, Ken Khachigian Files, box 8, RNPL.

15. Buchanan to Nixon (thru Haldeman), July 12, 1972, Contested, box 48, folder 8, RNPL.

16. Buchanan to Nixon, "The Jewish Vote and the President's Opportunity," July 23, 1972, Buchanan Files, box 3, RNPL.

17. Buchanan to Nixon (as requested), "The Vice President and the Campaign," July 23, 1972, Contested, box 48, folder 8, RNPL.

18. Buchanan to Haldeman (as requested), August 7, 1972, Buchanan Files, box 3, RNPL.

19. Buchanan to Haldeman (as requested), August 7, 1972, Buchanan Files, box 3, RNPL.

20. Buchanan to Nixon, September 6, 1972, Buchanan Files, box 3, RNPL.

21. Buchanan to Haldeman, Ehrlichman, and Colson, *Hearings before the Select Committee on Presidential Campaign Activities of the United States Senate, Ninety-Third Congress, First Session*, September 13, 1972, book 10, exhibit no. 194 (Washington, D.C.: Government Printing Office, 1973).

22. Buchanan to Haldeman, September 19, 1972, Buchanan Files, box 3, RNPL.

23. Buchanan to Nixon, "Political Memorandum," October 9, 1972, Contested, box 48, folder 7, RNPL.

24. Buchanan to Haldeman, Ehrlichman, and Colson, "Administratively Confidential/Political Memorandum," October 13, 1972, Buchanan Files, box 8, RNPL.

25. Buchanan to Nixon, "Political Memorandum," October 23, 1972, Buchanan Files, box 3, RNPL.

26. Buchanan to Haldeman, Ehrlichman, and Colson, October 26, 1972, Buchanan Files, box 3, RNPL.

Chapter 7. Watergate and the Second Term

1. Buchanan, *Nixon's White House Wars*, 306.

2. See Stanley I. Kutler, *Watergate: A Brief History with Documents*, 2nd ed. (New York: Wiley-Blackwell, 2010).

3. Buchanan to Nixon, November 10, 1972, Buchanan Files, box 11, RNPL.

4. Buchanan to Haldeman, December 11, 1972, Buchanan Files, box 3, RNPL.

5. Buchanan to Ziegler, December 14, 1972, Buchanan Files, box 11, RNPL.

6. Buchanan to Haldeman (via Larry Higby), December 21, 1972, Buchanan Files, box 3, RNPL.

7. Buchanan to Nixon, May 3, 1973, President's Personal File, Alpha Name, box 6, RNPL.

8. Buchanan to Nixon, May 16, 1973, President's Office Files, Handwriting, box 22, RNPL.

9. Buchanan to Haig, July 31, 1973, Haig Files, box 1, RNPL.

10. Buchanan to Haig, October 23, 1973, Haig Files, box 6, RNPL.

11. Buchanan to Haig, October 23, 1973, Haig Files, box 6, RNPL.

12. Florida banker and real estate developer Charles "Bebe" Rebozo was a longtime friend and confidant of Nixon's; he faced a congressional investigation during Watergate for a $100,000 campaign contribution he accepted on Nixon's behalf from Howard Hughes.

13. Buchanan to Nixon, October 25, 1973, Haig Files, box 6, RNPL.

14. Buchanan to Haig, October 31, 1973, Haig Files, box 6, RNPL.

15. Buchanan to Nixon, November 5, 1973, Haig Files, box 9, RNPL.

16. Buchanan to Nixon, November 10, 1973, Haig Files, box 9, RNPL.

17. Buchanan to Nixon, November 11, 1973, President's Office Files, Handwriting, box 23, RNPL.

18. Buchanan to Nixon, November 13, 1973, Haig Files, box 9, RNPL.

19. Email correspondence between Lori Cox Han and Buchanan, November 28, 2018.

20. Buchanan to Haig, November 26, 1973, Haig Files, box 9, RNPL.

21. Buchanan to Nixon, February 20, 1974, Haig Files, box 17, RNPL.

22. Buchanan to Haig, May 10, 1974, Haig Files, box 23, RNPL.

Bibliography

Alger, Dean E. *The Media and Politics*. 2nd ed. Belmont, CA: Wadsworth, 1996.

Berman, Larry. *The New American Presidency*. Boston: Little, Brown, 1987.

Boller, Paul F., Jr. *Presidential Campaigns: From George Washington to George W. Bush*. New York: Oxford University Press, 2004.

Buchanan, Patrick J. *Right from the Beginning*. Boston: Little, Brown, 1988.

———. *The Greatest Comeback: How Richard Nixon Rose from Defeat to Create the New Majority*. New York: Crown Forum, 2014.

———. *Nixon's White House Wars: The Battles That Made and Broke a President and Divided America Forever*. New York: Crown Forum, 2017.

Cannon, Lou. "The Press and the Nixon Presidency." In *The Nixon Presidency: Twenty-Two Intimate Perspectives of Richard M. Nixon*, ed. Kenneth Thompson. Lanham, MD: University Press of America, 1987.

Colfax, S. Thomas, ed. *"Deng Xiaoping Is a Chain-Smoking Communist Dwarf": The Sayings of Pat Buchanan*. New York: Ballantine Books, 1996.

Edwards, George C., III. *The Public Presidency: The Pursuit of Popular Support*. New York: St. Martin's Press, 1983.

Emery, Michael, and Edwin Emery. *The Press and America: An Interpretive History of the Mass Media*. 8th ed. Boston: Allyn and Bacon, 1996.

Genovese, Michael A., Todd L. Belt, and William W. Lammers. *The Presidency and Domestic Policy: Comparing Leadership Styles, FDR to Obama*. 2nd ed. Boulder: Paradigm, 2014.

Grant, George. *Buchanan: Caught in the Crossfire*. Nashville: Thomas Nelson, 1996.

Han, Lori Cox. *Governing from Center Stage: White House Communication Strategies during the Television Age of Politics*. Cresskill, NJ: Hampton Press, 2001.

Hufbauer, Benjamin. *Presidential Temples: How Memorials and Libraries Shape Public Memory*. Lawrence: University Press of Kansas, 2005.

Kutler, Stanley I. *Watergate: A Brief History with Documents*. 2nd ed. New York: Wiley-Blackwell, 2010.

McGinniss, Joe. *The Selling of the President 1968*. New York: Trident Press, 1969.

McInerney, Thomas J., and Fred L. Israel, eds. *Presidential Documents: Words That Shaped a Nation from Washington to Obama*. 2nd ed. New York: Routledge, 2013.

Milkis, Sidney M., and Michael Nelson. *The American Presidency: Origins and Development, 1776–2014*. 7th ed. Thousand Oaks, CA: CQ Press, 2016.

Miller, Warren E., and J. Merrill Shanks. *The New American Voter*. Cambridge, MA: Harvard University Press, 1996.

Nixon, Richard. *In the Arena: A Memoir of Victory, Defeat, and Renewal*. New York: Pocket Books, 1990.

Noah, Timothy. "'Acid, Amnesty, and Abortion': The Unlikely Source of a Legendary Smear." *New Republic*, October 21, 2012, available at https://newrepublic.com/article/108977/acid-amnesty-and-abortion-unlikely-source-legendary-smear.

Safire, William. *Before the Fall: An Inside View of the Pre-Watergate White House*. New York: Da Capo Press, 1975.

Scammon, Richard M., and Ben J. Wattenberg. *The Real Majority: An Extraordinary Examination of the American Electorate*. New York: Coward-McCann, 1970.

Short, C. Brant. "Patrick J. Buchanan." In *American Voices: An Encyclopedia of Contemporary Orators*, ed. Bernard K. Duffy and Richard W. Leeman. Westport, CT: Greenwood Press, 2005.

Small, Melvin. *The Presidency of Richard Nixon*. Lawrence: University Press of Kansas, 1999.

Stanley, Timothy. *The Crusader: The Life and Tumultuous Times of Pat Buchanan*. New York: Thomas Dunne, 2012.

Tebbel, John, and Sarah Miles Watts. *The Press and the Presidency: From George Washington to Ronald Reagan*. New York: Oxford University Press, 1985.

Wayne, Stephen J. *The Road to the White House 1996: The Politics of Presidential Elections*. New York: St. Martin's Press, 1997.

Index